# HENSLEY HENSON

# HENSLEY HENSON

## A study in the friction between Church and State

Owen Chadwick

CLARENDON PRESS · OXFORD

Oxford University Press, Walton Street, Oxford OX2 6DP

London  New York  Toronto
Delhi  Bombay  Calcutta  Madras  Karachi
Kuala Lumpur  Singapore  Hong Kong  Tokyo
Nairobi  Dar es Salaam  Cape Town
Melbourne  Auckland

and associated companies in
Beirut  Berlin  Ibadan  Mexico City  Nicosia

Oxford is a trade mark of Oxford University Press

Published in the United States by
Oxford University Press, New York

First published 1983
Reprinted 1984

British Library Cataloguing in Publication Data
Chadwick, Owen
Hensley Henson.
1. Henson, Hensley
I. Title
283'.092'4   BX5199.H/
ISBN 0-19-826445-3

Library of Congress Cataloging in Publication Data
Chadwick, Owen.
Hensley Henson.
Bibliography: p.
Includes index.
1. Henson, Hensley, 1863–1947.   2. Church of England –
Bishops – Biography.   I. Title.
BX5199.H448C47 1983   283   [B]   82-17824
ISBN 0-19-826445-3

Printed in Great Britain
at the University Press, Oxford

# PREFACE

The Dean and Chapter of Durham asked for a memoir of Hensley Henson and generously made the materials available. The unpublished documents are many and useful to the historian. Few people were more concerned than Henson with the tasks facing English Churches in the twentieth century.

But biographies should be written by persons who can see with the eyes of the man whose life they write. And apart from disagreements in principle, Henson wrote an auto-biography. The author of that autobiography is many things – cantankerous, decisive, courageous, difficult, clear-headed, truculent – but not lovable. Towards the end of his third volume is printed a letter from the ex-prime minister Lloyd George, who was then near death, telling Henson that nothing in his (Ll.G.'s) life gave him more satisfaction than his making Henson into a bishop. Did Henson really believe that Lloyd George, who invented the welfare state and won a Great War and created modern Ireland, put the making of a single bishop at the top of his list of achievements? Whether he believed this or not, why is such a letter printed?

Canon Charles Pattinson was Henson's chaplain; a delectable old clergyman, just the sort of clergyman that an honorary canon ought to be. He evidently loved Henson. He sat beaming at the table. He said that Henson's autobiography, seemingly so frank, seemingly so devoid of reticence, was not what it looked. It was an exercise in concealment of the self. 'I thought it was all nonsense. I begged him to throw it away and not print it.' If there existed a doctrine that a memoir was not needed because Henson did the job himself, the doctrine was false. A memoir was needed precisely because he did not write a true autobiography. He only gave the world the impression that he did.

So here came the stirring of a true problem in history. A diary in so many volumes must reflect a personality. It cannot be myth-making. It must be evidence, and first-class evidence. And yet a man with the best chance of judging said that out of it Henson made 'nonsense'.

So, among the many who helped with this undertaking I put at the head of the list Charles Pattinson, without whose sensitive persuasion that a mystery remained unsolved, this book would not have been written.

On several occasions Henson was accused of being a Victorian. He was not at all Victorian in one respect for he liked short biographies. At various times he mentioned books which he thought to be the proper length for a biography, and the longest is 223 pages and the shortest is only about 100 pages. When he edited a biography himself he kept it to 242 pages, and his cleverest efforts in biography were single lectures. Evidently he supposed that no member of the human race is sufficiently interesting to warrant extended treatment – until he grew to be a very old man. I have borne these ideas in mind but have not felt able to conform precisely.

I thank the Rockefeller Foundation for allowing me to write the first draft in the fairest of surroundings at Bellagio.

In the Chapter of Durham Canon Ronald Coppin took special care. I benefited from the knowledge and kindness of the Bishop of Durham John Habgood, and one of his predecessors, Bishop Michael Ramsey, with Lady Ramsey; from three Deans of Durham, John Wild, Eric Heaton, Peter Baelz; John Wild read several chapters in draft and commented; from Archdeacon C. J. Stranks, a learned authority on the Church in the diocese. Men who were ordained by Henson or who knew him when young, gave their memories; especially Archbishop Philip Strong; Bishop John Daly; Archdeacon H. S. Wilkinson; Canons and Reverends Gervase Markham, Leslie Morrison, John Hargreaves, Edward Lynn, R. H. Talbot, T. F. Taylor, J. P. Inman, L. J. Birch, Nat Evans, W. H. Blyth Martin, and T. C. Ledgard; others who knew him, Sir Olaf Caröe, Hugh Lyon, C. A. Lillingston, H. F. Macdonald; and among these I specially thank Nancy Wynne Willson and George Nimmins. Among librarians and archivists, the keepers of manuscripts at the Bodleian Library were generous with their time; John Sparrow helped me with the library at All Souls College; Dr E. G. W. Bill with the extensive material in the Lambeth Library; R. H. Harcourt Williams with the archives of the Marquess of Salisbury, especially the papers of Lord Hugh Cecil; Miss M. McCollum with the Ferens papers at the Department of Palaeography, University of Durham; Miss Penelope Morgan with the Hereford Cathedral Library; Robert Latham with the Benson Papers at the Pepys Library. Lord Butler of Saffron Walden, Mrs Evelyn Sandilands (Fearne Booker's sister), Audrey Bayley, and Canon Denis Payne cleared up particular points. Bishop Mervyn Haigh for whose second diocese I was briefly an examiner, long ago rewarded me by completing my edition of Henson's autobiography. He revered Henson. At that time I could not understand why.

# CONTENTS

# SOURCES

## UNPUBLISHED

Fearne Booker, after consulting the Bishop of Durham, gave to the library of the Dean and Chapter what papers Henson allowed to survive; the volumes of the journal and the letter-books and some boxes of sermons. Others afterwards sent thither letters or reminiscences.

In the Department of Palaeography, Durham University, are the letters from Henson to Cecil Ferens.

The Lambeth Library has various Hensoniana amid the papers of Davidson, Lang, Temple, Bell and Don.

The Public Record Office (LCO.2.261) has the enquiry into the constitution of Westminster Abbey while Henson was a canon.

The Bodleian Library has the papers of several correspondents of Henson; especially Selborne, Rashdall, Asquith, Sankey, and Sanday. It has the early minute books of the Stubbs Society.


## PRINTED

Apart from Henson's own works, including *Retrospect of an Unimportant Life* (3 volumes 1942–50), *Letters of H. H. Henson,* edited E. F. Braley, 1951, *More Letters of H. H. Henson,* edited E. F. Braley, 1954–, see the biographies of his contemporaries:

John Barnes, *Ahead of his age: Bishop Barnes of Birmingham,* 1979
G. K. A. Bell, *Randall Davidson,* 2nd edn. 1938
Adam Fox, *Dean Inge,* 1960
F. A. Iremonger, *William Temple,* 1948
R. C. D. Jasper, *George Bell,* 1967; *A. C. Headlam,* 1960
J. G. Lockhart, *Cosmo Gordon Lang,* 1949
G. L. Prestige, *The Life of Charles Gore,* 1935
Charles Smyth, *Cyril Forster Garbett,* 1959

and for a modern biographical study of Henson and three of these:

D. L. Edwards, *Leaders of the Church of England,* 1971

See also:

C. A. Alington, *A Dean's Apology,* 1952
Harold Begbie, *Painted Windows,* 1922
Timothy Eden, *Durham,* 2 vols., 1953

W. R. Garside, *The Durham Miners, 1919–60*, 1971
Roger Lloyd, *The Church of England, 1900–1965*, 1966
E. R. Norman, *Church and Society in England 1770–1970*, 1976
Charles Oman, *Memories of Victorian Oxford*, 1941
A. M. Ramsey, *From Gore to Temple*, 1960
—— *Canterbury Essays and Addresses*, 1964
—— *Preface to H. Hensley Henson, Ad Clerum*, 1958
Charles Smyth, *Church and Parish*, 1955
*Westminster Abbey Quarterly*, January 1939, pp. 17–25

Two articles by the present author:

'The idea of a national Church: Gladstone and Henson', in *Aspects de l'Anglicanisme*, ed. Marcel Simon, Vendôme, 1974
*Hensley Henson and the Durham Miners 1920–39*, Durham 1983

# 1. NOT AT SCHOOL

THE ORIGINS of a famous man are interesting moments. We want to know how many of his attitudes are explained. We wish to find his parents, and how much of his genius was heredity, and how much innate, and how much a capacity for taking pains.

This is difficult. The parents of a famous man are seldom famous.

In Hensley Henson's case the difficulty is worse. His father broke away from his father. Henson had a breach with, if not resentment against his own father. He wanted the world to know only that part of his origins which he liked to let slip and for the rest to guard silence. From the moment he became a young Fellow of All Souls College at Oxford he rejoiced to tell you all about himself, too much about himself, never was a man who (at first sight) talked so freely about himself. He regarded the election to an All Souls fellowship as his start in life. Of the self before then he will say little.

This was weighty in his psychology. A part of the strangeness in his character can be dimly discerned in what little we can find of his mysterious and vanished childhood; the childhood that never was; all his life he felt it a huge disadvantage that he was never allowed to be a boy.

The Henson family once lived at Porlock on the edge of Exmoor. By the time we first know anything about them, in the beginning of the nineteenth century they were small farmers at Morebath, south of Exmoor. Great-grandfather and grandfather farmed the land at Loyton Farm; god-fearing countrymen, each in his turn churchwarden of Morebath Church.

Thomas Henson, father of Herbert Hensley Henson, was born in 1812. When he was in his later teens he quarrelled with his father and left home, and went to London and into business. Though he once returned to Devonshire, it was only once. He cut himself and his family from its roots in the west country. Though our Henson's grandfather lived long, grandfather and grandson never met.

In the New Testament Melchizedek, priest and king, is described as without father, without mother, without a genealogy. Herbert Hensley Henson once wrote that this was how he felt. Intellectually he knew about Morebath. The boy felt sundered, as by a chasm, from his origins.

Thomas Henson his father, thus leaving home in a cloud, prospered in London. A baptismal certificate registers him as 'warehouseman', a census as 'outfitter'. He probably prospered by marriage. He sent one son into tea, a second into drapery, a third into tea. He prospered so that in 1865 at the age of fifty-three he was able to retire, and bought a property at Broadstairs on the north Kent coast, where he cultivated his garden and dedicated himself to religion. The house was called Vale Villa. He intended all his sons to enter trades.

Thomas Henson married young, and his first wife died young. He married a second time at Greenwich on 31 August 1852, a girl named Martha Fear. The eight children, six boys and two girls, of whom Herbert was the sixth child and fourth boy, were the sons and daughters of Martha Fear. Herbert remembered her as small and beautiful, *with dark hair, brilliant eyes, and a singularly graceful carriage, with an almost uncanny power over bees*. But she died when he was six and a quarter *and with her died our happiness*. He never really knew her. But she remained for ever a fragrant memory. As an adult he watched other mothers sacrificing themselves in a thousand ways for their babes, and he would marvel, and feel rebuked, and awed by something in the distant memory.

He later idealized the years from his birth on 8 November 1863 till his mother's death in January 1870. The years afterwards were so miserable that they cast a sunny light upon the earliest time when he was a boy in a big family with a roomy house and acres of garden. In his memory the garden was rich in fruit and gay with flowers, and these enchantments symbolized the glory of a lost childhood. He came to believe that his life was wretched and disordered from the day of his mother's death.

A widower cannot easily look after eight children, even though three of them have left home. The five that remained were all under ten years. Naturally there was a nurse. She made no impression on little Herbert. The house became gloomy, anarchic, quarrelsome; a child's hell. The two eldest, Arthur and Herbert, were sent to live in the house of the Congregationalist minister in Broadstairs, a mild scholarly man whom they liked with a wife whom they hated.[1]

The home was very religious. Sprung from a line of Devonshire churchwardens, Thomas Henson attached himself in London to the congregation of the famous evangelical preacher Baptist Noel. In the 1840s Noel was one of the magnetic preachers of evangelical London. In 1849 the folly of the then Bishop of Exeter threw all the Church of England into crisis. He refused to institute Mr Gorham to a Devonshire living because he believed Mr Gorham's doctrine of baptism to be heretical. And when a state court said that Mr Gorham was not a heretic, the shock at state interference lost the future Cardinal Manning into the Church of Rome, and lost Baptist Noel into evangelical non-conformity.

Baptist Noel took with him into dissent a number of his congregation; and among them Thomas Henson. Little Herbert was brought up in a family where father never formally ceased to be a member of the Church of England but rejected the Church of England in his heart and often worshipped among the nonconformists. Thomas Henson gave a piece of his land in Broadstairs to build a Congregational chapel, sent his two sons to live at the house of the Congregational minister, was very Protestant and very hostile to the Church of Rome and equally hostile to Anglo-Catholics, longed for the cause, not of Christian reunion but of Protestant reunion. Above all he refused to have his younger children baptized as babies. The future Anglican bishop was brought up in the home of an ex-Anglican with reasons for criticizing bishops sourly, and seeing all the good in Protestant non-conformity.

In another direction the father followed Baptist Noel. Noel was one of the leaders in the movement to free negro slaves. Herbert Hensley Henson was brought up to abhor slavery and what later came to be called racialism. The first novel which he remembered to have moved him was the epic of the American campaign against negro slavery, *Uncle Tom's Cabin*. (It may have been important that the real name of the original Uncle

[1] The minister was Augustus Frederick Bennett, minister 1869–86. Cf. A. Lister-Hetherington, *Congregationalism in Broadstairs* (1964).

Tom was Henson.) The future hammer of Fascists and Nazis was born.

The household had an outward piety; family prayers morning and evening, with the children reading the psalms. The shock of his wife's death drove Thomas Henson into a narrower and sadder religiosity; darker views of the human race, yet more puritan in code of life, still more Protestant, till the Congregationalist chapel looked too worldly and he separated to be a disciple of some Plymouth Brethren who came into the Isle of Thanet. The gloom of the house, the anarchy of its conduct, the puritanism of its way of life, the contempt for the world, the sternness and yet what Herbert called the *extraordinary waywardness* of the father, the absence of a mother, the misery of the children, the ill health of the elder daughter, the drudgery demanded of the younger daughter Marion as she grew capable of drudgery, together made a childhood purgatory worthy of the pen of a Dickens or a Bronte.

So vehement a desire to keep his motherless family unspotted from a corrupt world forced Thomas Henson into a decision with long consequences. He decided that the children must not go to school. The normal route of escape was blocked.

The career of the brother a year older than Herbert, the only other of the children to make a worldly success of his life, says something about the heredity and the environment. Arthur (born 31 October 1862) escaped into business as soon as he was allowed. He went out to India, was able and very hardworking, and became indispensable to his firm. At last he won the repute of being the rudest man in Calcutta, collected a large fortune, and retired to Minehead in Somerset; where he lived several years unhappily, with no interests, and no friends, and no conversation, and no religion except prejudice against Roman Catholicism and Anglo-Catholicism. He inherited father's hatred of Catholics while he reacted against father's religion. He evidently inherited father's pessimism about a corrupt world.

His fame for being rude tells something also about father, and may help to understand the younger brother.

The old puritans ordered plainness of speech. Say what is true. Do not make friends by a courtesy which you do not feel.

Say no pleasant things about anyone for the sake of politeness, but only if you can be sincere. And if you see the human race as corrupt, you will often need to say what is unpleasant. Brother Arthur's reputation for being the rudest man in Calcutta, and Brother Herbert's reputation for writing the most caustic diary ever written by a Christian bishop, are doubtless linked to father's horror at the ruins of humanity. Never curry favour by words. Speak the truth about this wicked world.

And especially say what is unpleasant (if it is true) at times when your worldly interest would be fostered by saying what your hearers would like to hear.

Herbert Henson was too young to flee into business. Deprived of school companions, deprived of games, deprived of holidays, deprived of everything but religion, brothers, sisters, and a good library, he escaped into the library. At an early age he became the voracious reader of the family.

The books in the house were theological. Foxe's *Book of Martyrs* was and is good reading for a boy, especially when embellished with woodcuts of martyrs being tortured or burnt to death. *Pilgrim's Progress* can easily be read with excitement by a boy. He learnt to love *Paradise Lost*. But soon the child betrayed precocity. Starved of children's books and then of boys' books, he was forced to read what stood on the shelves; and so mastered adult and serious theologians; some of them bizarre minds from a world of prophecies, and apocalyptic, and speculations about the number of the Beast in Revelation; but others from a world of serious ethical thought, and study of St. Paul, narrower but at times too fundamental to be merely narrow. By the age of fourteen this prodigious boy had read as deeply in divinity as many young men when they take holy orders.

Three years after the mother's death the plight of the family was improved because Thomas Henson, probably realizing that no nurse could look after these five children, took another woman. He married her, but does not seem to have married her by law – if so, the record of it has not yet been found and possibly the Brethren disapproved of legal ceremonies. He was already over sixty years old – one of the difficulties of the younger children was the age of their father, not only his religion. She was nearly thirty years younger than her

husband. She was a German from Stuttgart who married an
Englishman named Parker and after his death earned her living
as companion to an eccentric old lady.

Emma Theodora Parker, in the words of her stepson, re-
created the home. She could bring order into the housekeep-
ing, but no instant happiness for a disturbed family. She never
won the affection of the eldest boy still at home, Arthur. Even
for Herbert, whose future she made and who all his years
would think of her more as mother than as stepmother, she
never quite took the place of the real mother in the boy's
affection. He later said of her that he always found her presence
more challenging than consoling. She soon saw that Herbert
was clever. She fed his mind with a wider range of reading, the
novels of Walter Scott, historians in translation like
Thucydides and Plutarch.

The possibility of escape elsewhere than into the library
appeared. Thomas Henson decided that the boy, thirteen years
old, should follow his father and brothers into business in
London. He arranged that one of the elder brothers should get
the boy work in his firm. Herbert was excited at the prospect
of an office stool. The luggage was packed, the cab stood at the
door waiting to take him to the railway station, and the
Church of the twentieth century almost lost its strangest
bishop when a telegram came from the brother in London
saying that after all he could not have Herbert in the firm.

*Bitter was my grief.*

Perhaps this 'calamity' at last enabled the stepmother to
break the long resistance of Thomas Henson to the idea that
the boy should go to school. To achieve this end needed a
campaign of four and a quarter years.

Eleven days after his fourteenth birthday Herbert Hensley
Henson sat for the first time on the bench of a classroom. The
school was local, the Broadstairs Collegiate School, headmaster Richard Burbidge. The boy arrived suddenly, in the
middle of the term (19 November 1877).

Of this school the boy thought little. But no school is well
adapted for boys who have read adult libraries by the time they
are fourteen, can recite from memory long chunks of famous
sermons from past centuries out of Blair's *Lectures on Rhetoric*,
and think games a sinful waste of time. The other boys were

amused to find that the odd creature knew, in some subjects, more than their headmaster. Henson was shocked to find such adult ignorance and held his headmaster in contempt. The boys were also amused to find that while they were out on the fields playing games, the newcomer preferred to sit in the old lecture hall writing an essay or a sermon or a manuscript *History of the Russo-Turkish War* with lyrical eloquence on the Battle of Plevna. Though he went to school, it was too late for him ever to be a boy among boys. He found the school *detestable*. The extreme isolation of his home and a mind which already thought in adult literature, were like walls isolating him from his contemporaries.

Almost to the end of his life he could not bear to mention this school. It made a difficulty, filling in the entry *education* in *Who's Who*. To the end of his life and after, *Who's Who* carried only the word – *education: private*. It was true in one sense. But he was ashamed to print in *Who's Who* the name of the only school which he attended.

What he learnt at Broadstairs Collegiate School was quite a lot of Latin and a smattering of Greek; not enough to be an accurate classical scholar; making him shy of Greek and leading to an occasional howler even with Latin; but indispensable to his future career. The only schoolmaster whom he liked was an old Frenchman of courtly manners. D'Aubigné discovered Henson's wish to be a preacher, and made him a present of a life of the immortal French preacher Bossuet, which contained specimens of Bossuet's sermons. Henson was impressed. In his father's library he had never met a Catholic preacher and was excited by the grandiloquent style of the French baroque.

This later childhood, this education, he resented for the rest of his life. When from time to time he looked back upon it, he felt horror. By the time he was in his late teens and thinking for himself, he regarded sectarian evangelical religion as a monstrous evil to be fought with every claw. He had horror of the Plymouth Brethren – *poisonous schismatics* he once called them, several times by other opprobrious names, and never with tolerance. He had horror of over-emotional evangelical preachers, the missionaries of the later nineteenth century, the Baptist Noels of his childhood, the itinerant assailants of the brittle hearts of youth. Their doctrines made him (using some of his own phrases) a *lone wolf*; a *game-less man*; a man who was never a boy; a *predestined outcast*; *bound to be unintelligible to my coevals*; a man whom the world must think odd; *an enigma to my contemporaries*; hopelessly at sea when companions talked of test matches; a man against common talk; a man against common opinion; a man against.

Emotional sectarian religion he hated at a level far deeper than that of the rational mind. He hated it in his guts. It ruined his childhood and hampered his happiness all the days of his life.

Years later he asked himself what he owed to the religion of his home. Here was a man who was a famous Christian bishop, and born in a very religious home. What was the continuity between the two? The second caused the first? He must be wrong in his diagnosis but could not bring himself to allow continuity. *My home contributed nothing to my religious development but a strong repugnance* [*to my father's religion*] *and (oddly enough) the childish ambition to become a preacher. Both persisted – the repugnance deepened as I grew into boyhood, and I did become a clergyman.*

Something is here concealed, and we do not know what. The repugnance had a connection, to us unknown, with villainy; not by the Congregational minister with whom he was sent to live, and whom he respected, but by a leader of the Plymouth Brethren. The grounds for thinking this are threefold:

(i) his references to Plymouth Brethren are violent, all his life.

(ii) In adult life he became fascinated by the novel *Elmer Gantry*, written by the American novelist Sinclair Lewis. This is a repulsive book about an American revivalist preacher who used his power over women for the sake of money and sexual licence. It was not the sort of novel which the normal Henson would read. But *Elmer Gantry* he read at least three times, and referred to it again and again. The references when catalogued look almost like a little obsession. Something in the book fitted his experience and touched a nausea in the memory.

When he later came to read Thomas Hardy's novel *Tess of the d'Urbervilles*, the portrait which moved him was unexpected, for it was that of the sensual man converted to Methodism, whose conversion left him no less sensual.

(iii) As a young man he came to know the life of the Presbyterian leader of the seventeenth century, Richard Baxter. In voluminous and chaotic and enthralling *Reliquiae*, Baxter left an account of his own education. When Henson read of Baxter's education he felt their early experiences to be uncannily alike.

Baxter told how his father was much entangled in debt through gaming, so that the debt 'occasioned some excess of worldly cares before it was freed'. In the village were four readers in succession, ignorant men, immoral in their lives; the ordained men who were schoolmasters taught school and tippled on weekdays and whipped the boys when they were drunk. His father read the Bible alone, and oppressed him with the fear of sinning, until the boy suffered from 'a throbbing conscience'; stealing first from orchards, too addicted to novels, arrogant of his precocious learning, bold and irreverent towards his parents. He wanted to go to university but was kept from it and taught in school. His mother died and father married again, a pious and good stepmother.

Henson found the resemblance extraordinary. It reached right down to the most trivial details, even to stealing in orchards, for Henson never forgot how when he was five or six, his mother of the flesh caught him stripping the raspberry bushes in the garden at Vale Villa.

After Henson became part of the ruling élite of England, he suffered from a grudge that he never went to a public school. His chaplain used regularly to walk him round the great park of Bishop Auckland, and as regularly he would grieve at his inadequacies and attribute them to the monstrous nature of his education and say what a loss he bore by never going to a public school. With an equal persistence his chaplain would tell him that other men lacked this schooling and seemed not to mind. Nothing shook the belief. It was curious, for he regarded public schools as citadels of class privilege and as divisive in the social system; was inclined to attribute the complaisance and lack of principle among other ecclesiastics to their training in corporate spirit at boarding schools; thought that those schools repressed individuality and moulded men into types. Yet continually, even to tedium, he lamented that he had not endured this fate.

A part of the feeling consisted in a wrong diagnosis of his unease among his contemporaries. He had a sense that he did not easily make friends with the people most like himself. Another part was a dream about the glory of a classical education. He moved among men who could still recite fifty lines out of Vergil from memory, and instantly understood jests or references from the ancient world. He idealized the faculty, and longed, and knew that now he could never possess.

All this was only a symptom of an emotion more violent. He had a horror of his own education, and not without reason; for this was the same as horror at his early years at home.

He felt deprived of public school because he felt deprived of school. The worry was a superficial symptom of a deep self-doubt. He was apt to be envious of other people's boyhoods, and to imagine them paradisal. So often through the years he kept asking himself, what is the effect upon an adult if during his boyhood he was not allowed to be a boy?

During his education some person unknown helped him to a possession that comes to few. Whether it was stepmother, or mild Congregationalist, or Congregationalist's unpleasant wife, or Burbidge, or one of Burbidge's assistants, we do not know. But when his handwriting first appears on the stage of history, when he was twenty-one, it is already, and recognizably, the famous hand. It had not yet the artistry which made the letters of the adult Henson a joy to receive apart from their contents. But already it was firm, rounded, legible, and friendly to see on the page. Someone in his education must have helped. He never looked back upon this acquisition with a sense of gratitude, only with a pleasure at the shapeliness of English lettering and the magic of English words in their visible sacrament.

The growing influence of stepmother was suddenly marked when the boy was baptized.

A sailor named Captain Field came to Ramsgate to conduct a mission. He was noted for his breezy quarterdeck manner and full-blooded style of oratory. Herbert Henson attended his meeting. When Field appealed for the people who were unconfirmed to be confirmed, Herbert resolved to mark his discipleship by confirmation. But he could not be confirmed because he was not baptized.

The three young children, aged fifteen, fourteen, and thirteen, were all baptized at Minster parish church, away from home, without any preparation. Then Herbert was confirmed after an odd preparation; partly by a high-church rector and partly by a low-church Irish curate. He endured these last classes only because they were a gate to confirmation. He made his first communion at a large evening service at Christ Church, Ramsgate, and was not edified.

The boy was in rebellion against father's religion. His father hated papists. The boy was accustomed to walk over to the nearest Roman Catholic Church, St. Augustine's in Ramsgate, and was attracted by the *sombre dignity*, the curious charm of its stillness, and its uncanny remoteness from the vulgar distractions of the outside world. *It suggests a religion wonderfully unlike that which offended me so much in my Protestant home.* His visits were observed, and someone (*busybody*, he thought) told his father that the boy was thinking about becoming a Roman Catholic. The father challenged the son; who replied that there was no truth whatever in the story that he was about to become a Roman Catholic, and in prudence ceased to attend St. Augustine's.

When Thomas Henson moved to Pegwell Bay, he left Herbert as a boarder at the Broadstairs Collegiate School. Not for long. Though the boy had been at school so few terms, something about his ability, and probably a good deal about his character, caused the headmaster to make this studious adolescent of sixteen, who refused to play games and spent his spare time drafting sermons, into the head boy. The choice was not wise if the headmaster wanted a quiet life.

Boys in the dormitory misbehaved. The headmaster demanded of the head boy to know what happened. Henson told him what happened, but refused to say who were the culprits. At the age of eighty-three Henson still had no doubt of the axiom that the head boy would have been wrong to name the culprits. The headmaster summoned a meeting of the school, and in a scene of high drama accused his head boy, in the presence of all the other boys, of lying.

The puritan Henson family glowed with ardour for truth. To be accused of lying was the worst of insults, and to be humiliated in front of the school was more than Henson could bear. He flared up. At that meeting before the school, *there was a scene, in which I delivered myself with more passion than respect.* His situation was now intolerable. That night *I wrote to the exasperated pedagogue a scathing letter of farewell*, gave it to a friend to deliver, climbed over the wall of the school playground, and walked the distance of more than 5 miles to the new Henson house. He arrived home in the early hours of the morning, to a second scene of drama, *the amazement of my family* and the *indignation of my father.*

Here was a boy who had run away from school, and if he had not run away was sure to be expelled. Whatever the truth about the quarrel over the dormitory, no one could deny that the boy had failed at school. Relations between boy and father, strained already, came to breaking point.

In his memory afterwards he saw another barrier between father and son which he would hardly realize at the time. The intruder was education. Father came from a simple farming home where boys left school young. Father liked to read religious books. Son discovered for himself books. As he despised his headmaster for knowing so little, he could hardly respect the unsophistication of his father. And this was another plank in the remorse which afterwards he would feel about his early home. It is harder, he once wrote, *to be on terms of dutiful deference to one's parents when they belong to a lower social stratum than that to which we have been raised.*[1]

Discontented boy and discontented father were trapped within the same four walls. *I began to cast about for a way of escape.* A friend suggested that he apply through one of the agencies for a teaching post. The plan worked. Perhaps in his application he was not forced to state his age, or perhaps the headmaster was desperate for assistants; but whatever the case the boy, still only sixteen years old and looking young, found himself an assistant master or 'usher' at Brigg grammar school in Lincolnshire.

He found the school to be good. He liked the headmaster, a Mr Flower. The headmaster asked him what he meant to do with his future, Henson had no doubt of the answer. Already he practised preaching sermons, ever since the family found him preaching in a nightshirt. He said that he intended to seek

[1] *Discipline and Law*, (1898), 90.

ordination. He evidently added that he could not afford the money.

Flower was an Oxford graduate and for the first time opened the idea that to aim at Oxford University was not wild. Since a reform of 1868 it became possible for an under-graduate to attend Oxford University without also attending a college, and colleges were expensive. He could become a non-collegiate student. No doubt Flower saw the precocious brain of the boy and realized that if he were to be a clergyman he should certainly pass through a university and not along one of the still disreputable byways by which men could be ordained without a university degree.

Henson applied to his home. We can imagine the argument. A father who deprived his children of school lest their minds and morals be corrupted, and who himself had no experience of a university, would think a phantom Oxford to be the cess-pit of England. Moreover he was falling ever more into debt, the want of money hurt the family, he had three children more to bring up. Under such conditions how could Herbert be sent to a university, expensive even in its down-at-heel form?

The victory was won by the stepmother. She believed in the boy's ability and in the boy's vocation. She was also ambitious for his sake. The fight was long and hard, but at length she won. Thomas Henson agreed that the boy might be a non-collegiate student at Oxford. He made conditions. The boy must earn part of his keep, he might stay at Oxford only for the minimum period of three years necessary for the degree, and he must live as cheaply as possible.

So it was decided. Herbert Henson never forgot this trem-endous debt to his stepmother. There remained the problem of getting into Oxford, that is, passing the examination for matriculation. To a normally prepared schoolboy this was the easiest of tests. On theology and probably on history this boy knew more than any other boy in the kingdom. On certain other subjects, normal in most boys' knowledge, he was ignorant. A boy who spent less than three years at school, and who owed his knowledge chiefly to a theological library directed towards the nature of the Last Judgment, could hardly be well tutored in all the usual subjects. Oxford's demand for the Greek language made a hurdle. The headmaster of Brigg school added to his generosity by seeing that his young assistant was prepared to pass. The hurdle was not high. With the mellow wisdom of the centuries, Oxford required a knowledge of Greek from its applicants and then tried its hardest to see that they could not fail the test.

In October 1881 Henson matriculated at Oxford, and became an undergraduate, and entered a society remote from everything he knew. He was not quite eighteen, and looked still younger. This new undergraduate was affectionate, puritan in morals, very outspoken, very religious, hating Protestant dissent, anxious about money, with a distant reverence for a world of classical scholarship and a regret that he could hardly enter it, loving books, and aiming to educate himself to be a preacher.

The historian might expect a young man, coming out of narrow circumstances, to feel more than a little nervous. That was not what Henson's memory later told. He remembered his state of mind, in a carriage of that first train which he ever took from Paddington to Oxford, as over-confident if not arrogant.

Certainly this was a disadvantage. He appeared to have climbed into this new world by cleverness and obstinacy, owing nothing to an incompetent headmaster and winning a rebellion against the authority of his father.

The burden of the upbringing was heavy, and he must carry it through his adult life. To Henson the word *home* did not come bearing with it clouds of glory, except when he thought of his mother of the flesh. It came to him as a matter for his penitence, that he was so undutiful a son – the Oxford freshman son versus the ex-warehouseman father. Every son in the world wonders, after his parents die, whether he did for them what he could while they lived, and cannot but be touched with little memories of guilt. This heavy constituent of filial mourning loomed darker to Henson. It came to him like *a burden on the conscience, a shadow on the life, an accusation on the ear.*[1]

The heritage was not all loss. Years later he could write or speak with a rare sensitivity about the difficulties in family

---

[1] *Discipline and Law*, 95.

life, the moral pressures of the home, the kinship or the antagonisms of children and their parents.

The heritage had another consequence which some will think gain and some think loss. Men who grew easily and naturally in happy families are seldom interested in describing their own history. A boy with an unusual childhood never quite loses the feeling that in some way he is strange. He wants to understand himself, and see by what circuitous passage he came to be the person that he knows, if he knows. By an acquired necessity he is introspective. The natural auto-biographers are those whose paths in childhood turned corners.

Half a century later ten publishers competed for Henson's autobiography. By now he loved writing about himself and his state of mind. And yet he shrank back from the beginning – *I shall be forced to say much which it is horribly painful to parade before the public; and it will be difficult to speak frankly about my father without falling into impiety. Yet his character and conduct are integral to an understanding of mine.*

# 2.  OXFORD

HIS MEMORY that he arrived at Oxford confident did not mean that he lost his sense of shame. For most men who go to Oxford or Cambridge the college is as important as the university, often more important, the source of their friendships with other undergraduates, the chance of their stimulus from dons. When they list their education in *Who's Who* they do not simply put Oxford but preface it by the name of the college. Not so Henson. For all his later life and beyond, *Who's Who* carried the single word Oxford. He was an 'Unattached student', a 'non-collegiate', and he minded. These non-collegiate students were known to other undergraduates as 'toshers'. This was believed to be an inebriated attempt at 'unattached', and was contemptuous. Henson minded being a 'tosher'.

Until the system of modern grants, a class of students existed in the ancient universities known as troglodytes. They could not afford to come out of their rooms. If they came out someone might offer them a drink and then they might feel obliged to offer him a drink. They lived remote, in the cheapest possible room, up some high tower with an attic ceiling or distant lodgings remote from the rest of the university. They stayed with their books.

The unattached students were not by majority troglodytes. Sensible tutors gathered them into a loose society for games and rowing. But Henson regarded rowing and football as a sinful waste of time. He became a troglodyte; living in cheap lodgings in Cowley, *unduly absorbed* in his work, counting every penny, and feeling *terribly poor*. If Oxford was supposed to bring him happiness, he found that it belied his hopes. He was *isolated from the general life*. Hour after hour he stayed with his books.

Since his Greek was sketchy he could not read the Greats to which nearly all the abler Oxford minds still aspired. A future preacher might be expected to think of Theology. But Henson could hardly read Theology, which also demanded accurate Greek; and he knew that his father would regard Oxford theology with less than enthusiasm. He inherited something of this attitude. Theology at Oxford was likely to corrupt the faith of the young. Therefore he had to read the new honours school of Modern History, which many in Oxford regarded as an easy option for boys who at school were idle about learning their ancient languages. Modern History was just then over-hauling Classics as the course which attracted most under-graduates. But few of them were able.

He already knew a lot of history. Now he devoured books. Always his mind was highly organized, and for writing the English language he had a natural gift which he fostered by assiduous practice in exercise books. As at school he needed no schoolmaster, at university he needed no tutor. Books lay everywhere in Oxford. Henson ate them.

We do not know what regular lectures he attended nor who tutored him for most of his course. He heard Ruskin give a single lecture and thought him mad and incoherent. During his last two terms before the examination he hired a young clergyman to prepare him – E. W. Watson, later to be an Oxford professor; and Watson, though a shy man and a dull talker who delivered good matter in a sad monotone, read books with the hard determination of Henson himself and grew to be a friend as well as a coach.

The History School at Oxford offered choices, but its bias lay towards the history of the Middle Ages. When Henson came up to Oxford, the Regius Professor of Modern History was William Stubbs, founder of the systematic study of the English Middle Ages. A young man who at school had written *A History of the Russo-Turkish War*, and whose Latin was imperfect, might have been expected to head for the modern age. Henson, though he neither met Stubbs nor attended his regular lectures (though he heard him at least once), headed for the Middle Ages. With a passionate interest in church history, and an inherited dislike of popes and archbishops, he was not discontented to find that his special subject was the Life of St. Thomas à Becket, Archbishop of Canterbury. King Henry II, whose loose words caused Becket's murder in Canterbury Cathedral, became a hero to the young Henson. The under-graduate became a historian of the Early Middle Ages; clear-headed, able, ranging; with basic disqualifications for understanding all that he read, partly because it was all popery, and partly because it smelt to him of ignorance and superstition compared with the dream-world of Greek and Latin classics which he fancied to be so civilized and literate by comparison. All his life he saw the Middle Ages – not quite all the Middle Ages – as barbarous.

But now religious development affected the study of history.

On Sundays he attended the university sermons at St. Mary's Church. Here he heard most of the famous preachers of the day. Naturally the select preachers to the University of Oxford were never chosen from that extreme evangelical group in which Henson was nurtured and against which he reacted.

He thought these events memorable. When we look down the list of Oxford select preachers for those years we do not see why, since one or two of them were well known for being dreary in a pulpit.

But when we learn which preachers he mentions as specially memorable we see why.

The first came to Oxford and held a colourful kind of mission in the town hall only two days after Henson matriculated. He was a bizarre creature who by all the standards of rational history was trivial, a wandering eccentric – Father Ignatius Lyne – dressed in his own version of the Benedictine habit. He said that he was a monk and was reviving the monastic life in the Church of England. He claimed to have worked miracles. He could not have got leave from bishops to preach in parish churches after all the curious things that had happened. In later life Henson would have made short work of Father Ignatius. The freshman Henson was moved in heart as he listened to the passionate utterance and saw the black monk gesticulating on the platform with a total sincerity. In his mind he did not even put the noun *monk* into inverted commas. The words made *a kind of rhapsody* on the crucified Christ, and knew that over him at least they had *strange power*. Henson was still conscious of an appeal in the Catholic mass.

Any parent might have been disturbed if he knew that his son at Oxford sat at the feet of Father Ignatius, for the monk's reputation in the wide world was doubtful. Imagination boggles at what that extreme Protestant Thomas Henson thought or said if he heard about the sermon of Father Ignatius; and we may infer that he heard, because he taught his children to say what was true especially when it would be disliked by the hearer.

The next important sermon would make things no better. F. W. Farrar, then a Canon of Westminster, is famous for his book *Eric, or Little by Little*, the most sentimental novel about education ever perpetrated by a prominent man. Whatever charges can be lodged against the religion of Henson's family, no one could charge it with sentimentality. Moreover, during that first winter of Henson's time at Oxford, Farrar was the heretic in the Church of England. Naturally, the undergraduates of Oxford flocked to hear him when he came in the February of 1882, among them young Henson, who crammed himself into the crowded gallery. He afterwards felt that of all the sermons of his day in Oxford, this was the utterance which most moved him. It was thus far like the fervent oddities of Father Ignatius, in being an eloquent poem about the crucified Christ; rich in language, too rich, full of purple passages, but unlike Father Ignatius full of intellectual power. Afterwards he was certain that Farrar's notoriety as a heretic was undeserved.[1]

The third choice shows that the young man was growing. Farrar was a popular preacher, Father Ignatius too popular. R. W. Church, Dean of St. Paul's, could not draw the crowds, the church had plenty of room; for he was austere, quiet, gentle, reserved, almost shy, and scorned the tricks of the orator. He stood at the opposite extreme to a hell-fire evangelist like Father Ignatius. He was a high churchman to his fingertips, Cardinal Newman's intimate friend, a trusted and celebrated leader of that movement beginning to be called Anglo-Catholic. Henson looked up at him and saw *the unearthly refinement of a scholar-saint*.[2] All his life Henson remained faithful to the conviction that he never heard a more impressive teacher than Dean Church. When he started his own career he always kept by him the volumes of Church's sermons.

An itinerant monk suspect for being a Roman Catholic – a

[1] Cf. *The Value of the Bible* (1904) 243–4.
[2] *Letters*, 2. 100.

famous 'heretic' of the liberal school – a leader of the Anglo-
Catholic party – these are three of those who influenced his
mind by their words while he was an undergraduate at
Oxford. None of them could have pleased Thomas Henson.

This consuming religious interest began to make some of
his work for the history school look trivial. A man in quest of
religious transition finds higher things to do than trace the
careers of the murderers of Archbishop Becket.

Though he had no friends, and hid away in his lodgings, he
came to know a few other historians. We know the names of
two. During the early summer of his second year he attended
the Historical Seminar, where a young Scot of Balliol named
Cosmo Gordon Lang read a paper on the prime minister
Chatham. Henson admired Lang's handsome face, attractive
voice, and ornate diction; but even more admired the brilliant
eyes and learned comments of a member of the audience
named Charles Oman, then a junior fellow of All Souls. The
respect was returned. But with few exceptions Henson had
not time for friendships and did not regret. Later in life he
advised a young protégé going to Oxford that *Oxford is a*
*wonderful place for making friends but many of them are not worth*
*making*.

Meanwhile the religious unsettlement grew no calmer. It
was the age when men still argued about the truth of the Bible.
He kept away from the worst arguments because he kept away
from people. But his reading, and the sermons which he heard
so often, kept bringing before him the great debate of that day.
*As my knowledge increased, so did questions multiply and doubts*
*thrust themselves into my mind . . . In the atmosphere of a modern*
*university . . . the pieties of youth are sorely tried*. Two of his
brothers, reacting from their home, moved away from all
faith. The debate was impossible to avoid. From a society
where Adam and Eve were historical personages, and where
Balaam's ass spoke, and where Calvinism was all the truth that
mattered, he entered a society where hardly anyone thought
that a serpent really tempted a woman with the apples of the
tree of life, and where Calvinism was disreputable. Since in his
turn he was reacting against the religion of his home, he was
not disturbed to find that Oxford University did not profess
that religion. Nevertheless his foundations collapsed. A sensi-

tive conscience and immature youth suffered the uncertainties and emotions generated by being freed to ask himself what he believed about the world. Selecting a philosophy can never be other than uncomfortable. The only thing certain was, his religion would not be the religion of his father.

We cannot lift the veil on this internal debate. Probably it was more half-conscious than articulate to himself. He was more aware that important things happened than what happened. At one point in his private meditation in old age he raised a little fringe of the veil. He said that during his undergraduate years he discovered for the first time a poem which helped him as he wrestled with his faith. It was Robert Browning's *A Death in the Desert*; especially, said Henson, the epilogue. St. John, hunted and very old, lay dying in a cave in the desert. His friends watched at his side hoping that he would speak, while a Bactrian sentry stood on guard near the mouth of the cave, pretending to graze a goat. The dying man knows that he is the last survivor, who had seen, and walked, and handled, and could remember. When he goes, not one will be left. And the poem ends with a faith in the Lord whose power will survive the passing of all who had seen.

In June 1884 this hard reader and lover of books, with a clear head and a mature style, was placed in the first class of the honours school of Modern History.

At this point his history coach, Hutton of St. John's, gave him a piece of advice which caused him ever afterwards to look upon Hutton as a benefactor. Hutton said that he should enter for the All Souls Fellowship competition in October; for under their recent statutes All Souls were bound to offer fellowships to lawyers and historians by competition. Henson took the advice and entered. What his papers were like cannot be known, but the examiners were not unanimous and carried the election only by a small majority. On 2 November 1884 two friends from the historical seminar, Charles Oman and C. R. L. Fletcher, already young Fellows of All Souls, burst into his impoverished lodging in Cowley to tell Henson that he was elected. Henson found the news incredible. He was not quite twenty-one.

The undergraduate career at Oxford was formative both for mind and soul. Henson looked back upon that career as *wretched ruinous years.* He dismissed it all, from start to finish, in a single sentence. *I have always regarded my election to the All Souls Fellowship as the beginning of my Oxford life.*

## ALL SOULS

The government of England had lately changed the constitution of the universities and forced new statutes, and new aims, and better use of endowments, upon the colleges. All Souls, with plenty of endowment and only four nominal under-graduates (called Bible-clerks) scandalized every reformer; and during the later 1870s this public exposure started a war between parties among the fellows, conservatives v. reformers, with a radical or two in the wings. The Fellows of All Souls were a group of educated gentlemen, drawing a stipend, and coming from time to time for a feast – a few of them lived in college, and ordered the institution. They were a pleasant group of men. But the cold breezes of utility blew, and the members of the college must ask themselves whether the world could see their community as a justifiable modern use of an ancient endowment.

The fellows were not just country gentlemen. They included the leading European student of oriental religion; the Chichele Professor of Modern History in the university; the Reader in English Law; the Vinerian Professor of English Law (Dicey); the Chichele Professor of International Law and Diplomacy; and a strong tradition of legal studies which also meant that three of the fellows were Members of Parliament. The argument between the function of the college as endowment of learning, and its function as a place of research or education, was not simple and at times was tense. It was ended by the victory of moderate reform in the election in 1881 of a lawyer as Warden, Sir William Anson, the first lay Warden. The choice of clever young lawyers, or historians like Henson, was a sign of the new system.

Never before had All Souls elected a fellow like Henson; either intellectually or socially like. In his own person he was the widening of Oxford University; a historian instead of a classic, educated (if educated) at the obscurest of schools, lower-middle class by origin, and from a home getting rapidly poorer. The parents of another young fellow elected at the same time, Frank Pember, lived in a castle. A fellow elected the following year, the future Marquess Curzon, had an Hon. before his name and his parents lived in a stately home. Moreover Pember, though now engaged in legal studies, had behind him a brilliant classical career at Balliol. Curzon had a similar Balliol background, with a first class in Classical Moderations; and when the examiners placed him in the second class in Greats he was reported to have said, 'Now I shall devote the rest of my life to proving that they have made a mistake.' Pember and Curzon had an excellent education and were not tempted to suppose that they arrived at All Souls by their unaided brains. Henson suffered from the disadvantage that he had done it all himself. He sounded, and sometimes was, arrogant at his own cleverness. The Warden once said that he was the proudest man he had ever met. That was saying a lot, in a college where young Curzon was one of the fellows.

A man who for three years lived a hermit life in that gregarious university could not easily be absorbed into a humane society. He still looked a boy. He was on his best behaviour. His clothes were a little too dapper, his hair too neatly tended, his manners fastidious. He was not without suspicion, not without contempt, especially when he saw or feared irreligion. They found him angular in personality, liable to talk too much and too dogmatically. The training to speak the truth especially when the audience will dislike it made him an awkward denizen of a common room.

Being a civilized group of men, they began the process of mellowing. Under this treatment Henson warmed and responded. The fellows discovered that in electing this unusual creature, they elected not only a fellow unlike any they had ever met, but a friendly affectionate youth with a gift for sparkling talk and witty repartee. Never in his life hitherto had Henson a chance of experiencing anything like the friendships which now began. He came to regard the Fellows of All Souls as a several-headed substitute for a father.

The Warden came nearest to this status of foster-father. He was an unfailingly courteous and friendly person, able to reconcile old conservatives with young hotheads, too gentle for the House of Commons when he was given office there, but benign and stable in presiding over a changing society of unusual minds. His manner or appearance had something in it that was precise, even prim; but he relieved it by a twinkle and a drollery, and his affection was paternal. He did not idealize his young men. He condemned Henson for extravagance and disorderliness. But Henson was not the only young fellow to feel that the Warden cared personally about him and his future. When Anson died more than thirty years later, it was Henson who took time from a busy life to edit the *Memoir* (1920).

The portrait of Anson in the *Memoir* is not vivid, and was not idealized, for Henson learnt at home that you must not idealize even the dead. But the feeling of a son's affection is unmistakable to the reader of the dry pages.

Into the common room came famous men of Church and State, prime ministers and politicians, judges and civil servants. Henson met Gladstone; and one evening there came to dine the legendary historian of that age, Lord Acton, who knew everything and therefore wrote nothing. When Acton was in the mood, he was the best talker in the world. But this was not one of his conversational evenings, for all his life Henson kept the memory of a man with *the mysterious taciturnity and immobile countenance of an Assyrian monarch on an excavated monument*. Henson was invited to breakfast with the presiding genius of later nineteenth-century Oxford, Jowett the Master of Balliol, and surprised another guest by daring to contradict his host.

As he grew at home in common room talk his habits as well as his speech came freer. He would talk and talk, with sudden movement, cross-legged on the floor, or sitting the wrong way round on his chair, or climbing up and plonking his little figure on the end of the mantlepiece. His friends remembered an evening when Henson and the future diplomat Arthur Hardinge fought an argument from each end of the mantlepiece. They found his ferocity against nonconformists interesting if not alarming. Henson's name appears with a frequency (which he later smiled at as *indecent*) in the betting book of the common room.[1] Evidently he had parted, not only from father's religion, but from bits of father's code of morals.

---

[1] Charles Oman, *The Text of the Senior Betting Book of All Souls College* (privately printed, 1938).

Betting was not the only bit. Brought up to believe that games were sin, Henson could now be found playing tennis in the quad at All Souls, or walking in the Parks to watch cricket.

The betting-book reveals the interests of the little society, and of young Henson. For small sums they bet on marriages, or horses, or the next Archbishop of Canterbury, or the next election, or the next pope, or the weight of the fellows, or whether the word *college* is found in the Authorized Version of the Bible (it is, and Henson who made the wager lost his money), or the correctness of literary reference from Scott, or Dickens, or Gray. Henson lost his first shilling in a bet to decide who shot a rook in *Pickwick Papers*. Some of the bets could be checked on the spot and money changed hands instantly. Some (as on future marriages) were not paid for several years. Henson paid one bet twenty-eight years after he took it, on Frank Pember's future weight.

He was not the most numerous better in that book, for Doyle the librarian resided much longer and carried away the prize with 76 out of 590 wagers laid between 1873 and 1907. But in his own brief time of residence Henson carried off the record, 17 bets out of 36, or nearly half the total. He never betted on horses, only on a literary argument, or politics, or personal characteristics. The other fellows were amused at his signature in the book. It started as *H. H. Henson*. Soon it turned with a flourish into *H. Hensley Henson*. Knox bet him that it would alter again within the next five years. Curzon won a bet against Pember about the number of Henson's bets because he specified the signature *H. Hensley Henson*, and Pember paid his 2*s*. 6*d*. under protest when he discovered that *H. H. Henson* did not count.

Beneath this flippancy, and common room trivialities, and literary argument, and political prophecy, and university gossip, Henson was engaged in being serious. And the betting book shows that not all the fellows were certain how seriously they should take his seriousness of purpose.

The first and indispensable condition of Henson's happiness was his stipend, £200 a year for seven years. Here was freedom.

But it did not rid him of money cares. It came in a manner the most inconvenient possible. The old customs of an old

college were not only sacred but vexatious. In February 1885
he received the stipend for the last two months of 1884. Then
he got no more pay till the end of February 1886. So he must
live fourteen months on pay for two months. So long as he
stayed in college he could live 'free' – but not so free because he
must furnish his rooms. A fellow living in a college could
hardly behave as a hermit. But the pressure was worst from
outside. Thomas Henson was bankrupt, his property was
mortgaged, he could hardly feed and clothe, still less educate,
the younger children. The elder boys vanished overseas,
Arthur disappeared into India and severed all communication
with home, Frank failed in the draper's business, and meanwhile the youngest boy, Gilbert, was still to be educated and
there were the two girls, the only two people in the world
whom Henson loved deeply and emotionally. In the moment
when Henson began to earn so modest a stipend he must save
all he could for the sake of the five people back at Ramsgate.
He was their only resource. He needed more money than his
stipend. This sense of pressure never left him over the next few
years. It felt at its worst during 1886. He kept borrowing
money in advance from the bursar of the college. He disliked
this need and tried to avoid being a suppliant.

Therefore, after only five months of fellowship, he arranged
for a tutoring post for six months during the spring and
summer of 1885. His former private coach for the honours
school, Edward Watson, had just gone as a curate to
Birkenhead; and through him Henson arranged to spend the
months in Birkenhead coaching the indolent son of William
Rathbone MP in return for a fee of £150, which met his need.
In April he went to Birkenhead. On 12 May 1885 he began the
famous diary.

The author of the diary, as he at last emerges into the light
after the hidden years of childhood, is the most extraordinary
young man that ever was a fellow of a college.

That he hated the work of tutoring, or was a militant
Anglo–Catholic and stout Tory, might not be expected from
one of his origins. But something else perturbs.

The strong impression made by the diary is the hatred of
dissenters. He went round Watson's parish on *hunting expeditions*, sniffing out faith-healers, Salvation Army meetings, and

schism-shops, contending with prophets, recording blasphemy and tastelessness, registering his revulsion in the language of abuse and scorn. This nose for 'schism' was not all pain. Horrified by what he saw and contemptuous of what he heard, he nevertheless enjoyed the quest, like a beagle hunting its prey. *I find schism-hunting wholly destructive of my time. However there certainly is some compensation.* The language is so vituperative in an educated man that we can only account for it by that obsession of which we already know.

Secondly he looked back upon his six months at Birkenhead as important, but not by reason of his persecution of the sects. Hitherto his world was narrower than the world of any previous Fellow of All Souls. Thomas Henson never took his children away. Herbert Henson knew the Isle of Thanet well, London as a place for changing trains, a little town in Lincolnshire, the colleges of the University of Oxford, and the lodging houses of Cowley. He had never been anywhere else. The world consisted only of holiday-makers, landladies, retired professional men, undergraduates, and dons. Edward Watson, the curate of Birkenhead, changed this dramatically. Discoursing enchanting matter in his monotonous voice, he walked his friend through the parish, day after day. Henson at last met the people of England: docks, slums, rows of worker houses, demoralized, unemployed. Sometimes Watson took him inside the houses of the poor and Henson found that he was disturbed, even shocked. *Surely something must be wrong somewhere in the body politic if this state of things should exist. I'm afraid, if I stay here for the next six months, I shall become a Socialist* (18 May 1885).

The curate Watson gave him another kind of chance. Since the small boy preached in his nightshirt to the consternation of his family, Henson wanted to be a preacher. Watson had a schoolroom with a little mission service on Wednesday evenings and where therefore a layman (according to legal authority) might speak. Watson's oratory always sounded so sad (though its matter was not) that attendance was scanty. He enlisted Henson to speak; and the voice which later filled churches fuller than any other voice in England gave the first 'sermon' on 10 June 1885, to a handful of people. He still looked like a boy. When Watson went away on his summer

holiday, he left Henson in charge. It was the first effort at a
life's work. Henson enjoyed it vastly. He thought it made the
tutoring of Lyle Rathbone bearable.

Meanwhile he founded two societies.

The Stubbs Society at Oxford is the society where members
of the university (or visitors) read papers about history.
Henson founded it in the autumn of 1884,[1] and it flourishes to
this day.

The other society perished sooner. During the winter after
he returned from Birkenhead the Liberal Party attacked the
establishment of the Church in Wales. Henson hated dissent.
He therefore assembled a group in his rooms at All Souls on
10 February 1886 and persuaded them to found a society for
defending the establishment of the Church, to be called The
Oxford Laymen's League for the Defence of the National
Church. He became the secretary; enlisted in aid magnates of
the university like the President of Magdalen. When he could
get a prominent Liberal to appear on his platform he achieved a
coup, and so he persuaded the Warden of All Souls, who
believed in an established Church, and Thomas Hughes, the
author of *Tom Brown's Schooldays*. Rumours surrounded this
league. It was gossiped that Henson had founded a new order
of preachers; or that he intended to introduce an order of
Jesuits into the Church of England. The Anglo-Catholicism of
the young firebrand did not go unobserved. Even when these
rumours were dispelled, the cause attracted a little mild
mockery from the lukewarm. But Henson was ardent and
active. He went all the way to a village in Norfolk to speak at a
public meeting in favour of the league which he founded. The
meeting has this historic importance, that it was the first
occasion when a newspaper bothered to give a long report of
what he said (more than four columns of speech, and a leading
article, in the *Norfolk Mail* (16 November 1886). It was proof
that he could hold and excite an audience over an hour and
twenty minutes.

Broadstairs taught him that sects were pernicious.
Birkenhead taught him that the poor needed an endowed
ministry, they could not support chapels for themselves. Disestablishers were enemies of the poor. So he worked at the

[1] Bodleian Library MS Top. Oxon. d. 292/1.

problem; getting up subjects like tithe endowments, rates, charitable status. He became an expert.

To men like Anson, and to every member of a political party, he seemed odd and unpredictable. He was strong for the Tory Party because they defended the Church against disestablishment and therefore were the party defending the poor. But his passion for the poor, discovered in Birkenhead, made him propound radical courses which could not be agreeable to ordinary members of the Tory Party. The Warden, who was a famous Liberal, called him 'a Jacobin lacquered over to look like a Tory'. He felt, and was not silent about, the contrast between the squalor of the unemployed and these comfortable gentlemen living in college. Sometimes the fellows defended themselves against this onslaught with a 'tu quoque', taunting him with not practising what he preached. But they did not find his earnestness too solemn. Except when the discussion fell to serious talk, they found him amusing and light-hearted.

Behind the scenes he had an important experience, the day after he returned from Birkenhead to Oxford.

He walked along the river to Iffley and went into the empty church. In the silence the troubles of his family afflicted him, the illness of his sister, the disappearance of his brother Arthur, the burden which fell upon him to educate a younger brother, the poverty of his parents, and his depression of spirits over the tutoring in Birkenhead.

In the silence of Iffley church, with soft light falling through the stained glass, he spread all this trouble of mind before his Maker. Then by a sudden impulse he walked to the altar, passed the sanctuary cord, stood in front of the altar with his hand upon it, looked at the marble cross in front of his eyes, and took a solemn vow:

*I felt that I was accepting a life of struggle and sorrow: it was as if the Lord Christ had raised His hands and shown the nail-prints, and pointed to the cross, and called me to follow Him. There in Iffley church, and standing before the altar, with my hand upon it, I dedicated myself to God and the Church. Registered in the Archives of Heaven is my vow, and here also, in the time to come, a reminder to me not to forget.*

Though this contemporary record fails to mention it, the vow contained a vow to the single life for the sake of the poor. The nature of this pledge to celibacy was not very precise. As it grew in precision, it turned into a determination that for the sake of work among the poor he would remain unmarried for at least ten years.

Eighteen years later he told a friend – it was the only time, so far as we know, that he mentioned the experience to another – something more about the vow at the altar of Iffley church. What he said fits what we know about the mood at that moment. He told her that the words of the vow were these: *I would never let considerations of my personal reputation and advantage influence my public course.* This harmonizes with the contemporary evidence because of the miserable meditation on the family which immediately preceded, and in a manner caused, the vow. He came back from Birkenhead determined to dedicate his life to the poor of England by going among them and sharing their poverty. But how could he? How could he share anyone's poverty? He was the only bread-winner of a family in trouble, he needed nothing so much as money, the wants of the family pushed rather towards ambition than self-sacrifice. How can a man take a vow of poverty when thereby he sacrifices not only himself but a deeply loved sister hardly able to fend for herself, another sister being immolated on the altar of household chores and care for parents, and three other persons for whom he was an important stay? He could not help the ambition. In Iffley he vowed that that ambition should never influence his career.

The vow at Iffley was not a vow to take holy orders. He would be a layman, dedicating himself to the poor. But for a man like Henson, with his upbringing and environment, ordination was the only way in which the vow could be fulfilled. From time to time he contemplated being a member of a lay order of preachers which he and others would found. But by December 1885 he decided for ordination. This was partly caused by the discovery that vows are easily broken. The experiences of the Michaelmas Term 1885 did not appear suitable to someone who had just taken so solemn a vow in Iffley church. One week he threw off the very idea of a vow, the next week felt a traitor. This second feeling culminated in kneeling for two and a quarter hours in the chapel at Pusey

House (1 December 1885), with its principal Charles Gore kneeling at his side. After lunch he walked out again to Iffley and tried to renew his vow. But he was frustrated of the gesture of laying his hand upon the altar, for workmen were in the church. So he stood as near the altar as he could, and murmured a renewal of the vow. It was a rededication of his life to the poor; and, for a time at least, to be unmarried for that purpose; and not to allow the need of his family to divert him from the vocation. But now it included also a determination to seek holy orders. Ordination would be a public commitment for life, an inescapable sort of vow. And that meant, he must turn aside from his history, and embark upon the study of theology.

He felt like a crusader putting on the uniform with a cross on front and back. The garb might kill him, but wear it he must. *I will wear it though it prove a very Nessus robe.*

He would go back to being an undergraduate, and read for the honours school of Theology. This was a strange thing for a fellow of a college to do. However, he systematically dedicated himself to the syllabus; hired a private tutor; read St. Gregory of Tours with the new Regius Professor of History, Freeman, in his rooms in Trinity; went to hear Charles Bigg's Bampton lectures on the Christian Platonists of Alexandria; threw himself into the Biblical criticism of the New Testament, and for one from his background was not disturbed at the idea that the apostle St. John probably did not write the fourth gospel or that the apostle St. Matthew probably did not write the first gospel; attended a class in palaeography with the Lady Margaret Professor William Sanday, whom he found attractive as a man and as a scholar; heard lectures in theology and especially in church history; made a special study of the fourth century and the Church of the Roman Empire, and the battles over the creeds. Like Newman before him, his eyes were opened to Catholic antiquity by the study of the Fathers. Professor Sanday even tried to make him write a life of St. Leo the Great for a series and Henson accepted the task. This was a mistake for a man whose Latin was almost good enough but whose Greek was not. Neither of them remembered that Gore had already written just the little life of St. Leo which Sanday wanted Henson to write. Sanday was embarrassed, Henson did not mind. That Henson, son of the most anti-papal man in Kent, should have accepted the duty of writing the life of Pope Leo the Great, shows the cast of his mind in that year 1886.

We, who know what kind of a home he came from, and how as a child he aspired to be a preacher, and how he went to Oxford to qualify for holy orders, and what the hidden future held for him, are not in the least surprised at the decision to become a priest. But we have not understood the impression which Henson made in Oxford. The Fellows of All Souls were surprised by the news.

In their eyes he hardly looked an ordinand. Certainly he was stiff for the Church of England, stiff against dissent. Certainly he attacked them (and himself) for their comfortable way of life compared with the lot of the Birkenhead worker. But to them he was not solemn enough. He was amusing, devastating, cynical. He seemed a mocker of all things sacred or secular. He laid so many bets in the common room. And he sounded so anticlerical – strong for the Church of England, scornful of its clergy for their failure to live to its ideals. It was not only that he was a bubbling conversationalist, it was the kind of conversation with which he bubbled.

The Warden felt something incongruous. The historian, Doyle, refused to believe in him as a future clergyman. Early in 1886 he bet Henson 2*s*. 6*d*. that he (Henson) would *not* be a clergyman of the Established Church this day two years. Not many weeks later Duff must have changed his mind and said that if Henson was really going to be ordained he would be sure to end as a bishop; and Henson denied it, and they fetched out the betting book again, and Henson promised to pay Duff £5 if and when he were appointed a bishop.

He talked with passion of celibacy and the ascetic life. The fellows, watching him sip the port, could not bring themselves quite to believe. Arthur Headlam said that Henson was sure to be married inside the next ten years, and found himself bet by Henson 10–1 in magnums of champagne that he, Henson, would still be unmarried in ten years. Knox said just the same to him, and found himself bet 10–1 to the same effect, but this time in bottles of Apollinaris water.

The scepticism of the fellows had its effect. And their attitude had one practical consequence. They did not want a fellow of the college to sit the examination for the honours school of Theology. Perhaps they doubted whether his Greek was adequate, perhaps they doubted his expertise in Biblical criticism on which he had engaged for so short a time. They realized that he might not gain a distinguished place in the examination, and that the fair name of All Souls might suffer if one of its fellows failed to appear in the first class. They asked him not to sit the examination.

This reasonable request cast Henson back into the vacillation which the vow at Iffley stopped. He had no doubt about his vocation to the poor; no doubt about his wish to live in a Christian community among the poor. But again he doubted whether the clerical life could be the right way for himself. He was full of the early Fathers, and the first monks and hermits of the Egyptian desert; full of St. Basil and his little communities of celibate laymen serving the people; full of St. Francis, the little poor man of Assisi. Could a man be a loyal clergyman of the Church of England if he thought the Reformers *scoundrels* because they destroyed monasteries? He took his younger brother Gilbert for a little holiday in Wharfedale and they walked to Bolton Abbey, and found its ruins on the curve of the river lovely; and Henson's meditations at that spot were not friendly to the Reformation.

Was it probable, he asked himself in June 1886, that if he had a vocation to celibate life among the poor, he could only satisfy his moral ideal inside the Roman Catholic Church with its religious orders? Could he find such a community in the Church of England? Nothing but the real thing would do. He walked 6 miles out to see his friends at the theological college at Cuddesdon, which had resemblance to a monastery in buildings and way of life, and judged that, in comparison with what he wanted and the world needed, it was *elegant farce – an entertaining mask of monasticism.* He decided that, but for the abject *poverty* which threatened his family, he would become a Roman Catholic within twelve months – *Yet why? assuredly not because I believe in Roman Catholicism: perhaps because my restlessness spurs me on to change : . . My vocation seemed to be clear to me once, now it is all dark.*

Alternative careers lay open. Two of them he seriously considered.

Oxford University expanded its school of history among undergraduates but found it hard to acquire historians to teach those undergraduates. Henson was trained as a historian. Already he taught a few odd pupils from other colleges. For the second two terms of the academic year 1886–7 Oriel College hired him to look after their historians and made him a member of the Senior Common Room. He enjoyed it, and found the money valuable, for he could more easily make the grants to home and family. Two other colleges also used him as a tutor. In Oriel they wondered whether they should not take this fresh-faced man aboard as a fellow to be their permanent history tutor. The young men, who by majority were far from being intellectual, found that this tutor, who looked younger than they, brought history alive to them and that they enjoyed going to his classes. Nor was his merit only that of a teacher. A team of Oxford dons, producing essays on English constitutional history, knew that Henson studied the Venerable Bede, and even contemplated a book on Bede. They asked him to contribute the first chapter. That essay has this importance, that here for the first time Henson appeared in academic print.[1] His essay proves two things; first, that he was a serious student of English history; second, that he had not yet discovered his prose style.

This was no trivial side of his life. In a world where history was built as a successful subject, he might have a future.

The second possible alternative came through one of the senior Fellows of All Souls. A. V. Dicey was the Professor of English Law, an established scholar of international reputation. This grave lawyer was taken with 'the youthful vehemence and versatile sprightliness' of Henson.[2] The effect was astounding. Hitherto Dicey had never been seen inside the college chapel. After Henson talked to him he became a regular attendant and for the rest of his life never ceased to appear. The 'conversion' is the more remarkable by reason of the ages of the two parties. During the academic year 1885–6 Henson attained his twenty-second birthday, Dicey his fifty-first.

---

[1] *Essays Introductory to the study of English Constitutional History*, edited by H. O. Wakeman and Arthur Hassall (1887). The book was used, and brought Henson a regular tiny income over many years.

[2] *Memorials of A. V. Dicey*, ed. R. S. Rait (1925), 95–6.

Dicey saw his young friend's predicament. Possessing a nose for a future barrister, he advised Henson to be a lawyer, and Henson contemplated the idea. He realized that if he were not to choose ministry, a future as a historian attracted him more than a future as a lawyer.

Neither history nor law ever had a real chance – though one of the two was to have just a chance many years later. In 1886 the choice presented itself to Henson as a stark moral issue. He felt a duty to minister among the poor. He did not see how to do this, and (because of the need to help the family) he could not afford to do this. But he felt the call continuously to do something for the poor, who the year before moved him in Birkenhead and now moved him more and more on visits to East London. To be a historian was a sensible career, to be a lawyer a possible career, and in either he could help the family more easily. Between the stark either–or, which is the higher way, to sit in Oxford or to live an ascetic life among the slums of East London, Henson had no real freedom of choice. And the only sensible, perhaps the only possible way to choose London, was to be ordained.

His friends saw this and tried to bring the vacillation to an end.

On 29 June 1886 he took lunch with Charles Gore at Pusey House and afterwards they lay on cushions in the garden while Gore pushed him to make up his mind for ordination. After dinner in college that evening, a lay Fellow of All Souls, Hardinge, with whom Henson used to have marvellous battles of conversation, came in and told him to stop all this hesitation. Henson took the coincidence of Gore and Hardinge as a sign. He wrote a decisive letter to the Bishop of Oxford, asking to be ordained at the Advent Ordination, December 1886. *I have burnt my ships*.

He was not ordained that December. He continued to vacillate; but now, hardly more than any man who is nervous of a great decision ahead and wishes to be sure that it is right. To every honest man ordination is as big a moment as marrying a wife. It must commit the soul in perpetuity unless there is tragedy. Anyone may hesitate, as a fiancé may hesitate three weeks before his wedding and not dare to tell his bride.

Men of 1886–7, thinking of ordination, had a special reason

for hesitation. Could they believe the faith which the Church
of England professed? The eighties were the full tide of battle
between science and religion, and of anxious argument over
the truth of the Bible. If a man took orders, was he pretending
that he believed in Adam and Eve, or Noah's flood? Must he
believe from the depths of his heart that Jesus was born of a
Virgin Mother, or could he honestly take orders if his judgement did not know? An Anglican clergyman must subscribe
to the Thirty-nine Articles of Religion, drafted in the reign of
Queen Elizabeth I as the Anglican statement of a Protestant
creed. To subscribe these was not too difficult, because an Act
of 1865 made assent to the Thirty-nine Articles 'general' and
did not commit the future clergyman to every detail or every
proposition. But the Thirty-nine Articles talked much of justification by faith, or predestination. Henson had been brought
up to put the highest value on honesty in religion. Could an
honest man become a clergyman if he hardly knew what he
thought about such doctrines of St. Paul and who only knew
that Calvinists were puritans? One theory he was sure he could
never accept: hell-fire. He had cast off the flames of eternity
with his childhood religion and nothing should make him
believe it again.

So the hesitation now was different, and less passion-
fraught. He was sure that the Iffley vow should be kept. He
was sure that he was meant to serve among the poor. But
could he believe enough to be honestly ordained?

All this felt very painful, but was not more vacillating than
the mood of uncertainty which afflicts many men as they come
near to ordination. It felt more painful and more dramatic to
Henson because he came from so unusual a background, and
was still finding himself as well as his way in life. He sat in
Westminster Abbey, and looked up at the columns and the
vault of the roof, and wondered whether its beauty was all
consecrated to untruth. Sometimes he had what amounted to
an agony. Fate bore him along to ordination where he would
have to profess things which he did not believe – but this fate
was inescapable – and yet was it fate, or was it *some blessed spirit
who would save me from endless ruin*? He dreamt that he was
kneeling at the Lord's feet by an altar, and that the Lord
stretched out his hand and touched him and said *follow me*, and

called him to *sorrow and service, suffering and an early death*; and in his dreams he gave himself up in self-sacrifice, and received a blessing, and was sent out. *There are lots of reasons why I should not take orders. I scarcely think my belief is adequate; but one thing I know well, and that is this, that if I do not take orders I shall make shipwreck of my life.* (19 October 1886).

All the hesitation was blown away by a visit to Rome.

In the spring of 1887 he went with his friend Arthur Headlam to spend just over a month in Italy. Nearly three weeks of the time they were in Rome. Headlam was elected a Fellow of All Souls the year after Henson. He was uncouth, but Henson found him honest and of a kind heart. They were in Rome during Holy Week.

For Henson it was not a serene holiday. His state of mind was sufficiently evident for some of the English whom he met in Rome to be worried. It was even arranged that a visiting Anglican bishop should interview him and see if he could help with the mental turmoil. The bishop helped Henson not at all.

He heard a Jesuit preach a sermon for Holy Week to English visitors, and the preacher talked of the crucifixion like English preachers of his Protestant experience. He went up to the Convent of Trinità dei Monti, and heard the nuns singing, and was moved. But what went most to his heart was the Colosseum. He stood in the middle of the arena. His romantic imagination conjured scenes of Christian martyrs torn in pieces by beasts, and the clash of gladiators, and the monk Telemachus rushing out to his death to stop the cruelty.

Something in Rome cured him, not of doubt but of vacillation. Perhaps the assurance that, despite the yearning towards a celibate life and a religious order, he was not and never would be a natural Roman Catholic may have helped. He was pleased with All Souls Chapel on his return because the service was *delightfully intelligible*. He was decided now, to be ordained at the June ordination. He knew that he was a strong Protestant, and therefore did not need to believe all the dogmas which Catholics said that he must believe. He could be ordained honestly.

He found that he had only about six days to prepare for the examination. He had to pass a paper on Pearson, of whom he read no word. The archdeacon later told him gently and not to his surprise, that the Pearson paper was not good. However, they passed him on the examination. Anglican tests before ordination never demanded an unusual amount of knowledge.

He ordered two suits of clericals at Evans' and gave away most of his 'secular' clothes to the college boy.

In this swing of anti-Catholic mood, left by the visit to Rome, he did not seem to believe much. Even Charles Gore, at nearly the twelfth hour, doubted whether he ought to be ordained. *By Orders*, Henson told a friend *I understand a solemn taking the side of Truth as against Falsehood, pledging oneself to honestly seek for the truth, and not to say things one doesn't believe.* It was the ordination of a liberal intellectual. He did not suppose that the sacrament bestowed upon him any special grace. What was happening was (in his mind) a public declaration of himself. He was declaring his open allegiance to the *love* and *truth* and *light* and *honesty embodied* in Jesus Christ.

He still wondered, to the last minute, whether anyone would be scandalized by this view that ordination meant to follow the truth in Christ wherever it should lead, and had otherwise no doctrinal content. He had no sense of hopelessness, or of expectation. When with the other deacons-to-be he must subscribe the Thirty-nine Articles, he turned to his neighbour Ralph Nevill, and asked *Are you adequately honest?*

Prone to dramatic acts, Henson walked bareheaded in the meadows beyond Cuddesdon church the day before the ordination, and made his self-dedication. And in his present mood after the visit to Rome he gave the words of the dedication a slant which was undoctrinal. He promised God *to be loyal to the Truth, wherever I found it, wheresoever it should call me to seek for it.*

He was ordained deacon in one of the fairest village churches of England, Cuddesdon, on Trinity Sunday, 5 June 1887, by the Bishop of Oxford, Mackarness. Three of the Fellows of All Souls, Headlam, Hardinge, and Raleigh, walked out to the ordination. No member of Henson's family came.

He received two presents. The bishop gave him a Greek Testament. This he used every night till the last months of his life. Duff paid him half a crown for losing the All Souls bet that he would never be ordained.

## OXFORD HOUSE

In the Church of England a man must be ordained to a 'title', that is to a particular sphere of pastoral work, curacy or parish. By long tradition a fellowship at an Oxford and Cambridge college was regarded as pastoral work, and was sufficient. Henson had no other title but his fellowship at All Souls, which had almost no undergraduates. He was not even the chaplain at All Souls, though he began to help the chaplain.

We do not know what his earliest sermons were like. But we can infer. On 26 January 1885 General Gordon was murdered by the Mahdi's fanatics in Khartoum. With much of England, Henson saw him as a Christian martyr who died in the effort to kill the slave-trade and was let down by a weak Liberal government in London. During 1886 Henson wrote a lecture on Gordon which he delivered to several audiences in the London slums, and caused ecstasy or excitement among his hearers. As he then printed it, we know what it said. We can infer that Henson's early oratory was lofty, exciting, clear, passionate, romantic or over-romantic, panegyrical, and touched with such elevated moments of prose-poetry that the modern must think the paragraph artificial. Here is Henson on the watch-tower of Khartoum – *Long did it shine, that hallowed starlight of saintly heroism; it shone as if protesting against the Cimmerian gloom around, and men saw it, but they took no heed . . .* The style is so exuberant that it reminds the reader of the famous preachers in French baroque like Bossuet or Massillon. Part of it was authentic passion. A reporter had criticized Henson's speech at the Layman's League meeting in Wadham as 'fervid'. A working man who heard Henson orate in London praised him as 'a hot 'un'.

Henson's notes show that in the year before his ordination he studied the Fench baroque preachers. We find him meditating on the soothing melancholy of one of them as he walked solitary on the banks of the river by Godstow.

Old Bishop Mackarness of Oxford, who had no special reputation as a reader of books, saw the danger of artificiality. As an exercise of routine the ordinand must write a sermon for the bishop. The perceptive old man asked whether Henson studied the French baroque preachers. They fell to discussing

them, Henson found that Mackarness also had read them. The
bishop warned him against imitating them too closely, and
gave him the encouragement which was a salutary insult, of
saying that 'he showed signs of being a good preacher
presently'.

For a deacon Henson had extraordinary opportunities. That
October, four months after his ordination, he was a main
speaker at the Church Congress at Wolverhampton. During
that year he was the youngest preacher ever to occupy the
pulpit at Harrow School. And he still looked no older than the
oldest boys.

The reason why he was in demand was neither a repute for
oratory (though that repute grew) nor his fellowship at All
Souls. It was the office which he held as head of Oxford House
in Bethnal Green.

These were the years when the nation grew aware of the
plight of East London. Clergymen came out of the East End
and told audiences at the universities what they saw in their
daily life, and evoked among young idealists a strong desire to
help. In 1884 Oxford men founded the first two 'settlements'
in London, where young graduates might live among the
Londoners and see whether they could organize help. The first
was Toynbee Hall in Whitechapel, where the object was not
specially evangelistic but which wished to bring all good men
to work together for the common social end. The second was
Oxford House in Bethnal Green. Its founders believed that
religion and philanthropy were inseparable.

This was the start of a movement of self-sacrifice among
Oxford and Cambridge undergraduates. They delayed careers
to spend a few months or years doing what they could for East
London, and lived in sordid surroundings for the sake of
sharing the life of the poor. They sacrificed their evening
hours, were rarely able to pursue outside interests, and often
needed to delay marriage. They bridged the gap which
separated the classes. Out of the 'settlement' movement the
Churches won pastors. For although most of the young
laymen who helped in the clubs passed on to the normal
professions pursued by graduates, the need of East London got
hold of some of them, who then found their way of life in the
ministry of the Church.

The head of Oxford House was Jimmie Adderley. He was an Anglo-Catholic priest and an aristocrat. He dedicated himself to East London in a very Franciscan spirit. He was simple-hearted, as funny as any clown, and lovable. He wanted to found a religious order of unmarried men who should share a common life and devote themselves to the slums of East London. This wish was eventually fulfilled, and stands at the base of the revival of the Franciscan way of life within the Church of England.

Henson, reading for orders in Oxford, went to stay with him in Bethnal Green and was caught up as an ally. Adderley found that Henson also wanted a celibate order to help the poor. He acquired a speaker who could enthuse an audience of working men. Henson on his side found Adderley lovable and discovered an embryo organization for doing just what he felt called to do.

Adderley and Henson met frequently, and planned their community. Later in life Henson looked back and saw them both as *a brace of ardent fools*. At the time it was in dead earnest. They planned a rule. Henson called Adderley 'Abbot', Adderley called Henson 'Prior'. Later in life Henson saw Adderley as the true ascetic, himself as the backslider, too fastidious and comfortable to follow. He remembered one Ash Wednesday, as they walked together in Bethnal Green, when Adderley challenged him to eat a foul-smelling fish from a fishmonger's slab, and got *no* for an answer. Henson portrayed Adderley as the ascetic and himself as the ascetic-on-paper. We have every reason for thinking this picture false. They were both dedicated. They wanted, and intended, to be modern Franciscans in East London.

Henson's difficulty was not Adderley's austerity and his own love of comfort. It lay in the opposite direction. Adderley had a rich family. Henson had a family in debt. If Adderley lived in poverty it hurt no one. If Henson lived in poverty he hurt five other people. *It is treasonable inconsistency but I see not how to escape. It is not my will to remain in luxury: I long to throw aside all, and be an ascetic as was Francis: but I am not free to do what I would: I am not rich enough to be poor.* Or again: *It does seem hard that right across the pathway of my holiest hopes should be thrust the impassable barrier of the poverty of the family.*

In the summer when Henson was ordained deacon, Jimmie
Adderley moved from Oxford House to another East London
mission at Christ Church, Poplar. On 7 July 1887, a month
after Henson's ordination as deacon, the committee of Oxford
House met at Oxford House to appoint a successor. The
Warden of All Souls was in the chair. They appointed Henson
to be head of Oxford House from Christmas 1887.

Henson was so excited that he spent the afternoon riding
about London on the tops of buses.

He was excited because it opened the door towards what he
wanted. It brought him into East London, with responsibility.
It took him among the poor whom he felt a vocation to serve.
It brought him near Adderley and therefore nearer to the
Franciscan ideal. He could not doubt that it was right, so to
leave Oxford. He wrote himself a poem where he figured as a
medieval monk, *Father Herbert*, who is blamed for the folly of
going out into a desert of evil-smelling drains when he could
stay comfortable, and feel spiritual, inside his monastery walls:

> *By Bacchus!, if a monk may sware an oath,*
> *I swear it. Father Herbert, thou art mad.*
> *Stark, staring, startling mad, to cut thyself*
> *By one fell word from that which maketh life*
> *Worth living, and the Abbot's stall a throne*
> *Of slumbrous joys supernal! Thou art mad*
> *Changing the wine-cup for the living stream*
> *Of crowded Eastern Drains, whose myriad worms*
> *And slimy ancient eels, the rusty pipes*
> *Strain nigh to bursting! –*

Years later, Henson's enemies said that this was Mistake
number one. Henson, they said, was a deacon a month old;
with knowledge of East London only as a visitor; an academic,
not a pastor by training; had not yet reached his twenty-fourth
birthday; and was sent to a responsible pastorate where no
experienced pastor could guide. Never, it was afterwards said,
was the training of a young clergyman so bungled. The
Warden of All Souls must have considered the point about
training, which had weight. Every other criticism was wide of
the mark. At this moment of time, Henson's whole drive was
pastoral, though he wanted to use his academic equipment to
teach working men.

But not all the Fellows of All Souls agreed with their Warden. The sceptical Duff felt something incongruous between the man and his ordination. He now felt something incongruous when he saw a brilliant and irreverent young friend as the head of a London boys' club. He doubted that it could last. He argued it with Charles Oman, who loyally defended Henson and his choice of work. They fetched out the betting book. Oman bet Duff 2*s*. 6*d*. that Henson will be head of Oxford House, and residing there, this day two years. The day was 21 January 1888.

Oxford House stands large in red brick, looking over green grass to the Cambridge railway. The little chapel is at the top of the house, and in 1981 was clean and numinous except that the west end was used as a store for broken chairs; and on the wall a plaque to the Warden of All Souls, Sir William Anson, cries of the age of Henson. The inhabitants of the neighbourhood still know where it is, and what it does. At that time it was surrounded by some of the worst housing in London. Henson, whose nose was fastidious, found people living in rooms where he could hardly bear the stench. Landlords let their buildings fall into ruin because no one could afford to pay more than a tiny rent. Families lived in garrets with leaking roofs and stinking drains. The best work in the area was done, first, by the elementary schools and the forcing of children to attend; second, by voluntary organizations almost all connected with one of the churches, including the Salvation Army.

Oxford House consisted of four working men's clubs. It had a hall for lectures, a chapel, a club choir. Henson added a library, provided books and ordered silence. He also extended the work downward in age, creating the Webbe Institute in Hare Street, where boys of sixteen to eighteen had a gymnasium, a canteen, bagatelle, and where fifty boys could be housed in two long dormitories. Usually seven or eight helpers resided. Adderley left good assistants, and Henson added more from his Oxford friends. He talked often, to tiny audiences of working men. He spent a lot of time visiting patients in the London Hospital, and was distressed by what he found. For special occasions he had lectures by magic lantern,

a conjuror, a ventriloquist. He needed money for his exten-
sions. He gave some from his non-existent purse. Otherwise
he begged it – usually from Oxford dons or undergraduates,
but generous sums from a private benefactor, Walter
Scrymgeour. He edited a magazine, the *Oxford House
Chronicle*.

Part of the work was to interest Oxford men in the cause – in
short, to raise a social conscience in Oxford undergraduates.

He had a big meeting in New College with seven heads of
houses present, and his speech electrified, though it did not
please all of the audience. This speech has not survived. But a
draft of his utterance to Harrow schoolboys has survived, and
must have resembled the appeal to Oxford undergraduates.

The speaker talks of two nations, rich and poor, who hardly
know each other. He told how Christianity was supposed to
have abolished slavery, and yet the mark of the slave was still
visible on the foreheads of the mass of manual workers in
England. He told them that *civilization* is the property of a
small minority. In majority *England is pagan, barbarous, and
wretched*. But the connection of the two nations, civilized and
savages, is intimate. *The minority could not be civilized without
barbarizing the majority. The poor are crowded into the 'East End'
and the rich live grandly in the West . . . Even within the Churches
precautions are taken to prevent the possibility of contact between rich
and poor*.

I have simplified, he told them, to bring home what should
never be absent from your thoughts – *you owe to the poor the
possibilities of your life. Now, if this be so, with what feelings must
you learn that the poor are living in a condition of wretchedness,
monotony and vice, which severs them completely from the society of
the pure, the honest and the sincere?*

In Bethnal Green Henson engaged on a work which
perfectly suited his talents – the confrontation of atheists in
public debate. Near by was a Hall of Science, where atheism
was propagated. In Victoria Park atheist orators stood on
soap-boxes. The National Secular Society had an office in
Bethnal Green. On Sunday afternoons Oxford House organized counter-lectures in St. Andrew's Hall, and there secularists turned up to heckle or to argue. Henson was uniquely
well equipped. He had extended knowledge of biblical history

and church history. His work for the Laymen's League gained him understanding of tithes or endowments, on which atheist orators liked to harp. He was never at a loss for a word, knew already how to sway a crowd, had repartee which made short work of hecklers, and a darting wit which brought the crowd to his side in laughter. At a battle of words in Victoria Park a heckler called him a *fat purse-proud priest*, which played into Henson's hands, for he was slim, had no money, and was not yet a priest. A heckler in Victoria Park declared in a German accent to the crowd that all the evidence for the life of Christ was fabricated and that he never existed; and Henson enjoyed the riposte, for he could put over all that he learnt at Oxford with élan and sense of fun.

Not all the opponents were men of straw. Burns the celebrated Socialist came to do battle. Foote, the leader of the National Secular Society, gave a lecture which made Christianity responsible for slavery. Henson rose at the back to make 'some remarks'. These remarks portrayed Christianity more truly as the remedy for slavery. He turned what he said into a tract, and sold copies at the meetings, and this tract is one of the best little historical essays of his earlier years. Once the men at Oxford House advised him that a secularist speaker Rosetti was dangerous and begged him to go to confute. He went to the open-air station where Rosetti lectured and publicly challenged him to public debate, next Sunday, on the subject: 'Is Christianity of divine origin?'. Many turned up to witness the gladiators.

From this gargantuan debate, Henson learnt a lesson which he never forgot. When, at the bidding of his men he went to hear the atheist champion, he listened to an able lecture, informed and occasionally eloquent, criticizing Christianity as presented by the Churches in England. Then the lecturer turned to Christ and used the language of insult and ribaldry. Henson noticed that when the lecturer insulted the Churches, he had the audience at his command. When he insulted Christ he lost their sympathy and even attention until (Henson watched them closely) they felt towards the speaker something like repugnance. At the end Henson was allowed to address the meeting and had no difficulty in winning loud applause for a protest against such treatment of a person who lived to serve men and died to redeem. This was a lesson Henson never forgot. You cannot defend the Churches, they are indefensible; defend the Christ, and you are home.[1]

Young and younger looking, little of stature but lambent with fire; articulate and witty, never playing down to his audience, always treating the hearers seriously; with a gift of popular exposition; with a passion in his utterance, and a gift (if it is a gift) of scathing scorn for everything he hated – Henson won a name. Already, even before his ordination as a priest, one or two of the mighty began to wonder whether this leader of adolescent boys and hammer of atheists and master of the sermon should not be brought into some wider field than a club where he lectured to a handful on church history. They could not realize that inside the man turmoil still raged.

He lectured and preached everywhere. He took trouble to prepare. He ran four clubs, and created a boys club, and edited a magazine, and visited the hospital regularly. He must go to Oxford and rouse undergraduates. He must beg for money. He got less than six hours sleep each night. Though helped by young Oxford men, he overworked.

Something in the overwork was religious. Though not a new convert, he had the feeling of a new convert. He dedicated himself, every moment of time must be used for God's purpose among the poor. Nothing was mellow, nothing mature. He could not be still. He was a giant-killer; and the giant which he strode out to slay was too vast for the London County Council, let alone a single new deacon aged twenty-four. Six months after he took on the job several friends, including Sir Willian Anson, were so anxious about his health that they drove him to be overhauled by a famous London doctor.

Later in life he decided that most young clergymen who *are worth anything* commit this sin, and start *with gross mismanagement* of themselves, *attempting the impossible by substituting enthusiasm for common sense, and assuming that excellence of purpose can atone for neglect of the laws of health.*[2]

Tired, and bearing the cross of introspection which he must bear all his life, he suffered from sensations of unworthiness which at times became unbearable. He, the preacher, was a

[1] *Christian Liberty* (1918), 322–3.        [2] *Robertson of Brighton* (1916), 41.

hypocrite. He could not raise these men and boys unless he taught them something truly Christian, something clear, something dogmatic. What definite truth could he say? He had no doubt of a saviour of the world. He refused ever to appeal to hell. He had no doubt of the need of a Church as bearing the Christ. He had no doubt that dissent was bad. Preaching at Adderley's mission at Christ Church, Poplar, he saw a crucifix and found that it helped, and soon afterwards went out and bought a crucifix and kept it on his desk. But what else did he really believe? He sounded to his men as though he had faith in all the articles of the Nicene Creed. Had he? Was he nothing but the worst kind of hypocrite? The melancholy was very painful to one brought up to think truth so high a virtue.

In one of these moods Henson wrote a letter, which has not survived but which he afterwards regarded as lamentable. He sent it to Ernle Prothero, a lay Fellow of All Souls who always believed in Henson and encouraged his ordination. Prothero replied with a letter of spiritual direction. Henson found the letter beautiful.

In poetic language, Prothero put to him three suggestions. First, can excess of zeal be a hidden form of selfishness – working more for yourself than for Christ? Secondly, Prothero saw that Henson needed quiet, stillness. *If thou mightest multiply the hours of contemplation, thou mightest be happier.* And as to the 'hypocrisy', it is hard to teach men to be religious and moral without a living faith. But instead of introspection, and repeated questions to yourself whether you believe, look outward at the men and their need. *Gaze upon the cross through their eyes; look upward and out, and the words will flow pure and sincere.*

Henson was helped. The problem of the preacher-hypocrite troubled him all his life. He would not be Henson if he had not suffered tension in the days before his priest's ordination at Cuddesdon in May 1888. But the meditations before the ordination, which were very full, were no worse in their self-consideration than those of many ordinands preparing for a solemn commitment. They lay down ample safeguards that always he will retain his liberty of thought. But when he was ordained priest he believed in a body of Anglican doctrines which was a powerful message. Unlike the time before his ordination as deacon, he had no doubts whatever that he had a vocation to be ordained priest.

He expressed his most solemn profession in a satirical sentence: *I finally accept the Christian position: I part company with the amiable and attractive free-thinkers; I abandon all claim to be an 'original thinker'; I ally myself publicly with ritualists, reactionaries, re-vivalists, and ranters: nay, I become all these.* Near the end of his life, he dared to print this sentence and bring it before the public. But he could not quite bear to print every word of the last satirical sentence. It reads more gently: *I ally myself with the mingled host of religious folk — ritualists, reactionaries, revivalists, nay in some sense I become all these.* In his old age he could not bear to think that even in jest he once identified himself with ranters.

He spent his summer holiday from Oxford House as a locum in the parish of Ainderby near Northallerton in Yorkshire. To Ainderby came a letter (dated 13 August 1888) from Bishop Blomfield of Colchester, who said that the All Souls living of Barking in Essex was just vacant, and that it was *certain* to be offered to Henson. The bishop hoped that Henson would accept, and did not fail to remind him that soon his fellowship stipend would expire and that he would need pay and a house.

This proposal had almost everything to be said in its favour. It gave him a parish in East London where he could fulfil the celibate apostolate among the slums which was his dream. Incidentally it would ease the secret burden of his life, finding money for his family. What was to be said against it was, desertion of Oxford House only a few months after he accepted the work. *I am so deeply pledged to Bethnal Green that departure thence would be taken as a perfidious proceeding.* But the chance was too big to miss. A long interview at Hawkhurst with the Warden of All Souls, the nearest person to a foster-father that he possessed, calmed his scruples. Feeling that he was behaving basely, and that he would lose Oxford friend-ships, he decided to leave Oxford House. All Souls appointed him to Barking on All Souls Day (2 November 1888).

Critics of later years with hindsight, who grumbled that Henson was not the sort of clergyman that clergymen ought to be, argued that this was Mistake number two. Without any training during his deacon's year, without any assistant curacy, without any pastoral experience, without serving under any experienced parish priest, a young man of barely twenty-five years was made the head of one of the most important parishes in East London and incidentally the youngest vicar in the Church of England.

Bishop Blomfield of Colchester knew the parish, for formerly he was himself the vicar. Why then did he wish the young man to accept the offer? And he was not alone. His superior, the Bishop of St. Albans, in whose diocese Barking lay, was pleased that Henson accepted the parish.

Oxford and Cambridge colleges acquired in long centuries the right to appoint the incumbent of certain livings. When many or all of their fellows were unmarried clergymen, this assured them a future when they married; and even if they stayed long in college unmarried, the right to a parish could serve instead of the pension which did not exist. For the college it worked well. Whether it worked well for the Church was debatable and debated. Colleges tried to elect good men to their fellowships and therefore sent out good men into the parishes. But they acted on a doubtful axiom; namely, that all fellows were suitable for all parishes. Many colleges were in the habit of offering their parishes by rotation – to the most senior clerical fellow and if he refused to the next, and so on. If all fellows refused, the college could open the living to the world of applicants.

But since 1871 fewer fellows needed to be ordained men. When the parish of Barking fell vacant in the summer of 1888, All Souls had only two clerical fellows unprovided with livings. One was Cholmondeley, a pleasant man not prone to hard work and not likely to accept Barking. And the second was Henson, twenty-four years old and barely ordained priest. Everyone knew that Cholmondeley would refuse. The moment that the Barking newspapers heard of their vicar's resignation, they appointed Henson. Working people in Barking heard a story that Mr Enson was the oldest member of the college and so sure to accept. Certainly Henson was next senior; more than that, he was the last on the list. If he refused, the college perforce went out to the wide world of applicants.

Bishop Blomfield disliked what he heard about the only appli-
cant so far – *an outsider* – *a Cambridge man*.

To be fair to Bishop Blomfield, he sounded genuinely
pleased. All Souls might have sent him strange clergymen.
The last man they sent was a good man but could hardly cope.
Here the obvious choice, few in years and juvenile in appear-
ance though he might be, had already won a name for being
wonderful with working men, of whom Barking was full.
Not surprisingly Bishop Blomfield did his best to persuade
Henson to move from Oxford House. And he avoided a
Cambridge man.

In All Souls Charles Oman lost the bet on Henson's stability
in Bethnal Green and had to pay Duff half a crown.

# 3. THE PASTOR

## BARKING

I CAME to Barking Church on a cold Tuesday afternoon. It stood isolated in its grass sward surrounded by fast-moving cars and lorries. I stood under the arch of the curfew tower, which was the gateway of the old Benedictine nunnery, and tried to shut my ears to the sound of the traffic and to imagine its medieval peace. Over the wall lay the excavated foundations of the old abbey, which in Henson's day was not excavated. Away from the church to the east was the place of the vicarage, with its fourteen rooms where Henson cared for his family and entertained crowds of parishioners and taught the confirmation classes and wrote uncompromising letters. The three-aisled church with its historic windows attracted the aesthetic eye, a humane survival in the hard world of square blocks and combustion engines. The effect was of loneliness in an industrial world which moved too fast to notice what mattered. I remembered that in 1891 14,000 people could walk from their homes to the Church within fifteen minutes, and realized that to get home nearly a century later must take many more minutes.

By the 1971 census the population of Barking was 160,800. By the 1881 census, the last before Henson arrived, it was 9,000. It did not spread across the River Roding and open country divided it from London to the west. It was still a country town. But already it was a commuting town, for the station (London, Tilbury & Southend Railway) was convenient for workers in East London. And when Henson arrived it was growing in size between 1,000 and 2,000 new people every year. Though it still had farm-labourers among its parishioners, industry was dominant, a jute factory, a chemical works, Glenny's brewery, and above all the huge Beckton gas works, which supplied London with gas. The eastward expansion of London was delayed, as compared with the western, because of the marshy land along the valley of the River Lea. But now the railways had come, cheap housing for

commuters began, and the population grew with a speed
which alarmed organizers of every social organ, including the
Bishop of St. Albans, in whose oddly shaped diocese the
parish now lay. Once it had been a fishing port for the North
Sea trawlers. Henson was the last incumbent to receive a
present of fish when the fishing season was opened. So late as
1850 220 smacks in Barking Creek employed 1,370 men. But
railways killed the Creek as a port, and sixty Barking
fishermen were lost in a gale off the Dutch coast, and now
fishing was hardly more than a memory, and ceased to matter
to the people, for in 1865 most of the fleet transferred to
Norfolk ports.[1]

As well as the parish church he had a little chapel at Creeksmouth, regular services in a school room at Rippleside, and a
dilapidated mission room in Fisher Street. To help with these
four places of worship he had two curates, added a third four
months later and a fourth in the following year.

It was full of places of worship. The ordnance survey map of
1877 marks a Roman Catholic chapel, a Wesleyan Methodist
chapel, a Primitive Methodist chapel, two Congregationalist
chapels, a Baptist chapel, a Quaker meeting house (with
Elizabeth Fry buried in the grounds). There were three different groups of Plymouth Brethren, not numerous. The Salvation Army had a hall, for Barking was one of the earliest
centres of the work of the Salvation Army. That was a lot, in a
small town, for a new and ardent young vicar who believed
that, however good dissenters might be as individuals, dissent
was pernicious, with preachings of hell-fire, ranting in pulpits,
untrue fundamentalism about the literal truth of the Bible, and
the cause of uncharitable conflicts over education.

Henson had bounding energy, and was very articulate – that
is, even at the age of twenty-six he could give four or five
addresses in a day on four or five subjects. He began formidable, he continued formidable; and by preaching, visiting,
preaching, lecturing, preaching, presiding, preaching, rebuk-
ing, preaching and charming he won round himself a good
many enemies and a great band of disciples, until, one Thursday evening a year later, he could say, of a *weekday* service in a

---

[1] *Items of Essex Interest, no. 5* (ed. F. J. Braund), 1931; *Barking Abbey: 1300th
Anniversary*, 1966; *The London Borough of Barking*, 1978.

church with fifty-two women and four men, *wretched congregation . . . I suspect that there is treason in the camp. There was a
Christmas tree and Sale of Work in the Schism-den opposite.*

He said what he thought in the pulpit. He said what he
thought in people's homes, or in the schoolroom. No one
could be in doubt about his opinions, whether on theology, or
on parish life, or on subjects of public interest. He found that
he loved preaching, and that this was what he did best.
Though he visited, he hated visiting because he was embarrassed. He hated private interviews because he agonized with
the agony of the person who gave him confidence, and sometimes found it hard to bear. He visited the sick diligently, but
he hated the visit because he felt he had nothing to say, or
nothing adequate to say. Every form of communication he
enjoyed. But the pulpit was his joy and his throne. If he
preached for half an hour it was short, if for three-quarters,
rather long. He soon gained the experience to know when his
hearers listened. Sometimes he preached on a stool outside the
East India Docks, or in the vicarage garden, or in the park.
Sometimes he was exalted by his own sense of power; more
often he was depressed at failure or what he imagined as
failure, and melancholy under an overwhelming sense of
responsibility, and at bad times worse than melancholy.

His home was well managed. The vicarage was a large
house and his stepmother, whom he still called Mother,
moved from Kent to keep house, and was soon prominent as a
parish worker. They employed four young people to help
them in house and garden. The house and stipend enabled
Henson to look after his family. But his intention remained, to
get unmarried curates, have them live in the vicarage, and so
create a little community of unmarried priests. The large glebe
was a playing field. It had a beautiful old mulberry tree, which
provided Henson's table with mulberry tart, but suffered
grievously from raiders and died.

It was the age of very cheap gin and in the absence of other
amusements the age of flaunting drunkenness. In Bethnal
Green Henson gave up alcohol not on principle but for expedi-
ence. So many other Christian workers among the very poor
were devoted to the Temperance Movement that he did not
wish to seem to be behind. His early experience in Barking led

him to think that the Temperance Movement was to be backed. Perhaps his feeling had an element of policy, for he wanted to show that the Church could do all that dissenting chapels could do, and most of the chapels were dedicated to Temperance. But it was not only policy. On Trinity Sunday, 16 June 1889, under a very hot sun, he presided in cassock and surplice at a Temperance Mission in the vicarage grounds. *The speakers uttered the most astonishing drivel: but it is better that they should utter it under my sanction than against me.* About 1,500 people came, and he thought that most of them were dissenters. He would not take the pledge for life, but publicly undertook not to drink alcohol, except under doctor's orders, while he was Vicar of Barking.

The people were not so poor as in Bethnal Green but their life could be brutal. More than once he stopped a fight in the Broadway. Once he saw a bully hitting and stamping on a woman defenceless on the ground, watched by spectators who did nothing. He shouted at the onlookers, rushed up and *caught him a whacking blow over the shoulder with my stick: this diverted his attention and* – the man was big and Henson diminutive – *I thought I should find difficulty in reading my manuscript at Creeksmouth tonight.* But the bully thought better of it, and Henson helped the woman up and walked her away, and *expostulated with the hulking curs who looked on all the while.*[1]

In 1891 he caused an extraordinary scene, which the later Henson must have blushed to recall. He formed a children's branch of the Temperance Society. The schoolroom was crammed with children. He urged them to take the pledge, and not to drink the last sip of father's beer, and not to take a sip out of the jug when they fetched it from the pub. The children then, with papers from their parents consenting, went up to sign, and so many hundreds wished to sign that the wait was long, and the curate must keep the expectant children happy with funny stories, and the children were 'so late home that parents complained'.

His Watch Night Service, on New Year's Eve, was crammed with people, from regulars to ruffians. Harvest festivals

---

[1] In old age he mis-remembered it as an umbrella, and thought that it was broken on the man's back.

were crowded. The name-day feast of St. Margaret in July became a vast open-air festival, where anything from 2,000 to 4,000 children were fed at tables on the grass, and live chess was played with Henson as one of the live chessmen.

He raised money to restore Barking church. He opened the arches of the tower, removed the gallery, put in a floor into the tower for the bellringers, raised the level of the east end, improved the gas-light, made the chancel seemly with carpet and rails and candles, built a new vestry. He closed the mission and, begging the money, built a daughter-church, St. Paul's.

He created a series of clubs, for men and lads and women and girls; with gymnasium, library, refreshment bar (non-alcoholic), games room, reading room. He was fertile in ideas and not all of them succeeded, as when he invented an after-noon class for women and only one woman arrived, or when he had a men's class in Fisher Street and only two arrived, one of them *a half lunatic*. To an open-air service in June 1889 he got 1,100 people. If he thought the men lagged, he raided the pubs.

He could behave in a way which captivated his people. As he held at the church the first meeting of the restoration committee, the sudden resolution came into his head to begin now; and so all the committee, led with glee by their vicar, caught up the tools of the workmen who were repairing the tower and hacked their way through a partition to clear an old doorway to the west. Henceforth the committee were dedi-cated to church restoration. A month later, when workmen began to pull down the gallery, Henson appeared with his people to do their share of the pulling.

Henson was a first-class priest in charge of the parish. He filled a large church, sometimes he filled it so full that people could not get inside. He did this partly because he could talk, and was not afraid of being amusing, and was vehement against every form of immorality, and was a controversial person. But he also did it by very hard work, too hard work; organizing, sitting on committees, cajoling, bullying, persuading, leading; and by dedicated work as a pastor, knowing his people: listening, advising, sharing their confi-dences and their sufferings, caring for their children. Four years later, he began to be famous as a controversialist: and he believed that this wider fame among London newspapers

helped him in the parish. He felt that because of the controversial fame all doors in Barking were open. [1]

The vicarage gardens were extensive. He opened them on
Sunday afternoons and persuaded the town band to come and
lead their open-air services, and formed a committee of working men to control the proceedings except the sermons which
by his standards were short. These open-air services attracted crowds. They strolled about, and smoked. Not being
used to liturgies, some of them joined the service and still
smoked. The *Dundee Courier* called them the 'Sunday Afternoon Smoking Services'. Henson's internal pain may be
imagined, for he regarded smoking in any circumstances as
antisocial. On a fine day in summer the service became a
service for a multitude. Used to the soap-boxes of Victoria
Park, he knew how to make himself heard in the open air. And
in the open air he could be more amusing than he liked to be in
his pulpit.

An eyewitness is to hand. A young Oxford layman Cosmo
Gordon Lang came to visit Barking (May 1889). He reported
what he saw of Henson. 'He is exceedingly young – his only
experience was as head of Oxford House – but of a fiery and
contagious energy and most eloquent. He came six months
ago to a parish *dead* – 250 people a good congregation in the
church; and now, when he preaches, every seat is filled –
1100!' Lang admitted a doubt; of Henson's 'unruly tongue' and
of his 'power of denunciation and sarcasm . . . If these don't
spoil him, he will become a great cleric.'[2]

Statistics of Easter Communions:
     1891: 362; 1892: 388; 1893: 433; 1894: 490; 1895: 528.

Wherever Henson went he fought battles. These battles
were hard. He was never underhand nor malicious. His
weapon was public denunciation, from pulpit, in letters to the
press, in long private letters which do not read persuasively,
and finally in pamphlets which grew steadily longer. Always
we find him tilting, sometimes with humour but never in
mockery or sport, always in earnest.

In the parish of Barking lay the Beckton gas works. This was
the biggest employer in the area, paying more than 3,000

---

[1] But cf. *Cui Bono?* (1899), 4th ed., 26.
[2] Lockhart, *Lang*, 76.

men. The men had a union, the Amalgamated Gas Stokers. As this was the first trade union to be met by a man whose life was destined to be plagued by trade unions, what happened is important.

Between shifts the Beckton men had hours of leisure which they could not use. They stood idly at corners of the street, or drank for hours in the bars; on Sunday morning they stayed indoors, on Sunday afternoons they walked, Sunday evening they spent in the bars. In the summer they used Sunday to attend the union meeting, or to take a trip to the sea, or rather to a bar near the sea.

Trade unions were believed to be Socialist, and Socialism was believed to be against Christianity. Union leaders uttered hard sayings against parsons. The leader at Beckton, Watkinson, was believed to use pressure against the few churchgoers among the men. In the town of Barking men rumoured or assumed that the Union as such was hostile to the Churches. Watkinson was alleged to have said that he would burn all the churches if he had his way.

Promptly Henson invited all the union members to a church parade so that they could *publicly disclaim an hostility to Christianity*. The gas-stokers as promptly declined to go anywhere near his church. A fortnight later came a furious confrontation in the bar of the *Three Lamps*, where Henson went to address the men as they would not come to church. 'Why don't you keep to your church and leave the Union alone?' In March 1890 Watkinson said that for 'such men as the Reverend Henry [sic] Hensley Henson they were taxed from the crown of their head to the soles of their feet.' He declared that the early Christian Church was Communist and contrasted modern parsons. Henson was wonderfully well equipped to deal with the argument that Communism is the successor of the early Church.

In the autumn of 1891 the secretary of the Union, riled by something that Henson said, wrote an aggressive letter. He said that the Union would come to church if Henson preached on the text 'Every labourer is worthy of his hire', and challenged him to show in the sermon 'if he can' that he gets it. The offer was not meant seriously. Henson chose to take it seriously, and invited the men for 8 November, which was his birthday (aged twenty-eight). To everyone's astonishment, about 1,300 men crammed the church. They occupied pulpit steps, altar steps, seats of clergy, sanctuary step; stood shoulder to shoulder in the aisles and under the tower; displaced the choir from the choirstalls. A crowd stretched away in the churchyard, unable to get inside. The Salvation Army band sat on the steps by the communion rail, brass instruments piled inside the sanctuary. Many of the crowd had never been inside a church. They sang tremendously and behaved reverently except for once when a burst of applause ran round the church for something which he said in the sermon. The preacher felt *ravenous attention*.

They realized that for all his denunciations of appeals to greed or threats to break contracts, he was truly *a friend of the working man,* committed in heart to their side. They were right, for he held an axiom about priesthood, *the parson must always be on the side of the poor*. Three months later he had a magic name with the men. He could go to Beckton works and give addresses during the lunch hour in the lobby; fifteen minutes standing on a bench, with men standing round the walls or trying to hear through the door. He enjoyed this more than any other of his duties.

The gas-workers came again each year – November 1892 and 1893 and 1894. Each year they chose the text for Henson, such as *If any will not work neither shall he eat* (1892) (on which he gave them three-quarters of an hour). Again they filled the church, some standing, though without overflow. In 1894 they failed to fill the church, because the Union chose to collect for the restoration of the curfew tower, and some members objected to helping the Church of England so directly.

The sermons to the working men were double-edged. They said that the men were (almost always) wrong to strike. Strikes impoverished the nation and therefore themselves; especially strikes over trivialities. Violent remedies cannot but fail. Industries act upon each other. If miners strike and raise the price of coal they raise the price of iron, make it uncompetitive, and throw iron workers out of work. Higher wages for the one means lower wages for the other.

But: the Church is wholly in favour of unions. Itself it is a kind of union. Jesus Christ the carpenter taught the world the nobility of manual labour. The preacher showed the hatred of *rich men* oppressing their poor brothers, *idle men* whether they were loafers in the back streets or so-called 'gentlemen' hanging about clubs in the West End; his sense of loathing for landlords who grind, and debtors who drive little shopkeepers into ruin by failing to pay; his sense of suffering at the plight of the unemployed, and his recognition that they were justified in denouncing the Church. He demanded that employers should improve *immensely* the conditions of work, and should treat the employees not as *machines* but as *comrades*. He recommended to the State a whole programme which, from the lips of anyone but this hammer of Socialists, would have been called Socialist – the provision of chances for a better social life, of a medical service within reach of everyone, of compensation for sudden loss of employment by redundancy, and perhaps insurance against poverty in old age.

No wonder that the gas-workers came to church year after year. They found Henson to be 'their' man.

The world thought him an extreme Anglo-Catholic. He denounced dissent, professed celibacy, lectured on the grandeur of the monks, demanded an ascetic self-sacrifice of priests among the homes of the poor. Henson never applied to himself the word *Anglo-Catholic*. But he eagerly professed himself *Catholic*. He publicly criticized ritualists. He never wore a chasuble and never wanted to use incense. But he brought into Barking church, not without scruples by some, a cross and candlesticks. He introduced the old Jesuit service of the Three Hours on Good Friday. He led his congregation in that Catholic devotion which only reached England during the nineteenth century, the Stations of the Cross. He sometimes called the Holy Communion the *Holy Sacrifice*, or on occasion the *Mass*. He appeared at times in a cassock, and on occasion in a biretta. The world thought him Anglo-Catholic and the world was right. He disliked everyone in the English Reformation except Archbishop Thomas Cranmer, who drafted so lovely and so Catholic a book of prayer. His heroes were the Catholic leaders of the Church of England during the time of his youth. He was like so many of the dedicated slum priests of that generation – but unlike, in being younger, more articulate, better read, more trenchant, at times more scornful, and always cleverer.

He had a joy in the visible Church as a vessel of God's grace. He would not have it stained by worldliness or by immorality. When one of his boys got a housemaid with child, Henson excommunicated him privately for a period of penance. When the wife of one of his churchgoers rushed out of her house screaming because her husband beat her, Henson excommunicated him in due formality.

A mark of high-church devotion was the use of the sacrament of confession. Henson at first refrained. This disciple of Gore and Adderley never used a chief devotional aid commended by the high-church movement. His strongly Protestant upbringing, which almost everywhere else controlled his mind no longer, still made him dislike confession, and think of people who used it as spiritual weaklings. Yet he laboured under a sense of sin, sometimes intolerable, of his utter unworthiness before the Maker, of his ineffectual service as a priest – not all the time but in waves of sadness which at times turned into self-torment. Moreover a growing stream of parishioners used him as the priest before whom they made their confession. On 5 April 1893 he explained confession frankly to a candidate for confirmation, and suddenly was convinced that he must use it himself. *My conscience imperiously commands what my pride resists.*

He arranged to make his first confession to one of the Cowley Fathers at Oxford, Father Puller. His first confession was made on 8 May 1893; that year he recommended it strongly to all his candidates for confirmation; and in the Holy Week of 1894 he sat in church hearing numbers of confessions.

He took no pleasure in anyone's coming. It was a ministry impossible to enjoy. The sins of humanity are monotonous, and so Henson found. But he found something else which made him wonder whether he was really suitable as a confessor to his growing band of penitents. When the confessions were not monotonous – that is, when real tragedy or painful emotion was present – he felt too deeply. He could not be like a doctor, objective with a patient. His compassion ran too deep, his feelings too strong.

The future Henson – so unlike, apparently, the slum priest of Barking – cannot be understood without this background. Here apparently was a Church-and-State man; an establishmentarian; founder of the Layman's League; hammer of the Welsh Disestablishment Bill; scornful of Lloyd George whom, when he first saw, he called the *most nauseous Lloyd Jones*. Afterwards men often supposed that he imagined the Church to be only the religious side of the nation's life; that the idea of the Church independent of the State, with its own rights inherited ultimately from the New Testament, rights which even a Christian State could never rightly touch, was foreign to his mind. The error was pardonable. Partly from the non-conformity of his childhood, and partly from his acceptance of Catholic doctrine as a young adult, he assumed as axiomatic the Catholic Church and its rights in faith and worship, with which no State may interfere. He was still a vehement Church and State man. He still devastated disestablishers with his wit and information. But, underneath, he never saw the bond of Church and State as unconditional.

In the spring of 1895 the parish witnessed a contest for the office of churchwarden. A sitting churchwarden, regular in his pew, was opposed by a liberal politician who had not appeared inside the church for six years. The supporters of the new candidate (*bitter political dissenters and the drunken ruffians of the parish*) wanted control of the local charities. The contest was fought like an Eatanswill election, the vicar issued a printed pamphlet, ancient parishioners were brought out to the booth. Henson's sermons and speeches tore into pieces the doctrine that Englishmen who were not churchmen had any right, because they were citizens, to authority in the established Church. He spoke of the scandal of *an unbaptized Constantine interfering in the high religious concerns of Christ's Church*.[1] He won the poll after a recount, appeared at the window of the Town Hall to address a crowd of cheering supporters and a handful of booers and groaners, rang a peel of the church bells, and reinstalled his churchwarden. The alliance between Church and State was not unconditional.

---

[1] *Barking Advertiser*, 20 Apr. 1895; *Barking Parish Magazine*, May 1895. For the same anti-Erastian viewpoint see Henson's letters on Newman Hall in *The Times* 18 Feb. and 28 Dec. 1891.

Inside the man the travail of mind was not so stilled. First and
least important, he loved books. He bought good books and
read them and was sometimes up at 5 a.m. to read them and
knew that unless he read he would sooner or later not preach.
A big and growing parish, an ever growing congregation, a
growing demand upon his speeches or his sermons outside the
parish, consumed his unconscionable energy. He considered
whether he should let himself become a *bovine parson* and knew
that this could not be his vocation. But if so, how could he read
as he should read?

Secondly, he still worried, and needed to worry, over
money. The stipend of Barking was supposed to be £600 a
year. But nearly all was in tithe, the tithe could never be
collected in full, often the pay was more than six months in
arrears, normally it fell short by £100 or more annually. He
still owed debts, especially a very troublesome debt to his
predecessor for what he took over at the vicarage. Meanwhile
he lived as a Vicar of Barking ought to live, generous to the
charities, generous to the needy especially at Christmas,
generous in contributing to the raising of funds for church
restoration, and never stinting himself on books. He looked
and behaved like a reasonably paid incumbent, and each year
his debt mounted. His intimate friend at All Souls, Thomas
Raleigh, who often visited the parish and contributed largely
to its funds, saved him by a magnanimous secret loan. This
was not comfortable. *My career is to be quietly stifled by the squalid
pressure of domestic burdens.*

Against the background of outward success and inward fire,
against the portrait of a priest who seemed to be wholly at
home in his parish, fulfilled in his pulpit, living a ministry for
which he had prepared himself since boyhood, the waves of
melancholia poured over him. We must be cautious of these
descriptions because of the nature of the Journal. Sometimes
he used it as his outlet, whether for penitence or for pent-up
feelings, and therefore what he wrote has selectivity. If a man
uses his diary as a release for certain feelings, we cannot deny
that the feelings exist but need to beware of supposing that the
feelings filled all the waking hours of that man, who seldom
bothered to record ecstasies and enjoyments. Looking back he
knew that this was the best time for his ministry; the con-

temporary record is partly of depressions beyond the lot of many. The descriptions are the language of a man of highest ideals who knows that he does not live fully to those ideals; in part the language of mere weariness after long days; in part the spreading out of trouble of mind before the altar of God. But the descriptions show more than these normal causes of temporary depression.

He was living in a strain; probably a strain too tense for his physical strength. He was pouring his soul out upon a great parish, and with the fault of the young idealist overtaxing his physical capacity. He was very emotional, and felt everything in his heart, and agonized with those in agony. He was a warrior, and struck doughty blows, and wielded a broadside; but he had no tough hide, and when his enemies retaliated with abuse, or slander, or malevolence, he could not shrug it lightly off his shoulders. This priest fought a campaign at an intensity which could only be kept up for a limited time.

The sense of hypocrisy came, not more than occasionally now, but terrible when it came. *There seems no way of escape. I am just chained to the wheel, and must go circling round in an orbit of pain and shame till the link snaps, and I am removed from the torture, because its torture is not felt* (16 June 1894). The old Calvinist feeling of depravity came over him without any consoling conviction that he was a chosen soul. The worst time was one Easter day at 6 a.m., when he was almost overwhelmed with the sense that he was unworthy to be there, and could hardly complete the service. Sometimes the mood was just restlessness. He would make acts of faith, and try to make acts of hope, but at such times they rang hollow in his ears. At times he would help himself to such consolation by writing poetry: *Why*, he asked himself,

> *Why thoughts of Heaven jostle thoughts of Hell,*
> *Why the sweet ardours of my love for Thee*
> *Are elbowed ever by foul blasphemy?*
> *I know not how it is, yet this I know*
> *That I do love thee best of all below.*
> *And yet is it some madness of the thought?*
> *Some devil rioting in a mind distraught?*
> *I know not: yet I would that I could know*
> *Whence come the tyrants which torment me so . . .*

This was written in a mood of depression on holiday, at a café in Munich. True penitence looks outward and upward at light. Henson had that vision. But at times he had a touch of the pseudo-penitence which is excess of introspection and can be egoistical.

To dissenters as individuals Henson was caring and courteous – unless he stood in public dispute with a controversialist. But he filled Barking church. The newcomers were not all heathen. Chapel congregations sank. And Henson refused to conceal his opinions. The chapels were in schism, their ministers not true ministers, their people misled. These utterances failed to endear him to the numerous dissenters of Barking. And we, who know of the 'huntsman' of Birkenhead, cannot help predicting disaster as inevitable. He really did think the people to be misled, he had a vocation to guide them aright, and if he did not prune a speech by careful preparation, his language ran away with him, into scorn or fury.

The disaster happened at Brentwood on 17 May 1892. In duty bound he attended the diocesan conference of the St. Albans diocese. Speeches at diocesan conferences seldom electrify their hearers, and Henson was bored. Then two laymen in succession criticized the work of the Church of England in country parishes and praised the work of the dissenting chapels. Henson rose impromptu, *in a towering passion*. He worked himself up, his words ran away, his eloquence bit, and he ended by calling dissenters *emissaries of Satan*. He knew that the speech was foolish from the moment that he sat down.

He was humiliated; must apologize next day abjectly; was nevertheless rebuked publicly by the bishop for using 'language which neither youth, nor inexperience, nor excitement could for one moment justify'; and was in disgrace. The newspapers took up the cry. He was pilloried. He felt like John Henry Newman when his name was posted up on Oxford buttery hatches like a dishonest servant. In the provinces men asked for laws against parsons like Henson, so that bishops might instantly deprive such a man of his benefice.

He was very penitent, felt degraded by the abuse, hated himself for his loss of self-control – *I deserve all that they say*. He had nightmares – that he might die a violent death in a street riot.

The reader of Henson feels that this calamity was pre-destined. Sooner or later such an incident had to happen. Imbibing scorn of dissenting Protestants with his hatred of the religion of father; habitually using reckless language; using his diary to set down in ink the fiercest language against *sectaries*; hunting nonconformist meetings through the back streets of Birkenhead; determined to empty the chapels and fill the church in the parish of Barking, he led up to this kind of utterance both in private and at times in the pulpit. Only a month before, he reproached the Salvation Army, to his pri-vate self, as *that weapon of Satan*. In Birkenhead these ex-tremisms of a young graduate went unsung. In Barking, at first, they brought him not worse than abuse or jeers in the streets or ferocious letters in the post. They also brought crowds into church. But then the immature firebrand moved onto a wider stage, where the ardour of youth appeared before the world. The Brentwood diocesan conference brought him up with a jolt that left a permanent scar in his memory. He forgot neither the pain nor the lesson.

It was the earlier of two loose utterances which with some men destroyed his reputation. *It hung about my neck with the depressing effect of the dead albatross about the neck of Coleridge's Ancient Mariner.*

He was publicly identified as an uncharitable fanatic. This made it hard to get the kind of work which he wanted. Prospective patrons shrank from a bigot. It made it hard to get the curates whom he needed, for prudent trainers of ordinands did not wish their fledglings to learn these habits of utterance. All his life he was sure that the Brentwood speech inflicted lasting injury on his reputation and therefore his influence.

In the short run it hurt nothing of his work in Barking. The gas-workers of Beckton cared as little about chapels as about churches and were content to see the name of their unofficial chaplain in the newspapers. Dissenters came to church no less to discover what their critic said. The organizations still prospered, the roll of communicants rose, the work increased, the devotion seemed deeper. Dissenting lecturers came into the parish to assail his standpoint, and lower the repute of the

Church of England, and to be assailed is to be noticed.

But in the longer run it probably helped to drive him at last from the parish. Henson overtaxed his energies for his people, and no one could have worked at this pitch indefinitely. When on top of this the clash of arms was never silent, the strain led to more frequent self doubts.

And money would hardly allow him to stay much longer in Barking.

On 24 April 1894, after a strenuous week during which, among other duties, he heard about thirty confessions, he made his own confession to Father Puller at Cowley, and then saw the Warden of All Souls, to tell him that he had decided to leave Barking *because the strain was too great physically*, and that he would like a place at Oxford.

Henson would have made a wonderful pastor to undergraduates. But Oxford would not have him back.

He would have liked the university church of St. Mary's. The appointment would have been ideal. But the Fellows of Oriel College chose his junior Cosmo Gordon Lang. Balliol College needed a chaplain – but they refused Henson and chose a temporary chaplain, Hastings Rashdall, who was a learned historian and philosopher but had not Henson's genius with the young. Merton College wanted a clerical fellow, his friend Arthur Headlam suggested Henson, the Warden of Merton wrote to him, but they would not have him. Instead they chose a learned friendly obscurity with perfect manners. Henson frightened people – celibate by profession, Anglo-Catholic by notoriety, bigot by ill fame, denouncer of sectaries at a time when Oxford University welcomed nonconformist undergraduates. So three Oxford colleges in succession refused to have the only man who combined extraordinary gifts as a pastor with sufficient academic quality of mind. Colleges have high walls and are timorous about inviting controversial men into their tranquil towers.

A few miles to the north of Barking lay an almshouse, St. Mary's Hospital at Ilford. It had a clerical chaplain or warden, whose duty was to look after a few old men or their widows, but who had a reasonable stipend. That summer of 1895 its chaplain turned Roman Catholic, later to be dignified as

monsignor. On 24 July 1895 Henson accepted the chaplaincy
of Ilford Hospital.

The step looked paradoxical; the most hard-working young
vicar in England retires to a sinecure with a dozen souls.

Ilford gave him a chapel on Sundays, a small house for his
parents and sisters, a stipend of £350 a year not dependent on
hazardous collectors, and leisure. He described it to himself as
*a clerical Fellowship in the country*. He would have time to read,
chances to be in Oxford, a pulpit with freedom from the
harassments of a strenuous pastorate. And none of those who
doubted the change could know of Henson's letter to his bank
manager which borrowed more money and told him that he
*retired to Ilford partly in order to pay Barking debts*.

It would not be like him to go out like a lamb. He preached a
farewell sermon like no farewell sermon before or after.

*. . . The appeal of sensuality is clamorous, and they yield – from end to end of
Barking they yield – until the streets of this ancient Christian town have
become as the highways of the City of the Plains.*

He painted a portrait of Barking as a corrupt city like Sodom
and Gomorrah – prostitutes in the streets, local government
corrupt, apostles of hatred propagating hatred, everywhere a
reign of suspicion –

*I turn from this degraded parish which has spurned and broken me to the
Church which has relieved the darkness, and shall, by God's mercy in the
end redeem the whole life of Barking.*[1]

Instantly the reporters were at the parish. Was it true that
Barking was so immoral, or the streets so degraded, or the
municipality corrupt?

Was Mr Henson so calamitous a failure as Mr Henson said?
The passers-by whom the reporters asked gave various replies:
'we all know Mr. Henson by this time', 'clerical froth' – 'he
came to *boss*' – 'he never spared himself in work but has rather
increased the evil for he has quarrelled with almost everybody'
– 'his ideas of social and religious life are purely medieval.' The
chairman of the urban district council said pompously, 'The
reflections upon the virtue of its girls are most undeserved.'

[1] *Star*, 12 Nov. 1895.

The congregation, curates, and bishop rallied to his aid. A full meeting on 28 November presented him with an illuminated testimonial and a cheque for 50 guineas, accompanied by an ill-delivered speech. These warm-hearted proceedings were fairly reported in the local press.

Henson made a grim note: *Though they* [the enemy] *are now so confident, all the world knows that not a man of them had dared to apply the word failure to my ministry had I not myself placed it in their mouths.*

Reminiscences of others about the early life of a man who afterwards became famous are seldom reliable. But for what they are worth, the memory which Henson left in Barking was this: a sincere and formidable young priest who created a teeming congregation and filled the church; a man whose vestry meetings were stormy and controversial; the opener of the vicarage garden to crowded open air services where the music was provided by the town band; a vehement critic of the trade union and yet 'a great man for the working man'; a vicar who held crammed services for the gas-workers where the men chose the text for his sermon.

One of the early Franciscans of the Anglican revival looked back upon Henson as the founder of his vocation. Henson heard his first confession, gave him his first communion, and took him over to visit the Society of the Divine Compassion which was the earliest form of the revived Franciscan life within the Church of England.

Later he always looked back upon the time of Barking as his best years; the spring-time of his life; the time when *I discovered both my defects and my capacity.* He used to wonder whether to accept such a load at the age of twenty-five had been rash; *perhaps sinfully rash, I do not know.* Much later he met someone of the name Herbert Hensley Henson Hearne, and found that he was the son of one of his Barking club boys who expressed his devotion to his former vicar by alliteration at a christening.

That November Henson acquired his first dog. Unenterprisingly he named it Jack. The next day he lost all his time for study in trying to comfort the dog's homesickness.

## ILFORD

When I came to Ilford, I could not find the hospital. Knowing
that it stood near the station, conveniently for a chaplain who
often wished to visit Oxford, I applied to the drivers in the taxi
rank. None of them knew. At last I found someone who
suggested doubtfully that it might be the old building near the
main crossroads. At the crossroads queues of cars waited
stationary in four directions. I threaded my way among the
exhausts and saw a building of dark brick, which at first sight
looked neglected, and at second sight charming and historic in
its neglect. Then I remembered that Adeliza the abbess of
Barking founded it in Norman times. It looked as though a
person or persons did much to it during the nineteenth
century. From the crammed pavement I pushed at a door and
found myself in a little courtyard, with the chapel in front and
low houses to right and left. It had quietness amid the fumes
and shoppers, and the sad air did not destroy the instant
sensation that here is a place to do with God. The chapel was
locked, and on the door a paper was pinned, which said
'Service on Fridays in Lent.' I rang the bell of the house to the
left and got no answer; peered through the window and saw
rooms denuded of all furniture but a ping-pong table. I rang
the bell of the house on the right. An ancient lady in carpet
slippers shuffled to the door, and suddenly I was glad that in
her nuns' heaven the Norman abbess Adeliza has joy to see her
almshouse still caring for the elderly poor.

On a spring day of the 1980s the incongruity between that
place and that chaplain shouted in the ears. Never was a chapel
at a busy crossroads so unknown. Even the cabmen opposite
had no idea what it meant. Henson had a mission to the young,
the male, the worker, the crowd. His energy was restless. To
think of him, at the age of only thirty-two, ministering the
sacrament to a handful of old folk, one of whom troubled the
congregation with audible sighs of disgust, was pain to one
who remembered what it was like in Barking. Everything
spoke not only of quietness but of frustration. It was a vision of
an artillery man priming his gun within an old hermit's cell. I
blamed Henson for coming here – until I remembered that
ogre, the manager of his bank. Then I remembered too how

he loved the quietness of the monk's ideal, and exalted St.
Benedict in his historical imagination, and for all his unquiet
spirit felt a kinship with men who looked for God in a place
apart; and the reproach faded. But he could hardly find tranquillity at so traffic-laden a crossroads. To his extreme vexa-
tion he discovered after his arrival that the crossroads was the
customary pitch for barrel-organs and Salvation Army bands.

The almshouses were designed for men. The men brought
their wives and died, and no one would turn out the widows,
so most of the houses were occupied by females. As they aged,
they grew squalid. At one time the congregation helped. But
under the previous chaplain the congregation left or quarrelled
over ritual, and the survivors took no notice of the almsfolk.
Into one house an entire family, rough, dirty, noisy, and
drunken, moved. One of Henson's first duties was to eject the
lot. Later he persuaded Lord Salisbury to send him £78 a year
so that the almsfolk need not receive poor relief, which they
and the congregation felt to be a blot upon their name. When
his stepmother came to live with him, she made the almsfolk
her special care.

I was not the only person to suffer from scepticism about
Henson at Ilford. Several months after he went there to be
chaplain, his friend Cosmo Gordon Lang left the university
church at Oxford after too short a tenure, and again Oriel must
look for a vicar. Lang wanted Henson, and saw no bar in the
circumstance that he was hardly settled at Ilford. Other
weighty advisers likewise saw no obstacle. But during the last
two years the Fellows of Oriel College had not grown bolder.
No doubt they knew that this non-collegiate 'tosher' was not
fond of colleges. Laying about him with his club, and uttering
a truth which should not be cried from rooftops by persons
eager for a college fellowship, Henson thought of an Oxbridge
college as a *little suburban coterie*, with the *monotony of its interests, the narrowness of its range, and the pettiness of its concerns*,
and soon afterwards was willing to say all this in print.[1]

All Souls knew Henson better. One of their fellows even
laid a bet with the chances only 7–3 against Henson one day
becoming a bishop; odds which the Fellows of Oriel College

---

[1] *Quarterly Review*, 185 (1897), 260–1.

would have found absurdly favourable to Henson; and indeed
another at All Souls was willing to bet on the improbability of
that future. But they saw that he had leisure, and needed
libraries, and intended serious study. In summer 1896
they re-elected him a Fellow of All Souls – the proposer was
Compton, the same who carried his original election in 1884 –
and henceforth Henson normally spent weekdays at Oxford
among his books and weekends at Ilford among his 'parishioners'. A short time later the college appointed him
chaplain, with the understanding that the former chaplain
should take the Sunday services while he was at Ilford. The
pay was £20 a term.

Even Henson doubted whether Ilford was the right place to
stay. He had two discomforts. The unexpected discomfort
was noise. Seeking a quiet place to say his prayers, and to study
the workings of God in the world, and to write, he found that
he lived in one of the noisiest places in England, with traffic,
organ-grinders, evangelistic mission, brass, Salvation Army
bands, on Saturday evenings dancing in the street outside the
near-by pub. At times he could not work in his study but
retreated to the vestry of the chapel. He tried to persuade the
Marquess of Salisbury to let him borrow to build a *library* in
the garden at the back, so that he could work further from the
road. His patron was polite but he got no library.

The half-expected discomfort was nearness to Barking.

Three people, whom Henson wanted, refused the parish of
Barking. All Souls then appointed a fourth, and over this
appointment Henson almost quarrelled with his foster-father,
the Warden. Slowly the parish sank, vitality faded, devotions
grew formal, organizations failed. Henson was too near. To
watch this happening was agony. He took no pleasure in this
proof of his pastoral genius. He cared for the people.

But the discomfort was worse than watching. He was too
close to be a mere watcher. On the borders of their parish the
citizens of Barking could find their former leader. Discontented curates walked over to consult him, old parishioners
came to pour out their troubles, men or women who ought to
have appeared in their pews at Barking pained him by wor-
shipping at Ilford chapel. The congregation at Ilford grew. His
Bible classes swelled, the women to fifty. Henson was not

always sure that they ought to grow, at least in that way. He mourned that his chapel was *a cave of Adullam*. His existence at Ilford increased the difficulty of his successor's work; and it would have been hard for anyone to succeed Henson even if he had emigrated to New Zealand.

He was still the parish priest, though without parish organizations; with his confirmation class, and Bible class; hearing confessions regularly; with leisure to go out, and lecture and preach. Lent 1896 must be unique in Anglican Lents. Henson gave four different Lent courses (not with common materials), one of them as far away as Hemel Hempstead (eight hours away each week, back about 1 a.m.). In Lent 1898 he also gave four Lent courses, one as far away as St. Albans Cathedral (home at midnight). He conducted the Three Hours at that sanctuary of the high-church movement, All Saints Margaret Street. Occasionally he still confronted atheists on a soap-box at Victoria Park. He conducted his first retreat, at the Clergy School in Leeds. Decades afterwards old men recalled how unforgettable to them were the words which he spoke in that retreat.

His daily life was marked by two mechanical innovations. He began to use a telephone. He never mastered its complexities, grew frightened of its buzzings, and soon stopped. On one of his visits to Oxford he bought a bicycle, and then a special bicycling suit. At first he kept falling off. His spills were so frequent that he congratulated himself if he returned without sprained muscles. He smashed a hired bicycle by running into a dung-cart in the Mansfield Road, came back ignominiously from Little Milton in the village cart with *my faithless and futile machine*, and scratched himself sorely by charging into a hedge to avoid ramming a cart. Once mastered, the bicycle became his regular exercise, and a widening of the visits which he could achieve round Ilford.

In later life he often looked back upon Barking as the happiest time. He never felt that about Ilford.

While at Ilford Henson changed his mind dramatically. When he came to the hospital he was a dedicated and celibate Anglo-Catholic priest. When he left five years later, he was famous as a Protestant controversialist.

This turnabout was not the only dramatic turnabout of

Henson's life and therefore not to be ascribed only to the events of that time.

Nothing is more honourable in Henson's character than the desire to see the truth and then act, whatever the consequences to himself. His mind was able but not subtle. He could not easily discern nuances, and when he saw a truth he saw it with a dazzling clarity, sometimes oversimplifying what he saw, but also seeking to penetrate to its essence. When he grasped such a truth, he saw it in such illumination, and acted upon it with such force of conviction, that he could not understand how anyone else could see it differently once they knew the facts. As a young don reviewing books he was like all young dons before they learn how difficult it is to get anything in the world right; he pulverized, and growled, and slashed, and gave his critics the sensation that this is a knowing young man. Authors who were woolly, or sloppy, or sentimental, or muddle-headed, must fear castigation from the warden of Ilford Hospital, who would accept no plea that nevertheless they meant well.

This was the combination of qualities which made his turnabouts dramatic. What he held, he held with force. Simultaneously he had moral conviction that truth must be followed where it leads; and if new truth came upon him, so that he proved himself wrong, nothing stopped him burning what he once adored. He saw perfectly that such change hurt his public influence, and made some men doubt his character. This he minded. But he must act because it was immoral to refrain from following the truth. The turnabout could not be quiet slow growth of mind. It could not but be dramatic. The outside world was sure to think, though it thought errone-ously, that this champion swung in a moment, overnight, from one forcible conviction to another forcible conviction.

For this crux of his spiritual and intellectual life, one motive leaps to the eye. His predecessor at Ilford filled the chapel with incense and bells and vestments and statues, and then became a Roman Catholic. Henson was sent to Ilford to keep the chapel part of the Church of England. Therefore the debate with Rome was the battle of the years at Ilford. And therefore Henson became a Protestant controversialist, and so lost, little by little, the ideals and doctrines of an Anglo-Catholic priest.

This was the only motive for turnabout which he himself allowed.

A tiny handful at Ilford preferred their old warden to their new. A new Roman Catholic priest in Ilford almost succeeded in converting, or perverting, a girl under Henson's religious care. The Essex newspapers were full of the war between Henson and his predecessor, between Henson and his rival. Henson got the better of these arguments. He was a master in the skirmishes of the street.

Two European events made impact upon his mind. Pope Leo XIII condemned Anglican orders, and this did not raise his reputation in Henson's eye. And then came the Dreyfus case. A mass of evidence exists to show that what resurrected the anti-Catholic partiality of Henson's childhood was the trial of Alfred Dreyfus before a French court martial.

Dreyfus, who was a French Jew and an officer in the French army, was convicted of betraying military secrets to the Germans, and sent to Devil's Island. The case did not yet touch Henson, nor most of England. But gradually doubts rose in French minds, whether justice had miscarried. If so, it could only have miscarried because other French officers forged evidence. Therefore the debate became entangled with the honour of the French army, which was determined that somehow Dreyfus was guilty. And because Dreyfus was a Jew, the debate was marred by a shrill French anti-semitism.

On 13 January 1898 the novelist Émile Zola published his letter *I accuse*, a tremendous indictment of the French war office for suppressing evidence and conniving in the grossest injustice. The end of that month saw riots in the streets of Paris and scuffling in the French Chamber, and a demonstration of 20,000 people against Jews. Zola was convicted of libel and went into exile in London. Then Colonel Henry of the intelligence department confessed that he forged one of the documents of the prosecution and on being sent to prison cut his throat.

The French government at last consented to a retrial. Dreyfus was brought back from Devil's Island and in September 1899 tried again at Rennes. By now almost all the world, including almost all the British, were convinced of his innocence. The court martial shocked the world by bringing in a second verdict of guilty. The news sent Henson straight to bed *in an unspeakable rage*. But the court also pleaded extenuating circumstances, reduced the term of imprisonment to ten years; and soon the French government took the course (in justice unsatisfactory) of 'pardoning' Dreyfus.

Months of this case roused anti-clericalism in France, and fed anti-popery in England. For the French army and the French Church appeared to be allies and bedfellows; like Caiaphas, suppressing an innocent man for the alleged good of the State. Two of the worst anti-semitic books were written by French priests.

Henson's emotions were not engaged on Dreyfus's side very early. But he loved underdogs, and hated injustice. Dreyfus enlisted his sympathy partly because he looked alone against all the organs of power, partly because he was a Jew. Henson's sermons of this time began to be filled with pointed references to Dreyfus, and the crime of the French Catholic Church. Zola, whose novels repelled him, came as a saviour of Catholicism from outside the Catholic Church. The Church of France, the Church of St. Louis and St. Francis Xavier and Bossuet and Pascal and Fénelon and Vincent de Paul, had given *a spectacle of moral bankruptcy which shocks the world*. What revived all his childhood fear of Rome was the suppression of truth. Bishops and clergy joined with army officers in putting their welfare before justice, and trampled upon *the inherent sanctity of truth*.

For controversy at a more educated level he was not yet so well equipped. He took on the Jesuit Father Herbert Thurston, about the moral record of the Jesuits; and that was rash, for Thurston was a dedicated scholar who had just begun his long career of refuting every variety of anti-Catholic or anti-Jesuitical legend. After various knocks the Protestant champion lay flat upon the floor of the ring.

When we contemplate Father Herbert Thurston in the library at Farm Street in Mayfair, spending day after day in the effort to track the source of some hostile story, we cannot help wondering whether that was the best use of his time, and how many works of scholarship we lost because he thought controversy his vocation. But here he may have helped the Church of England. With anti-Catholicism imbibed at childhood; with evidence of unscrupulous conduct by a local Catholic priest; with a conviction that the Dreyfus case proved corruption in the Church of a neighbouring nation; and with such memories of his own ordination that any pope who condemned that ordination must be unworthy – this young Anglican could have degenerated into a hammer of popes. We shall see one pamphlet much later in his life, which will remind us of this moment. But Father Thurston brought him up with a jolt.

Meanwhile, the argument over Catholic rituals inside the Church of England widened into a national rift, taken up not only in conferences and synods, but in every man's conversation, in tea-parties and dinners, in speeches from platforms, even in Parliament. If anyone fancied that the nineteenth century made religion less interesting to the common man, he must change his mind when he saw what happened in England during the year 1899. It was like those old days of the early Christians when, so it was said, if you went to have your hair cut, the barber would at once engage you in theology.

The heirs of Newman and Keble and Pusey had widened and deepened worship in England. Often they were not much concerned with ritual provided that they could secure reverence in the way of prayer. But on the provisions of the Prayer Book they reintroduced confession and the wearing of vestments at the sacrament of holy communion. And a much smaller number of Anglo-Catholic clergy acted on the principle that what the Prayer Book does not forbid is allowed provided it conforms to the practice of the Catholic Church in all the centuries. On this principle several churches in London, and a few outside, introduced the use of incense and the practice of reserving the elements of bread and wine in an aumbry at the side or a tabernacle on the altar, whether to be ready for an emergency of sudden sickness, or to foster the sense of the presence of God among those who said their prayers in the church. In addition, at certain special days in the year like Holy Week, they felt free to use the ceremonial of the Roman Catholic Church, at services outside the canonical services and translated into the English language.

The unaccustomed practices grew visibly. All attempts to stop them failed.

A large body of ordinary opinion disliked what happened
and thought that the bishops ought to stop these 'extreme'
churches if they could. The bishops as a body had the same
opinion but knew that they could stop them only by persuasion. A resort to the law meant a resort to a system of courts
where, under the then establishment of the Church of England, the supreme court was the Judicial Committee of the
Privy Council. And priests of Anglo-Catholic parishes knew
that a State had no right whatever to interfere with the way in
which a people prays, and thought that the Judicial Committee
had no more status in this matter than the Tsar of Russia or the
Nizam of Hyderabad. Therefore if a bishop, or anyone else,
prosecuted a 'ritualist' in the law courts, the ritualist took no
notice of the courts and went to prison for contempt of court.
This did more harm to the Church at large, and gave more
encouragement to ritualism as a movement, than any other
course of action that could have been devised.

The bishops possessed a veto on prosecutions. After several
imprisonments they began systematically to prevent prosecutions, either by veto or by threat of veto. So they preferred a
small number of churches where they regretted the way of
worship to a handful of clergy-martyrs in prison for so conscientious a cause. In this they were as wise as could be.

The Church Association was founded in 1865 with the aim
of stopping ritual practices which were illegal. By 1892 the
plan floundered, for the bishops would not permit prosecutions, an attempt to prosecute Bishop Edward King of Lincoln
was hardly upheld by the Judicial Committee, and the failure
did the Church Association and their cause vast damage.
But this made part of the barrel of powder on which the
bishops sat. Good men, not extremist men, who cared for the
Church of England, and had emotional feelings against sudden
innovations in ways of worship, felt repelled from their parish
churches; and felt also that the national Church, their Church,
was being brought back little by little to the popery which in
their hearts they associated with the fires of Smithfield, with
the Spanish Armada, with an attempt to blow up all Parliament, and with a Stuart desire to kill the liberties of Englishmen. They had a grievance but no redress.

And because they had no redress, some malcontent or

fanatic was likely to try some form of direct action. So sensitive minds began to fear.

In 1895 and 1896 two other events, apart from the reports of what went on in London churches, swelled the anxiety of Protestants. Lord Halifax conducted negotiations with the Pope over the recognition of Anglican orders as the first move towards reunion between the Church of Rome and the Church of England. These negotiations ended in fiasco. The bishops were not so firm in repudiating them as might have been expected. Secondly, the Church of England was invited to send a representative to the coronation of the Tsar in Moscow. The archbishop chose Creighton of Peterborough, who was bearded enough for any Russian bishop, and encouraged him to appear in cope and mitre. In the cathedral at the Kremlin Creighton looked magnificent in red and gold and the visit of so intelligent a historian fostered ecumenical fraternity between the Church of England and the Russian Orthodox Church. But neither the magnificence nor the fraternity escaped the eyes of those who feared that a famous Protestant Church was being led to betray its Protestant heritage.

John Kensit was a Londoner born not far from Liverpool Street who after a time as draper's assistant and then as stationer, set up a Protestant printing house in Paternoster Row which began to flourish on the sale of anti-Catholic tracts. During the early nineties he became a comic figure with fanatical utterances, and yet a menace. He appeared at Church Congresses and wherever else publicity might do good. But when he appeared in Bow church to protest against the confirmation of Bishop Creighton to the see of London (15 January 1897) Creighton had never before heard his name. This protest was equal to a brawl in church, at the least very unseemly. It was ominous for the new method of direct action.

Not far from Kensit's printing office was the church of St. Ethelburga, Bishopsgate, where the new ritual was used. Towards the end of January 1898 unseemly noise and arguments and pushings began on Sundays in St. Ethelburga's. Thenceforward the scale of operations mounted.

In May 1898 this unpleasantness turned worse. The fanatic Kensit was only important because a large number of unfanatical Englishmen agreed that he had cause for his fanaticism. In

May the protesters found at their side the weightiest assailant ever to attack Anglo-Catholicism from his place in the House of Commons, the leader of the Liberal Party in the Lower House, Sir William Harcourt.

Harcourt was the truculent son of a truculent canon of York Minster. The political scene alone was not sufficient for his stock of pugnacity. Though no brawler, he felt with Kensit that the Church of England was betrayed, that the bishops were to blame and that Parliament had the duty to intervene. Harcourt turned ritual brawls from a police matter within a few churches into a national argument. Between July 1898 and March 1899 letters from his pen appeared regularly in the pages of *The Times*. Every letter abused the bishops for inaction. He was not afraid of personalities. He pilloried the Archbishop of Canterbury and held up the Archbishop of York to contempt. The resulting furore came to be called The Crisis in the National Church.

The danger was obvious. Harcourt called upon Parliament to act since the bishops would not. If Parliament passed a law to forbid certain rituals, or order a certain kind of liturgy, a large number of people, who had no use for the rituals, would rally to those rituals because they would think the intervention of Parliament a monstrous interference with the liberty of the Church of England. Harcourt was under the illusion that Parliament could do what Henry VIII had done. Therefore a real act of Parliament would do one or probably both of two things; divide the Church of England in an unhealable schism and precipitate an irresistible campaign for disestablishment when a main body of Anglicans found the State nexus so intolerable that they joined hands with dissent to bring it to an end.

This crisis in the National Church changed Henson's life. It made him think out his Anglo-Catholicism. It revived his strenuous contention for establishment, and made him think further his notion of a national Church. And it made him famous, and so opened the door to the longed-for departure from Ilford.

As the agitation grew hot during June and July 1898, Henson was away on a long solitary holiday to Germany and Vienna, partly to recover from the melancholies and moods caused by Ilford. He entered the national fray for the first time in July. By the end of November he was so well known that the *Guardian* headed its leader in capitals, 'Mr. Henson on the Situation'.

His interventions did not lack courage. Kensit held a public meeting in the main street at Ilford. Henson published a stalwart article defending the use of confession (*National Review*, November 1898), and this was almost like daring Kensit to blaspheme in the Ilford hospital. He took on that heavyweight Sir William Harcourt in the columns of *The Times*, and was not worsted.

Every possible policy looked wrong. Should we back a House of Commons, totally unfitted for passing laws on ways of worship, in passing such laws? To the contrary should we fight for freedom, and therefore for the provocative freedoms of the ritualists? Or should we go for disestablishment, which would deprive the poor of many churches and narrow the broad tolerance of the Church?

In November 1898 Henson published a short book or long pamphlet entitled *Cui Bono?*[1] At bottom, this was a plea that establishment mattered. That was ground which Henson well understood. It took rank as an able and persuasive piece which may still be read with profit. Its author felt strongly and wrote cogently. The chaplain of an obscure Essex almshouse was discovered to be a power in the land. The *Guardian* talked of his singular force and eloquence.

We must not risk disestablishment. That would mean a narrowing. Establishment safeguards a breadth of opinion and practice. Only establishment protects toleration. He summoned his experience as a pastor in Barking, and remembered how every door opened to him because he was the parish priest. And this marvellous place of the parish priest, the strength of the Church, is being risked for the sake of ceremonies which may or may not be good but are not necessary and provoke. He begged the high churchmen to give up reservation of the sacrament and the use of the word mass, and to deal tenderly with the people's reverence for the Bible, and for the keeping of Sunday. He begged the whole Church

[1] 'Who will gain?'

meanwhile to trust the rulings and leadership of the bishops and especially of the Archbishop of Canterbury.

Naturally, this unpopular-making stance was not likely to make its author unpopular among bishops and archbishops.

The force, the wit, the raciness, the power of writing – that was what no one knew and *Cui bono?* disclosed.

We should not exaggerate the impact. The pamphlet went through four editions at once but each edition was only 250 copies. People who call their books by Latin titles cannot intend a large public. And the Latin title had another aspect. People to whom Latin is a familiar language do not bother to use it in the titles of their books. People who went little to school, or acquired their Latin the hard way, are proud of the acquisition.

But in arriving, he separated himself from many Anglo–Catholics who looked to him as their ally. They were of another opinion. If Parliament debated a bill that no Anglican should call the holy communion *mass* they would never again call it anything but *mass*, lest they be seen to obey a tyrant.

Sir William Harcourt, precipitating turmoil in the Church of England in a manner revolting to Henson's sense of Catholic devotion, made a catalyst which helped Henson to know his own mind.

We cannot so leave the diagnosis of Henson's turnabout. He dedicated his spare time from the Ilford Hospital to reading. He read widely, unsystematically, mostly in the history of the Church which was his love, but also in the study of the Bible. And he found that the truths of the Bible were less secure than he expected.

As a young graduate at Oxford he comfortably adjusted his intelligence to modern criticism of the Bible. He cheerfully sacrificed the idea that the early books of the Old Testament were historical in all their parts, and willingly accepted the evidence that St. Mark was written before St. Matthew. But at Oxford he saw no need to question the main lines of the history narrated in the New Testament.

At Ilford his reading raised doubts. Could the usual portrait of the Christian ministry in the New Testament be defended in the light of the new historical evidence? He had believed and taught the apostolic succession of bishops. Could he teach it now? And even more, how much could we know for certain about the life of Christ except the single overwhelming fact that the earliest Christians confessed Him their Lord and their God? His outlook began to be more radical than the outlook of his Oxford masters. And this was an intellectual contribution to the turnabout. Formerly he condemned dissent in unmeasured language and declared their ministers invalid because they did not stand in historic succession from the apostles. But now – was the modern study of the New Testament showing him that nonconformist pastors were just as valid ministers of Christ as himself?

With the third reason for the turnabout we enter a realm of speculation into the mystery of a personality.

His father was already senile. Early in 1896 his sister Tennie went mad and in April died. In September 1896 the family sold perforce the house in Broadstairs and received no money, which went to pay debts. His stepmother brought his father and surviving sister Marion to live at Ilford. This was the time when his stepmother, whom he called Mother, first came to be known on paper as *Carissima* (dearest). On 8 November 1896 his father died.

No son ever felt more guilt at the death of a father. *I discover too late how much he was to me.* He accused himself of *harsh misjudgment,* of *hard lack of sympathy*. He was filled with remorse. The sense of guilt never left Henson. He had revolted against his parent, the only parent of his flesh whom he had ever truly known. He did not like to remember the days of his sonship. In his spiritual teaching to others he would urge them that the oblivion of past sin is a healing to the soul. He did what he could to forget. But he never forgot.

A psychohistorian, therefore, may guess that this death was connected with the ensuing change of the son's mind. While father lived, and was a stern puritan and perfervid Protestant, Henson was an Anglo-Catholic. When father died he realized what he owed, and knew how much came through to himself of the stern puritan and fervid Protestant.

On 1 November 1900, at All Souls where he went for the gaudy, he received a letter from the Conservative prime minister Lord Salisbury. It invited him to accept a vacant canonry at Westminster Abbey, saying that it would offer a wider field for his gifts as a preacher. Henson was so prostrated by this letter that he spent next day prone, in bed or on a sofa. He thought it *almost miraculous. I have received an utterly undeserved promotion, and am called to a work quite beyond my powers. Have mercy upon me, O God, and enable what Thou dost demand.*

A last hurdle must be leapt. To enter the canonry he must pay fees of over £50 and had no such money. This time his old aunt, Emma Hensley Long, from whom he inherited the name Hensley, stepped in and paid.

He was installed as canon on 24 November 1900, and as Rector of St. Margaret's which went with that canonry, on 9 December. He was thirty-seven but looked absurdly young to be canon of anywhere. Whether or not he was right in thinking himself unpopular at Ilford, a large number of persons failed to get inside Ilford chapel to hear his farewell sermon.

# 4. THE CANON

THE SEVENTEEN years between the installation to the canonry at Westminster and the consecration to a bishopric look to the external eye like the serene epoch of Henson's stormy life. Intending all his life to be a preacher, he found himself with one of the famous pulpits in England and turned it into the most famous of all. He had a cause to advocate, and knew what he wanted, and suffered few of the endless scruples of the past, and made his journal more objective, less passionate, and duller. It was a new world, a comfortable upper-class world, of ecclesiastical politics at a national level, or of social engagements in London. He would not be Henson unless the waves of melancholia came over him and found expression in his journal. But they were far less frequent. To an external eye he seems to be a man with a happy home, a work which suits his capacity, sufficient controversy to make him content but not such poisoned controversy as to destroy his assurance, a programme ahead in which he believed and for which he could contend. All the recipe for happiness was there. And Henson was happy. Being Henson, he was never happy unreservedly. And though he occasionally wondered in his later career why he was such a fool as to leave London, he never looked back upon this time as the most fulfilled decade of his life.

Journal, 11 December 1904:

*A white mist enwraps Westminster and a black fog covers my own soul. It is strange how capricious and how despotic are one's moods. They are the whips of the Furies who deal out punishment to men's folly and fault; and then most do their strokes fall when the naked and quivering wretches can least sustain them.*

The Canon of Westminster inhabited a world a long way from Ilford. The slum priest of East London was translated into a preacher who might see under his pulpit the prime minister, the Archbishop of Canterbury, the Speaker of the House of Commons, the Chancellor of the Exchequer, Field Marshal Lord Roberts, or F. E. Smith. His income and environment befitted a member of the upper class. For the first time in his life bank managers were deferential. As Rector of St. Margaret's, the church attached to his canonry, he had the duty to conduct fashionable or famous weddings. His home was a large rambling house with unusual rooms. The Athenaeum became the club where his friends gathered. He easily met powerful politicians or leading ecclesiastics, spoke in Convocation, sat in the gallery of the House of Commons. He also loved to hold confirmation classes, and show parties of schoolchildren and working men round the abbey. But the one-time vicar who rampaged into the pubs of Barking to fetch out males for his congregation, or challenged the workers of Beckton to public battle, was hard to recognize in the well-dressed acceptable handsome churchman of the Establishment with his youthful looks and witty conversation.

The private journal changed. It became less introspective, more confidential, more ecclesiastical, at once important and dreary.

This change of state was fostered by his marriage. The courtship was one of the shortest on record. The vow of celibacy vanished. Not without trace.

On 7 July 1902 he dined with Charles Stuart Parker, a former Liberal colleague of Gladstone, and biographer of Sir Robert Peel. At the dinner he met Parker's niece and *found her a very charming companion*. Four days later he proposed marriage. She was Isabella Dennistoun, daughter of a west-Scottish squire. She was thirty-two, he thirty-eight.

He needed to defend his conduct. *I also have to confess myself*, he told a friend who asked, *too craven for the unaccompanied journey*. In the days when clergymen were not allowed wives, Archbishop Cranmer of Canterbury was said to have smuggled his wife in a black box, and Henson wrote smilingly to a friend that this was the method that he preferred.

On Sunday afternoon, 19 October 1902, he spent his last day of bachelor freedom preaching for his friend the Vicar of Chigwell and by ill fortune preached one of his own published sermons which the Curate of Chigwell had preached the Sunday before. The next day he married Ella in Westminster Abbey.

Ella was a gentle, affectionate lady of grace and good works.

She had nothing like her husband's speed of intelligence, and that made a little problem for her even before she began to go deaf. They remained affectionate all their lives. He diligently recorded their disagreements, sometimes with laughter and sometimes with grief. But he tried to write to her every day when he was away. She was of the Scottish upper class and in one sense helped his career, partly because she was so obviously a suitable and good wife for a Christian clergyman, and partly because through her connections he came to know a new range of powerful people. He did not marry money because she had little income.[1] If the Chaplain of Ilford Hospital moved up among the British élite when he became a Canon of Westminster Abbey, his marriage confirmed him in that place.

The needle pricked him. Was he an upper-class clergyman, of the sort he despised? Was preaching sermons to Lord Roberts, or to the Archbishop of Canterbury, the equivalent of the apostolate to the poor of which he dreamed and which he had fulfilled? Was the world of fashionable weddings the field where he was supposed to minister?

This little needle took the special form that he never quite forgot the ideal of celibacy – or at least he lived with it so long that at odd moments it afflicted. He even suffered from the occasional sense of humiliation that he might have chosen the less sacrificial path and by his marriage abandoned the truest and highest ideal of the priesthood. To the Anglican canon no longer an Anglo-Catholic a little touch of his Anglo-Catholic past intruded. All his life he could devastate young curates contemplating marriage. Most of his life, almost to the end, he held it an evenly balanced debate whether a Church did better with a married or a celibate clergy. Just as he was critical of clergy and tolerant of laity because he applied higher standards to the clergy, so his pen recorded the least hint of what should be disapproved in parsons' wives; and above all bishops' wives, who must be very special people to escape his demolition.

Ella went into labour on the evening of 7 January 1905.

---

[1] Wife's unearned income, tax year 1921–2: £158 14s. 0d.

*About 5 a.m. the doctor came to my study to say that the end had been reached. Ella was well, and the child was born dead. So ends another, surely the last of my dreams. The whole house mocks me at every corner with futile preparations for babyhood. I went to church, and celebrated at 8 a.m. with an effort; and twice I preached, fighting the while a desperate battle against the contemptible weakness which would sit down and cry.*

*I looked at the dead boy: he is fashioned completely, and fairly proportioned though small: his tiny face had a care-stricken and sorrowful look which sufficiently confessed its father. It is no 'still-born infant' that I mourn, but my own son.*

Tuesday, 10 January 1905: *Kirshbaum* [Henson's curate] *accompanied me to Norwood, where the poor little body of my dead child was buried without other liturgy than its father's grief.* On 15 July 1905 Ella had a miscarriage.

These two calamities revived for a time the doubt whether he ought to have married.

Ella never again conceived. To them both, the state of childlessness was heavy disappointment. When their silver wedding came, Henson wrote that this childlessness had been the *greatest shadow* in their married life. Sometimes he wondered whether if he had been blest with children he would have been a better as well as a happier man. It gave him private pain to attend a children's party at Christmas in a friend's house, or to preside at a meeting in aid of a maternity home. *Without a family*, he wrote sadly when he was nearing his eightieth year, *not even conjugal love can create a home*. Only half-humorously he grew accustomed to say, that *while there was much to be said for a celibate clergy and much for a married clergy, there was nothing to be said for a childless married clergy*.

They never thought of adopting. But each, in a different way, compensated for the void. This was easier for the husband. He could find promising young creatures everywhere, in the choir at St. Margaret's, or in the congregation, or by the numerous ways which a clergyman is brought into touch with families; and then he would foster, and keep in touch by letter, and pay the fees for a better education. In this way some seven boys and then young men were brought into a filial relationship. Henson believed that his own non-boyhood disqualified him from understanding boys. On the contrary, few men understood them better; and it is possible that the element of sublimation in this work gave it a finer point. Certainly it gave him intense satisfaction, even though he grudged the minutes which so busy a man needed to spend in keeping up regular letters with distant protégés. He was conscious that these letters were a compensation for the baby that died.

Ella had not this resource. For a time the loss of the child was so grievous that she was attracted to mediums who offered communication with the dead. From this sprang part of Henson's hostility towards spiritualism. But then in 1916 a girl, Fearne Booker, came temporarily to the house, and helped with the secretarial work and the driving. Soon she was permanent, a sort of unofficial companion to Ella, really a daughter, named at last in Ella's will *my acting daughter* and inheriting from both the Hensons. She was intelligent, small of stature, with bright hazel eyes and sensitive hands.

Friends gave them another dog, which instantly died; and then an Aberdeen terrier, christened *Logic*, and soon famous among the cloisters of Westminster. When *Spy* drew a cartoon of Henson for *Vanity Fair* (Henson thought the cartoon *villainous*) Logic appeared trotting jauntily at his heels. Apart from Logic and his friends Henson lavished affection on birds, and always watched their antics and their nesting with pleasure. Photographs still exist of men engulfed amid scores of pigeons because Henson was worried about their diet in severe weather and paid for supplies of bird-food. Not being musical, he had a curious fellow-feeling for rooks.

Ella helped Henson. She was a kindly manager, and loved an open house, and almost every day they had guests at their table, usually three or four but rising on occasion to parties of seventeen or eighteen. She therefore needed to be good with servants and succeeded. She cared little whether the guest was a Member of Parliament or an errand boy whom her husband picked off the Embankment. She liked having all the choirboys to tea, and married a housemaid from her canon's house. She had the boldest possible taste in decoration, but the boldness was not tawdry nor vulgar, its only defect was expense. She was gentle, and good at parish visits. What she was bad at was intelligent exchange. At times guests at her side found it hard to listen to her *nice weather* conversation when if they strained their ears they would be sure to hear a memorable epigram coming from the other end of the table.

Henson came to Westminster with the name of rebel. He liked, and liked to live up to, the reputation. His arrival put the conventional on tenterhooks. They expected trouble, and Henson preferred that this expectation be not vain. Before long he was the best-known rebel, and with opponents the most disliked clergyman, in all England.

He was an unusual rebel because he had that mental paradox in him, to be a *rebel of the establishment*. He was no dissenter, disliked nothing more than dissent. In many ways this gadfly of high ecclesiastics was a thorough ecclesiastical gadfly. He dressed with perfect convention, and looked like a canon and rector though apparently too young to be either. Being exceptional in his cast of mind, he was less dangerous than he looked to opponents, because he could never have many disciples. All his life he made men think, admire the originality of his opinions, and seek to refute his arguments. But not so often could he convert. Seeing the weakness in every party he belonged to no party. If you rode with him as leader you might find the turnabout, logical at the front of the column, too nimble for the vanguard to make the change of direction.

Nevertheless this was a rebel with weight in the punch.

St. Margaret's was a home of musical worship, where men came rather to hear than to take part, and where God was found through beauty. Henson was ill adapted by nature to accept this doctrine of the purpose of a parish church. Henson could conceive no function for St. Margaret's except as a place where a *congregation* worshipped, and was sure that *to preach* was the reason why he was sent to St. Margaret's. Accustomed to crowding his churches, he could never fill the pews of St. Margaret's only with a musical élite. He soon drove out the organist, and got a new musician whose ideas fitted his own. The congregation at St. Margaret's changed. Those who came for music vanished. Others came in larger numbers.

Legend had it that afterwards many MPs sat under his pulpit at St. Margaret's. Henson heard the legend, and knew that MPs were few. Legend had it that young people crowded his church as once at Barking and Ilford. But young people are not wont to travel distances to church. Eyewitnesses reported that the congregation was grey-haired and respectable and intelligent.

We have several descriptions of Henson preaching at St. Margaret's or in the Abbey. Since in Edwardian England the sermon was still an important and might be a newsworthy utterance, a little knot of reporters would often gather under the pulpit and asked for his notes at the end of the service. He soon got the habit of leaving summaries of his next day's sermon at the offices of *The Times*.

Whether in the Abbey, or in St. Margaret's, or before a university, Henson usually preached for thirty-five or forty minutes. He thought forty-five minutes on the long side, twenty-five minutes scandalously short. He once preached for fifty-five minutes by a choirboy's watch. Sometimes Ella talked suggestively of the value of wrist watches for preachers. He wrote the sermon out in full, and preached it from the text but delivered it as though he was not tied to the text. Most Sundays he preached twice, sometimes three times, but if he ran out of time for preparation he was not afraid of re-preaching old sermons, even sermons which he had printed, and very occasionally a published sermon by someone whom he revered, like Dean Church. Almost all his intellectual work of the week was dedicated to the preparation of sermons. The books which he published during the time at Westminster were nearly all collections of sermons. He did not like to invite visiting preachers. *Let everybody be fairly sure of finding the preacher in his place, and then there is a chance that he may draw about him a company of people who are genuinely concerned to hear and understand his teaching. By this means there is a possibility that he may succeed in building up some coherent view of faith and duty in the public mind.* He would not permit either humour or slang into his sermons, on the ground that they lowered the dignity of the pulpit. That was a change of taste from his Barking days.

If a man is to preach to a nation he must marry a need of his times. Newman's sermons became national because in the romantic age they summoned dry Anglicans to a new warmth and depth of Catholic spirituality; Spurgeon's sermons, be-cause the newly educated and urbanized lower-middle classes needed a simple gospel; Liddon's sermons, because in an age when traditional certainties dissolved before the advance of knowledge, he preached those certainties as still certainties, with an exceptional intelligence. Henson marked the next stage in intellectual development. He knew that the certainties were certain no longer; that the message about Christ which he must deliver had to be a liberal gospel; that the old language must be restated in the light of new knowledge; and yet that the result must not be Christianity and water, but still a message that transformed lives. Henson, with a half Plymouth Brother for a father, and a devout Lutheran for a stepmother, and an Anglo-Catholic celibate priest in his immediate past, knew that the certainties were certain; he knew himself a Christian, an Anglican, a liberal – and his mission to be the preaching of a liberal Christianity that was still Christian. Ordinary preachers found their words difficult to adjust to the axioms that the early Old Testament was legend or that words ascribed to Christ might be interpolated; and in their difficulty they dripped platitudes of morality and abandoned *force* to the extremists, evangelical or Catholic. Henson was a liberal, and still had *force*. He gathered people who wanted to hear a gospel which their intelligence could receive and which was still the Christian gospel.

One man's impression of a preacher is but two-eyed and partial. Yet the witnesses are in harmony. And the portrait which they drew of Henson the preacher was as follows:

He had restless, brilliant eyes, which looked straight at the people. The face was boyish, with its pointed chin, flat hair, thin lips, and slanting cocked eyebrows. In the voice was something purposeful and mordant, but it was not a beautiful voice, for it had a reedy quality, at times even rasping, and the power in the utterance depended hardly on the timbre. Yet somehow it was a provocative voice, by sounding lay and unclerical amid such religious surroundings; a voice that did not draw but made uncomfortable. The face was pale, and gave a mixed impression between ardour and impassivity, so that the passion seemed not to be emotional but only intellectual and therefore cooler. The speaker gave an impression of driving energy and determined will, and of believing wholly in what he said. His hands fidgeted and at times distracted attention from the words. It was not sleek, nor

smooth, the sermon did not purr like the engine of a Rolls–
Royce, it had not the attractiveness of a quiet and persuasive
eloquence. On the contrary, against a background of sedate
Anglican music and liturgy the sermon was too different, a defiance of conventional ideas made to seem the more
defiant by contrast with its conventional environment. The
violence was not in the delivery, this was no speech of fury, the
tone remained quiet, and yet it still felt a violent intrusion. The
language could be brilliant. Yet all the witnesses are agreed
that it was more brilliant than persuasive, that sometimes the
brilliance of the phrases detracted from the convincing power.
There was no charm, no magnetism, such persuasive force as
existed lay in the appeal to the intelligence. All the witnesses
are agreed that it was a high form of the preacher's art and
doubted whether it was the highest.

Was this determination and will–power and shattering of
convention fixed upon a goal which was truly deep enough, or
spiritual enough, or ultimate enough? Henson's sermons
reminded one not unkind witness of the doggerel:

> O Nancy Brown I love you dearly
> My heart is yours – or very nearly

that is, he did not seem quite willing to rise up towards
ultimate surrender; and we who know the fear of the mission
preacher which was rooted in his childhood may wonder
whether this was not a sensitive appreciation. Perhaps his
horror of the extempore word, and his consequent determination always to prepare a written text and not depart from it,
may have contributed. One of the witnesses talks of the
preacher as 'rigidised' by this need of a manuscript.

In 1909 Henson formalized his theory of preaching. He
went to America and gave the Lyman Beecher lectures at the
University of Yale, published under the historical title, *The
Liberty of Prophesying*.

Parts of the book contain the normal theory of the
preacher's office. This might be a Fénelon talking. Every man
who is made to stand on a pedestal is thrust into moral danger,
and even a low pulpit is a high pedestal. Be yourself: that is, do
not try to be the kind of preacher which your own past will
never allow you to be, but use your natural endowments and

develop them if you can. Never forget that you are in that pulpit to declare the Word which is not your own, and that the Word is not to be identified with any man's explanation of that Word. Read hard; men who speak must have something to say, and therefore must gain a store, and that store must be of general knowledge, not particular knowledge looked up a few hours beforehand for a single sermon.

Henson was the first to unfold the special difficulty of a preacher's sincerity. *You are in that pulpit to declare a word which is not your own.* Must you be able to make it all your own? Are you like a king's messenger who bears no responsibility for the content of the message?

In a congregation of 1908 – even a London congregation of 1908 – a lot of people still believed every word of the New Testament to be historic. They expected their priest to think alike. They heard him using prayers which agreed with their faith. Yet any preacher likely to be heard in St. Margaret's studied divinity and knew that this was not true. The preacher was no longer certain whether all the words spoken by Christ were spoken by Christ, or whether Lazarus walked out of his tomb, or whether the water was turned into wine. If he thought the story of Lazarus legend, could he say so from a pulpit? If he said so, he offended the minds and perhaps the souls of people in the congregation who associated high endeavour of their conscience with the evidence of the New Testament; that is, he could hurt some people's religion in weightier matters than the historical point at issue. If he kept silence, and allowed his people to assume that he shared their axiom on Lazarus, was he conniving at insincerity if not a lie?

All Henson's instincts told him to answer that the truth must be spoken whatever the consequences. But his head told him that this was not the highest morality. Men easily deceive themselves that they know the truth. In a pulpit he must beware of turning his private opinion into dogma, especially when it disagrees with the opinion of all well-read men or with that of all the Christian centuries. Modesty may not be the cardinal virtue of a preacher, who is required to be bold. But it is a virtue of a preacher's mind. To correct an utterly unimportant item of historical error can do no good; in the context of the early 1900s it can weaken moral imperative.

These admissions Henson set out with pain. He saw the danger of what he allowed; the *degradation* of an insincere mouth booming out of a pulpit; the complaisance of a speaker, looking to say what pleased an audience instead of the truth; the man for whom *the frown of society is as the curse of God.*

Early in his career Henson felt horror at Robert Browning's poem *Bishop Blougram's Apology.* More than once in *The Liberty of Prophesying* (and many times throughout his years) he came back to Bishop Blougram; where a Roman Catholic bishop of the early 1850s does not believe all the doctrines of his faith and argues, cynically but ably, that nevertheless he is right to continue being a bishop, combining public belief with internal disbelief. The arguments of Blougram, though not heroic, were cogent; the needs of the Church, the importance of not weakening simple faith, the impossibility of eradicating hypocrisy from any part of life or society, the need to face reality. The arguments of Blougram were all rational; and Browning thought them contemptible, and Henson thought them blasphemous. When in doubt, to speak out was always right.

This was the worst for his mental argument; the thought that, in an age of swiftly moving ideas, a teacher could be valued by the taught because he seemed to believe what he disbelieved and could not considerately say that he disbelieved.

All his life, after coming to Westminster Abbey, he wrote out his sermons and preached from the written text. The witnesses are agreed that this diminished his quality; that the man was a magnetic, captivating speaker when he suddenly spoke without preparation, on a subject where he felt moved. Even the English style was more compelling when it poured from his lips impromptu. Nothing and no one could persuade him to abandon the rule of written sermons.

The reason was, he knew that if he spoke impromptu he became too exciting. He responded to the feeling of the audience. They stirred him to potent language. *The congregation acts on the preacher almost as powerfully as the preacher acts on the congregation.* He could feel himself magnetized by the expectations of the hearers to talk more forcibly than he meant. Therefore he must draft the sermon beforehand. Then the words were written in the quiet of the study, away from the invisible spell of men and women in pews.

The Biblical critics gave a marvellous aid to understanding Christ. They purged the Church of appeals to the lower morality of the Old Testament; they made Jesus live, as a historical person with a lifelikeness known to no previous generation of Christians; they made Him even more the centre of the Bible; they brought a freedom in divinity which was weighty in teaching moral duty in the modern world. Henson saw the gains, and showed the Churches how to be grateful.

Is a man a Christian if he cannot believe that Jesus was born of a virgin? The question began to be debated during the last two Victorian decades. The mode of birth and the Incarnation of the Son of God appeared to most men inseparable. They found it probable that so unique a person entered the world uniquely. Their affection for Mary was touched. They saw the birth as a sacrament of the new beginning for humanity. They were accustomed each week to say the Apostles' Creed and from childhood affirmed their faith in the Virgin Mother. Upon that theme hung a lovely ideal of purity; and round it artists and composers and poets created a treasure of song and painting and carols, one of the fairest heritages of Christian worship.

But men are part of an age. The science and history of the nineteenth century made stories of nature-miracles harder to believe and demanded, if not a law of God, at least a law. And then the critics said that the evidence of the New Testament was doubtful, and that no historical evidence of such a matter could be other than uncertain. And, like so much from the Biblical critics, this was a relief to some minds, who saw that the Incarnation was God-in-man, and believed that man was no man unless subject to the universal conditions by which men live.

What a layman believed was his responsibility. But could the Church ordain a man as a priest who disbelieved the Virgin Birth of Christ? By 1902 most members of the Church still thought this impossible. But already, with willingness or reluctance, several bishops ordained men of this faith or non-faith to the priesthood, provided that they were reverent, provided that they intended to teach what God revealed, and

provided that it was their private doubt, and they had no wish
to disturb their people.

When Henson was ordained, he had no difficulty on this
point. But during the years of 'leisure' at Ilford, his reading of
the radical critics sowed doubts in his mind. Never for an
instant, all his life, could he question that the Christ is the Son
of God and the true revelation of God and in Him God became
man. Never for an instant, all his life, did he think that someone who rejected this faith could rightfully remain a Christian
minister. But now he doubted the historical circumstances –
the nature of the birth, or what exactly happened after the
death. Yet, though he was not sure about the history, he was
sure that he was a disciple, and had no need to resign from his
ministry, and could still repeat publicly the historic words of
the ancient creeds hallowed by the centuries – 'born of the
Virgin Mary . . . the third day he rose from the dead', and
might honestly understand them as poetic words to express a
mystery beyond human knowledge.

Therefore he must show his people, and the Church at large,
that Christian faith need not depend on these historical
circumstances; and he must defend any priest who proposed
himself a Christian but could not affirm his faith in the
miracles of the New Testament. Bishops were very unhappy if
their priests denied such events publicly, and threatened prosecution, or took away a licence to preach. Every such priest
under threat from his bishop found Henson rushing to his aid.
And since Henson never feared consequences for himself, and
wrote in language that never minced, he was a stout defender
of such men. And because he was so stout a defender, he made
himself suspect for heresy, and unpopular with numerous
ordinary members of his Church, and popular with many of
the intelligent laity of his Church because they were
themselves agnostic about miracles.

A preacher at Westminster Abbey preached against Henson
in his presence. A canon in the York Convocation accused
him of 'treason'. The Bishop of London went down to Ely
Cathedral and made remarks too pointed at Henson. The
Church Association, a litigious body, brought a charge of
heresy and quoted sayings. The fashionable author of the day,
Marie Corelli, wrote a novel in which appears an atheist

Canon of Westminster Abbey. A rude minor canon, sitting immediately under the pulpit in the Abbey, read ostentatiously during the sermon, to show that he would not listen while Henson preached. Henson wrote humorously to an Ilford godchild authorizing him to deny that his godfather robbed the Bank of England or kept dynamite in his possession or poisoned his father or strangled the dean or contemplated wife-murder or coining or arson.

All this left Henson a marked man. Conventional minds regarded him as dangerous. They therefore flocked more numerously to his sermons, and when they found the sermons to be worth hearing they brought their friends. But when he saw a multitude beneath him at the Abbey he suspected most of it of not being Anglican. *The churchgoing public abstains from the heretic* (19 November 1905). This was not true.

Simultaneously he gained a different kind of repute. He rose to be the prophet of Protestant union.

What are we doing, we Christians, quarrelling, when London is a byword for immorality, and quarter of the British people are underfed and crowded into unclean dens, and drunkenness rampages, and a world cries aloud for conversion? Under the threat of Turkish invasion centuries ago, Christendom put aside its disputes and rallied. We are under a threat like that, the coming of secularism and materialism as a philosophy of life. Christianity is the one barrier. On it depends humanity, compassion, and at last civilization. It has to render this supreme service to mankind. How can it do so if it is riven, and if Churches forget their mission to society while they battle with each other?

Therefore denominations must accept each other as fully Christian. They must find a simple common basis of faith. Then they can freely invite each other's preachers to their pulpits, freely invite each other's communicants to their holy tables, freely recognize each other's ordinations, cease to talk about validity or efficacy, and agree on a syllabus of religious teaching in schools.

He never quite saw the predicament clearly. His solution hung upon all the high churchmen of England – a strong and numerous body – ceasing to teach what they regarded as essential to a Christian devotional life; and whether that out-

come was probable he did not consider. Nor was it probable
that the high churchmen on one side, and many orthodox
dissenters on the other, would be persuaded by an astringent
voice issuing from under a shadowy nimbus of heresy. What
he saw was England's plight; the children of the slums waiting
ignorant while the Churches quarrelled over the way they
should be educated; the Establishment, which was the
guarantee of religion and morality among the poor, threatened
because churchmen stood rigid against dissenters and dissenters fought to overthrow the Church, neither side seeming
to care what would afterwards happen to the people of
England.

Reading Henson at this time of his life, and in that moment
of English history, you often feel that in the long view he was
saying something that needed saying and had a future, and that
in the short view he weakened his influence by appearing an
impracticable theorist, knocking the world for its sins.

He gained in stature because he took on anyone, however
eminent; and yet needed to recant more often than was consistent with skilful controversy. In a single year of 1902–3 he
made three public withdrawals, one because he seemed to
blame the Bishop of London, most unsubtle among souls, for
sharp practice, and another because he accused Lloyd George,
whose speeches against the Established Church were savage,
of political dishonour. He fought hard and steadily. He banged
away at the Church of England to grab less in its attitude to
nonconformists, and at the nonconformists to come and help
the Church instead of undermining what good it could do. He
fought by speeches, sermons, articles in journals, letters in
newspapers, and by five short books.[1] The books were not
widely read. They knocked about too swingeingly for the
academic reader, and had too many long words for the popular
reader. His lips were mightier than his pen. He never ceased to
fight. No attack could discourage him, no imputation gave
him pause. He made himself popular with hardly anyone. And
beneath his pulpit in Westminster Abbey, the crowds grew.

Many nonconformists warmed to him. When he went to

---

[1] *Godly Union and Concord*, 1902; *The National Church*, 1908; *Reunion and Intercom-
munion*, 1909; *The Relation of the Church of England to the other Reformed Churches*, 1911;
*The Road to Unity*, 1911.

the Wesleyan West London Mission (1902), they received him with an ovation of cheering. The two Presbyterian Churches in Scotland warmed to him. When he attended the General Assembly of the United Free Church in Edinburgh they gave him an ovation. The Scots long believed that English and Scottish churchmen were brothers of the heart, separated only by bigotry. They would never dream of accepting bishops, but wanted to be accepted as equally Catholic though they had no bishops, and could not see anything in charity or in divinity that spoke to the contrary. And here was an eminent ecclesiastic of the Church of England saying what they longed to hear. The name of Henson was famous in Scotland. The University of Glasgow made him an honorary doctor of divinity.

But not many Anglicans were so persuaded. They had a civil war in their folk memory. That taught them to value bishops not as administrators but as keepers of the faith and of the sacraments of the Church. Henson, the new Henson, said that this was a rigidity which divided Churches. This was not how it felt to most of the leading English churchmen of that day. The historic ministry, stretching back down the centuries, stood for continuity in truth, and for all those high aspirations of the conscience which focus upon the Christian sacraments.

No one knew that Henson had a father who for many years was a Protestant nonconformist and an acting mother who was a German Lutheran.

This generous attitude to dissent happened at that moment of British history to be important in politics. The nation debated its education. An Education Act of 1902, an Education Bill of 1906, divided the people of Britain. Should the State contribute the money of the taxpayers to schools which taught the religion of one of the denominations in the State? On this subject each side had a strong case, and each side used violent language. Nearly all the leading Anglican clergy stood on the side of the Conservative Party. Henson, though strenuous for an Established Church, wanted to treat dissenters as part of the Establishment, and therefore was far more friendly to compromise than other Anglican leaders. A sermon of Henson was quoted by a speaker in the House of Commons;

and when his name was mentioned, howls rose from the
Conservative benches. It is not known how many other
sermons of the twentieth century have been quoted in the
House of Commons but probably the event was rare if not
unique.

While he was canon, he entered a new sphere which slowly
affected his life and reputation: the Lower House of the Convocation of Canterbury.

This body was of negligible importance. It consisted of representatives of the clergy not bishops, and was overweighted by
archdeacons, deans, and canons. As it could decide nothing,
but could only argue, fewer than half the members bothered to
turn up. It discussed the form of words at cremation, or the
dilapidation of vicarages, or local ecclesiastical records. It had
this weight, it was the only representative body for the clergy
of most of England. An old rule ordered that if anyone says
that Convocation is not the true Church of England by repre-
sentation, let him be excommunicated and not restored until
he revoke his wicked error. This was still the law. But although
all the members of the Church of England, bar a handful,
thought Convocation to be unrepresentative of the Church,
nobody was excommunicated.

Nothing seemed less likely to be a natural outlet for Henson;
except that it met in Church House, just across Dean's Yard
from his canonry. He was frequently bored by the proceedings
and as frequently refused to stay.

But he was a debater. He had never lost the art that once
served him in the fights of Victoria Park. He could think on his
feet and never stumbled over grammar or hesitated for the
right word. He understood the facts – on tithe, and non-
conformity, and the history of the Church. These data he had
at his finger-tips. Someone would get up and make an inaccu-
rate statement. Henson had no need to check the inaccuracy in
the library. He had the information ready in his well-stored
mind. The clergy of the Lower House of Convocation were
not accustomed to this sort of readiness, or this clarity and wit
of expression. He sounded not at all like a usual sort of canon.

For Christian assemblies have this demerit, that they think it
their duty to be kind to the last speaker. They are quick to
forgive nonsense provided it be warm-hearted, or earnest, or

pious. Henson had no such feeling. If the last speaker talked folly, it might affect the course of events; and therefore that folly should be exposed and nailed. He took on his superiors as well as his equals. Henry Wace, the Dean of Canterbury, who led the evangelicals in Convocation, had a particularly rough time, but Wace was well able to stand up for himself.

  Henson began to be quietly influential, and in an unusual way. He was no one's ally, a member of no party. Suspect for heresy, certainly a friend of heretics, he seemed to want to deliver the Church of England into the hands of the nonconformists. As such he could not be a leader. But in that small group of debaters, he acquired stature. He had information which they needed. He always went straight to the point. His common sense could never be diverted from the main issue by emotion, or sentimentality, or red herrings. All assemblies are liable to the sin of woolliness, but Christian assemblies are specially liable, because they have faith that somehow all will come right by charity. If a bad speaker be a good man, we must forgive him his confusions. Woolliness of mind had no chance of getting past Henson. Therefore, though still a loner, he became a maker of policy. They wanted to know what he thought.

## PUTUMAYO

Putumayo was a high remote district in the upper Amazon. The Putumayo Company collected rubber. The general manager sat by the Amazon seven to ten days from the rubber districts. He visited only once in the three years 1907–10. His subordinates were uneducated whites who knew nothing about rubber and were paid by results – the more rubber sent, the more pay. Indians who would not work rubber, or worked slowly, were therefore a threat. Quickly the Putumayo won the repute of a haven for criminal whites. Supervising labour meant driving slaves. No one knew who was the government. Peru and Colombia both claimed the area, and while their claims were arbitrated both sides withdrew their police. It was a no man's land. By 1910 Peru had two civil servants in the area, both in the pay of the Putumayo Company. The quickest way from the area to the government

in Lima was not by crossing the Andes but by sailing all the
way down river to the Atlantic and through the Panama
Canal.

In the autumn and winter of 1907–8 local papers charged the
company with slave-raiding, flogging, burning, and shoot-
ing. An American civil engineer named Hardenburg happened
to pass through immediately afterwards, was robbed of his
possessions, and when he reached civilization, gave sworn
depositions to the Secretary of the London Anti-Slavery and
Aboriginal Protection Society, who caused them to be printed
in *Truth*.

The Putumayo Company produced evidence that
Hardenburg forged cheques and blackmailed. This evidence
persuaded few. But everyone needed to be careful about the
law of libel. In a speech at Caxton Hall the Dean of Hereford
said that gentlemen bearing titles and honourable positions
in our country had shares in a company which committed
abominable outrages. The company's solicitors took instant
action, and forced the Dean of Hereford to humiliating
apology.

The Foreign Office applied to the government of Peru,
which moved leisurely. The Foreign Office also asked the
English directors of the company, who pooh-poohed the
stories as fabrications. And it sent the consul-general at Rio de
Janeiro, Roger Casement, up the Amazon to investigate.
Casement had already made his name exposing colonial
exploitation and brutality in the Congo.

Casement spent eight weeks in the Putumayo during 1910.
His report was horrifying enough; Indians whipped,
mutilated, raped, tortured, murdered, or in several cases burnt
in a flag or cloths soaked in kerosene; with all manner of nasty
detail. The company started to sue Casement for blackmail
in the Peruvian courts. But whatever was discounted for style
or bias in the narrator, the indictment was stamped with
truth and confirmed by sufficiently independent witnesses. Sir
Edward Grey, the Foreign Secretary, said in his place in
Parliament that this Blue Book made 'the most horrible' reading that had ever come before him.[1] This villainy was not

---

[1] Parliamentary Papers 1912–13, lxviii. 819 ff.; 1913, xiv. 3 ff. i; Hansard, xli, 2352.

simply the concern of Peru, though mainly of Peru. Three directors of the company were British. None of them had ever visited the Putumayo. Were they responsible for what was done by Peruvian citizens whom they could not control? Yet on their name depended the reputation of the company in the international market. They guaranteed the good faith of a prospectus.

The law of Britain was not sure that they had done anything for which they could be brought to court. Everyone refrained from mentioning their names lest they lose large damages for libel. Henson boiled over at the idea that directors of a company could sit comfortably in London and take no responsibility for horrors which their employees perpetrated upon enslaved Indians.

On Sunday, 4 August 1912, Henson preached on Putumayo for three-quarters of an hour, with *the gloves off.*

He said that the Blue Book contained *the most terrible indictment of modern commercial procedure ever drafted*; that Casement had *added some pages to the world's literature.* And he was willing to generalize. This member of the Conservative Party showed his streak of anti-capitalism, the imperialist showed his hatred of corrupt colonialism. The iniquity in the Putumayo was unique only in its extreme character. Throughout the backward world peoples were maltreated and exploited by the European adventurers free of control from a responsible government. He demanded a change in commercial law to make it impossible for those who make money from the oppression of native races, to wash their hands of all responsibility for the crimes of their agents. *Is it not the irresistible demand of justice that these men be brought to public trial?*

There was talk that English Franciscans might be sent on the Roman Catholic mission. Henson begged the great congregation in Westminster Abbey to support this mission.

*This is no time, when the Indians are perishing, to debate the merits of Churches – I prefer to recall the glorious achievements of Roman Catholic missionaries in the past and in the present. I refuse to see in them any other character than that of fellow-Christians called to an urgent and heroic work. I rejoice to aid their effort, and pray God to bless it.*

All this last utterance must have surprised members of the

congregation accustomed to regard Henson as a critic of the Church of Rome. We who know that once he wanted to be a monk, and that he could not look upon the Benedictine habit without a sense of reverence, and that St. Francis of Assisi was one of his heroes, are not so surprised.

The tension of the sermon came when Henson read out from the pulpit the names of the three English directors. Others avoided their names for fear of being prosecuted, he pointed to them as individuals. From the pulpit he sensed the breathless feeling in the congregation, as though he excommunicated souls and delivered them to Satan.

Two days after this sermon, Lord Robert Cecil in Parliament asked the prime minister (Asquith) whether he would not consent to appoint a Select Committee to enquire into the responsibility of the directors, and determine whether any changes in the law were desirable. Asquith consented.

A week later began an acrimonious exchange of letters between Henson and the solicitors of the company. Realizing that they could not win a case against Henson for defamation, they sought to pillory him before the public in violent language – 'It is without precedent that a minister of religion of rank in his Church should use his church to utter, on such a sacred occasion as a sermon from the pulpit, the most outrageous slanders against honourable gentlemen . . . envenoming the matter by pronouncing their names from the pulpit and suggesting that they be brought to public trial.' They said that his conduct was unworthy of a clergyman of the Church of England – unworthy of a gentleman – unworthy of a man. Then they accused him of dishonesty in stating his case against their clients. They could hardly have used fiercer language. If they could not prosecute Henson for defamation, they realized that Henson would have no wish to prosecute them for defamation, and could therefore do their utmost to lower his reputation before the public.

They failed. The damning facts remained; first, that they were responsible for a company whose agents tortured and killed; and second, that they failed to prosecute their assailant. Innocence must have sued. Not to sue was a confession. *The Times* (24 August 1912) summed up the controversy in a leader, which acquitted Henson and damned the directors.

In his old age Henson used to look back down the years, and think of so many words said, so many useless words said, so many harmful words said unwittingly. But three utterances of his life never failed to bring pleasure and gratitude to the memory, three moments when he spoke for a nation's revulsion against wickedness. Of these three utterances the sermon on Putumayo was the first.

## PREFERMENT

Since he proclaimed his charitable invitation about nonconformists – that there should be free exchange of sacraments and pulpits – nonconformists kept inviting him to preach, and could hardly understand why he obeyed the laws of his Church and refused. In 1909 he accepted an invitation to preach at an institute attached to Carr's Lane chapel in Birmingham – knowing that he could not preach in the chapel but could say what he liked in a hall. The Anglican incumbent protested. The Bishop of Birmingham, now Henson's old friend Gore, *inhibited* him from preaching. Nevertheless he preached (31 March 1909), and so added a repute for lawlessness to his other notorieties, and became a hero to nonconformists and to liberal Anglicans who liked charity in churches. To his dying day he kept Gore's inhibition framed on his study wall.

Henson never ceased to be a Tory, in most of his political attitudes. He owed his hospital and his canonry to the leader of the Conservative Party. Yet his next four offers of preferment – a professorship, a deanery, and two bishoprics in succession – came from leaders of the Liberal party. At first sight that is strange. Liberal prime ministers may have found it odd to be promoting one with his attitudes on establishment, or trade unions, or even on Ireland. But on what mattered he was now their man. He wanted Anglican leaders to befriend dissenters who made a force within their political alliance. By preferring Henson they gained the credit of picking someone who happened to suit their political needs while simultaneously they gained the kudos to be won by nominating someone not of the right political party and thereby showing that religion is above politics.

Henson followed with interest or acerbity the exercise of the patronage of the crown by successive prime ministers. He had no high opinion of their endeavours. When Asquith became prime minister in 1908 Henson was alarmed; a friend of *the High Church faction*, an advocate of disestablishment; committed to a licensing bill and old-age pensions, *projects in which the sacerdotalist fanaticks will support him*; likely to encourage *the futile cry for autonomy*, and to treat the Church as *an episcopalian sect*; moving towards disestablishment with the aid of the high-church party.

The prime minister had to find a Professor of Church History at Oxford. He wrote to Archbishop Davidson (17 July 1908) 'Would it be possible to find a place there for the restless and able Hensley Henson of Westminster?' The archbishop was not encouraging. But who else might Asquith find? The prime minister thought the field of candidates thin. He was afraid that he might even be 'driven' to offer it to Arthur Headlam.

Henson was startled to receive a letter offering him a professorship. Among the many things that he might become he had never conceived the idea of being a professor. Asquith seemed to think that Oxford needed stirring. 'The waters at Oxford', he wrote to Henson, 'are somewhat stagnant, and it is time they should be moved.'

The selection was not very sensible.

Henson gave all his time to being a preacher, and was now a leading preacher of England. He had published an essay on early English constitutional history. The medievalist and constitutional historian left the Middle Ages and Anglo-Saxon world and became a general reader. But then St. Margaret's gave him a special interest in the seventeenth century, for the church was important during the civil war. Here he read widely, both in original printed sources and in the historians, and was well capable of judging whether a historian was critical. None of Henson's work was research. He expanded well what he learnt from others, and often from an unusual point of view. He came to love Richard Baxter, the Presbyterian leader of the seventeenth century, whose childhood and youth resembled his own, and was important in the public rediscovery of Baxter. He wrote an essay, *English Religion in the Seventeenth Century* (1903), first given as lectures in St. Margaret's. The originality lay not in the sources but in the selection of neglected subjects, and the independence of mind as he treated his themes. The book was ill received by the professionals. He made one rashness, by saying that 5,000 witches were executed under the Commonwealth; and when controversialists distrusted Henson for other reasons than his history, they were apt to resurrect some unslaughtered witches as a sign that he was unreliable.

The reader of Henson's sermons is occasionally half-convinced that this man ought to be a professor. But he was not a technician of history. And his cast of mind was that of barrister. He could not be detached like an academic. History was important to him not as the story of bygones but as a weapon in contemporary war.

Henson was curiously attracted to the professorship. His wife wanted him to go. The Archbishop of Canterbury thought that he ought to go, his foster-father the Warden of All Souls urged him to come. When he discovered that he would lose £300 a year in income and thought that he could not afford to accept, the Warden blasted this material objection into nothing.

Behind was a graver objection. He knew that a leading candidate, who wanted the chair, was his old friend who instructed him in history at Oxford and taught him the plight of the human race at Birkenhead, E. W. Watson. Every qualification that Henson had not, Watson had: erudition, research, a tiny but sufficient list of publications, inability to open his mouth without sounding dull. Moreover Watson, told that his name was put forward for the professorship, consulted Henson, who eagerly approved, and did what little he could to help his friend's candidature. Watson needed the post, Henson did not. Yet who could know whether Asquith would choose Watson if Henson refused?

On 16 August Henson went before breakfast into the chapel of All Souls and spread out Asquith's letter *before the Lord*. After breakfast he went to service in Christ Church and after service went to see the Dean; for to the professorship was attached a canonry at Christ Church. The Dean, Thomas Strong, told him how he would be welcome at Christ Church.

Overnight his mind cleared. He must refuse. Part of the motive was certainly Watson, part of the motive realism about his own gifts. But as he meditated on the interview of the Sunday it dawned on him that despite the kindness and welcome, the Dean had a touch of uneasiness. Whether this was Henson's imagination, or whether his antennae sensed something in Strong that his words did not express, he realized that Strong, who was a high churchman, could not welcome the coming into his college of the hammer of high churchmen. This became the final argument that weighted the balance.

That Monday, 17 August, he wrote his refusal to Asquith. Three days later he wrote again to Asquith recommending Watson. A fortnight after that the newspapers announced the appointment of Watson. And Watson's tenure of the chair was as predicted, being erudite and unexciting.

Ella was very disappointed, even *grieved*.

The Warden of All Souls was a reliable judge of men and of academics. He wanted Henson to accept, and told him that he need not worry about the fear of failure. He well knew Henson's mind and capacity. This is a weighty opinion. Henson wondered to the end of his life whether he did right to decline. But dryasdust professors of history cannot doubt that he was right.

Henson was again restless. When the Dean of Westminster, Armitage Robinson, with whom Henson never got on in chapter, resigned the deanery for the deanery of Wells in 1910, Henson wanted to succeed him and was disappointed. He was a man who needed the stimulus of change. Ten years as a preacher in St. Margaret's and the Abbey was a long stint for Henson. He felt stale, and looked at the heaps of old sermons with disgust (2 June 1912). To his wife's grief he kept refusing her demand that he spend money on improving the house in Dean's Yard, suspecting that the money would be wasted, because he would move as soon as it was spent. As Asquith's government was busy trying to disestablish the Church in Wales, Henson knew that it was his duty to say publicly what he thought even though he knew it would be unpopular with Asquith. He watched while the see of Oxford went to Gore, the see of Birmingham to an obscure clergyman whose merit seemed to be that he was half a Socialist, the deanery of St. Paul's to Inge. *But truly* (he consoled himself) *we know not what is best for ourselves, and our wisdom is to look well to our steps in the path wherein we are actually treading.*

Coming from so narrow a background, he could not but feel some of the drive forward towards place and power. But in justice to Henson, he had a coherent campaign with its three prongs – strengthen the establishment by including dissent, be as brotherly as possible to dissent, and restate the doctrines of the Church of England in such a way that they will not offend intelligent men – and saw that a higher place would provide a higher platform from which to promote this campaign. And although we see from his diary how he wanted preferment, his public acts did whatever could be done to destroy the favour of the mighty. When a policeman was shot dead chasing an armed gang of Irish bandits, Henson not merely sent a subscription to the fund for the murdered man's family, but accompanied the cheque with a published letter that *the State of Ireland reflects infinite discredit on those responsible for its government.* Any prime minister must be embarrassed if he were seen to offer promotion to a man who spoke so loudly of the *infinite discredit* of his government; and when Henson attended a reception at the Admiralty two days later it could hardly surprise that the Chief Secretary for Ireland (Birrell) cut him or that Asquith *was distinctly cold.*[1]

Asquith had a forgiving nature. He could not make such a gadfly into a bishop. But he recognized the stature and the ability, and began to think of deaneries. In 1910 he half-suggested to Archbishop Davidson that Henson might become Dean of Lincoln, when Davidson told him that they needed a preacher.[2] In February 1912 he invited Henson round to Downing Street and entrusted him with the task of preparing his daughter Elizabeth for confirmation. If Asquith was not willing to entrust this turbulent priest with the deanery of Westminster or the bishopric of Oxford, he was willing to

[1] *Spectator*, 13 Feb. 1909; Journal, 15 Feb. 1909
[2] Bell, *Davidson*, 852. Campbell-Bannerman as prime minister hesitated over Henson's name for the see of Truro in 1906. Earlier Henson refused to be considered for the see of Pretoria.

entrust him with what in his eyes must have been far more responsible.

Four month's after Elizabeth's confirmation, Asquith offered Henson, who was then in America, the deanery of Durham. Henson knew nothing of Durham but accepted unhesitatingly. He afterward said that by 1912 he was *bored* by London.

The prime minister evidently expected a little trouble, because he later (5 December 1912) told Henson that he was *surprised and pleased* by the way in which the choice was received. Not quite everyone was pleased. The *Manchester Guardian* praised Asquith for preferring so broad-minded a man, a correspondent in the *Guardian* wondered why no one said anything about heresy, and Henson's enemy the *Church Times* thought the appointment lamentable. A local northern paper introduced him with a damning nickname, the Reverend Coxley Cocksure, and provided him with a comic coat of arms. But on the whole the world approved.

Henson kept up the record established when he left Barking and when he left Ilford. At the evensong (29 December 1912) when he preached his last sermon of nearly forty minutes at St. Margaret's, many hundreds of would-be hearers could not gain admission.

# 5. THE DEAN OF DURHAM

THE DEANERY is one of the historic houses of Britain. Its most venerated room was the kitchen off the old Norman undercroft, built for the Benedictines in the fourteenth century and once the kitchen of the monastery. Nearly 37 feet across, it was excellent for roasting oxen, less satisfactory for boiling an egg. The dining room had a wall of the same date. The prior's chapel was the dean's study and an appended sitting room. King Edward III lodged in the house on one of his expeditions towards Scotland. King James VI and I slept in it as he came south to receive the crown of England. The hallway into the dining room had panelling of the fifteenth century. The drawing room was the prior's solarium. And everywhere were bosses, and coats of arms, and joists of old roofs, and traces of ancient windows now blocked up, or corbels of former arches. Everything about the house was lovely, except comfort.

Henson's predecessor, Dr Kitchin, revered every inch of the house and had no wish for change. He expressed his duty thus: 'neglect is bad' but 'far more terrible is virtuous improvement'.[1] This was not Ella Henson's idea of her mission.

For five months the improvements proceeded and the Hensons could not sleep in the house. The wonderful improvement, and now a treasure which no future dean may alter, was the hand-painted blue-green wallpaper of the prior's solar or drawing room; a true enchantment with tall shoots of bamboo, delicate pink blossom, on a hummocky sandy grassland, with partridge hovering in the trees, butterflies and dragonflies, and with crested birds of paradise, blue with drooping tails, brown and green peacocks, little blue kingfishers, and hanging in the trees, two decoy caged birds. No doubt Ella intended it as a chinoiserie to go with the Chippendale chairs and Chinese cabinet. It is not unlike the Chinese bedroom wallpaper at Blickling Hall. It startles the eye and then ravishes; and after the long reign of Kitchin who hated

[1] *The Story of the Deanery, Durham, 1070–1912* (1912), 97.

refinements, it must have startled the first Durham visitors who came to sip decorous cups of tea with the new Dean and his wife.

Henson was Dean of Durham for a month over five years, and yet the time seems an interlude in his career. He was a good dean, and in circumstances of unprecedented difficulty for the cathedral.

He was now a person of consequence. The new consequence is best illustrated by statistics (see Table).

*Staff in the deanery on 1 April 1913 (excluding gardeners)*

| Name | Office | Monthly Wages | | |
|------|--------|------|------|------|
| | | £ | *s.* | *d.* |
| Mrs. Berry | Cook | 3 | 6 | 8 |
| Caroline | Head Parlour Maid | 2 | 3 | 4 |
| Sarah | Head Housemaid | 2 | 0 | 0 |
| Olive | Parlour Maid | 1 | 16 | 8 |
| Lily | House Maid | 1 | 13 | 4 |
| Hilda | Kitchen Maid | 1 | 10 | 0 |
| Ada | Kitchen Maid | 1 | 6 | 8 |
| Mrs Braithwayte | Laundry Woman | 2 | 3 | 4 |

Total bill for domestic service £16. 0s. 0d. monthly

Servants were happy in the Henson household. This was due to the calmness and gentleness of Ella. But it was also due to the unpretentiousness of Henson. He consciously used his dog as a way to the hearts of the staff. Logic the Aberdeen terrier accompanied the dean whenever possible, became a public figure in Durham. During 1916 Logic became Logick because for unknown reasons Henson then turned Catholic into Catholick and Bishopric into Bishoprick. After more than six years of companionship Logick disappeared mysteriously and was never found.

The community, though divided into we and they, was happy. During the twenty-six years during which Henson had a numerous domestic staff, they had only one crisis, when a footman got one of the maids with child. One of the girls stayed for years until she moved with them to be a solitary solace in their retirement. For Ella the younger maids took a little of the place of the daughters who did not exist.

Henson loved the house, its history, its quiet, the garden

with its rooks, the southern aspect from his study window, the rural peace instead of the roar of London; and the tranquillity was only marred by the doubts inside the man, whether rural peace was where he ought to be, and whether he could satisfy his restive conscience that one who was called to be a slum priest could justify living in such a house.

*Self-judgement is difficult and misleading, but so far as I can judge myself, I was a better Christian as Vicar of Barking than as Dean of Durham. Partly, perhaps, the reason lies in the fact that the one position was more congruous with Christianity than the other* . . . (30 May 1915)

With this staff it was his duty to entertain – the chapter, the clergy, the county, distinguished visitors to cathedral or university, Ella's too numerous Scottish friends and relations. On 27 January 1915 Henson gave lunch to thirty people – canons, minor canons, honorary canons, and others. And the occasion, which was a commemoration of benefactors, has only this importance, that we know from it the size of the table in his dining room, for he noted that thirty was as many as his table could *comfortably accommodate*.

What was he doing in Durham? Of the two careers between which he had to choose, the slum apostolate, and the academic student, the first could hardly be the reason for Durham. Perhaps he could revive, he wondered, the old tradition of learned deans, and use his leisure to gain that scholarship for which (he imagined) he longed. Perhaps at last he could write a learned history. Perhaps he would write a History of Episcopacy, to show the rigid theory of apostolic succession to be baseless. From Durham University he received his second doctorate of divinity.

These plans were illusion.

The dean of a great college like the Durham Chapter, with one of the glorious buildings of Christendom under his care, with a historic link to the university and the school and the teachers' training college and other communities round about, was an administrator. In addition, Henson was incapable of refusing any invitation to preach or speak. The Dean of Durham was in constant demand – not only in the pulpits of churches of the diocese, or on platforms against Welsh disestablishment, or at meetings of literary societies, but in

London, or Windsor, or Cardiff, or Manchester, or York, or
Oxford, or Edinburgh, so that he travelled frequently and
long. Always he prepared these utterances carefully, worked
hard at his books, and acquired much information which he
needed. He knew a lot about everything, but if to be learned is
also to know everything about a little, he had no chance. In
these conditions his published books could only follow the
pattern of his time at Westminster and be collections of public
addresses.

This time of his life was mellow. He was widely respected
and doing work for which he was perfectly fitted. He did not
feel a rebel nor even a lone wolf. The old Henson always
looked back upon Barking as the happiest time of his life. The
reader of Henson's letters or journals wonders whether this
brief time as Dean of Durham before the deluge came, was
truly the serene time of so unserene a nature; with platforms in
plenty, leisure to prepare what must be said from those
platforms, responsibility but not an agonizing load of responsibility, and the satisfaction of bringing harmony to a not
harmonious chapter.

Not quite for the first time he came up against the women
campaigners. On Monday, 14 April 1913, the Chief Constable
of Durham called at the deanery. The Secretary to the Home
Secretary had just telephoned that they had received anonymous information of an impending attack by suffragettes on
Durham Cathedral. Dean and chief constable went immediately to inspect the cathedral and see that no suffragette
concealed herself in the building before it closed. They found
nothing. Henson searched it again at 11.00 p.m. on the
Tuesday night, a vast black echoing space with plenty of holes
to hide. On 3 May 1913 they were to have the service of the
installation of the new Chancellor of the University, the Duke
of Northumberland. They suspected that suffragettes might
seek to damage the building beforehand or riot during the
service. They took stiff precautions to see that no one got in
without a ticket, and all was well.

History finds it hard to know whether suffragette militancy
fostered or hindered the coming of votes for women. They
were economically independent and highly educated and had a
social need and sooner or later they would gain the vote as part

of a general extension of the adult franchise. But the Liberal Party, then in power, was nervous because women were believed to be more conservative than men. Asquith's government carried bills as far as a second reading and no further. Not only Liberals but members of all parties were specially nervous of granting female suffrage in Ireland, then heading for civil conflict, because they believed that power in women would strengthen the political power of the Roman Catholic Church and so weaken the link with England.

Henson was not specially interested in the constitutional arguments. He thought of women as non-political beings. If he heard women talking politics he always disliked the experience. This he never argued but accepted tenaciously. He believed in the equality of women – that is, one of the grand moral claims of Christianity was its elevation of the female sex to its true equality in society. But equality did not mean identity of function. His idea of a woman's place was formed by his stepmother Carissima and his self-sacrificing domesticated sister Marion; and then by his wife whose mind was not interested in everyday arguments of politics. Women are equal to men, that was Christian doctrine. But whether women should have votes was just like the question whether members of universities should have two votes, or at what age men should get votes – it must be answered on purest expediency, in an effort to get the best government for the country. For himself he was sure that they should not have votes. He was sure that feminine votes would increase the emotionalism of politics. His evidence was derived from the connection between women's votes and the campaign for total prohibition of alcohol in the United States.

His intimate friend from All Souls, Dicey, with the weight of a famous constitutional lawyer, argued the same point more articulately (*Letters to a Friend on Votes for Women*, 1909, 2nd edition 1912). The problem of democracy as a constitution is the difficulty of getting sensible capable people and not demagogues to the top. The curse of democracy is sudden waves of emotion forcing government into a spasm instead of a reasonable decision. Since women are 'proved' to be more emotional than men, their possession of the vote increases the probability that decisions will be taken on waves of feeling.

Moreover, government rests on force. It is no good for Parliament to pass a law unless it can in the last resort compel the
disobedient to obey. But a minority of men cannot force a
majority of men; and therefore women with votes create the
possibility that a majority in the country, consisting of a
minority of men and a majority of women, will pass a law and
then be unable to compel the majority of men to obey that law.
'Votes for women' is a way to imperil the sovereignty of
Crown and Parliament.

This attitude grew sharper with the crimes of the militants.
Henson called them *frenzied females*.

It pained him that not all clergymen agreed. His friend and
former parishioner, Lady Frances Balfour, was strong for the
feminine cause. The Anglicans founded a Church League for
Women's Suffrage, Roman Catholics founded a St. Joan's
Alliance. Both these bodies represented the suffragettes as
Christian crusaders. That parsons should be drawn towards
cranks who chained themselves to railings or smashed
windows systematically in London streets or set fire to mail
boxes filled him with astonishment if not horror. He took little
notice of them until that spring and summer of 1913, partly
because of the supposed threat to Durham Cathedral, and
partly because the nation woke up with repugnance when on 4
June 1913 Emily Davison, who two or three times tried to kill
herself in very public spots, achieved the most dramatic of
ends by tackling the legs of the King's horse, Anmer, as it
raced in the Derby.

That summer suffragettes began to interrupt church services.
Freelances disturbed congregations in St. Paul's Cathedral and
Westminster Abbey, and tore up an altar cloth in the church at
Llanberis. Someone tried to burn down St. Bartholomew's at
Southsea. Whether or not they thereby lost votes, their managers believed the scuffles useful, for that autumn Ethel-
Smyth informed the Archbishop of Canterbury officially that
henceforth disturbance in churches was policy. In the midst of
the litany at St. Paul's Cathedral twenty women stood up amid
the kneeling congregation and sang their own lesser litany,
beginning 'Save Emmeline Pankhurst', refused to leave
when asked, and were ejected. St. Pauls' suffered again two
months later, when the women organized simultaneous dis-

turbances at St. Paul's, Birmingham, and Norwich Cathedrals, and another at St. Luke's church, Kensington. The mode of disturbance was to chant prayers for suffragettes in prison and then refuse to leave. At St. Paul's they clung to chairs, gave a verger a black eye, and one kept screaming as she was carried away. Dr Oesterley nevertheless continued to preach his sermon on the patience of Job.

In the mood of that moment the Church Congress of 1913, held at Southampton, made the subject its leading theme. Henson was invited. It was not his favourite platform. *I hold strongly that there is too much organized talking in the Church of England.*

What was new about the Church Congress at Southampton in 1913 was the prominence of women among the speakers. A woman first dared to speak from the floor of the Church Congress in 1881 and in the following year a woman was invited for the first time to speak from the platform. They were not yet common as speakers. Though the majority of persons in the pews, they were not yet invited to be members of diocesan conferences or ruridecanal conferences. The feminine chairman of a London diocesan committee on women's work was not able to appear in person to present her report to the diocesan conference.

While, outside, the suffragettes' organizations held meetings once a day, and a procession of bishops and clergy was faced with high placards, and members going in and out of meetings were handed leaflets or newspapers, the Church Congress of 1913 took a series of themes where feminine speakers must contribute – the Kingdom of God and the sexes, the ideals of manhood and womanhood, marriage. Twenty-one speeches in all were made by women, several from the platform, more from the house. For the first time complaints appeared in the daily press that man's point of view was not adequately represented. For the first time a woman stood on the platform at the 'Men's Meeting', annually designed to draw the working-men of the city. The speaker was Maude Royden. Whether because she was a controversial lady, or because she was a lady, the lovable Bishop Talbot of Winchester was roundly abused for putting her on the platform. By common consent Maude Royden's utterance was the speech of that week of speeches. She talked of prostitution, and sexual frankness, and the double standard of sexual virtue for men and women, and whether harlots were necessary to the comfort of society, and the futility of negative attitudes towards sex, and the horror of using people as animals instead of people; all this extraordinary at that date from the mouth of a woman in public, painful in the ear at times, but said with delicacy as well as courage and stirring the audience to their hearts. The unforgettable impression was heightened by the mere effect of a solitary woman talking to more than 2,000 men.

Henson failed to hear this speech. On the invitation of Gertrude Bell he had agreed to take the chair at a simultaneous meeting in Southampton of the Anti-Female-Suffrage Society. The meeting was rowdy. *The Suffragettes attended in force.* Henson does not seem to have minded taking the chair for a member of Parliament, Arnold Ward, who uttered sentiments which every right-minded suffragette must heckle. Arnold Ward begged parents not to allow their daughters to become militants because after their appearance in a police-court they would go back to their homes *very much damaged articles in the matrimonial market* (Voice: *What about the blemished men in the matrimonial market?*). Further pontification was punctuated with loud interruptions and the chairman's lot was not happy.

On the Sunday, at St. Luke's, Southampton, he preached to a large congregation on a very Hensonian text, *They marvelled that He was speaking with a woman* (St. John 4:27). He said that Christianity was the cause and safeguard of women's dignity and women's equality and that Christianity had nothing to say for or against the political franchise. He denounced clergymen who were not ashamed at this moment to embarrass the government by applauding the militant suffragettes.

For the rest of his life Henson refused to alter his opinion. Nearly thirty years after the vote was conceded to women, Henson still thought it a mistake in the development of the British constitution.

## WAR

Europe had known a long peace. The Boer War, however exhausting against expectation, and taking a toll which first made war memorials frequent in English churches, was still a colonial war fought with a professional army. Men imagined that civilization and culture progressed so far that war was only a blot upon backward peoples. And now the Christian peoples of Europe found themselves locked in a struggle of which no one could see the end.

Most churchmen had no doubt that to fight was right. The Germans tore up a treaty in breach of moral obligation, and invaded peaceable countries, the closest allies of Britain, by an act of naked aggression. Unless a man took the pacifist view that Christ's words made it impossible for a Christian to fight, all agreed that to fight was moral because it stood for justice, and that Christian men in resisting German invasion were but policemen resisting robbers and murderers on behalf of a just society. It was a loathsome and painful but necessary and conscientious act.

This was the common view, and though Henson disliked taking the common view he shared it instantly. He was wholly behind the government going to war, for the sake of Belgium and the rights of the treaty, and thought that nothing could be more Machiavellian than German policy. He was only anxious because at that moment his sister and stepmother happened to be in Göttingen and he wondered how they could get home.

The patriotic Dean of Durham enlisted among the recruiting sergeants, and went round platforms in the county and in village squares –

*It is perhaps unusual for a clergyman thus directly to associate himself with these warlike preparations, but surely it is not really unfitting . . . If enlistment is the duty of young Englishmen at this serious juncture, who could more fitly bid them enlist than the man, whose official character is precisely that of the advocate and exponent of human duty? Accordingly, I propose to exert myself as a recruiting sergeant!!*

His sermons did what they could to convince his hearers of

the righteousness of the cause, and to maintain their conviction. One of his best little volumes of published sermons was *War-Time Sermons* (1915). It was dedicated to the Durham Regiment, and contained many utterances given before parades of troops, sometimes amid the storms of coughing which were his worst distraction when preaching. He found that people at first could hardly listen, and he could hardly preach, on any subject remote from the burden of the moment; bereavement, the shadow of want, the nature and efficacy of prayers for other people, prayers for the dead, the providence of God in history despite mass killing. He tried to eschew the violence of language which some of his hearers wanted. Posterity has doubted the link between Christianity and patriotism during 1914 and 1915. It has felt revulsion from the crude crusading speeches of Bishop Winnington-Ingram of London who turned himself into a martial priest. The reader of Henson's *War-Time Sermons* may regret phrases or passages but will never doubt that this was a Christian man trying to speak in a Christian way in the midst of very un-Christian circumstances.

The Churches at first felt the benefit of war. People came to pray. The spirit of community was aroused, men sublimated their individual selfishness in a common aim, self-sacrifice was evident, men soon talked of 'the spirit of the trenches'. A common opinion held that paradoxically an un-Christian war helped the Christian Churches. Men near death, women whose men are near death, are not far from a sense of eternity.

This opinion Henson could not share. He doubted the moral gain. He thought that a growing obsession with death promoted unhealthy cults. Extreme situations produce fanaticism and drive away reason. He soon thought that he could detect a rising of superstition.

The superstition which he denounced was the widespread belief in the Angels of Mons – that British troops retreating from Belgium under overwhelming German pressure saw the heavenly host at their hand. Henson's bishop, Moule of Durham, was inclined to believe. On 25 July 1915 Henson, happening to be preaching in Westminster Abbey – for the worst thing about Durham was the obscurity of its pulpit –

condemned the Angels of Mons and what to himself he called *episcopal prayer-wheels*. He did not seem to disturb the Archbishop of Canterbury who sat in the congregation.

Even so, on occasion he was troubled by the ethical contradiction, that war was fiendish and evoked moral quality:

*Letters from Gilbert and Reggie* [two of his 'boys'], *both expecting to be sent to the Front immediately and exalting in the prospect. Thirteen months ago they were decent Christian lads, feeling malicious to nobody: now they are obsessed with a desire to slay Germans! And the strange thing is that they are both greater, mentally and morally, than they were! Was ever moralist confronted by such paradoxes?* (2 September 1915)

A wave of feeling which he felt specially called to resist was the drive towards making everyone teetotal, if not towards making the consumption of alcoholic liquor illegal. He admitted the evils of drunkenness. He rejected the methods and axioms of the campaign.

In March 1915, during the Dardanelles campaign, Sir Edward Clarke addressed an appeal to the clergy, asking them to set an example. Bishop Handley Moule of Durham, who had been teetotal for forty years, sent this letter, with a note of blessing, to all his clergy, and so it came to the Dean of Durham.

A dean does not usually denounce his bishop. Henson's letter to *The Times* (printed 19 March 1915) was given prominence in its front page.

Less than three weeks later it was announced that the King had resolved not to drink alcohol for the duration of the war and on 8 April the archbishops and Cardinal Bourne appealed to the nation to follow the royal example. It later turned out that the royal doctors would not allow the King to keep his pledge. Henson could not know that till much later; but meanwhile the Dean of Durham won a large national reputation as the *brewers' friend*. This was one of the controversial reputations which he specially enjoyed. But he was alarmed to find brewers using his name in their advertisements and making into an advocate of unrestricted hours of drinking a dean who wanted licensing laws. Since the world by majority preferred to drink alcohol, the Dean of Durham, for one of the few times in his long life, was at one point of 1916 in danger of feeling popular.

At a girls' prizegiving he told the girls that much drunkenness came from indigestion, which was the result of bad cooking. He begged the girls to learn how to cook. This sally also found its way, via the local papers, into the national press.

By national emotion, young men of every sort and profession were swept up into the fighting services. Women argued with young men of military age who had not volunteered, and sent them white feathers to accuse them of cowardice. Posterity, especially the leaders of 1939, many leaders even by 1915, saw this as a mistaken policy, and that sensible planning demanded discrimination to maintain the home front. But how they could have fought the war without this wave of emotion is not easy to see. They believed that they could not impose conscription; partly because British tradition and opinion hated the idea, and partly because no one was sure whether it could be enforced in Ireland. They needed large armies; fancied that they could not or should not compel men to join; therefore they must engage in a vast moral pressure to volunteer. And hence the dean felt it right to stand on a platform as though he was a recruiting sergeant.

What was the duty of young clergy? As the wave of other young men rolled towards France, young clergymen could not wish to be behind and sometimes were liable to the unpleasant attentions of recruiting women or themselves open to a charge of cowardice or a white feather. A few resigned and enlisted as combatants. Others went as chaplains. Henson accepted the doctrine of long centuries, a doctrine publicly stated by the Archbishop of Canterbury, that the sacred calling of the clergy made it wrong for them to be combatants. But everything short of killing he thought that they should do, and certainly should not be exempt from national liability to duty. Dedicated all his ministerial life to the proposition that religion is for men, he was pained to hear rude talk that because the clergy were not combatants Christianity could hardly be a man's religion. Virility was a quality needed at the moment by the nation; and for the first time the virility of parsons became a snide abuse – the effeminacy of the young curate. Henson went to St. Michael's, Cornhill, and spoke humorously. He said that clergy were prohibited by the canons from bearing weapons, and from fox-hunting, and by an old custom they had precedence in society.

When government at last agreed to conscription (single men and widowers, January 1916, universal, May 1916) Henson made himself a propagandist for the rightness of conscription. He thought that Archbishop Davidson made an error in securing the exemption of the clergy from conscription, and after a very rare series of vacillations, in which he even tossed a coin, sent a letter to the *Spectator* on *the Clergy and Military Service*. His motive for sending it appeared to be that if he did not send it he would be doing something prudent to his own career and that if he sent it he would *prejudice my chances of a bishopric* (19 June 1917). So he sent it, and the letter appeared in the *Spectator* of 1 July 1917. Certainly the letter contained strong medicine. *Why should the clergy be legally certified as the only Englishmen who need not be ready to die for England in the hour of England's danger? What generous youth aflame with patriotic sentiment will be able to endure such an exclusion from the national life?* The letter caused him to be denounced in an anonymous letter as *a kind of clerical Winston Churchill* and even as himself *a shirker*. A vicar in Deal, who lost two sons in the fighting, appealed to Henson to lead a campaign against the exemption of clergy. But he would lead no campaign, for it was too late. He resented the axiom that 'priests' were separated from the main body of the citizens.

As war reached its peak of bitterness, the call sounded in the nation for reprisals, especially in air raids on civilians to retaliate for the Zeppelin raids on London. Archbishop Davidson was strong against such clamour and (February 1916) got a motion passed *nem. con.* in the Convocation of Canterbury that such reprisals would lower the standard of honourable conduct between the nations.

Henson – anti-pacifist, militant, crusading, unsentimental by nature – had a concealed reason for believing in a good Germany somehow misled, whether by Kaiser, or General Staff, or Prussians. Down in Kent he had a German stepmother whom he thought of as mother. He was grieved when he heard how the police had intruded to make sure that she was not a hostile alien. Throughout Henson's long life of resistance to German militarism, the existence of Carissima must never be forgotten. However harmless civilians might be killed by Zeppelins, or atrocity stories come out of Belgium, or passenger liners wantonly sunk by submarines, or Nazis behave vilely to Jews, Henson continued to believe in the German people. Whenever he could reasonably be sceptical, he tried to disbelieve the stories of German atrocities.

In October 1915 he was already under fire for saying at a sermon in London that the talk about reprisals was un-Christian. A gentleman of Birmingham wrote to order him, 'For God's sake get out of the Church: you are out of place there', and Henson turned him a mild cheek. This was only the first of a volume of savage letters. In the midst of these letters he had the courage to preach about *the greatness of the German people*.

> *We must not allow ourselves to think meanly of the German nation. Are you a student of philosophy? . . . Kant . . . Hegel . . . Are you a lover of music? . . . Handel, Beethoven, Mendelssohn, Mozart, Wagner and Bach. Are you a student of poetry and literature? . . . Schiller, Goethe and Heine. Are you a historian? . . . Ranke, Mommsen, von Sybel . . . Are you a student of science? or a lawyer? or a theologian? You will own your teachers in many illustrious Germans . . . The German nation . . . is one of the greatest and most richly endowed of all civilized nations . . . How is it that this great and eminent people has been carried by its rulers into this criminal War?*[1]

Such language was unwelcome, and to some was repulsive. But Henson continued to give Archbishop Davidson his strong support.

In May 1917 he joined other eminent men in a public campaign against reprisals and received another vile anonymous letter. He found himself arguing with an Italian friend about the justice of an air raid on Freiburg. If it was thought necessary for the successful conduct of the war, it could be defended. If its intention was to propitiate public opinion and slake men's thirst for revenge, it was indefensible. He found that the Italian lady was far readier than he to believe the stories

[1] *War-Time Sermons*, 117.

of German atrocities. Wherever he went he tried to pooh-pooh the excessively martial utterances of Bishop Winnington-Ingram of London. He argued with commanding officers. In cathedral services he avoided cursing passages in the psalms wherever he could.

In close connection with the campaign for reprisals ran a harsh attitude towards conscientious objectors, both by tribunals and by individuals. Henson thought this disgraceful and un-Christian and was willing to say so publicly. He had no disposition to minimize the ethical difficulty, for he saw how tribunals and the military resented the release of men who at a crisis in the history of the nation refused to do anything. On 13 September 1917 he sent a short letter to *The Times* (printed 15 September) because *it seemed base to hold one's tongue when these 'early Christians' are in gaol*, and even the Warden of Wadham College wrote his *amazement* that Henson should *champion* conscientious objectors.

Even he was not exempt from the quest for scapegoats. Who had corrupted this great people into such shocking aggression? His anti-popery made him hard on the Roman Catholics of Germany, and once to multiply ignorantly the number of Roman Catholics among the German people. Carissima came of southern Germany where no one specially loved Prussians. And Henson was inclined to put all the blame on Prussians, barbarians out of the East, never truly converted to Christianity. For one who was nearly a professional historian, his history of Prussia was comically dubious.

This attitude to Prussia was shared by others who wished to distinguish between Germans good and Germans atrocious. And some of them went on to blame Martin Luther. Since England entered the Reformed camp during the reign of Elizabeth, Luther was never admired uncritically. Now they saw how north-German Protestants were the makers of German imperialism, and how Luther was creator and hero of north-German Protestants. In wartime England the repute of Luther sank.

On this point Henson's history was better. He assailed the claim that German militarism had an ancestor in Luther. *The attempt to exploit the present disgust of Prussian Statecraft in the interest of the polemic against the Reformation had best be abandoned, alike in the interest of historic truth and of common sense.*[1] He realized that while the critics looked as though they used Luther to whip the Prussians, they really used Prussian violence to whip the Reformation.

During 1917 a decision led to consequences unforeseen, and cast his restless spirit into a new stratum of unhappiness, and brought to an abrupt end the decade and a half of confidence in himself, his programmes, his aims and his vocation.

Part of the reason for the decision was the tiny size of Durham congregations.

For the first time in his life, he had no congregation to listen to his sermons. The normal congregation at the cathedral was small. War made it smaller. It grew no larger because its famous preaching dean entered the pulpit. No little knot of reporters sat under the pulpit busy with their shorthand, no suppliant journalists waited to bear away the notes, newspapers had less paper to print sermons and more agonizing news for the newsprint which they were allotted. We know that melancholies were always liable to sweep over his soul, and now the sadness became associated with this backwater in which he found himself. Once he was a national figure, now he was but the Dean of Durham. *If my life had ended ten years ago, it would have seemed a greater thing than it looks now* (10 August 1917). Here was a man whose vocation was preaching, who had been accustomed to crowds, and now found himself orating before handfuls. Whenever he got the chance he accepted invitations to lecture or preach away. The memorable utterance was a centenary lecture on *Robertson of Brighton*, 1916. He was very discontented with this lecture, but it was brilliant. Robertson, himself in a backwater at the chapel of a watering place, was a Victorian liberal preacher who could speak to educated men and women without watering down his gospel. Henson felt rapport with his subject, and allowed his personal feelings to give point to the lecture. He understood the needs of preachers, was a historian well read in the Victorian age, a liberal concerned with the force of liberal

---

[1] *War-Time Sermons*, 272: Cf. also *The Reformation: A Sermon preached in the Crypt of Canterbury Cathedral on the Occasion of the Annual Thanksgiving for the Reformation, 10 October, 1915.*

divinity. Henson attained the peak of his literary style, clear, not over-written, cogent, in short sentences.

The leading Congregationalist church in London is the City Temple. The secretary invited Henson to preach on 25 March 1917. Bishop Winnington-Ingram begged him not to accept, but in vain.

We have seen that hitherto he always refused such invitations to preach in nonconformist churches. The exception was the Carr's Lane Institute at Birmingham, and this was an exception because it was not the chapel.

He never made clear why he changed his policy and accepted.

*We . . . went to the City Temple for the fell purpose of kicking down one old rotten convention which blocks the way of Christian fellowship.* He preached both morning and evening, to vast congregations, wearing his Anglican robes. He had the rare experience that once or twice applause broke out. *The Rubicon was crossed in matters ecclesiastical.*

It was like teetotalism again. A batch of insulting letters arrived daily. The *Church Times* called it a 'somewhat histrionic appearance' and an 'eccentric ecclesiastical escapade'. The *Guardian* had no quarrel with the words and said that he could well have launched this appeal for unity from the pulpit of Durham Cathedral, but that the act was a serious breach of Church order. Bishop Talbot of Winchester disapproved, Inge liked the sermons, the Easter Vestry of the parish of Chesham Bois sent a special resolution of thanks to the Dean of Durham, Hodder & Stoughton refused to publish the sermons.

The two sermons at the City Temple, morning and evening, finally persuaded a large number of leading members of the Church of England that the Dean of Durham was not only a *schismatic* but a *heretic*. That is a fate which Deans of Durham may bear with equanimity provided they are willing to continue being Deans of Durham. But the chance existed that a Liberal prime minister, or dissenting prime minister, might try to turn this powerful orator, who symbolized the plea to cast down all the barriers between church and chapel, into a bishop. And though a dean may endure the charge of schism and heresy, a bishop may not – that is, if he is to be a successful bishop in his diocese; partly because he is a representative figure in his diocese and needs to be seen as such; and partly because his duty is, and is seen to be, an endeavour to drive away schism and heresy from his people.

Fifty-two years later the Archbishop of Canterbury preached a sermon at the City Temple and no one found it odd.

But for Henson, outwardly trenchant and inwardly sensitive, the sermons at the City Temple prepared an unhappiness which threatened to become unbearable.

# 6.  THE HEREFORD SCANDAL

IN 1916 the ill success of the war forced a change of prime minister from Asquith to Lloyd George.

Lloyd George understood less about the Church of England than any prime minister before him or after him. Brought up in a dissenting environment in North Wales, losing his faith during his teens, making his name as a lawyer in vindicating the rights of non-conformity against the Church in Wales, he was the first person not an Anglican (for Rosebery and Balfour and Campbell-Bannerman behaved as Anglicans when in England) to be responsible for the patronage of the Crown. This was a new development in the relations between Church and State in England, and might be expected to lead to unusual nominations in the Church.

He had helped Asquith to pass the act of 1914 to disestablish the Church in Wales, though the act was not to take effect until the end of the war. Ever since Welsh disestablishment came into the political map, the diocese of Hereford concerned the Liberal leaders. It was the most rural and the most Anglican of all the dioceses of England; yet it pushed out towards Wales and had Welshmen along and within its borders. When the see was last vacant, and the prime minister happened to be Liberal, Lord Rosebery nominated to the see John Percival, one of the very few leading clergy in England to believe in the rightness of Welsh disestablishment; and this against the strong scruples of Queen Victoria who doubted, and was right to doubt, whether John Percival had the necessary gifts for so rural and conservative a diocese, and anyway disliked him as a 'disestablisher'.

This attitude was the foundation for the notion that the see of Hereford was suitable for Henson. No one stood more prominently before all England as a man who befriended dissent. Although he believed strenuously in establishment, he believed in an establishment which included the dissenters; and it might be presumed that during the next bishop's term of office the Act of Welsh Disestablishment would take effect. Against this singular virtue all other considerations paled – that the place was very conservative in churchmanship which

Henson was not, that his entire previous experience had been in cities, that his pastoral attitudes came out of those of the slum priest and Hereford possessed no slums, and that to send him to a place like Hereford would, as Asquith remarked of Henson in another context, be like sending a destroyer into a land-locked pool.

Nevertheless Hereford happened to be vacant. And the prime minister had another consideration in his desire for more harmony between Church and Dissent. He wanted to make Henson a bishop. That the see should be Hereford was accidental. To Lloyd George it was more important that Henson should be a bishop than that he should be Bishop of Hereford.

We have evidence of another motive for the strange choice. To the Lloyd George of childhood and youth, the Lloyd George of Portmadoc, the Lloyd George of Welsh culture and Welsh tradition, preaching was the supreme work of the Christian pastor. He formed the opinion, doubtless on the smallest possible evidence, that the bishops of the Church of England were not good at sermons. Here was a man agreed by his confidential advisers to be suitable for a bishopric and known to be one of the leading preachers in all England. We cannot know whether this motive was really weighty. It was what the prime minister afterwards told a group of churchmen who protested to him against the appointment of Henson.

Archbishop Davidson of Canterbury was a wise and experienced man who worked with many prime ministers. He was horrified – the word is not too strong – at the arrangements which Lloyd George made to supply himself with information. 'He has installed in Downing Street' he told Henson 'an army of inexperienced and arrogant neophytes, who perform their work inefficiently and offensively. These defects are at their worst in the particular case of ecclesiastical patronage.' Davidson saw the prime minister, as a manager of business, to be 'unprecedented, dilatory and scandalous'.

Lloyd George had a secretary, Sutherland, who treated the ecclesiastical side of his duties with ribald contempt which Davidson found repugnant. He remonstrated to the prime minister against Sutherland's jesting ridicule, and found that he could not get a hearing. And together with this distaste, came a certain cavalier inefficiency among the staff. Thanks to one of the secretaries, Captain Evans, Lloyd George offered one man the deanery of Norwich without first asking the King, and found himself in trouble. On top of the weakness of the secretariat, the prime minister was engaged in winning a war. Years later Winston Churchill also found that, while winning a war, he found it hard to be as diligent as he ought in the matter of ecclesiastical business.

Lloyd George had formed an alliance with Ernest Pearce, an Anglican clergyman who became a Canon of Westminster in 1911 and therefore a colleague of Henson. Pearce was a friendly man who had known Henson for some twelve years. He had a fund of common sense, was a good judge of men, and could hold his tongue. This caused men in office to turn to him for advice, and they might have done worse. Lloyd George inherited him as an ecclesiastical adviser, found him trustworthy and sympathetic, and in his own infinite ignorance trusted him to excess. War made martial clergymen more influential and Pearce took work as assistant chaplain–general, with the rank of a brigadier. He became so indispensable that he was even allowed to read the files of ecclesiastical patronage in 10 Downing Street. He found himself the principal ecclesiastical adviser to the principal adviser of the King. He had this special merit or demerit, that he thought the Archbishop of Canterbury far too cautious an adviser. 'Cantuar' he told Henson, 'wants a quiet time, but it isn't good for religion in England that he should have it.'

From July 1917 Henson began to take an interest in the use of Anglican patronage by the Welsh ex-Baptist, and to be conscious that his own name was discussed. In mid–August these rumours took a formidable turn. Pearce wrote to him to say that the impending vacancy at Hereford was under discussion. 'You are well to the fore: so don't complicate matters by any irruption marked by your usual cogency.'

Pearce was not the only person engaged. At the end of September Henson heard that some bishops pressed his name on Lloyd George as a possible Bishop of Hereford. Davidson's papers show that these bishops were Nickson of Bristol and Burge of Southwark. Burge once worked with Henson in the Laymen's League at Oxford and carried weight with

Davidson as a humane and sage adviser. Henson also heard that Lord Curzon, who was elected to his All Souls fellowship the year after himself, and was now eminent in the government, exerted himself to the same end.

To give the Archbishop of Canterbury his due, he was not against Henson being a bishop. He had often sat under his pulpit in Westminster Abbey and St. Margaret's and knew how deep was his religion, how the controversial character assumed before the world was a veneer compared with the inward faith and affection and compassion towards the human race. But the archbishop thought that this moment, when Henson was famous as a 'heretic' and 'schismatic', was not the diplomatic time. He warned Lloyd George more than once that if he nominated Henson he would have protests. Lloyd George pooh-poohed the objection. He had lately nominated the Modernist Rashdall to the deanery of Carlisle. The archbishop had warned him of protests. Lloyd George received nothing but praise. The archbishop had cried 'wolf' and his warning now went unheard.

Archbishop Davidson had another point. He thought that of all the sees in England, Hereford was the least suitable for Henson. The man was an expert in urban parishes and ought to go to an industrial diocese. His parish experience lay in London slums. Why should you send a voice, whose clarion cry could raise the dead, into a place where even the living were deaf to clarion cries?

The discussion went on and on. Henson made it more complicated. Bishop Burge of Southwark came to him, almost directly from Lloyd George, and told him that he would probably be offered the see of Bristol. Henson said that as a man with no money he could not afford to accept the see of Bristol, which was poorly endowed. *There would not be enough to pay the railway fares.*

On 5 November a letter arrived from Burge saying that he, Burge, had been offered the see of Hereford. He was disinclined to go, but he would go if Henson would accept the resulting vacancy at Southwark. But he doubted whether Henson would accept Southwark.

Henson said that he would not accept Southwark. He did not believe his physical strength sufficient.

Thus the sensible plan to get Henson into one or other of two urban dioceses failed, through Henson's choice. This should not be forgotten when Lloyd George is blamed for sending Henson to Hereford, an armoured car into an orchard of apple trees.

Earnest Pearce was on tenterhooks. He was engaged in delicate persuasion that Henson, despite the possible row and the obvious unsuitability of the see, ought to go to Hereford. But at any moment, Henson might get up on a rostrum, say something which captured the headlines, and undo all the good work. When Pearce saw Henson's name billed to appear on a public platform, he suffered extreme nervousness. For the second time he wrote a letter to Henson begging him not to be indiscreet. Despite their acquaintance of twelve years Pearce did not know his Henson. The letter was likely to drive him into *blazing indiscretions*.

On 2 December, which was Advent Sunday, Henson lunched at Canterbury with the Davidsons and afterwards went for a walk with the archbishop. Davidson said, 'I hope when you become a bishop, you will go to a much more important bishopric than Hereford. That is a poor little country place.' Henson inferred (correctly) that Davidson had advised Lloyd George not to recommend him for Hereford. He noted the asperity, rare in Davidson, with which the archbishop talked about Lloyd George.

But Davidson was overtaken by events. All that first week of December rumour was prolific. Out of Hereford came announcements that Henson was coming, reporters kept asking him whether it was true, an auctioneer offered to help him purchase the furniture of the late bishop. A congregation at Durham eyed a visiting preacher, who happened to be Arthur Headlam, as though he came with the possibility of being Henson's successor as dean. The prime minister, or the prime minister's office, or the prime minister's advisers, were monstrously indiscreet. *The Times* even announced the offer on its front page when it was supposed to know nothing about the matter.

At 11.15 p.m. on the night of Saturday, 8 December Henson returned to the deanery of Durham and found awaiting him the letter from Lloyd George. It was an odd letter. It

said that Hereford was not quite the most suitable diocese.
'I should prefer to see you grappling with the needs of some
large and industrial population.' But a more responsible diocese could be 'in due course' vacant; and if so, 'I trust you will
have proved your powers of governance and guidance in such
way that I may have the privilege of suggesting your
translation.'

In short, the prime minister was very frank. It was more
important to have Henson a bishop than to have him Bishop of
Hereford. And if he did well at Hereford, the prime minister
gave a half undertaking to promote him higher.

Certainly it was an odd letter; on the high old-fashioned
doctrine of the marriage between a bishop and his see, a
scandalous letter.

The bishop in the Church of England is both a diocesan
pastor and a national counsellor. Henson's reasons for becoming a bishop were more national than diocesan. He saw the
national Church going down the Gadarene slope, as he conceived it, into being a denomination among other denominations, and therefore wished to brake the slide, to hamper the
movements towards synods, church assemblies, and autonomy from Parliament. He wished to be a Modernist bishop,
thus far at least, to show that a man who was agnostic about
the great miracles of the creed might lawfully be not only a
priest but a high priest, and that such agnosticism had in it
nothing either insincere or disloyal. He distrusted the Anglo-
Catholic movement headed by bishops like Charles Gore and
Cosmo Gordon Lang, and wanted to counter its influence
which he thought disastrous. He observed the growth of
Christian Socialism, of which the protagonist at this moment
was young William Temple not yet a bishop, and wanted to
stem that tide. Thus his motive for being a bishop was to play
an influential part in the national policy of the Church of
England, and he had a feeling of being an Athanasius against
the world, of being a champion with few enough comrades
fighting at his elbow, and such as there were, weak and timid.

In Hereford, and along the Welsh border, and in vicarages
among the hills, people had souls. To be a bishop was to take a
responsibility that those souls be shepherded.

Of these religious matters the prime minister was not

aware. Otherwise he would hardly have hinted to this dean that he need only go into rural exile for perhaps a few months, but he ought to do well there so that he could then be promoted. The attitude had something in it that was scandalous. 'He will be learning his job' the prime minister wrote defensively to Davidson 'in what ought not to be a very hard school.'

Lloyd George's letter kept Henson awake most of the night. He knew that for national reasons he had to accept but wondered whether he could possibly make a good enough bishop. He sent his acceptance next day and the newspapers carried the news four days later, though (such the indiscretions of Downing Street) he had already received shoals of congratulatory letters through the post. He told Archbishop Davidson, *I shrink from the episcopate with a kind of terror.* That was not at all to say that he did not want to be a bishop.

Two days after that the trouble started.

The leaders of English Christianity, of all denominations and not only the Church of England, were not reconciled to the idea that a man could disbelieve the Apostles' Creed and remain a faithful and sincere Christian. Whatever private arrangements might be made, this could not apply to public profession. The more conservative bishops interviewed their candidates for ordination and if one said that he could not accept the Virgin Birth of Jesus, or his bodily resurrection, they would refuse to ordain him; for they thought a belief in these miracles essential to a belief in the Incarnation of the Son of God which was the heart of Christianity. By 1917 this conservative attitude, so far (at least) as concerned the birth, became the stance of a minority. Men allowed that, in these complicated days for the intellect, sincere men might have doubts and yet remain Christian men. But if after interview bishops consented to ordain such men, they did so with the understanding that the new clergyman would not parade his difficulties before his people, for he would disturb their general and diffuse faith and therefore, perhaps, their moral attitudes. Six years before the Bishop of Oxford refused to ordain William Temple because Temple could not affirm the two miracles of the Apostles' Creed. Archbishop Davidson interviewed Temple and then ordained him. Temple never thereafter paraded his scruples before the people and came before the end of his life to believe that Jesus was indeed born of a Virgin.

But Henson had paraded. He had proclaimed, in lecture, in sermon and in print, the right of other men to *deny* the two miracles of the creed and still hold office as priests in the Church of England; and his own claim, not to deny but to be agnostic about the same two miracles. And now he was to be consecrated to be a bishop, the guardian of truth. If Henson became a bishop despite this opinion which he made public, it became official teaching in the Church of England that no one need believe literally either of the two miracles enshrined in the creed. Therefore the Henson case was a test case. To the leaders of the Anglo–Catholic party like Charles Gore, now Bishop of Oxford, to the leaders of the evangelical party like Dean Wace of Canterbury, only three things could happen. Henson must recant. If he would not recant, he must not be made bishop. If he were made bishop without recanting, the Church of England was finished as an authentic part of the universal Christian Church.

Therefore, a campaign, with all the unpleasantness of a campaign; meetings of clergy, resolutions by ruridecanal chapters, resolution by the committee of the English Church Union, letters to the press, extracts from Henson's writings, sometimes taken out of context but sometimes fair, warnings by bishops, support for Henson from men so extreme as to lose him thousands of votes – and always a demand upon Henson, both publicly and by many private letters, that he should help by making a statement, a profession of faith, a reassurance to troubled minds. More extreme men hoped that when the chapter of Hereford met to elect its bishop (4 January 1918) they would refuse the prime minister's nominee, and were disappointed when the minority in chapter was derisory, fifteen out of nineteen prebendaries voting to elect Henson; not so derisory when men realized that ten other prebendaries stayed away from the meeting.

To Henson it felt lonely to be pilloried through England as a heretic. The All Souls men stood by him – Frank Pember now the new Warden, W. P. Ker, Prothero, old Dicey. Inge, the

Dean of St. Paul's, was a tower of strength except that support from Inge lost votes. James Adderley, with whom once Henson was nearly a monk, disagreed with him and stood loyally at his side. In French and Belgian trenches men were locked in a terrible winter war and the people of England hardly knew or minded. Even godly men cared much more that at that moment the holy city of Jerusalem surrendered to a Christian army, after so many centuries of Muslim rule. Many intelligent laymen wanted clergymen to possess the intellectual liberty for which Henson stood. And the canons of Hereford proved that, whatever their leaders said, many clergymen were content with a conceding of that liberty.

Therefore the agony fell on two people: Henson and Archbishop Davidson. Henson was in agony because he was a target, felt isolated, at times shunned by his former friends – Lord William Cecil, Bishop of Exeter, known to Henson and all his friends as Fish, who in Barking days helped Henson with money and good-will from his parish at Hatfield, now was cool and asked for reassurance; Father Puller, who in hearing Henson's confessions had given him some of the sacred memories of his life, now bustling about in the campaign against him; Bishop Winnington-Ingram of London, who married him to Ella, now asking for a profession of faith; Charles Gore, at whose side he had prayed in the chapel of Pusey House and who was as responsible as any man for his decision to be ordained, now the heaviest opponent whom he possessed. Henson enjoyed controversy. No one must think that he enjoyed *this* controversy. It was the agony of his career.

For the opposition he had no understanding. He regarded them as conspirators. The tension made him waspish. Archbishop Davidson saw him at breakfast on 19 December, was disappointed at his 'self-satisfaction', and thought his denunciation of the opponents 'rather venomous'. When he saw him again on 7 January he found in him the same curious mixture, tryingly cocksure but pleasant to deal with. 'He is also strangely sensitive to criticism, while he proclaims his complete indifference to it.'

The Archbishop of Canterbury was in pain for a different reason. From personal experience, and from listening to his teaching, he was satisfied that Henson was a reverent and Christian man. Just as he had ordained William Temple over the head of Temple's bishop, so now he thought it right to consecrate Henson to a bishopric. But he was the responsible head of the Church of England. In duty bound he must try to prevent irreparable damage to his Church by a schism. Charles Gore was a very powerful man. He represented not just extremist ritualists, but a large body of moderate high churchmen, many of whom made up the strength of the Church of England. He was clear-headed, learned, strong, godly and greatly revered – everything that an Anglican bishop at his best ought to be; and these qualities made him very influential. If Davidson consecrated Henson against Gore's formal protest (written 3 January 1918), and then Gore resigned his see and said that the Church had lost her faith, Davidson foresaw a disruption that could destroy the Church of England. Davidson was always inclined to be alarmist; or, put better, he was the most prudent archbishop ever to occupy the see of Canterbury, and his foresight told him that they approached a precipice.

What could he do to avert? He must persuade Henson into some kind of profession of faith, which Henson steadily refused to all other requests. For this purpose he had only three levers. One was his office, to which Henson would naturally give heed. The second was his trust in Henson, his belief in Henson's faith, and conviction that Henson should rightly be a bishop. The third was a threat. He could resign his own see rather than consecrate Henson. This would not legally stop Henson being consecrated if, as was probable, the State could find three bishops complaisant to consecrate. But it would make Henson's position in his future diocese impossible, and in effect force Henson to withdraw his acceptance of the prime minister's nomination.

As the tension mounted, Davidson began to talk of the possibility of resignation. Men in the know heard of it with alarm. On 7 January 1918 Davidson invited Henson to Lambeth and mentioned to him the chance that he might need to resign rather than consecrate him 'in the teeth of a really weighty protest from the bishops'. Henson said that if the archbishop resigned, he would himself need to resign from office in the Church of England. *How* (he said) *could I go back to my Deanery, discredited and disowned, to teach without authority and to be the mark of every insult?*

To believe that Davidson really would have resigned if Henson had refused to help him is very hard. It was a step of a gravity and decisiveness which by training and habit of mind Davidson was unfitted to take, for it would precipitate the crisis in Church and State which he dedicated his life to avoiding. But he was no insincere person, using a Machiavellian threat to force Henson to help. That also was out of character. He was a man who worried. He saw the shadows of tigers behind all the bushes in the jungle. Certainly he imagined that to resign was as practicable a possibility as it was a theoretical. Yet it is difficult to believe that Davidson, in the crunch, would have resigned. He would have contradicted his life.

Still, he had a hard time. Father Puller (18 January 1918) appeared at Lambeth armed with books and papers and in the company of Darwell Stone, the Principal of Pusey House, and told him, 'There is no doubt that bishops who consecrate a heretical bishop incur anathema.' He turned to a paper, and with a loud impassioned voice, on the authority of St. Paul and of the Fathers, declaimed to Davidson that it is the duty of the faithful laity to save the Church from faithless bishops. He talked of their need to break from the Church and found a true Church, and they would call upon all faithful clergy and laity to separate. Then he surprised Davidson by his profession of loyalty to him the archbishop, and regret if they had to part. Darwell Stone said nothing, but sat in silence, with a stern air of resolve.

Father Puller then surprised the archbishop even more. He said that he and Henson had once been on terms of great intimacy. Davidson could not imagine in what circumstances this intimacy could have occurred. But he took his chance, and told them of Henson's simple Christian teaching, and his belief that Henson was truly orthodox. And Father Puller most earnestly expressed his pleasure at hearing this said about Henson.

The Archbishop of Canterbury was in a very painful place. Only a handful of people could know what he thought of Henson. He appeared – or at least, he was afraid that he appeared – to be a careless man consecrating an unbeliever merely because the State ordered him to consecrate. The only person who could help him out of this agony was Henson. But how could he ask Henson to make any statement compromising his integrity?

Henson's consecration was fixed for the feast of the purification, 2 February 1918. At the confirmation in Bow church on 23 January – a legal waste of time, proved since 1847 to be mere ritual – two protests were handed to the presiding lawyer who ruled them out of order. By that date a long list of bishops, headed by Gore of Oxford, had declared that they would not take part; and they included Winnington-Ingram of London and Fish Cecil of Exeter and the evangelical leader Watts-Ditchfield of Chelmsford; eight certainly – but probably Lang of York would not come though he would not say why, Hoskyns of Southwell was known to be vehement against Henson, and his own bishop, the sweet-natured Handley Moule of Durham, said that he would come but would not feel able to present Henson to the archbishop.

On the day of the confirmation in Bow Church, Gore withdrew his protest. He had received from Archbishop Davidson a profession of faith by Henson.

Upon this profession of faith hangs the historical argument never yet settled. Did Henson withdraw, as Gore claimed, the doctrine that a sincere Anglican bishop could disbelieve the Virgin Birth and the bodily resurrection, and recant his assertion that he himself was agnostic on those two points of fact?

At a meeting on 15 January at Lambeth, Davidson, saying that he wanted to explain Henson's position to Gore, drafted a little statement of faith which Henson accepted, though he did not sign. He disliked the procedure, but Davidson made him a personal appeal for the relief of his (the archbishop's) conscience.

This personal appeal is mentioned in Bell's Life of Davidson. When Henson saw that book, which he helped Bell to write by lending him his journal for the Hereford episode, he felt that Bell unwittingly did him, Henson, an injustice by weakening the fervour of the archbishop's appeal. Henson was determined to retract nothing. He was faced by an archbishop telling him of his own agony. Davidson said that people told him how on trains and omnibuses they heard people talking about an atheist being made a bishop. He said how perturbed he was in his own mind, and how something should be done to correct so injurious a rumour. He begged Henson therefore to accept the statement which he had drafted. Confronted with this troubled supplication from the head of his Church, Henson accepted the statement of faith.

Two days later at another meeting at Lambeth, Davidson drafted a letter to Henson and a reply from Henson, which Henson signed with a small amendment, to the effect that he was *astonished* that any candid reader of his writings could entertain *so dishonourable a suggestion*, that he did not believe the creeds. On 18 January the newspapers carried Davidson's letter to Gore explaining Henson, plus the letters between Henson and Davidson, both drafted by Davidson. [1]

Both parties drafted their statement with extreme care. Davidson did not ask Henson to profess a belief in the two miracles, a profession which Henson must refuse. He asked Henson for two things: that Henson profess faith in the creed and that he declare himself to have no wish to alter the words of the creed on the Birth and Resurrection. To profess a belief in the creed is not to profess belief in a particular interpretation of all its clauses. To say that you have no desire to alter the historic wording of a clause is not to say that you believe that clause as your father believed. Davidson asked Henson for nothing which he could not sign. Yet simultaneously he must give the world a vague impression that Henson was more orthodox on the miracles than was alleged. In archiepiscopal prudence came a point where skilful drafting verged into

---

[1] Letters printed in Bell, *Randall Davidson*, 874, and most contemporary newspapers. The vital clauses of the letter from Davidson to Henson ran as follows: 'I am receiving communications from many earnest men of different schools who are disquieted by what they have been led to suppose to be your disbelief in the Apostles' Creed, and especially in the clauses relating to Our Lord's Birth and Resurrection. I reply to them that they are misinformed, and that I am persuaded that when you repeat the words of the Creed you do so *ex animo* and without any desire to change them . . .'

The vital clauses of the reply, of which the first part was drafted by Davidson for Henson, and the last sentence added by Henson at his own volition, were: . . . *What you say is absolutely true. I am indeed astonished that any candid reader of my published books, or anyone acquainted with my public Ministry of thirty years, could entertain a suggestion so dishonourable to me as a man and as a clergyman.*

sleight of hand. And Davidson could plead as his justification, that while he asked nothing of Henson which in a literal sense Henson could not concede, he saved the Church from calamity.

To make this repugnant act tolerable to himself, Henson also had to draft with care. He must not be seen to recant his past. His books stood. They might contain errors or extremisms to which he could not now adhere, but in substance he had nothing to retract. He must insist on his books as part of the past by which his mind must now be judged. Thus he reaffirmed his old opinions. And yet he reaffirmed them in the context of a request by the archbishop that he should show himself to be orthodox despite what the world said. Henson could do it because he believed himself to be orthodox and that orthodoxy did not include faith in a physical birth from a Virgin Mother.

When he read the newspaper Henson wondered whether his letter read *like a cowardly surrender*, and was inclined to think that all was well. Many people read it as a recantation. Gore found sufficient reason to withdraw his protest. Whatever Henson actually believed, the protest achieved that the Church need not be seen officially to teach that a sincere clergyman might deny the two gospel miracles.

Some people were pained that the result was indecisive. Henson's extremer opponents like Frank Weston, Bishop of Zanzibar, wanted the archbishop to have refused because then he would have 'cleared' the name of the Church of England from the suspicion of heresy. Modernists, like the novelist Mrs Humphry Ward, lamented the issue and thought that the only satisfactory answer would have been a trial for heresy, and then Henson's acquittal would have ensured legal freedom for everyone. But these opinions of regret were held only by the strongest on both wings. Most people sighed with relief.

This act saved the Archbishop of Canterbury, and quieted the worst of the hurricane. But its memory remained part of the ineradicable bitterness of these days. Some laymen thought it dishonourable, a man professing what he did not believe in order to become a bishop. Even the wording by which Gore withdrew his protest suggested that Gore had a doubt on the sincerity of the undertaking. By the needs of the

Church, and his respect for an agonized archbishop, Henson did something which made him suspect for that insincerity which all his life taught him to regard as the unforgivable sin. And this internal horror was brought upon him by people whom he saw as *unscrupulous*, the worst kind of ecclesiastical agitators.

This was not in the least true of the leaders. No one could be less unscrupulous than Gore. The best of the opposition to Henson was shown by the record of a revered bishop, Talbot of Winchester, who was the alternative choice for the see of Canterbury when Davidson was nominated and now was Davidson's close and influential adviser. On the day when the newspapers carried the letters between Davidson and Henson, Talbot wrote a brochure entitled *The Appointment to the See of Hereford*. There he wrote that he saw the choice of the Dean of Durham with grave concern and regret, for he knew how it would trouble the Church; partly because many disagreed with him on important matters of Church principles and policy, and on the social responsibilities of the Church; partly because he is known 'mainly as a controversial gladiator, wielding a very sharp and fluent pen, and often in scornful opposition (or what seemed so) to the convictions and feelings of the great body of Church people'; partly because he advocates Christian union on a plan more likely to divide than unite; partly because such an appointment, of a man unwelcome to the body of the Church, puts a strain on the relation of Church and State and so increases the probability of disestablishment and the possibility of disruption; and above all because of his willingness to stretch disbelief to cover the two great miracles of the New Testament.

Nevertheless, wrote Talbot, he (Talbot) refused to join the protest of Bishop Gore. Why? Because Henson is a wholehearted believer in and has borne very telling witness to, the truths of Incarnation, Trinity, and Resurrection; a more influential witness than all but a few in our time; because behind this lies a sense of pastoral responsibility little suspected by those who only know him in the newspapers. 'We have to do with an earnest Christian apologist and preacher. It would be bitter indeed to have to treat him as a deliberate and convicted heretic.'

Therefore, wrote Talbot, we should give him the benefit of the doubt. If he (Talbot) were Archbishop of Canterbury, he would well feel that he was not warranted in refusing to consecrate. He (Talbot) would satisfy his own feelings by not taking part in the consecration, but prolonged controversy was intensely harmful and he hoped that now it would cease. Meanwhile it was clear 'that the uncontrolled autocracy of the Prime Minister is, in such a matter, hardly tolerable' and he pressed for change in the system.

No one could think of Talbot as unscrupulous. Afterwards Henson's friendship with Talbot was not impaired. And yet — if it was right for the archbishop to consecrate, as Talbot confessed, and therefore Henson was to be a bishop in the Church of England — was it right to hurt the future work of that bishop by so publicly staying away from his consecration?

Henson was consecrated Bishop of Hereford in Westminster Abbey as the Bolsheviks gripped Russia, the day before they disestablished and took all the money of the Holy Orthodox Church. He found the liturgy neither devotional nor edifying. He prevented his stepmother coming. At this tense moment he was afraid that the press would discover her to be a German, and he did not wish her to see unseemly interruptions. Archdeacon Hough, who was being consecrated suffragan Bishop of Woolwich, made it too plain that he was sorry to share his consecration with a heretic. Dean Inge preached a beautiful uncontroversial sermon paying a tribute to Archdeacon Hough, calling Henson his dearest friend, and telling how the people of the north 'say that no one ever understood them better, or won their confidence more completely'. Henson loved the sermon and was grateful to Inge, but even in his affection felt a nagging prick because he knew that the archbishop had bowdlerized the sermon. The archbishop did not aid his devotions because he looked harassed and nervous.

Henson could not say his prayers at the most solemn moments because his ears expected to hear irreverent shouts of protest that never came. At near-by St. Matthew's Church a priest preached a sermon against all that was happening in that hour at Westminster Abbey. Henson was grateful to the seven diocesan bishops who came to join the archbishop, especially Burge of Southwark, and Ryle, the Dean of Westminster, who presented him; and yet with a rueful smile that one of his strongest supporters, Bishop Hicks of Lincoln, stood for nearly everything which otherwise he disapproved – *a feminist, a total abstainer, and three parts a pacifist.*

At the time Henson was not sorry about the plight of Archdeacon Hough, whose consecration to a bishopric was made hideous by a controversy in which he had no concern. Much later Henson was sorry about Hough. He need not have worried. Hough retreated into a modest house at New Cross, refused a larger stipend, preferred buses and trams and tubes and never owned a car, and was beloved all over South London, especially among costermongers who knew this bishop as Mr Uff.

The opponents demanded a new way of choosing bishops. One Henson was enough. Two would smash the Church. A bishop was representative. A prime minister, whose power in this matter was an accidental survival from the power of the godly prince of the Reformation, chose a man whom the Church would never choose. The old arguments, that good prime ministers, a Gladstone, a Salisbury, a Balfour, an Asquith, chose people best for the Church, were destroyed overnight by Lloyd George. Prime ministers cannot be trusted, it was said, to use their power responsibly. And even if they could be trusted, why should a non-Anglican choose the leaders of the Church of England?

This feeling was not widespread among most of the laity of the Church of England. They were happy to see Henson a bishop and the system by which prime ministers chose bishops was not a whit diminished in their eyes. But the feeling was widespread among the clergy who were heirs of the Oxford Movement, and among some others, and was shared by several bishops. It was aired, inevitably, in the Convocation of Canterbury. And there it became embarrassing (1 May 1918). Bishops were forced to argue that the system of selecting bishops was bad, in the presence of the person whose selection caused them to think it bad.

Bishop Gore of Oxford stood up and said that the situation was alarming and abnormal; that no one could deny that 'the position was intolerable; that at any moment the highest officers of the Church could be appointed by one who, for the time, was its enemy.' He admitted that the system worked excellently under previous prime ministers. But the training of the present prime minister, said Gore, 'had not been such as to give him an intimate knowledge of what was going on in the Church of England, and what its best interests were.'

Then he turned to the manifest anomalies. The confirmation of the bishop–elect was a farce. The election was by the wrong people, for the dean and chapter were obviously unsuitable. He recalled the two precedents of the seventeenth century, when the Crown agreed to be advised on the choice of bishops by a body of churchmen. He (Bishop Gore) wondered whether the system might be revived; and asked the archbishop to appoint a committee to consider this plan.

All this was said in the presence of the archbishop and twenty–two other bishops including Henson. A considerable majority of the twenty–two other bishops had failed to appear at Henson's consecration. It was embarrassing.

Henson was not a man to sit silent. The consequent passage of arms between himself and Gore caused blushes among the company. But then he turned to the proposal and stripped it bare. What was proposed was to abolish the way of choosing bishops which prevailed in the Church of England for many years and to find a new way which would express 'the mind of the Church'. He told that meeting the history of bishops' elections in Christendom, how they had been stained by scandal, riot, bloodshed, and murder; he said that since the Reformation the worst appointments of bishops had been the rare cases where bishops were chosen by the clergy. *The appointments by the boards* (of the seventeenth century) *were not conspicuously successful*, and Henson claimed them as evidence that *appointments were bad in proportion as they were made by Church people in what they conceived to be the Church's interests*. Why? Because such appointments were always partisan. When people talk of the need to express 'the mind of the Church', what is this mind? What they mean when they talk of the mind of the Church, is the mind of their party in the Church.

And there was something more than the Church. By history

the English bishop is more than a churchman. He is national. *They could not dwarf and shrivel him into being merely the leader of a sect. He was one of the great historic figures of the English people, and the attempt to warn off the national authorities from any real concern in the appointment of bishops was only a way of saying that the English Church had committed suicide and was content to be reckoned a mere sect.*

The Prime Minister, said Henson, advised the Crown not because he was nonconformist or secularist or churchman, but because he represented the English people. He acted under conditions which made abuse *almost impossible*. He had access to the best advice. This was the place where the national character of the Church of England found its expression.

Thus Henson articulated the long modern argument of the relation of Church and State. Next day he regretted this speech. He realized that everyone felt him to have provocation, and that everyone, including himself, wished that he had not answered Gore. And yet the debate of the two gladiators, Oxford and Hereford, rose far above the personal question.

For more than fifty years afterwards, Henson's name was still the symbol of the argument. Was it absurd that a prime minister, who need not be an Anglican, had almost the final part in selecting bishops of the Church of England? In the abstract it looked absurd. But did Englishmen mind about abstract theory? Were they more likely to ask, does it work? And when they came to ask, 'does it work?', they would often fasten upon the name of Henson. If the ecclesiastical organs of the Church of England chose bishops, Henson would never have become a bishop. Opinion always believed, and the archives amply confirm the belief, that no purely ecclesiastical mode of election could have elevated him to a see. He had few ecclesiastical backers. Yet by common consent he became one of the bishops to lend lustre to the Church of England during the twentieth century.

In the long constitutional argument over Church and State, and the place of crown patronage in the Church, the nomination of Henson was never forgotten. The Church resisted as they had resisted no choice of a bishop for more than seventy years. And afterwards the Church knew that it was glad at what happened. In the Reformation Henry VIII forced upon the Church an archbishop whom no one wanted and in future generations Cranmer became the most beloved of archbishops and even appeared in the calendar of saints. Something curiously like this happened in the twentieth century; though no one will ever propose Henson as a contender for the calendar of saints.

This was not the only public onslaught upon the new bishop in his presence. Was he a heretic? Ought we to reassert in his presence the need for Christian men to affirm that Jesus was born of a Virgin and that his body rose from the tomb?

Were men distressed and alarmed because the bishops failed to speak? Bishop Watts-Ditchfield of Chelmsford, who was not an intellectual, thought that the bishops must speak. He brought a petition (10 July 1918) to the Upper House of Convocation, and the petition was signed by some who were intellectuals. Henson reacted even more fiercely than when he assailed Gore. And this time the bishops were openly on Henson's side. They could not share his opinion but they disliked this repeated harassment.

Frank Weston, Bishop of Zanzibar, was the stoutest missionary in Africa; an angular, enchanting personality, with a belief that he might save the Church of England from itself. During 1919 he published a strange book, _The Christ and his Critics_: a lot of which was a direct attack on Henson for heresy. But the book persuaded no one. The argument with Henson seemed at last to rest upon the extent to which human 'personality' could rightly be ascribed to the Christ, and the controversy tailed away into subtleties which looked irrelevant to the twentieth century, and the book lumped all the bishops of England in a common damnation for sitting with Henson on the Bench. Wise men said that if this was Henson's heresy, then the hunt was a heresy-hunt in the worst sense.

Henson was worried by the book lest it bring more trouble upon him but relieved that it was so bad a book as not to need an answer. He called it privately _the Zanzibarbarian fulmination_.

Were men distressed and alarmed, as Bishop Watts-Ditchfield said? Some of them, undoubtedly. The argument, whether a good Christian man, and especially a good Christian teacher, might be agnostic about what happened in the

two great miracles of the New Testament, continued to raise
its head until the Second World War. And since, in the intellectual climate of that age, philosophical and scientific,
some people were bound to be agnostic about the miracles
though in all other respects they were godly Christian men,
the Church must accept the possibility of such reverent agnosticism if it were not to cut itself off from the mind of
European society. In this partial retaining of its hold upon the
intellect of Europe, the Church owed a larger debt to Henson
than it usually realized. Perhaps he compromised a little before
his consecration, for the sake of helping an archbishop to climb
out of a barrel full of gunpowder. But he vindicated
sufficiently the liberty of thought which he claimed. And he
could not have achieved this if he had been in truth a half-
Christian. Archbishop Davidson believed in the depths of his
authentic piety. To anyone who listened to him, even occasionally, this was impossible to doubt. He believed in the
Christ as the Saviour of men and never wavered. That blunted
the force of all the petitions, the excommunications by
Weston, the circumlocutions of Watts-Ditchfield. In difficult
years for the Christian intelligence, shall we exclude from
ministry in the Church a profoundly Christian man because he
had to say that he did not know what happened at the birth and
after the death?

These battles left a permanent mark on Henson.

He was a man of anniversaries. Hitherto the anniversaries
stirred him to religious meditation; his birthday, the day of his
ordination, the day when his mad sister died. The consecration
was a new anniversary. As each year he remembered the self-
dedication of his ordination, and recorded his penitence that
his priesthood was not all it should be, so he began to record
each year his consecration to be a bishop, and with a like
feeling of sadness and repentance.

But this new anniversary was not like the old. He remembered not only the commission, but the horror. What
should have been a treasured memory brought recurring resentment. In his worst moods – 1921, 1922, 1923 were the
worst, but horror came in other years, 1926, 1932, 1933 – the
memory made him shiver with rage, and provoked a revived
sense that the bishops treated him ill. In some years the mood

was godly and self-critical, but hardly ever other than sad. The mind's eye saw it all vividly; his heart could feel the tension as he waited for the raucous irreverence that never came; seeing again and again the look on the face of the archdeacon who was consecrated at his side; realizing that Lang of York, once his friend, once a fellow of the beloved college, refused to come; recollecting with pleasure Inge's generous language and rueing that the language was altered in draft. Only during his seventies could the memory mellow. In his last ten years of life the day fed no resentment. But to the end it carried a special air of sadness which was not quite the sadness of true devotion; godly sorrow in large part, but not godly without admixture. And in younger fiercer years it was hard to bear. In 1922 he told the other bishops that the day of his consecration to be a bishop was *the unhappiest day of my life.*

Apart from this annual melancholy, the event had weighty consequences.

The first, and probably the chief, was the destruction of his self-confidence. As a child he learnt the hostility of the world. Then the friendships of All Souls, and success as a slum priest in Barking, and fame as a preacher in Westminster, gave him assurance. The event of 2 February 1918 revived the old fear that the hand of man was against him; that people eyed him with suspicion; that his influence was weakened because men distrusted. As he once put it to himself on one of the fatal anniversaries (2 February 1932), *it is not good for any man to be, or to be thought, an Ishmael.*

This word *Ishmael* to describe himself was not his own invention, a reviewer seized upon the name. Probably in his earliest years as bishop this renewed feeling of being a lone wolf affected not only his intimacy with some of the other bishops but his mental gymnastic. In 1919, while he was Bishop of Hereford, he published a lecture given in London among a collection of lectures (*The Church of England: its Nature and Future*). The reviewer in the *Guardian* read the lecture and then described Henson's mind in words some of which might have been taken out of Henson's own mouth, or fitted his mood in the months after his consecration:

We need not take Dr. Henson seriously when he is in this particular mood. His history is unsound; his deductions are faulty; there is not a paragraph in the lecture which does not bear the evidences of a strangely perverse and twisted habit of thought. Admire his great abilities as we may, it is useless to deny that he seems to delight in posing as the Ishmael of the Church. He belongs to a party – but it consists, if one gets to the real secret of things, of nobody but himself.

Then, the affair of consecration seemed to destroy his relationship with 'the bishops'. From his father he learnt to be against bishops. Then he defended bishops as successors of the apostles. Then he valued them as leaders in the national Church. But now 'the bishops' caused him to be suspect in the country, and made his future work as a bishop far more difficult. He said to himself that he *despised* bishops. Something of the inherited anti-bishopism of childhood reappeared.

These were 'the bishops', a mysterious corporate entity. Individual bishops he distinguished. To despise 'the bishops' was one thing, to despise Charles Gore another, for no one could despise Gore. Burge he always admired. Men not yet bishops at that time but afterwards bishops were accepted as individual friends. Arthur Headlam, then on the point of becoming Regius Professor of Divinity at Oxford, defended Henson with a hurricane of common sense which blew away all the opponents (*Church Quarterly Review*, April 1918); and when he was soon a bishop, despite an awkwardness in social relations, and a shouting match about Hitler, he remained cherished by Henson to the end. *The bishops* were not the same as a lot of bishops. In all that concerned the bishops as a corporate body, Henson never relented.

He would not go to devotional meetings of bishops. He did everything possible to avoid staying at Lambeth Palace. At bishops' meetings or at Lambeth Conferences, he was an astringent individualist. He never quite lost the sense, *I am an incongruous element in the episcopate.* Davidson he never resented. If one individual bishop summed up his critique of 'the bishops', it was the other archbishop, Cosmo Gordon Lang. *I feel like a fish out of water in the company of the bishops.* Even two years after these events he wrote a sour letter to William Temple calling himself *The Outcast of Hereford.*

The last consequence of the consecration was more distant. It turned him into an autobiographer. Even a few months after the event, he thought that he needed to publish an apologia for his life and regretted that he saw no fitting opportunity. As he looked backwards he saw this dreadful thing huge in the past, and fancied that to everyone else it was as huge as it loomed in his memory. And men (he imagined) could not understand, they accused him of recanting for the sake of office, or of bringing the storm upon himself by seeking publicity, or of not being a true and sincere Christian. No clear project formed in the mind. He had other things to do. But he began to think that some day he would write a defence of himself.

Meanwhile the journal grew again more interesting, but for the wrong reasons. Once it was a fascinating document because he fought with demons in East London. Then it became respectable, a document of the establishment. Now it added new touches of sourness. Friendly to laymen, generous to his friends, tolerant even about politicians, it had always been frank about clergymen, especially bishops. Now it became franker. He began to use the journal, at times, as a relief and a release for exasperation. That makes it sometimes more entertaining, sometimes more boring, and on occasions distasteful. His own epithet for this production was *severely candid*.

Long ago in the All Souls common room he betted Duff £5 that he would never be a bishop. He could not pay the debt because Duff was dead fourteen years.

To become Bishop of Hereford cost him in clothes, fees, and moving house £1,000. After such an outcry he expected to remain for ever at Hereford. He stocked the garden with fruit trees, put the drains in order, and extended the electric light. He looked so young that someone mistook the bishop for an ordinand.

He expected trouble. When he arrived at Hereford he could still see anti-Henson placards on walls and telegraph poles.

He soon saw that the country folk of Herefordshire were unmoved by what had happened. They thought the Church of England ought to be as by law established, and heard that their new bishop was a strenuous advocate of establishment against its assailants. They thought that bishops ought to be kindly and tolerant towards dissenters (of whom they had few) and heard that no bishop in England was kinder to dissenters than their new bishop. They liked men not to be too narrow in their attitudes to the mysteries of faith, and heard that their bishop stood for liberty. They did not want men to be attacked by bigots and they rallied to support anyone who might have been persecuted. They liked their bishop to be famous and could hardly distinguish fame from notoriety. Henson even wondered whether parents would keep their children away from his confirmations. No such idea entered their heads. Though he had no notion of it, he started with vast advantages.

He had two other advantages by reason of his equipment. A bishop is judged by his appearances on platforms, before meetings, congregations, schools. Henson was trained to talk. Many minutes though he might talk, he was worth hearing. The second advantage was easily forgotten. In contemplating Henson, controversialist and national scandal, men easily forgot that he had been a first–class parish priest and pastor. Not for a long time had Hereford a bishop with such unusual experience of parochial life.

For a few months he was nervous of opinion. Early he said *I move in an atmosphere of treason in an unknown land!* (6 June 1918). He was not well, sprouted boils, had to preach in pain and without a collar, looking (he said) like *an episcopal scarecrow*, needed an operation on a carbuncle, had to have several teeth extracted (dentists tortured him for the rest of his life) and the doctors diagnosed him as run down and hinted at a connection with his recent experiences. Yet he kept being surprised by the kindness and the welcome of the clergy as well as the people of Herefordshire. And not only in Herefordshire. His bookman in London said to him 'When I think of you, sir, I always picture all things peaceful and beautiful.' Henson at first thought that this might be flattery and then realized that the man spoke sincerely. It seemed to him an amusing portrait of *the most cynical and battered old gladiator in the Church* (11 September 1918).

At first sight a bishop seems removed from the people. But this is not true. Though he only sees them at confirmations, he sees both children and parents at one of the receptive moments of their lives. What he says may live in the memory because hallowed by association with a precious moment of growing life. Henson became a bishop for a national reason; he wanted to help guide the policy of the Church, and through it to affect the moral well-being of all England. But instantly he was at work, laying hands on the heads of very simple country folk, and because he had a caring heart, he was as moved when they knelt before him as they were moved who knelt. The sophisticated preacher of a fashionable London church or a northern deanery was suddenly close to the people of England, almost as close as, so many years before, in Bethnal Green or Barking or Ilford.

The people found a certain stiffness to overcome. Then they began to enjoy the personality, his courage of speech and directness of manner. They knew that he was an intellectual, and were surprised that he never talked down to anyone, but treated all the world as if they were his equals. They admired his abounding vitality. They often disagreed with what he said. He denounced reprisals against Germany, and raged against a blasphemous parody of a New Testament text, *Father forgive them not, they know what they do.* But the people of Herefordshire found him generous and warm. Hereford was not accustomed to housing one of the five or six best orators in England. And the ending of the Great War produced occasions when they valued this gift. At the commemoration of the Armistice; or at the dedications of war memorials to the fallen in squares or on village greens; at the putting into effect of the delayed act for the disestablishment of the Welsh Church; at public meetings to support the plan for a League of Nations – their new bishop could be relied on to say what commanded or inspired the audience.

He was younger and faster than his predecessor. He also had a mechanical advantage. As once his pastoral range in Ilford was extended by a new bicycle, he was the first Bishop of Hereford regularly to use a car. The car was not quite reliable. It brought him embarrassingly late to engagements more than once. But the clergy were not used to a bishop, never in all history had been used to a bishop, who could appear in so many places so rapidly.

The Anglo-Catholic clergy were likely to be suspicious. They judged him, correctly, to be a vehement Protestant, and did not know that he could understand them because once he shared their ideals. They were therefore surprised. They found that he used his patronage impartially, and was as willing to promote Anglo-Catholics as any other kind of churchman. An Anglo-Catholic priest applied to him for leave to use incense in services. Henson replied that incense was illegal, but that he believed its use to be *congruous with the mind of the Church of England* and would *acquiesce* if the representatives of the parish could be shown to want the use. The Anglo-Catholics discovered that however he disagreed with them he would treat them with a total fairness; fairer than they would find in numerous other dioceses; fairer than under his predecessor.

Henson was not to remain long at Hereford. Bishop Moule of Durham died in 1920.

The moment that Archbishop Davidson heard the news of Moule's death he knew whom he wanted as the new Bishop of Durham. It was Tommy Strong, the Dean of Christ Church, Oxford. Durham, the archbishop told Lloyd George, needs a scholar of the first order and one who understands university life. Strong was in former years chaplain to the two scholar-bishops of Durham.

Lloyd George replied to this plea through his secretary Captain Evans. He wanted the Church to increase its hold upon the people, he said. He implied that Tommy Strong, delightful, godly, musical to his finger tips, academic, quiet, and quaint, was not a man for the people. He said that he could not see him rightly placed amid the miners of Durham. Lloyd George mentioned again the need for preachers. Then he suggested Henson; well known and liked in the Durham diocese; a scholar, already possessing strong links with Durham University, and 'a strong personality with great gifts of preaching'. Lloyd George evidently found the choice obvious.

The Archbishop of Canterbury was very disturbed when his chaplain (Bell) read him this letter over the telephone. He expected a new storm. The Lambeth Conference was about to meet, Bishop Weston of Zanzibar was on his way, and the archbishop hardly liked to think what would be said if this supposedly heretical bishop received a new promotion.

Archbishop Lang of York was even more disturbed. He wrote to Captain Evans begging the prime minister to recon-

sider. He said that he was not moved by personal feeling, for
Henson was one of his oldest friends. He confessed Henson's
abilities, and that the diocese needed a strong bishop urgently.
But Henson's appointment would bring 'disappointment,
division and friction' in the diocese.

The archbishops refused to take any responsibility for the
choice of Henson as Bishop of Durham.

This must make a prime minister pause. In her later years as
sovereign Queen Victoria achieved the constitutional innovation that prime ministers would not proceed without the
assent, though not necessarily the warm good wishes, of the
Archbishop of Canterbury. Under King Edward VII the
custom was continued. King George V did not like to interfere
so decisively. Lloyd George accepted the practice which he
found. But here both archbishops refused even to assent.

And yet their arguments were weak. Canterbury was afraid
of another storm. Was it necessary to be afraid of a thunder-
cloud out of Zanzibar? York was afraid of friction in the
diocese. These were fears for the future, not yet proven. And
to the contrary, the prime minister had compelling arguments, only one of which need be concealed. Durham knew
and wanted Henson. He was an excellent bishop in the diocese
of Hereford. He had a quality more valued by the Welsh
dissenting prime minister than by the two archbishops – he
could preach. He was strong, and after a long weak reign
Durham needed firmness. Incidentally, he had in his pocket a
letter from the prime minister almost promising a rapid move
from Hereford.

Despite the archbishops Lloyd George offered Henson the
see. He continued to show discourteous ignorance of protocol
by making the offer through a secretary. Henson hesitated not
for a moment in accepting. He had served in Hereford for two
and a quarter years. Durham was a senior see, with a seat in the
House of Lords. The see carried high prestige. It was preferment. Therefore it vindicated, a little, himself and his causes. It
showed that after all he was no outcast, no Ishmael. Besides,
he loved Durham, and knew that many in Durham were glad
to see him return.

The Archbishop of Canterbury was a false prophet. No
storm blew. Even when that menacing figure out of Africa,

Frank Weston, appeared at the Lambeth Conference that summer, everyone was astonished that Weston and Henson became close friends.

The warmth was not universal. The *Church Times* (18 June 1920) accused him of being discontented with his rural diocese and of casting backward glances upon Durham; and in this the editor was malicious, for Henson's private journal, so candid about his feelings, shows not a sign of backward glance or of ambition for Durham. (His single backward glance longed for good old days as Canon of Westminster.) As was his way, he cast himself into the work before him, which was the diocese of Hereford. The insinuation caused fury among Henson's friends, and a public letter of gratitude to him from all the available leaders among the Hereford clergy. Another critic accused him in a public speech of aiming to become Archbishop of Canterbury and this caused him nothing but laughter.

Henson entered Durham with feelings very unlike the feelings with which he entered Hereford. *I knew, and felt, that I was welcome.*

Looking back later, Henson often wondered whether any other prime minister but Lloyd George would have had the temerity to nominate him to a bishopric. The question was usually accompanied by a scruple, whether Lloyd George did well or ill. And then, sometimes, he would end with a modest little act of faith, that neither Lloyd George nor himself could lie outside the concern of the divine wisdom.

# 7. THE MINERS

DURHAM DIOCESE sat upon a coalfield. In many villages the men were almost all miners, the vicar and the minister of the chapel might be miners' sons, the shop a miners' co-op, almost the only employment below ground. Durham was one of the earliest products of industrial England. Till the coming of the railway it prospered by sending coal on coastal barges to London. In the mid-Victorian age this dominance slipped. Then came the Great War and the mines of 1920 entered a very difficult time of competition.

Russians no longer bought coal. Belgians and Germans dug more of their own coal. Englishmen improved their methods of producing gas and needed less coal. And everyone began to use more and more oil instead of coal. The Royal Navy alone used nearly 2,000,000 tons of coal in 1913–14 and less than a quarter of a million tons in 1929.

A great industry, one of the foundations of British wealth, was suddenly in direst trouble.

No one adapted easily, nor could adapt easily. The miner's father and grandfather worked happily in his village. He expected to do the same, and fancied that this trouble was a hiccough caused by war. The coal owner lived on the memory of prosperity and export and abundant royalties. In less prosperous conditions the only way to maintain profits was to lower wages. Throughout the 1920s they assaulted the level of wages, and thereby cast the miners of Durham into an attitude of continuous resistance.

Henson arrived at Durham just when the county was set for twenty years of unpleasantness, poverty, unemployment, and social disruption. It remained to be seen how the boy of a Kentish watering-place, the Oxford don, the East London slum priest, and the upper-class London dignitary, would cope with the mountains of slag and idle devastated machinery which stood for tragedy in so many lives.

He had a singular qualification, and a singular disqualification. The qualification was, that he easily got on with everyone except other dignitaries in gaiters. He could walk out into his park, sit on a bench with a miner, and converse in equality, with pleasure to both parties. The disqualification was, he was a stalwart member of the Tory Party with obsolescent Tory principles. Whatever was to be done for the Durham coalfield, could only be done – though this was not yet clear – by massive interference on the part of the State. To this friend of Professor Dicey every interference by the State was at first suspect.

The case of the employer ran as follows: if we go on as we are, mines close and everyone will lose their money and everyone will be out of work. To live, we must sell coal. To sell, coal must be cheaper. It can only be cheaper if miners (until better days) accept lower wages or work longer hours for the same money.

The case of the miner ran as follows: we are already near the level of subsistence. We can hardly give a decent life to our wives and children if wages are reduced even by a few shillings. They had the slogan, '*Not a penny off the pay, not a second on the day*'. They could not believe that the coalowner could not afford increase. John Lambton, the Earl of Durham, confessed that in 1918 he drew £40,522 from coal royalties and way leaves, Lord Londonderry confessed that he received £15,334, or about 4½*d.* for each ton of coal brought to the surface.[1]

The miner had weapons with which to fight. His union, the Durham Miners Association, was one of the oldest effective unions in the country. But it was not rich, and any prolonged strike looked likely to destroy its reserves of money. It belonged to the Trades Union Congress. And the TUC might sometimes be persuaded to back it nationally.

Secondly, the miner began to acquire defenders in Parliament. In the General Election of December 1918 only two out of seven miners' candidates won seats. In the General Election of 15 November 1922 the Labour Party won ten of the county divisions, and the miner J. Ritson, with whom Henson afterwards had several tussles, beat a Conservative to win Durham. From 1922 the Durham miners had a body of representatives in the House of Commons. Was it possible that they could persuade or force government to pay subsidies to the miners to tide them over till better days?

[1] Garside, 109.

The parish priest of Barking fought the Gasworkers union and drew them all into church and convinced them at last that he was a lover of the working man. This was the experience which from his past he carried into the north of England and the worst industrial troubles ever known to English society. During the summer of 1920, when he accepted the offer of the see of Durham, England looked to him near revolution – windows in London broken by demonstrations of unemployed workers, violent incitements in the radical newspapers, the Bolshevists in Russia held up as examples of the way in which Labour should go, a government hardly able to cope; and Henson remembered his old Barking dreams, that one day he might be killed in a street riot, and wondered whether it could happen to a bishop who became responsible for the most tormented area of English industry. As he watched tension rising, he felt that revolution was almost upon them, since (he thought) the country had a power capable of resisting Parliament, the might of organized labour, which tried even to dictate the nature of the country's foreign policy, yet represented only a minority of the nation.

From the beginning he was harassed by the precedent of successful mediation by a Bishop of Durham in a strike. His predecessor but one, Bishop Westcott, helped to settle the great coal strike of 1892 by summoning miners and employers to Bishop Auckland, bringing them together, and appealing to their better judgements. This mediation got into the history books and was famous. Its existence brought continuous pressure to bear on Henson, made public men ask him to try to bring the sides together, and perplexed his conscience to know why he did no such thing.

When he asked himself why Henson could not do what Westcott did, he was inclined to minimize Westcott and to think that the achievement was only possible because the sides were ready at the moment to settle; to say that the circumstances of the 1920s were very different from the circumstances of the 1890s; to diagnose the labour movement as more extreme, and more organized, than the miners' leaders of Westcott's day; and sometimes he added, when he wanted to defend himself, that parsons ought not to interfere in what they do not understand and they do not understand economics.

He did not mention one big difference in temperament. Westcott thought opposites always nearer than was supposed, Henson saw no possibility of harmonizing opposites. The one was a mediator by instinct, the other by instinct thought mediation impossible. Henson saw the miners' leaders as wrong. Such a mood had no place for mediation.

The miners started by being friendly to Henson. When he went walking in the Park, and sat with strikers upon benches, or upon the grass, or escorted them to see the chapel, and enquired into their opinions, he met with nothing but courtesy.

From 31 March 1921 was a lock-out, which grew more bitter as time passed.

Sunday, 1 May 1921, which was Labour Day, was a turning-point. Miners and mine owners gave Henson a chance to mediate. They organized a large meeting at the Empire Theatre in West Hartlepool, and asked Henson to speak on a platform with employers to his right and miners to his left. He was warned that Communists were likely to heckle his speech but no one interrupted as he went on for forty minutes and the audience listened decorously.

Westcott, reconciler to his marrow, suspicious of clarity as superficial, would have poured out a series of elevated, charitable, and unintelligible obscurities. Henson could not be obscure if he tried and thought it immoral to try.

Since this speech was fatal (if it is fatal for a bishop to be unpopular among miners) we must give a summary. It praised the unemployed miners, unemployed through no fault of their own. Many served their country nobly in the war, many *are among the best of our citizens.* But now the miners were using a weapon which ought to be ruled out of civilized usage. They were loyal, and generous and kindhearted, but were isolated, and did not realize the effect upon the community. A great strike is like a blockade from within; as though an enemy blockaded our ports. After a dreadful war we have to build this country again into prosperity; and a prime condition is, not demanding higher wages than an industry earns. *Increased wages means depreciated values. What is the good of an artisan having large wages if he can buy nothing with them? . . . A strike is the worst business in the world. You may gain sixpence, you will certainly spend half-a-crown in gaining it.* And then he said (it was not necessary to his argument but this was a moralist denouncing immoral behaviour when he saw it) that one effect of the minimum wage was to stimulate *shirking* of work, *ca'canny*, which in southern English meant go-slow. He said that some men went down the pit and cut only so much coal as equalled their free allowance. And then he rose to a noble appeal, for an end to false ideas of a class war, and a working together by all the community to maintain the leading position of Britain in the world.

The audience, mining or owning, were pleased. The committee asked if they might print the speech as a pamphlet (printed as *The Blockade from Within*). Press reports fastened, not upon the praise of miners but on shirking and ca'canny. From Friday 6 May the newspapers filled with controversy. The word *shirking* roused miners to resentment, as though he applied it to all of them and not to a few. Henson wrote to the newspapers to defend himself (*Durham Chronicle,* 13 May 1921). He had no doubt, he said, that the majority of miners worked honestly and shared his disgust at shirkers.

The police started to take unobtrusive measures for the bishop's protection.

At Wingate on the Sunday after Ascension (8 May) which was locally known as Trades Sunday, the miners refused to attend to hear the bishop. In the streets they stared at him as he passed in the car but did not look unfriendly. He found the miners forthcoming whenever he talked to them as individuals, and wished he were a rich prince-bishop so that he could feast them in crowds. When on 10 May he confirmed at Cassop, two or three police constables attended in case someone demonstrated, but nothing happened.

At Ferryhill on 12 May 1921 he confirmed eighty candidates in an overcrowded wooden church. As he left the miners demonstrated, jeering and booing. He stopped, and standing up in the car started speaking to the crowd. They heckled him as he went on for half an hour, but when he got back into the car and drove away, no one booed. The police inspector's report was even friendlier to Henson:

By the time he had finished speaking, a crowd of about 500 persons had collected, and they were so pleased with what he said – and he

did not mince matters – that they cheered him loudly. The bishop
then left in his car. I believe the bishop did more good by that speech
than all the speakers who have come to Ferryhill since the strike
started.

The local papers next day printed accounts under 'Jeers and
Cheers'.

Three years later (15 May 1924) he confirmed again at
Ferryhill – 138 people in a low-pitched building once a skating
rink, a dense crowd in the over-hot church, close attention,
candidates reverent; and as he drove away, nothing but
friendly greetings. This kind of occasion was very moving to
the outwardly stern and inwardly emotional Henson. At
Trimdon Grange (15 May 1924) *the sight of these big pit-lads
bending their heads for the laying on of hands, with a look of resolute
purpose on their faces, is a spiritual tonic.* At Consett (4 April 1923)
he preached at the funeral of some killed pit-workers and
found himself weeping in the vestry afterwards with their
families. He quite fell in love with the miners as individuals.
He found them *the most attractive of men, polite, cheerful,
generous,* but not amenable to argument.

So continued this curious harmony between private compassion and affection for individuals, and mutual respect when
bishop and miners met, with public denunciation of strikes
and biting phrases, for Henson was an orator, and understood
the dictum of the old Roman who said that if your speech is to
move to action it is not enough to prick with your needle, you
must drive the needle home into the flesh.

Henson was not critical of social reformers. He was critical
of Christians who said that the first duty of the Church was
social reform. For Henson the first duty of the Church was to
change souls, to make consciences sensitive, to keep wills
moral. Its duty lay with individuals. Its doctrines were no
more useful to determine economic policy than any other
general principles out of relation to the predicaments of an
age. He noticed that the reformers – he especially criticized
William Temple and the COPEC Conference of summer 1924
– exaggerated the evils of the present to promote, if not a
better, at least a different future. One of the COPEC men
described the working men as 'bled white of all true humanity
by exhausting toil'; and Henson read the phrase and then

looked at the miners whom he saw walking in the Park and thought that he had never met a more vigorous and cheerful set of men. The language seemed to him absurd.

But it was not only a fear of pretentious words. Henson was a Victorian individualist. He never accepted the belief that you can make men better by law. The growing body of evidence, which showed that if you altered the structure of society you could further moral growth, was not evidence for Henson. You cannot make men better by changing society, you can only make society better by changing men – that was a traditional belief which Henson carried with him to his grave.

But now came a calamity.

The Dean of Durham did not approve of his bishop. Dean Welldon was a man with a distinguished past, a young headmaster of Harrow, a Bishop of Calcutta. Nevertheless he was unscholarly, and liked jests in the pulpit, and enjoyed playing to the gallery; at least, that was what Henson thought, but Henson by nature disapproved of bishops and, being diminutive, specially of bishops when they were large in stature. Bishop Welldon had 6 ft 5 ins of height, a waist of 63 ins, and a tiny voice. He had a rollicking gait and exploded with gusts of laughter. On a visit to the royal family, Henson was told by little Princess Elizabeth that when she went to the zoo she most enjoyed the rhinobottomus. This became Henson's nickname for his dean. Welldon was not Henson's kind of dean, and Henson was not Welldon's kind of bishop.

Two men cannot appear to differ because one is small and the other gigantic, or because one likes and the other hates popularity, or because one mind trundles over undulations and the other mind darts straight ahead. The difference between dean and bishop came to centre on a point of policy: drink.

Dean Welldon was a leader of the temperance movement. And at this moment of British history, in the idealism of the aftermath of war and the new confidence in the votes of women, it was powerful in politics. Henson loathed the idea of prohibition. His experience of the United States made him realize it to be politically disastrous and unenforceable and a recipe for crime. He resented it on principle as an attempt to make men better by coercion.

Dean Welldon found it hard that his bishop should be the ecclesiastical leader of the campaign 'for drink'; hard that Henson should make speeches in the House of Lords or on Sunderland platforms; hard that he should turn to a gloomy and silent Bench of Bishops in the House of Lords and tell them that no one should manufacture sham sins; hard that the brewers claimed the Bishop of Durham as their champion; hard that he should hear his bishop called by the nickname The Liquor Bishop; hard that Henson should revive the Victorian cry, in a new and amused form, that he would rather see England free than England sober. These griefs led the dean into a sin which deans ought not to commit. He made a speech against his bishop.

Every July or August the Durham miners held their gala. This was a celebration half a century old. Thousands of miners crammed the streets, escorted by wives and children, with brass bands and a flag for each colliery. It was a festival, yet intended to demonstrate the solidarity of the miners. At the gala of July 1924 Dean Welldon attended, and was invited to speak; and said that he looked to the Labour Party to solve the drink problem in Britain, and criticized Henson because he was the Liquor Bishop; so that the *Northern Echo* (21 July 1924) gave the affair a headline, 'DEAN'S ATTACK ON BISHOP'.

During the summer of 1925 the discord between owners and miners grew angrier. Coalfield and government moved into that conflict which led to national crisis all over the land. On 30 July 1925 the coal owners gave notice that they would end the wages agreement on 31 July and that an eight-hour day (instead of a seven-hour day) was essential.

While fury raged, Henson wrote an article for the *Evening Standard* (8 July 1925). It appeared under the headline 'The Coal Crisis: an Explanation and a Warning', with a photograph of a young and well-groomed bishop.

Not a compulsive seeker after print like his friend Dean Inge, he nevertheless enjoyed appearing in the newspapers. At that moment he was engaged on a series of articles for the *Evening Standard*. His conscience – whether it was the donnish conscience or the episcopal conscience – was not quite at ease over writing a series of articles for the *Evening Standard*. He felt the need to justify them to himself. He pleaded that he used the money, first to repair the historic church at Escomb, and secondly to pay for the education of one of his 'sons'. But the awkwardness of promising a series of articles lay in the need to pronounce on the issues of the hour; and the issue of June 1925 happened to be the demand of the miners for a *living wage*.

In his article Henson paid the Durham miners, as human beings, warm tributes. But of a *living wage*, he said that it was *plain folly* to insist unless the industry could pay. Otherwise to insist meant closing mines, throwing men out of work, wrecking the industry. And he accused the miners' leader, A. J. Cook, of wanting to bring the mines to deadlock. He asked for a ballot act for trade unions as the only way of preventing a minority from dominating the majority of honest workers.

When he read his own article in the *Evening Standard* he was dismayed. *I am not sure whether it can do any good. I am disposed to think it may do harm. Why then did I write it?*

It did harm. In the House of Commons the Durham miner MP Ritson referred rudely to Henson and begged the Tory Party to keep him in order and talked of bishops drawing huge surpluses in coal royalties. 'The day has passed when we had to take off our hats to the squire and bow to the bishop, whether it was Welldon or the other.' Outside the House Cook told Henson to mind his own business, and accused the Church of propping capitalism.

Two and a half weeks later, on Saturday 25 July, the miners held their annual gala. The speaker was a past and future prime minister, Ramsay MacDonald. The public houses were open most of the day, candy-rock was sold in gargantuan quantities, sword dancers leaped, gas balloons soared into the sky, drummers twirled their drumsticks, a hundred brass bands escorted the miners to the race course by the River Wear, banners were carried from different localities, one from Chopwell with the names of MacDonald, Lenin, and Marx, another ominous little banner inscribed 'To hell with bishops and deans! We want a living wage!' On the platform at the race course Ramsay MacDonald talked in his speech of the recent article in a London newspaper and contrasted Henson's attitude with Westcott's. Just at that moment a vast bishop was seen approaching. It was Bishop Welldon, the Dean of Durham, escorted by Canon Lillingston. As a leader of teetotalism he had been invited by the miners' temperance group to address a smaller meeting after the main assembly. Cries went up, 'here he comes!', and hisses and boos.

Quickly the cries changed – 'Keep him off' – 'Put him in the river' – 'Duck him' – and some miners made a headlong rush at the dean. Welldon smiled and waved them away. They swept onwards, driving dean and canon out of the enclosure and on to the river bank. Stones and sticks were thrown, the dean's top hat and umbrella disappeared into the mass and then the hat sailed through the air into the river, the dean was struck on the head and kicked in several places. He was borne relentlessly to the river. The police arrived just in time, hailed a motor launch which happened to be passing, and got Welldon into the launch and away down river, threats shouted after as he was rescued.[1]

That evening the dean said that he could not understand the attitude of the miners, because he had always been in full sympathy with them in the struggle for the improvement of their condition. The Labour leader Emanuel Shinwell took a different view. Next day he addressed a miners' demonstration at Chester-le-Street. He 'deplored' the incident but seemed not to deplore excessively. 'Little blame' he said 'attached to the miners, for with no other means of curbing the tongue of a dean, it was the sort of thing that they might be expected to do.'

To throw a dean in the river seemed so out of keeping that another theory was soon floated – the miners thought the dean to be the bishop. No one ever knew whether the miners intended to throw Welldon in the river or whether they meant to throw Henson, or whether they just felt a need to throw a gaitered dignitary in the river and did not mind whom. People assumed that they thought themselves to be rabbling Henson.

Henson was unsympathetic to his dean. *He only gets his deserts. He has given abundant provocation by his incessant and untimely talking: and his folly in appearing at the demonstration was in all circumstances gross.* But he worried at the increased risk of physical assault upon himself. Unlike a dean, a bishop must go

---

[1] Good accounts (e.g.) *Durham Chronicle* 1 Aug. 1925; *Northern Echo* 27 July 1925. Welldon had made an alarmist speech against trade unions at the Bishop Auckland Rotary Club on 21 July.

about among crowds. He thought his article in the *Evening
Standard* to be hard for the miners to accept, but not impossible. When read in the light of what the dean said, it became an
offensive attack on the working man. By the end of the month
there was public rumour that Henson had said, in the mood of
Marie Antoinette when she was alleged to tell the people to eat
cake when they had no bread, that *a shilling a day is enough for
miners*. Henson was forced to contradict the absurdity.

Henson believed the rabbling of the dean to be a disaster for
himself. It was too dramatic. A handful of miners united with
the rashness of a dean to make the world think that the working people of Durham hated their bishop. He thought this to
be untrue. When he went in the Park and talked with the
miners, he knew it to be untrue. But meanwhile the world
believed it true; and in believing it true, destroyed what political influence for peace he might be able to exert. No moment
of this terrible thing was later allowed to appear in his frankest
of autobiographies.

Durham had a few revolutionaries. But this incident helped
to make the rest of England think the county to be seething
with revolution, the red heart of the class war.

On 31 July 1925 Baldwin's government stepped in to avoid
the stoppage of the mines. They agreed to maintain the
miners' wages at their existing levels until 1 May 1926; and
during the nine months a royal commission should issue an
impartial report on the future of the mines. Henson regarded
this subsidy from the taxpayer as a Danegeld; a bribe by which
the government bought nine months of peace, and forced
themselves to fight in May 1926 when they should have fought
in August 1925.

In March 1926 the royal commission reported that a continued payment of the taxpayers' money was indefensible, and
assumed that a reduction of wages was inevitable. Government also used the nine months to prepare ways of keeping the
nation going if they were faced with a General Strike.

Henson watched the two sides sparring warily before the
battle, and ruefully looked at his own busyness as the Church
argued heatedly over the revising of the Prayer Book. *Nero's
fiddling was by comparison an act of grave and responsible importance.* He found the world about him growing strange to what

he stood for. *I am filled with fear as to the possible development of this coal-strife. In the best event, it means a further dwarfing of all that the Bishop of Durham symbolizes, represents, and expresses in that great population. And in the worst event?*

On 30 April 1926 the miners struck against reduction of wages. Four days later the workers in transport, gas, electricity, printing, building and heavy industry struck in sympathy with the miners, and Britain faced the General Strike. Ports and shipyards and power stations stood still. The distribution of food and milk was allowed.

The country disliked this method of bringing pressure to bear upon the government. The leaders of several unions were opposed to the strike. After only nine days it was called off, leaving the miners to fight on alone.

At no moment of Henson's life was illness more of a blessing to his mental comfort and even to his safety. It silenced him at the most tense moment of the Durham conflict.

At a Congregational chapel in Westminster (7 March 1926) he preached a sermon in an asphyxiating atmosphere (*like Nebuchadnezzar's furnace*) with bad toothache and a neuralgia to split his head. Earlier in the day he had preached in Westminster Abbey and was already exhausted. Half an hour into the sermon, and only three minutes from the end, his voice dropped and he fell forward onto the desk of the rostrum. He was brought water but could not drink. Then he tried to continue, but the words were meaningless, and a doctor came forward to stop the sermon.

A doctor in Harley Street diagnosed excess of work and strain together with poisoned gums. All Henson's teeth were removed, and he found false teeth *the most disgusting experience in the world*. He was not therefore in good shape when the strike broke out; ordered by the doctor to spend more hours than usual in bed and always to have an hour's rest after lunch and take a whole day off every week.

On the morning of the General Strike he walked round to the County Court Office to offer what help he and his could give in the strike. They told him that he could probably go on with his confirmations, and that the strikers of Durham County seemed to have small enthusiasm. He went back to his study, and sat at his desk, and could not work: *the utter futility of*

*everything on which I have been engaged, and to which I am pledged,*
*overwhelmed me.* In the evening he motored to Trimdon and
confirmed. The miners who gathered about the entrance were
civil. But he thought the strike to be criminal, and very likely
to end in civil war. He hated it when other bishops made
mediating noises, for they seemed to condone the strikers.
When Bishop Winnington-Ingram of London offered Fulham
Palace as a neutral meeting-place between strikers and
employers, Henson only commented, *feather-headed prelate.*
He himself felt as useful as one of the posts in his Park.

To sit and remain silent for long was impossible. On
8 May he wrote a letter to the *Northern Echo* to the effect that
no one could gain by the General Strike and that to call it off
was necessary before negotiations could begin and that meanwhile all good citizens should support the government,
especially all Christian citizens. But this was a more wary
Henson than usual, for he sent it to the editor asking him only
to print if he thought it advisable. If the editor decided not he
would have done no harm, if the editor decided yes he would
increase his chances of a martyr's crown and have delivered his
soul.

The editor refused to protect Henson and indeed the article
said just what the editor wanted and which few other public
men had the courage to say. In a newspaper largely type-
written, and full of reports of hooligan outbreaks and police
using batons, Henson's article occupied the very centre of the
page, the first thing upon which the eye fell, under the headline
'Who can possibly gain by it?' The article ended: *No Christian*
*man is free in conscience either to break contracts, or to molest his*
*neighbours, or to resist the lawful requirements of the State.*

Bishops must motor, and motors met pickets. The Durham
miners tried to stop traffic. They felled trees across roads.
Several cars had tyres slashed, others had 'blackleg' scrawled
on them in large capitals, by 8 May no traffic moved in the
areas of Chopwell, Houghton-le-Spring, or Annfield Plain.
But Henson, out in a car nearly every day, met no trouble
before 9 May.

Henson asked himself whether a General Strike could be
justified as a moral act. He compared it to one of the Pope's
interdicts, and condemned it as liable to the same objection,

that it hurt all the innocent with the guilty. *It also overrides all the reconciling influences of neighbourhood and personality. . . . Will the tyranny of the Trade Unions perish as that of the Popes perished under the disgrace of its own excesses?*

He was silenced in his diocesan journal the *Bishoprick* because the printers struck. He loathed the ending of freedom to speak and print. He loathed equally the sense that he must think several times before he said anything. *What I have to consider when I make a speech is not whether my words shall be true and relevant, but whether they will embarrass the government, or even endanger my own safety! The last consideration might be ignored, but hardly the first.*

For the evening of 9 May he had to prepare a sermon at All Saints, Bishopwearmouth. This was in Sunderland, where violence had occurred. He was forced to put his head into the lions' den and growl at the lions and not look nervous. He found it hard to draft. The feeling of incongruity between bishop and poor man popped up its head again. He said to himself that this would be easier work if he lived not in Auckland Castle but like John the Baptist in the wilderness, clothed not in gaiters but in leather and camel hair, feeding on locusts and wild honey. The address must tread a narrow line. He must say that he abhorred the whole idea of a General Strike. Yet he must not appear to be *the paid apologist of the capitalists*, as A. J. Cook had scornfully asserted. He felt unusually anxious about drafting this sermon for Bishopwearmouth. In crises where something must be said and nothing said too plain, politicians know no gift more useful than bumble. Henson could not bumble. He used too many long words but never too many words.

By the afternoon he was feeling ill. He travelled to Sunderland in pain, the pain increased during the service, and when the time came to mount the pulpit he could only crawl out of the church on his chaplain's arm, and be driven back to Bishop Auckland in agony. There the doctor ordered immediate operation for appendicitis. Late at night he was driven, for the third time that day, along the road to Newcastle, still in agony – *it was truly a via dolorosa*. The doctor and the chaplain, who went with him, knew that the road was picketed by bands which were stoning vehicles and blocking roads with railway sleepers. Henson refused to ask for police protection. They kept passing knots of strikers. As they passed through Birtley, where strikers and police had been fighting, and police had made several baton-charges, strikers stoned the car. No one was hurt. The doctor later gave evidence that Henson gave no sign of indignation but was grieved that miners should be so misguided. The appendix was gangrenous, his life was for a time in danger, his weight went down to seven stones ten ounces. In Durham Cathedral they prayed for his life. He spent several days in semi-delirium. Always in his nightmares he travelled along in a car between rows of watching miners.

A week later he came out of the worst and was able to sit up and take an interest and start to convalesce. But he was im-mobile during the worst part of the General Strike. He started to worry about clergy in mining parishes – the parson at Dawdon who wrote letters against the coal owners as capital-ists, the parson at Hamsteels who denounced Socialism and whose miners stopped or insulted parishioners going to his church, the parson at Shotton who retained all his popularity and to whose wife the miners brought bags of coal. By 3 June, from his bed, he was able to write another letter to the *Newcastle Journal* (also a letter which he repented after it was posted), this time not against the miners but against the well-meaning efforts of the Archbishop of Canterbury to mediate in the dispute.

Archbishops of York may be what they like, but Archbishops of Canterbury ought to be reconcilers by nature as well as by grace, and Davidson loved peace and harmony in the nation. As early as 7 May he presided over a small meeting of bishops and free churchmen to consider whether they could issue an appeal. They asked for a renewal of negotiation, on the basis of an end to the General Strike, a temporary renewal of the subsidy to the miners, and the withdrawal by the coal owners of the proposed reduction in wages. Archbishop Davidson planned to make the appeal on the radio that evening. The dictatorial Director-General of the BBC, John Reith, banned the broadcast. He pleaded that he was afraid lest government take over the BBC. Winston Churchill refused to print the appeal in the *British Gazette,* the strike-breaking newspaper. In shortened form it got into the shortened *Times.* Lloyd George attacked the ban in the House of Commons and finally it was broadcast four days late, on 11 May. But, engaged in winning the battle, government insisted that the strike must end before they would negotiate. A lot of Conservative stalwarts were very angry with Archbishop Davidson. A lot of Labour stalwarts were surprised and delighted.

Henson could not dress or shave without help. He was in bed most of the day and felt rotten. He read Scott and Trollope and Trevelyan's *History of England*, but he had not enough to do and missed his ministry. His illness gave him a jaundiced view of everything, nation, democracy, miners, Church, bishops, and himself. He could not preach in interruptible pulpits or speak from hecklable platforms. However, he could still write letters to the newspapers, and his suffragan Bishop Knight worried that this prostrate man could still put the windows of Auckland Castle at risk by writing a letter from his bed.

A vicar from West Auckland came to visit the sick man and disturbed his moral sense. The vicar met a railwayman on strike and said, 'You are a churchman, how can you reconcile your conscience to breaking the contract under which you are employed, and joining in action which you know to be illegal and suspect to be calamitous?'

'You see this house' replied the railwayman, 'it is my own, and represents the savings of years. If I were to stand out of the strike it would be wrecked, and I myself might be knocked about.'

This story shocked Henson. Men who had no wish to strike were forced to strike by fear of illegal violence. Was this a free country? The trade unions, he told himself, and soon told the world, *have got off their true purpose, and have grown into a formidable menace both to industrial freedom and to public order. They have come to be the mocking caricatures of anything that could be described as democratic.* What sounded persuasive under the name of peaceful picketing, was *a sordid and hypocritical form of organized bullying.* He wanted government to take strenuous measures to reform the system. He refrained from saying how.

When he was fitter and on a convalescent holiday, he went to see the prime minister at Bewdley. He told Baldwin that it was absolutely necessary to reform the laws of trade unions. Baldwin agreed, but did not see how.

Orators in London talked of the many mining royalties which that capitalist the Bishop of Durham received from the Durham mines. At a mass meeting at Rainton in the county of Durham the miners' leader Cook jested that Henson denounced subsidies but lived on subsidies all his life. (The Ecclesiastical Commission received £400,000 a year in coal royalties, much of it from the Durham mines. Only a tiny bit of this came back to Henson.)

Nevertheless, the contrast between Christ's poor and Christ's bishop kept troubling his spirit. He always reached the conclusion that he was in a straitjacket. The scene was encumbered when he arrived. He had to make what good he could out of what he found. Once, outside his diocese in Scotland, Ella and he got out of the car to picnic by the roadside, and afterwards gave the rest of the sandwiches to two lean and hungry men who looked more like unemployed than tramps, and who took the sandwiches eagerly. *Their appearance cast a shadow on my mind, and oppressed my conscience with a grossly offensive paradox – Christ's declared representative at his ease in a Wolseley car, making holiday, confronted by Christ's true successors, the outcast poor, sitting homeless and hungry by the roadside.* He could not see any way out of the dilemma. *It can spoil one's earthly happiness: it cannot suggest any way of escape.*

Meanwhile, from bed or from convalescence, letters did what could be done to hamper other bishops who wanted to mediate in the coal strike.

For the good of the country Baldwin must win. For the prosperity of the county of Durham Baldwin must win. To keep mines from closing Baldwin must win. To feed the young miners of the future Baldwin must win. Any attempt to mediate made the miners think that Baldwin might yield and so prolonged the strike. That was how Henson saw the scene. To the miners' leaders he looked ultra-Tory, a capitalist, the coal owners' friend and the miners' enemy. To himself he felt the burden of the future – these miners when they are older, and their children when they grow, will have no mines to work in unless they lose their misguided strike. His head never wavered. His belly was not quite so sure. *My heart with the men, my head with the masters;* or again, *I am personally the woefullest man in the world, for my mind is with the economists, and my conscience with these fatuous Socialists.*

In August 1926 miners in other parts of England began to drift back to work. In October Durham miners began to drift back, not without violence against blacklegs at Silksworth colliery. The strike was breaking, and the leaders knew. On 30 November 1926 they called off the strike.

Certainly, as the miners at last settled, there was an anti-clericalism in their leaders:

> Have you heard the parson preaching,
> Have you listened to his teaching,
> How the slaves in Egypt suffered long ago?
> But you heeded not his patter
> As you felt it didn't matter,
> For of mining how could any parson know?

The time had its discomforts for the inhabitants of Auckland Castle. Watts, the Anglo-Catholic Vicar of Shildon and a fervent Christian Socialist, held a meeting of miners and their wives at Ferryhill, where five years before Henson was jeered and cheered, and took Henson's philosophy to pieces, point by point, not without insult. Then the coal in the Park of Auckland Castle gave anxiety. The miners were in the habit of digging illegally for open-cast coal in the Park. Above the River Gaunless is a steep slope, known as the Cliff, with narrow seams of coal. They usually came in the early hours after midnight, and used the timber of the Park for props in their workings, and left unsightly marks on the face of the hill. Patrols of police occasionally caught two or three, the magistrates would fine them 10s. and a few shillings costs, and the miners clubbed to pay the fines.

In these centralizing days the Park belonged, not to the Bishop of Durham, but to the Ecclesiastical Commissioners in London. By a mischance of timing the secretary of the commission told Henson (26 June 1926) that they needed to take action to satisfy the police but did not like to act without his approval. Henson cannot have welcomed this request that he approve prosecution. But confronted with the need to decide, he was sure that prosecution was right, they owed a duty, both to law and order, and to the protection of the landscape for posterity. During the remaining months of that year of the General Strike twenty-three men were prosecuted and fined. If only twenty-three were caught it is not hard to imagine the number who stole. It made no difference. The only sensible deterrent was to blow in the workings whenever they were discovered. When caught the miners made remarks like this: 'We are married men with three children each, and on the dole, and we haven't a bit of fire on.'

The miners were hazy about the difference between the bishop who was the nominal owner and the Ecclesiastical Commissioners who were the real owners of Auckland Park. Henson was uneasily aware that he sanctioned the prosecutions. For a few weeks he found no miners to talk with on his walks in the Park.

In that autumn of 1926 Archbishop Davidson fell ill, and instantly the rumour was widespread that Henson would be the new Archbishop of Canterbury. The rumour was natural. Baldwin was prime minister, and this was the single bishop who stood up against 'meddlers' in the strike like William Temple of Manchester. The gossip appeared in Canadian newspapers, even in Berlin. In England it had about it a breath of the Tory extremist. Someone wrote to him to say that hundreds of thousands of English Christians were praying, 'May you be a second Latimer, and be true to Israel against his enemies, and you will never know Latimer's martyrdom. It will be to us a sign that God has not deserted us when he raises you to the see of Canterbury.' All this was distasteful to Henson, especially when the *Daily Express* (16 November 1926) ran him as its leading horse in the race. Its philosophy of selection ruled out the other leading bishops because they were greasy with the oil of mediation between miners and coal owners. It printed a photograph of Henson, looking young, alive and bristling. It called him 'one of the great forces in the Church'.

After the failure of the General Strike Durham County was quiet but not happy. The stoppage impoverished families. Unemployment rose steadily, the Communist Party gained adherents, more men and boys were made redundant – 172,026 miners in May 1924, 107,938 miners in December 1931.[1] On 1934 figures the average weekly wage of the Durham miner was lower than that of any other miner in the country. The cottages were some of the most overcrowded in Britain, though, or because, many lived there rent free. The sanitation of these houses was primitive and caused worry to the officers of health. Some villages had privies standing in a row like sentry-boxes down the middle of the street, and when not wanted for the needs of nature they were used by the children as a playground and sometimes as a theatre, costumes made from toilet-paper. At Birtley 2,000 people lived in huts built for Belgian refugees during the First World War. In Henson's own Bishop Auckland, more than half the insured workers were unemployed by 1934 when government designated the region as a Special Area, with a fund for economic development. The children grew used to being unemployed. One child, asked what he wanted to be, said that he wanted to be on the dole like his father. To grow up in an atmosphere where father and elder brothers hung about waiting for and not finding work was not good for the boys. The men had the pink 'un, a bet on whippets, and sipped long beer; the teeth of the children were looked after because of the school; and mostly the mood was listless.

In April 1928 the Lord Mayor of London launched a fund to aid the distressed in Northumberland, Durham, and South Wales. The government gave £150,000 and promised £1 to every £1 subscribed. These welfare schemes brought in large sums of money. Institutes were erected, sports fields laid out, boys' clubs started, reading-rooms opened. They helped the boys and women. The adult unemployed miner took little notice. The increase of pithead baths after 1926 made much difference to the comfort of miners who still worked.

For everyone who cared about men's souls the age-old problem tormented the conscience. Henson knew that charity must help. He started to organize a lot of charity. But he knew that charity applied in certain ways could destroy character. It troubled him that the nation fancied itself to solve the ills of Durham by keeping everyone alive, when the only solution to be more than temporary was to create work. He began to

[1] Garside, 248.

move away from his origins and to demand action by the
State. From early in 1929 he issued a series of warnings on the
danger of the dole to the character of the nation and a demand –
a neo-Tory demand from a Tory – that the State should act to
make work.

These utterances were more courageous than popular. To
say aloud that dole is bad for the character when so many men
live on the dole is a message likely to cause resentment even
when it is true. His most unpopular utterance was a lecture to
the Individualist Club at Northumberland Avenue in London
(18 June 1930) and printed under the title *The British Lazzaroni*,
the Lazzaroni being the beggars of Naples. This brought him
many hostile remarks, a shoal of anonymous letters, and two
abusive Open Letters, one from a future Labour cabinet
minister. His repute was of hardness, as though he said, dole
corrupts, take away dole. This was not what Henson said.

Meanwhile he did what he could to encourage the charity
which he condemned as not enough. He lent part of the Park as
a sports ground for the unemployed and paid anonymously
for the equipment. He appealed in *The Times* (13 December
1932) for money to help the unemployed with boots or shoes
and won many donations or gifts in kind, and took his chance
to voice his admiration of the way in which the Durham
unemployed maintained their standard amid adversity. He
opened work centres for unemployed, visited camps for unemployed boys, directed public attention to an organization
for opening sports fields, and an institute where the unemployed were trained to make furniture and to cobble shoes,
and a public scheme for creating allotments, and another
scheme for the keeping of poultry, and a fishing boat available
at Hebburn for the use of unemployed men.

The worst trouble for this master of the mordant phrase
came in July 1932 through an unmordant utterance in the
House of Lords. He had no need to make, and should not have
made, that speech. He was politely clapped at the end, and the
Lord Chancellor (Sankey) beckoned him to the Woolsack and
congratulated him that he had never heard a better speech, nor
a speech that more completely captured the House. The Labour
minister Philip Snowden hobbled over on crutches to the
Bishops' Bench and said 'Your speech won't please your

friends in Durham; but it was all true. You are a courageous man to speak like that.'

If these eminent peers did not flatter – and neither Sankey nor Snowden was famous for butter – this evidence shows something of Henson's oratory. In the cold record of Hansard which is all that the historian can see, it was not much of a speech; not very coherent in structure, nor cogent, nor spiritual, nor persuasive. The Lords debated public expenditure, and Henson attacked the extravagance of local councils, and said that Durham was now equipped with main roads far better than it needed, and that the ruin of great empires came from financial mismanagement.

Henson hardly expected this to offend. He had said far more unpalatable things at the time of the General Strike. But this charge of extravagance and mismanagement mortally offended the members of local councils in County Durham. The Labour leader George Lansbury said that the Durham miners 'hated' Henson. A Labour MP attacked him in the House of Commons and the Conservative MP for Houghton-le-Spring, who was a man of character and heard his conscience whispering to him to rise to defend the bishop, did not dare. In *John Bull* Hannen Swaffer printed a caricature of Henson sneering down at a frightened little man, under the heading 'Why despise the common man?'. In his final apostrophe he besought Henson: 'Come out on the people's side, my Lord! You have the brains to help them to the things they want. Speeches such as yours will not only retard progress; they will bring down, amid the ruins of many other things, the Church of which you could be such an ornament.'

The nastiest attack of Henson's life came that autumn in the *Weekend Review*. This represented the Bishop of Durham, sitting remote behind castle walls, a Dives caring nothing for the sufferings of Lazarus at his gate, cold and heartless, occupying his time writing pharisaic letters to *The Times*. If there were truth in Henson's doctrine that a faithful apostle is always unpopular, during the second half of 1932 he was at his most apostolic.

Normal abuse he endured with a measure of equanimity. If he were worth all this spattering of powder and shot he must count. But he was miserable under the lash of George

Lansbury that the miners hated the Bishop of Durham. In the depths of melancholy he went out into the Park and found *two little blackguard boys* floating a little ship in the beck. He stopped, and joined the game; and as he gave out a sixpence, said to one of them *Do you love the bishop?* The boy said, 'O yes, I always did'. Henson pathetically set the boy in the Park in the scales against Lansbury. Less than a week later his morale was back. *I could almost wish that the miners did hate the bishop, for their hatred would at least indicate a consciousness of his existence.*

For all that Henson did for the unemployed in the county, the conflict was never stilled so long as he was Bishop of Durham. In Durham, men said, bishops always stood against the tide. Tunstall tried to stem the Reformation, Morton fought against triumphant puritanism, Van Mildert resisted the reform of the parliamentary constitution. And now Henson was an old-fashioned individualist in an age when individuality perished, a man who distrusted majorities in an age when the committee was infallible, a mind which never went with the crowd in an age when the crowd fashioned the public mind. And he did not realize that courage and clarity and refusal to conform could win another kind of respect and even an affection and in the long run a different kind of 'popularity'.

A weighty authority on the history of Durham has expressed the view that Henson's time as bishop was a calamity for the Christianity of the working population of the country and that he should never have been made Bishop of Durham, because the Church still suffers from the gulf between worker and clergy which he helped to dig – perhaps, did most to dig. Another equally weighty authority has taken a contrary view, that miners care nothing about opposition in the long run and give their allegiance, though not their agreement, to a stout heart and sincerity and compassion.

The question has no answer and yet is of importance. In human history a dramatic moment comes to symbolize the underlying social movements of an age. Jenny Geddes threw her stool at the preacher and divided Scotland from England – the theory is too naïve, for Mrs Geddes would have been ejected as a brawler unless her brawl symbolized what Scotsmen felt but had not expressed. The Roman Pope's ambassadors marched to the altar of Santa Sophia and laid upon it a shocking excommunication of the Patriarch of Constantinople and all his supporters; and so divided East from West for ever – and yet the high drama only focused long and heart-felt differences which over four centuries drew East apart from West. A lone knight errant, without even a Sancho Panza for his groom, Henson went into battle with the trade unions of England, on moral grounds – the sanctity of a contract, the wrongness of breaking it because other men order it to be broken, the interference with liberty necessary to picketing, the encouragement of social bitterness and class struggle, and the self-interest of a powerful minority of the community without regard for the interest of the total community. Whether the high drama that ensued – the attempt to pitch a gaitered dignitary in the river, or the public statement by the leader of the Labour Party that miners hate their bishop – dug down the trench which divided Church from working man, or was only a symbol of a trench which was dug over decades, perhaps for two centuries or more,[1] is a question which men of guesswork must try to divine. The bias of the historian expects underlying movements over decades to be more likely to determine a course of events than the moment of drama. To throw a bishop into a river was to throw a bishop into a river. In the parishes miners still brought bags of coal to their vicar's wife.

[1] Stanhope 1818; affray between the keepers of the Bishop of Durham and the Weardale lead miners. The bishop's men arrested two poachers and their friends rescued the poachers, knocking out the eye of a bishop's man and injuring severely three others, kicking them as they lay on the ground and hitting them with their gunstocks. The bishop was Shute Barrington.

# 8. CHURCH AND STATE

HENSON WAS the famous advocate of the establishment of the Church of England. Whatever else changed in his opinions and conduct and faith, he maintained this conviction without compromise for the first sixty-five years of life. The people needed God, and by no other means could God be brought to all the people, especially to the poor people.

In ardent youth he aimed to drive the dissenters back into the Church of England by conversion. Then came the revolution of the year 1900. In that embattled year he saw the unpopularity of the Anglo-Catholics, and realized that Protestant England would never back an Anglo-Catholic England. Therefore the established Church must include all the Protestant Trinitarian groups, from Anglican to Baptist. All Protestants were members of the Church of England because it was the Church of the nation. The Reformation made the State the governing body of the Church. And that was right. Representatives of the nation should govern the Church of the nation. The only body to be the authentic voice of the baptized people of England was the House of Commons. He had no sympathy for those people who said that because the House of Commons now contained atheists or nothingarians it was unsuitable government for a Church.

This remained his opinion for more than a quarter of a century after the volte-face of 1900. He found himself in an increasing solitude. Large numbers of laymen thought as he. But if you wanted to find another leading ecclesiastic of this opinion, you had to ransack the cathedral closes of the country; and if other bishops shared this obsolescent opinion they were too prudent to say what they thought. The only man who publicly consistently and cogently argued for the power of the House of Commons in the affairs of the Church of England was the Dean of Durham and then the Bishop of Hereford. We must remain the Church of the nation or what will happen to the poor? And if we are the Church of this nation, the nation has rights and interests.

The trouble was, this did not work.

The Bishop of Winchester was anxious that he failed to shepherd his huge diocese. He wanted to make half of it into a new diocese, or two new dioceses. He will need to ask Parliament. How many years will he need to wait until busy government finds time for a bill in which it has no interest? The Bishop of Winchester will have to possess the patience of a saint to bear frustration while prime ministers, party, government, and opposition care nothing. This was preposterous. Parliament and prime ministers and home secretaries had their time occupied. To say that Parliament governed the Church of England was to say that no one governed the Church of England.

The battles over ritual in 1900 produced an agonizing species of this difficulty. Parliament demanded that the national Church 'set its house in order'. What did that mean? No one knew, and each man had his opinion. But the demand included at its centre an end to ritual 'illegalities'. And the bishops of the Church of England committed themselves to meeting this demand. They would amend the Prayer Book, and make everyone conform to the amended way of worship.

The demand, thrown out by a popular assembly moved by political interest as well as emotion, thus caused a promise which, made under threats, was difficult if not impossible to keep.

To change the Prayer Book! – it was written by a master of English prose-poetry, it moulded the English language, martyrs died in flames for the sake of its use, men stood up for it with courage against a rough soldiery during civil war, and it carried for three and a half centuries the aspirations of the English conscience. Its author, Archbishop Cranmer, lovable, hesitant, scrupulous, and a genius at ways of worship, was the only Anglican bishop to be revered by every member of the Church of England and by many outside the Church of England.

With the tops of their heads everyone admitted a book of prayers to be less sacred than the text of the Bible. But the bishops promised Parliament to do something which in the hearts of churchmen was nearly as difficult as altering the Bible. A form of prayers begins by being a careful draft. By repetition it grows hallowed, because used at moments when the conscience is awake, and then it can come to be powerful in the deepest needs of humanity, like pain or death. To mess about with an accustomed mode of prayer is to ask for trouble; and this trouble is certain to come, not only from a handful of the hidebound who think that all change is to be resisted, but from liberal minds who nevertheless feel that something important, both to them and their children, is put at risk. The bishops promised Parliament what they would not find it easy to perform.

But perhaps very small changes would satisfy? One of the saints was a misprint, he did not exist even in legend, should we spell him right? The purpose of marriage was to avoid fornication, brutally expressed, many clergy left out the offensive clause illegally, should we have a positive sentence? Saints outside the New Testament were male or virgin, women are godly, should we have a mother to remember? Brides were compelled in marriage to promise to obey their husbands, was it indispensable to insist on this vow when everyone could see that the bridegroom was about to spend the rest of his life obeying his bride? The Athanasian Creed threatens that you will perish everlastingly unless you believe that those that have done evil will go into everlasting fire. Must we condemn persons who hope even for the wicked ultimately? Many clergymen quietly failed to use the creed on days when it was ordered. And yet, could it be said that the removal of an ancient creed was only a very small change in the Prayer Book?

The name of Cranmer, the hallowing of time, the martyrs, the history of a nation, cast an aura over a whole book, and failed to notice that inside that book appeared bits, phrases, opinions, which were unedifying, unintelligible, or untrue.

Parliament was promised ritual order. Three pieces of ritual were in question: the use of incense; reserving the sacrament, that is, placing consecrated bread and wine from the holy communion in a cupboard aumbry or tabernacle, usually with a light burning in front; and the coloured vestments for the minister at holy communion. Some Members of Parliament thought that all these should be made illegal by law, or that they were already illegal by law and the law needed only to be enforced.

The bishops knew more than Members of Parliament about the Church. They knew that an Act of Parliament to make reservation illegal was the only certain way to encourage the practice of reservation. Whatever else Parliament might control, no one, certainly not Henson, believed that it could alter the doctrine of the Church or its prayers. Parliament had made legal a body of doctrines, and a Book of Common Prayer, which the leaders of the Church had agreed. No one suggested that Parliament could alter the Athanasian Creed, or tell brides in church not to vow to obey their husbands, or canonize a new saint. It could only do so if the leaders of the Church so proposed. Henson shared his opinion with every-one else, it was obvious. Whatever else the House of Commons presumed to be, it never dressed up as a synod.

In this way the demand of Parliament – 'put your house in order' – included (though members of Parliament failed to realize what they asked) a confession that they must concede alteration in the historic constitution of Church and State.

Early in the Victorian age the organs of Church opinion, embryo synods, took shape. The Convocations of Canterbury and York revived their meetings; which were historic enough to be as old as the Commons. Because these Convocations were clerical, a House of Laymen was added not long before Queen Victoria died; that is, though the Convocations still met separately, they also joined together with the laymen in a less embryo synod, the Representative Church Council. During the years after 1905 this body became the nearest thing to a synod which the Church possessed. Its resolutions had no power. It was nothing but a forum of discussion. Sometimes Henson was appalled at the quality of its speeches. All men find some virtues harder to practise than others, and the virtue which Henson found hardest was to sit patient while foolish men talked interminably. But if anyone was to 'put the house in order' he could hardly do it now in any way which the Representative Church Council disapproved.

Henson eyed this debating body with suspicion. He saw how unrepresentative was this body which called itself Representative. He feared that an assembly drawn from a single denomination would be narrower in its attitudes than the old government under Parliament. He saw that in such a body an Anglo-Catholic leader of stature, like Charles Gore, had weight – in short that any conceivable synod would be friendlier to Anglo-Catholics than any conceivable House of Commons. He thought that if a synod won the right to replace Parliament as the government of the Church, it would turn the national Church into one denomination among others.

Therefore his isolation – not as a dean or a bishop but as a church politican – became always more solitary. Henson stood against any self-governing assembly for the Church of England. But the force of history drove the Church of England into some form of assembly; for without it they could no longer administer the pastoral needs of the Church, nor could they obey the bishops' promise to 'set their house in order'. Someone had to say (for example), it is not compulsory so many days in the year to consign so many people to hell by reciting the Athanasian Creed. Parliament could not say that. Therefore some kind of 'synod' must exist. This was the only time in his life when Henson looked like Mrs Partington brushing vigorously away with her mop to roll back the incoming tide, until the day when he cast the single vote recorded against the plan for the 'synod' that had to exist.

Under the guidance of Archbishop Davidson of Canterbury, and with the complaisance of the government of Lloyd George who as an ex-Baptist thought the plan right so far as he was interested, the Enabling Act of 1919 received the royal assent. This allowed the Assembly, with its three houses of bishops, clergy, and laymen, to propose measures to Parliament. The measures went before a committee of both houses, the Ecclesiastical Committee. And if this committee so recommended, the measure of the Church Assembly became law without passing through the stages of a bill, but solely on the resolution of House of Lords and House of Commons, followed by royal assent.

The Dean of Durham was vocal in the early discussions, the Bishop of Hereford lamented that as a junior bishop he had no seat in the House of Lords while the bill passed through Parliament and became law. To compensate for his lack of a parliamentary platform he published during 1919 no fewer than ten letters to *The Times*, some of which took much space and none of which was expressed obscurely.

Once the bill became law Henson worked loyally within the new system. But he did not see why he should not try to alter it for the better.

Parishes had an electoral roll of baptized parishioners who elected a parish council. The parish council elected members to a diocesan conference. The diocesan conference elected members to the National Assembly. This was not quite democracy because too many stages happened between the baptized parishioners and the National Assembly. But it was the nearest thing to a representative system that was practicable.

Naturally the persons who did not go to church except to be christened, or to be married, or to be buried, were unrepresented by this system. Yet some of those were sure that they belonged to the Church of England, and might even pronounce the words 'C of E' with a rueful pride, and were sure that they cared what happened to the Church of England. And they were not the only people not well represented. Some parishioners, devout, church-going, communicants, never dreamed of attending a church meeting or signing their names to belong to an electoral role which was new-fangled. Henson was hardly surprised to discover, by a visitation of his diocese during 1924, that the Anglican population was about 600,000, the number of electors 156,138 or just over a quarter, the number of people who attended the annual meetings 8,832, and the number of elected councillors 6,828, so that this allegedly representative system meant that in most parishes twenty or thirty persons attended the annual meeting and elected nearly all of themselves to the council. In the democracy of the nation seven out of ten took part. In the alleged democracy of the Church one out of sixty-five took part.

The claim of the National Assembly, wrote Henson, *to speak the mind of the laity cannot reasonably or prudently be conceded.* He was afraid that a small minority of Anglicans could impose on the general body of the Church of England a sectarian attitude out of keeping with the broad tolerance in the tradition of the Church, or which could be manipulated in the interests of an ecclesiastical party.

He wanted direct election to the Assembly, like the national elections to Parliament; and did not face the difficulty that an election with large bodies of ignorant electors is far more easily manipulated by partisans and with far more distasteful results. What mattered were not his remedies, which never had a chance, but his warnings. The rights of a man who seldom went to Church but was proud to be 'C of E' were still rights. A crowd of inarticulate souls must not suffer spiritual domination from a caucus of ecclesiastically minded laymen who saw only what their group saw and had nothing but a contempt for anyone who was only 'C of E'. Henson had a strong faith in the underlying religion of Britain. They might sound secular, but in their moments of agony and conflict they still cared, and this caring was not contemptible, but a precious spark of divine faith to be fostered, whether for the sake of the Church of England or for the sake of England.

As Bishop of Durham he had a seat in the House of Lords. When he accepted the see he looked forward to that seat, knowing that it would enable him to play the part in the national life which he saw as the attractive role in a bishop. He soon found that this hope was mistaken. To be influential in the House of Lords a man must be often in the House of Lords. He must sense the atmosphere, be known, win respect, walk the corridors, eat in the restaurant, gossip with peers, be behind the scenes as well as on the stage, stay out of bed later than is good for morning prayers. A Bishop of Durham, amid confirmands ordinands patronage miners, could not spend that time. He was too distant. The adorable Lady Scarbrough gave him a prophet's chamber in her house in Park Lane whenever he wanted. But he could not use it often enough to be a regular Member of Parliament. The utmost that he could do was to attend debates on key issues of Church and State or Christian morality.

From this seat he almost succeeded in destroying a plan to divide the historic diocese of Winchester into three dioceses. Archbishop Davidson, who had no wish to divide, nevertheless did what he could in the Lords because this was the decision of the Church Assembly and he must be loyal. Henson had no such feeling. The nation as well as the Church Assembly had an interest in the see of Winchester.

Then the Church Assembly decided to make a new diocese

of Shrewsbury out of the Shropshire end of the see of Lichfield, and the northern part of the see of Hereford. Henson told them how the Vicar of Barking had friendly relations with two successive bishops but he had *never felt that palpitating desire to have the diocesan always on his vicarial doorstep;* and though as bishop he had affectionate relations with his clergy, he *really did not think that he would care to have them always tumbling in on him.* His scathing ridicule in the House of Lords swung votes – high-minded but mistaken men, pouring out money on bishops when some clergy were near to starving, and breaking the most efficient diocese in England. The supporters of Shropshire tried to mock the speech as a flight of rhetoric. But it was more than powerful, it was a recent Bishop of Hereford pleading eloquently for his people. The House of Lords rejected the Shrewsbury Bishopric Measure by 61 votes to 60, and Henson was a hero in all Herefordshire. Everyone attributed to him the failure of the measure.

The situation had danger. On the one hand he made a name for himself in the Lords, his advocate's mind commanded the ear of the peers, the course of debate was turned. On the other hand a speaker in Parliament may not read from a prepared text. He must speak with notes in his hand. When Henson had only notes, devastating phrases came pouring into his mind and out of his mouth, and made him far more witty as a speaker than when he read a script. This was one reason which caused him always to read from a prepared text when he preached a sermon, for the prepared text might lose in spontaneity but gained by excluding the unprepared epigram. In his speeches in the Lords Henson was nearer to the recklessness of his conversation at table, and farther from the gravity of his pulpit homilies. As old Dicey saw in All Souls, the man was a genius at pleading. In his diocese he was seldom invited to show this side of his mind. His place in the Lords invited him, even compelled him, to be a counsel for the prosecution. And when he prosecuted, he riddled the other side's case with words which streamed out, as one hearer remarked, like bullets from a machine gun.

To demolish the other side in a lawcourt is to win the case before the jury. To demolish the other side in a Parliament, a synod, a Lambeth Conference, may not win the case, nor be the best way to win. For you still need the votes of those whom you have just slaughtered.

The Church Assembly was given power to run the pastoral machinery of the Church of England with only a veto conceded to Parliament. The creators of the Church Assembly expected Parliament not to use that veto. They expected Parliament to think that its time was better occupied than with the trivialities of diocesan boundaries, or that it would feel unwillingness to intervene in a matter which evidently concerned Church and not State, where the organs of the Church had decided. What happened was not foreseen. By campaigns against the division of the see of Winchester, and then against the division of the see of Hereford, Henson reminded Parliament that it possessed, and ought on occasion to exercise, its veto. This was more troublesome because in the case of Hereford certainly, and in the case of Winchester not improbably, Henson was right about the merits of the case. He called Parliament to show that it still ruled the Church. He reminded Parliament, and the Church Assembly, and everyone else, that when the Church Assembly was founded, and inherited its prophet's mantle, it received no double portion of the Pope's infallibility.

But as a new Prayer Book drew nearer, this predicament, to which Henson thus contributed, bred a growing discomfort. What would happen if the Church Assembly proposed a new way of worship for the Church of England and then Parliament threw out the measure? It must lead to the worst form of crisis between Church and State, that crisis which the apocalyptic Henson predicted when he opposed the making of the Church Assembly so relentlessly.

In the preparation of the new Prayer Book Henson sat on committees and took a modest part. His nearly mortal illness of the early summer of 1926 took him away from important meetings, but the work in which he engaged he did loyally. His religious heart was not quite in the work. One of his heroes was Archbishop Cranmer and he was not quite sure about meddling with words so hallowed. But his pastoral mind was in the work. He felt the ritual confusion to be a stumbling-block in the parishes, perhaps only a few parishes in each diocese, but troubling souls out of all proportion to their fewness.

The process of revising a prayer book could not be only pastoral – that is, remove unintelligible words or rubrics which no one obeys. Men talked of 'enrichment' – that is, to make it a better, fuller liturgy, still Cranmer's book of prayers, but expanded to meet the needs of modern hearts. That they were revising during the General Strike led them to insert prayers for industrial peace. Because it was the age of the League of Nations they wrote a prayer for the League, which put into a prayer book intended for a century an institution which was to have eleven more years of effective life. It was the age of the Empire; and that old imperialist Henson drafted the prayer for the British Empire, and the prayer is good, if now, like the prayer for the League of Nations, it dates the revision:

Almighty God, who rulest in the kingdom of men, and hast given to our sovereign Lord, King George, a great dominion in all parts of the earth: Draw together, we pray thee, in true fellowship the men of diverse races, languages and customs, who dwell therein, that, bearing one another's burdens, and working together in brotherly concord, they may fulfil the purpose of thy providence, and set forward thy everlasting kingdom. Pardon, we beseech thee, our sins and short-comings: keep far from us all selfishness and pride: and give us grace to employ thy good gifts of order and freedom to thy glory and the welfare of mankind; through.

Among the prayers came a change of doctrine. Because medieval man ran into superstition when he prayed for the dead, Cranmer avoided all praying for the dead. Catholic minds in the Church of England long thought this a weakness in Cranmer, since to pray for a beloved who has just died is the most natural of Christian acts. Because the doctrine was linked to old memories of Catholic versus Protestant, it remained absurdly controversial; until the massacres of 1914–18 made almost everyone think it natural to pray for the dead, and ended controversy except among fanatics, and so brought the bishops to insert it into their amended prayer book. Henson was grateful. He thought that the general acceptance of prayers for the dead was one of the few good things to come out of the Great War.

What else were they to allow? They allowed extempore prayer – we know that Henson approved but he hated extempore prayer as vehemently as extempore sermons. They allowed vestments at the eucharist because many bishops thought them legal under Cranmer's Prayer Book, and some bishops wanted them, and nearly all bishops knew that they could not get obedience if vestments were forbidden. Against Henson's wishes (he was absent ill) they allowed reservation of the sacrament but only for the sick. They would not allow reservation in churches to help private prayers. They would not allow incense.

In these deliberations it was hard to determine how far the voting went with one eye on Parliament. Henson knew that the people of England were more Protestant than the members of the Church of England. If the representatives of the people were confronted with a permission for Catholic practices like vestments, reservation, incense, would they behave with more Protestant zeal than the Church Assembly and veto what was proposed, thereby causing a battle between Church and State over the most sensitive nerve in the Church, its manner of prayer? Archbishop Davidson allowed that Parliament had full right to vote a negative so frightening. Henson believed nothing of the kind. He did not deny the constitution, that Parliament had an actual power, as it had power to do anything, but Parliament was not a synod. Nevertheless bishops in committee could use Parliament as a threat. If such and such were permitted, or if such and such were not permitted, they would think the new Prayer Book impossible and might oppose it, not only from their place in Church Assembly but their place in Parliament. Henson himself was willing to oppose it in Parliament if any other reservation but that for the sick were allowed. When afterwards he tore the House of Commons into shreds for its folly, he could not deny that its members possessed the constitutional right to be fools.

The calamity which lay ahead, both for the Church and for Henson, perhaps on one view for the State, was fostered by the little half-forgotten sore place in Henson's origins on the Isle of Thanet. The revised Prayer Book was carried through the Church Assembly by overwhelming majorities, so overwhelming that a rejection by Parliament would look like a blow in the teeth of responsible churchmen. But in the course of debate it became clear that extremists of both wings –

evangelicals determined to resist vestments or reservation in the Church of England, Anglo-Catholics determined to resist a book which would stop reservation and incense – were united to fight the book; incongruous allies, agreed on nothing but the badness of the book; and willing to carry the fight against the book beyond Church Assembly into Parliament.

This strange alliance of opposites hurt Henson at that innermost ulcer of his childhood. His dislike of Anglo-Catholic extremists was famous. But this alliance resurrected his boyish sense of nausea at extreme evangelical religion. As he worked, up and down the country, in meetings or in print, the scathing phrases sprang to his lips; the *Protestant underworld* uniting to obstruct the religious mind of the Church; the evangelical party as *an army of illiterates generalled by octogenarians, a description more unkind than untrue;* Bishop Pollock of Norwich who led the opposition and who happened to be the least pastoral bishop in the Church of England, reminding him of that *rather enigmatic but extremely interesting figure, the stylite or pillar-saint of the primitive Church, whose aloofness was as impressive as his attitude was apparent*; supported by *moribund societies*, whose members cannot be argued with but *must be left to the slow but sure process of extinction through moral and intellectual penury*; Pollock, enduring *the applause of these deplorable fanatics; thousands of elderly incumbents hitherto unknown to fame have abandoned their parochial duties in order to preach a crusade against the book*; opponents of the book who are the *Bourbons of English religious life* – the searing indictment went on, in newspapers, Convocation, Church Assembly, Parliament, periodicals, raising delight and glee in the central body of churchmen; fetching in the crowds, so that when men heard that Henson was on his feet they tumbled into the chamber; greeted at the end with cheers, laughter, rapturous applause, not only for the wit but for the inspiring conclusion, for this was not only a slayer of Goliaths but the evangelist of a historic English way of prayer; and simultaneously making enemies, of anyone who was an evangelical, almost anyone who opposed the Prayer Book, anyone who was an octogenarian, and several who never attended a university and fancied that by *illiterates* Henson meant people without a degree. The Marquess of Lincolnshire, who was eighty-four years old, talked mournfully in the House of Lords of the atrocious crime of being a very old man and asked their Lordships whether they could approve the language of the Bishop of Durham.

In Anglo-Catholic mood the *Church Times* denounced the new Prayer Book and therefore lamented that Henson suffered from a 'venom' regrettable in a prince of the Church ('It has often been said that his bark is worse than his bite but his bark is certainly terrifying'). In evangelical mood the *Record* denounced the new Prayer Book and therefore regretted the tone and temper of Dr Henson, and accused him of a 'superiority complex'.[1] In moderate mood the *Guardian* supported the new Prayer Book and therefore praised Henson for his humour, vigour, and sincerity, always noticing the high sentiments and depth of feeling which the wit set into relief.

The detection of humour is an enigma for the historian. A man speaks a sentence, in a literal sense stinging, outrageous. The sting and outrage are made harmless by the manner, the droll expression of the face, or the smiling eyes. The hearer sees and knows that it is humour, and laughs, and does not think it outrageous because he knows that it is not meant solemnly. But the historian has only the minute, the printed record. He cannot see the eyes or (on Henson's face) the cock of the eyebrows. Unless he is careful he takes the utterance as formal.

This difficulty for the historian is also a difficulty for anyone not present. When Henson talked at Convocation of *the Protestant underworld* (*Chron. Conv.* 29 March 1927, 92) no one in the audience seems to have suffered shock. When it was cited in print weeks later, the memory of the occasion, where he pulled the leg of Bishop Pollock of Norwich, was lost. Newspapers cannot quote eyebrows.

When afterwards he was blamed, up and down the land, for talking of a Protestant underworld, he recanted no word. Partly he begged his critics to have a sense of fun. *I do not desire for that party* [the evangelicals] *anything worse than a keener interest in the things of the mind, and a more adequate sense of humour.* Partly he thought it true. He did not identify either the evangelicals or the opponents of the Prayer Book with an

---

[1] *Church Times*, 1927, 735; *Record*, 1927, 314.

underworld. But the existence of violent fanaticism could not be denied. It shouted down the Archbishop of Canterbury at a Croydon meeting. It printed scandalous little tracts against good men whose only offence consisted in being bishops and wanting a new Prayer Book rather more tolerant of diversity than the old. Who could deny that the underworld existed and was nasty?

Henson never observed, or never showed that he observed, that for a large body of men religion and humour are strange bed-fellows. If you are in deadly earnest about the worship of God and the prayers of the common people, ought you to compare the Bishop of Norwich to a sparrow sitting alone upon the housetop, well placed to survey the countryside but unable to see what went on inside his house which was the diocese of Norwich? The souls of some of his hearers were so constituted that they saw how light the utterance and could not imagine it to set off a passion for a devout and Biblical mode of prayer. Yet the power in this range of speeches lay not only in the experience of a practised orator and the wit of a sparkling mind, but in compassionate concern for the prayers of the people of England as heirs to Thomas Cranmer's gift.

When the measure came to the House of Lords the managers of the proposal were conscious that Henson was the best speaker whom they possessed in either House; though they were also aware that the best speaker was not always the most persuasive. The speech which he made (14 December 1927) was one of his ablest. By the highest standards of parlia-mentary debate this was a great speech.

To summarize its body is to lose its flavour. He withdrew any suggestion that by his phrase *the Protestant underworld* he scourged the body of evangelicals, for whom as a whole, he said, he had no sentiments but those of respect and regard. Then he quoted passages from the sort of nasty tracts which he had in mind, tracts abusing the Archbishop of Canterbury (*pardon me your Grace*) as silly, and abusing the Archbishop of York (*pardon me your Grace*) as pompous and swell-headed. And when he had tried to put himself right with the Pro-testants, and charmingly demolished his opponent Bishop Pollock of Norwich, and dismissed the speech of Lord Carson from Northern Ireland (whose speech only showed how

Protestant was Ulster) he rose to a lofty exposition in which he attributed much to the effect of the Great War. The Church of England had learnt not to be insular. Its members had learnt a breadth which gave them a disgust of a rigid or narrow uniformity. They saw a picture rising of a truly Catholic Church *not pinched in the bondage of a cruel intolerance*. It stretched its claim as wide as the religion of Jesus Christ and wanted to use and make its own every element which is validly contained in the Christian tradition. And in this scientific age of critical enquiries, are we to hold everyone to every word of a Prayer Book drafted before modern science and modern criticism?

In the debate Bishop Pollock's brother Lord Hanworth, the Master of the Rolls, drew attention to Henson's own evidence that the Church Assembly was unrepresentative of the laity of the Church of England and inferred that because the Church Assembly wanted the book by such large majorities it did not follow that the general body of laymen wanted the book. Lord Hanworth was right. Henson did not deny that he was right. But he had an astonishingly effective argument. The House of Lords, beyond all other assemblies, would not deny that at certain times and for certain purposes the unrepresentative assembly expounded the national mind more truly than the representative assembly. And this measure is about the service of holy communion, and that is where the wishes of communicants themselves are what matter. He could not see how the House of Lords could rightly hinder the Church of England from doing what it wanted without injustice. He reminded them of Stalin persecuting religion in Russia and of the anti-Christian flood spreading westward, and asked whether this was a time to hamper the Church of England. *The Church of England asks of your Lordships nothing more than justice.*

Archbishop Davidson confided to his diary that he did not quite relish the tone of this speech, and yet could not deny its quality:

Henson of Durham spoke with a brilliant oratorical power and effectiveness, but with not exactly the kind of arguments which I like best as coming from a bishop on a solemn issue, but no one could fail to admire the speech and there was nothing in it to which I could legitimately take exception.

Davidson and his colleagues carried the measure to approve the Prayer Book by 241 votes to 88, a far smaller minority than was expected; for Protestants and Anglo–Catholics in the constituencies had bombarded the members of Parliament.

On the following evening the House of Commons rejected the measure by 230 to 205 votes and so changed the subsequent history of the relations between Church and State in England.

Historians have inconclusively debated the cause of this unforeseen débâcle. Everyone is agreed that the debate went badly; that the advocates of the measure spoke dismally, and its enemies spoke with persuasive hostility. Its chief enemy was Joynson Hicks the Home Secretary, a devout evangelical. The argument, 'I am conscientiously opposed to these Anglo–Catholic innovations in my Protestant Church', was a more convincing argument than the plea of expediency, 'if we have this revised book we shall have less anarchy'. Here appeared to be a battle between religious feelings and ecclesiastical policy, and in such matters feelings are a hundred times as strong as policy. And Parliament represented not only the people of England but of Scotland and Wales and Northern Ireland. Some presbyterians of Scotland, some dissenters of England and Wales, could not vote for a book which brought the Church of England the smallest step nearer to the Church of Rome and therefore, they presumed, dug a deeper ditch between the Anglicans and the 'reformed' Protestants. The head of all the Celts, Lloyd George, Welsh ex–Baptist, voted against the measure.

But the most emotional of these non–English speeches came from a Presbyterian of the extreme left, the member for Paisley, Rosslyn Mitchell. This was a rant against popery worthy of the seventeenth century. When posterity reads Mitchell's speech in Hansard, it cannot understand how the orator could be other than ridiculous in the year of grace 1927, and thinks it a blot upon the prestige of the House of Commons if such a speech gained a single vote. But all the witnesses are agreed, that Mitchell's rant swayed many votes.

A majority of English members voted for the measure.

The House of Commons had not intended to order wives to go on promising to obey their husbands or clergymen to go on condemning to everlasting death all who failed to believe that

bad men are burnt or the Church of England to go on celebrat-
ing a saint who did not exist because he was a misprint. But
this was the legal effect of refusing the measure.

Henson was not in the House to see what happened, for he
needed to go back to his diocese to institute a vicar. And the
words which he wrote on the morning after registered the
second big change of mind in his life –

*The episcopate can hardly sink so low as to accept a policy from a majority of*
*the House of Commons.*

In these words he threw overboard, without marking it, the
theory of Church and State which he advocated for more than
quarter of a century; the theory that because the Church of
England is a national Church its government lies rightly with
Parliament. Anyone who reads the speech of Rosslyn Mitchell,
and then hears the evidence of its potency, must drop any such
theory in the small hours of a night. On 15 December 1927 the
House of Commons disqualified itself as a sober and responsible government of the Church of England.

Henson diagnosed some personal causes for the rejection.
He thought that the bishops were unpopular, and that some
Members of Parliament voted not against the book but against
the bishops who approved the book. The Conservatives still
resented the attempt of Davidson and his friends to mediate in
the General Strike of the previous year. The more Protestant
members still resented not so much the inability of bishops to
control ritualists but the encouragement which a few bishops
gave to ritualists – Winnington-Ingram of London because he
encouraged all good work and had the charitable illusion that
everybody did good work, Michael Furse of St. Albans
because he was a high churchman by conviction. Henson
thought that some more Christian members of Parliament
resented the Modernist utterances of Bishop Barnes of
Birmingham, whose sermon at St. Paul's Cathedral, a month
before, was interrupted by a brawling canon.

These personal diagnoses by Henson have small probability
and lack confirmation from other evidence. That other evidence shows a resentment against one bishop whom he failed
to mention, himself. Several witnesses are agreed that his

phrase the *Protestant underworld* gave lasting offence. Instead of seeing that he meant, as he intended, the Rosslyn Mitchells of the world, they assumed that he lumped the entire evangelical movement, heirs of the Reformation, under this damning phrase. Several witnesses believed that the Prayer Book was lost in the House of Commons because Henson talked with contempt of the *Protestant underworld*. That judgement is very unlikely to be correct. But it rests on more basis in contemporary documents than Henson's own doctrine that the offending bishops were Winnington-Ingram, or Furse, or Barnes.

History sees that the causes of rejection were not personal. The people of England, most of the members of the Church of England, were content with Archbishop Cranmer and his book, and the way in which it was modified, illegally but with pastoral care, by their vicars. They had no desire to see change in the Prayer Book. They hardly thought the battle worth fighting if any weighty body of opponents scrupled.

Henson was not quite exempt from blame for the situation in which he found himself. By the time he became a bishop the Gadarene descent of the Church authorities had begun, and he made but hesitant efforts to check its rush. The bishops had been blamed – most unreasonably blamed but still blamed – for not keeping ritual in order. Therefore they committed a series of blunders. They brought to Parliament a Prayer Book which two out of the three responsible Church newspapers abused; forced the House of Commons to argue its contents and so to prove itself (what no sensible person doubted beforehand) a deplorable body for debating ways of prayer; and put the book forward in conditions where members of the House of Commons could plead that by voting down the book they were saving the Church of England from itself. The bishops provoked a crisis in Church and State, and rubbed the nose of the Church of England in the dust, for a book which few people wanted badly. When we study the consequences of this far-reaching disaster, and remember the man-hours which afterwards resulted for commissions on Church and State, and are disturbed that new liturgies are called by inappropriate names like Series 2 or Series 3, our instinct is to pillory Saklatvala the Communist Parsee because he voted not merely

against a different Church but against a different religion, and
Rosslyn Mitchell because he hardly ever entered the House of
Commons and dabbled in theosophy and had no manner of
understanding for the subject of which he talked with such
passion. But on reflection we cannot praise the bishops for
tactics.

For the sake of very small gains, and without real backing as
distinct from backing in Church Assembly, they risked a
constitutional crisis and invited speeches and snide articles and
anonymous letters from fanatics. They did this because:

(1)  militant Members of Parliament twenty years before, in a
     forgotten epoch sundered from the present by world war,
     demanded that ritual be controlled;
(2)  because bishops met 'illegalities' in their parishes and their
     consciences were uneasy that they neither could nor would
     call offenders to order;
(3)  because the Church Assembly was new and had no political
     sense and was full of ecclesiastical laymen who represented
     a small minority of the real Church;
(4)  because they were led by an archbishop with the experience
     of a Solomon and prestige of a Cranmer, but whose
     axioms were formed between 1870 and 1890 and whose
     most painful memories touched the ritual troubles of late
     Victorian England.

Four days after the vote Archbishop Davidson summoned
the bishops to Lambeth to consider what they should do. The
newspapers were filled with contempt for the Church as
creature and slave of the State, and the atmosphere was
emotional. Davidson was always at his best in such a crisis for
he could not be swayed by the heat of a moment. It was
possible to try again; that is, slightly to modify the book, pass
it again through Church Assembly, and expect that the House
of Commons would be too ashamed of itself to wreck again.
They could make a strong declaration that the House of
Commons had no authority over the worship of the Church
and the bishops would administer their dioceses as though the
new Prayer Book was law. This second plan had the demerit
that it could do nothing to cure the 'anarchy' in parochial
worship and looked like too hostile an onslaught on the State.
They could set up a committee to consider what alterations

ought now to be made in the relations between Church and State. And finally, at the extreme, they could lead a national campaign for the separation of Church and State, that is for disestablishment.

The bishops tried the three first of these plans in succession. They carried a slightly modified book through the Church Assembly, though with smaller majorities (27 April 1928), and saw it rejected a second time by the House of Commons (14 June 1928). They then made a strong declaration that they would administer their dioceses as though the book had passed; and appointed an Archbishops' Commission on Church and State to consider what changes in the relationship should be proposed. To gain time and diminish emotion, Archbishop Davidson of Canterbury resigned his see on the plea of age (he was eighty, and the word 'octogenarian' had been bandied about), the first Archbishop of Canterbury for 650 years voluntarily to break the marriage between himself and his see. The resignation gained valuable months. Even the most hot-headed enemies of the State's behaviour could not expect anything to be done till a new archbishop sat in the chair of St. Augustine.

Henson stood just before the tumble. But at this moment his prestige stood higher than at any other point in his life. About March 1927 Cambridge undergraduates played the game of caricature-letters to *The Times* and produced a limerick:

Dear Sir,

The affairs of the realm
Demand a strong hand at the helm,
A hand, Sir, that I
Am prepared to supply.

Yours faithfully,

Herbert Dunelm:

At that moment many members of the Church of England valued this strength. They saw that the House of Commons committed outrage, and wanted one of their leaders to say so, and found their mouthpiece in Henson. When Archbishop Davidson retired, a few people pressed hard that Henson should succeed to the chair of St. Augustine, and imagination finds it hard to conceive what would have happened. That was an impossibility. Lang of York succeeded naturally to Canterbury. But Archbishop Davidson and the Crown came under far more serious pressure that Henson be moved from Durham to be Archbishop of York. This was not the idea of Stanley Baldwin the prime minister. Baldwin thought that the greatest service which he could render the Church of England at this juncture was to get Winnington-Ingram out of the see of London, and had to be discouraged from the plan to use the see of York as a pawn in that game. Discussion produced the superlative advice of young William Temple for the see of York. Henson liked Temple and did not mind. He admitted to himself that to *refuse* the see of York would be pleasant but had no wish to change sees.

In these circumstances of the second half of 1928, when the House of Commons rejected the revised book for a second time and Archbishop Davidson resigned to gain rest for himself and a breathing-space for the Church, one part of the future was predictable: a bishop, probably several bishops, though a small minority, would regard the present link between Church and State as an intolerable restriction on Christian liberty and ask for disestablishment. This expectation was fulfilled, but in two surprising ways; first, only one of the bishops took this way; and second, that bishop was hitherto the staunchest defender of establishment, the advocate to the limit of parliamentary power in the Church because the nation had an interest in the national church.

More than anyone else Henson lost the battle.

Archbishop Davidson could and did resign, anyway it was time. Archbishop Lang was in favour of the book and saw that Parliament could not stop him using it and hardly minded that the book was illegal, it was no more illegal than many of the things they already did to everyone's comfort. The Commons told them to put their house in order and when twenty-five years later they twice proposed how to do it, the Commons refused any such proposal and they might as well get on with their work and cease to worry.

Bishops went ahead, allowing the more sensible changes, so that clergy need no longer consign so many millions to the flames and the Church of England could celebrate a real though still lamentably obscure saint instead of a printer's error. If the newspapers said that they were governed by Parliament that was not their experience. They went happily on, as though the thunders of the House of Commons had nothing to do with the matter. Practical men before 1927–8, they were practical men afterwards.

Henson alone was suffering from shock. He had a theory of Church and State not shared by other bishops. The House of Commons not merely tore up his theory but danced among the shreds.

Rosslyn Mitchell in the House, and all the anonymous letters in the post-bag, contributed. For quarter of a century Henson advocated the happiest relations with the Protestant denominations. But now Protestant denominations, or their fanatical members, behaved disgracefully towards a Church which wished to make a few modest adjustments in its prayers. And this resurrected the latent passion from Henson's past. Before 1927 his attitude was, these godly and sensible Christians of the Reformation ought to have their say in our national Church. After 1928 his attitude was, these bigots must have no part in our Church and the only way to get them out is disestablishment.

Perhaps heredity had nothing to do with his swing in mind from one extreme to the other. Yet we do not forget (what no one then knew) that his father left the Church of England because the State interfered in the truth of its doctrine.

Henson's private papers show a concealed motive at work.

On 11 May 1927 – that is, half a year before the Revised Prayer Book came before Parliament and therefore nothing to do with what happened in the House of Commons – Henson made an entry in his diary. He said that he was reconciling himself *to the abhorred necessity of Disestablishment. The fact is that I cannot endure the possibility of the Crown patronage in the hands of a Labour prime minister.*

Bishops had not much concern over patronage. They all accepted office under that patronage. They hardly minded if the prime minister was not an Anglican, for they knew that he consulted the Archbishop of Canterbury, that he must get his recommendation past the King who must be an Anglican, that the chosen must be elected by a majority of the canons of the cathedral and then consecrated by other bishops. The system had plenty of safeguards. Henson not merely accepted two sees in succession at the nomination of an ex-Baptist but was proud and saw nothing wrong and was grateful to Lloyd George. A man chosen by the leaders of the nation is more honoured, and afterwards wields more influence, than one elected only by a denominational committee. At no point in his life, whether before or after 1928, did Henson denounce on principle the patronage of the Crown. Indeed, before he died, he accepted another appointment from a prime minister.

But Socialism! He associated it with the secularists whose heckling he fought from soap-boxes in Victoria Park, the atheists of the Gasworkers Union in Barking, the Bolsheviks of the Russian revolution and Lenin's demolition of the Russian Church, the political support for breaches of contract which he thought to be inherent in the General Strike. With the government of Ramsay MacDonald in 1924 he lived under a Labour regime and was not able to think that anything very awful happened – Hewlett Johnson to be a dean but Hewlett Johnson had not run the red flag up the towers of Manchester Cathedral, Barnes to be Bishop of Birmingham and Barnes was confessedly a middling bishop and a clumsy theologian but nobody could think him a bad man or a bad mathematician. This fear of Socialist prime ministers was not the result of past experience. Yet it ran in Henson's make-up. He could not have conceived that the next Socialist prime minister after Ramsay MacDonald would be an Anglican who exercised the patronage of the Crown with as conscientious a sense of responsibility as any prime minister of the twentieth century.

As the revised Prayer Book came nearer to Parliament the thought recurred: *I could almost wish that Parliament would reject the Prayer Book Measure, and thus give a fair and ample plea for advocating Disestablishment, for the prospect of the Crown Patronage in the hands of a Labour Prime Minister is terrible indeed* (17 November 1927).

The conversion of Henson to disestablishment was the second turnabout of his career. In 1900–1 he publicly threw Anglo-Catholicism overboard to be a liberal Modernist and the leading defender of establishment in England. In 1927–8 he publicly threw overboard the theory of establishment and for the rest of his years advocated the separation of Church and State.

This conversion astonished everyone, from Archbishop Davidson downward. Some, it shocked. Even now, the reader of Henson's mind is startled at the suddenness, in mental terms the *violence* of the swing. To remain established on the present terms is *spiritual treason*; the Church guilty of the criminal folly of selling its birthright for a mess of pottage.

From the earliest moment that this state of mind peeped into public, as early as December 1927, Henson began to worry those who saw subtleties. King George V was less capable than Henson of perceiving nuance. He was equally capable of seeing the obvious, and with a soldierly eye discerned what touched his throne. At his side Lord Stamfordham knew well, as the King's less experienced mind could not, that the place of the Church in the historic constitution of Britain was delicately near to the place of the monarchy. Stamfordham tried to persuade Henson that the Enabling Act could be amended so that Parliament need not control worship, and that this promised a less perilous way forward than raising the issue of disestablishment. Henson thought such a way forward to be a cul-de-sac, and could not see why disestablishment might affect the crown adversely. Later he had a private conversation with Stamfordham, who besought him, 'Think of the King!' Henson replied that the King stood to gain rather than lose by being dissociated from the Church of England, and be set in an equal relation to all his subjects. Lord Stamfordham could only shake his head mournfully.

At the meeting of bishops in Lambeth Palace soon after the vote; in a series of speeches and sermons, of which the most potent was an electrifying sermon before Cambridge University on 29 January, 1928;[1] in several articles and two short books – *The Book and the Vote,* and *Reflections on the Crisis*, and finally in his *Second Quadrennial Charge* (December 1928), Henson declared that the establishment must be *mended or*

[1] At one of the sparkling phrases in this sermon a guffaw was heard from the gallery and downstairs an undergraduate thought that he could not mistake the voice and that it belonged to Michael Ramsey of Magdalene College. Michael Ramsey said many years later that this sermon was one of the most powerful and persuasive utterances he ever heard; that they all knew whither Henson was leading them, and yet he kept them on tenterhooks, eager to hear what would come next.

*ended*. In saying this he was not unique. Other bishops believed the same. The archbishops were engaged in appointing a commission to advise them how to mend. The anxiety which Henson caused among other bishops was not this *mend or end,* but the overtones in what he said.

From the first he plainly believed that *mending* was a dream and *ending* a duty. Not without a touch of cynicism in his speech, he voted for the motion to appoint the commission on Church and State. But he too evidently thought it a waste of time, and refused to give evidence at the invitation of the commission. He suspected, and made no effort to conceal that he suspected, this commission of being no determined effort to mend, but a way of cooling heat and gaining time and allowing the Church to forget the disgrace. And this was the second overtone. We have little time. To talk of mending is to talk, and to postpone an urgent need to an invisible future. We need to mend *now*; and since we cannot mend *now*, we need to end *now*.

This was not realistic of Henson. The British are a stable people, and have a habit of mind with their constitution, that though in course of time it is bound to need change, it is best changed little by little, adapted, one step at a time. To demand a constitutional revolution is to try to force a break in history; and once we embark upon so radical a disturbance of our axioms we may find consequences which we neither expected nor wanted. Therefore in the adapting of a constitution we should refuse to thrust out upon a dark sea where we cannot see the reefs ahead, but remain on the ground that we know and attempt to cultivate it better and get rid of the weeds.

In the shock and anger and emotion of those first months, men talked of schism in the Church of England, and suggested that if the bishops did not cure the constitution at once they would form their separate Anglican Church which would be in control of its own worship. Henson believed that he could put himself at the head of a movement to demand freedom from the State. He was quick to discover that his head had no tail. His own dean, Bishop Welldon, said that nobody wanted the Revised Book anyway, why should anyone make a fuss about the loss of what no one wanted?

By the end of January 1929 Henson was aware that he had

achieved the unenviable situation of being a leader without any followers. He felt ridiculous, and sad. The feeling did not make him change his mind. For the rest of his time as a bishop he could hardly make a speech without a reference to the need for disestablishment if the Church was to be healthy. Any ill which he saw, like a ritual brawl in Marazion in Cornwall, he fancied could be mended by disestablishment. But he knew himself to be a *lone wolf*. In February 1929 he felt himself to be as unpopular as in December 1917.

It was a big change. Henson reached the height of his national influence during 1926. Then he was a leader in the revision of the Prayer Book, he had the ear of the House of Lords, his speeches on temperance or education were heard with respect, even on strikes and Labour his common sense and honesty won attention. Men talked of him as perhaps the right person to succeed Archbishop Davidson in the day, certain to be soon, when he died or retired. Three or four years later all this had vanished. He was *unstable*: changed his mind in a moment; was not just a radical but an eccentric radical, an *episcopal Jacobin, the imp of the Church of England*. He was conscious that he was no longer a leader in meetings of bishops, but an individualist. Once he was Archbishop Davidson's lieutenant. Now he was Archbishop Lang's critic and gadfly, remote in sympathy and feeling from Lambeth. Men listened with interest and amusement but refused to follow. *The sense of failure has taken hold of me, and on all hands I find myself 'at a loose end'. I don't see the direction in which I ought to turn. The control of ecclesiastical affairs has passed out of my hands: and I am conscious of having lost such 'following' as I had* (19 January 1930).

More than once at this time he wondered whether he did right to accept a bishopric, whether his temperament was suited to a bishop's work.

This melancholy must not be taken too seriously. When reading Henson's melancholies we should always be conscious that from time to time depression swept over him and he used his journal as a release for the demon of the dark. But this fits other evidence of the time. He believed that the series of events cut short his public career – *reducing me to the nowise impressive situation . . . of an extinct volcano*. On 27 June 1929 he reached his nadir by avoiding the ceremony at Durham University which gave Stanley Baldwin an honorary degree, because his presence might be unwelcome.

The hardest to bear was Ella. She could not see what he was at. Conscious of disapprobation when he went abroad, he felt it harder to feel disapprobation when he came home. She could not see why he should want to impoverish his clergy, or move out of Bishop Auckland, or lose the seat in the House of Lords whence he did so much good. She persisted, and this was painful. He sadly noted little marks of declining status. On the first Sunday in January 1931, for the first time, no reporter bothered to bear away the notes after his sermon in the cathedral.

He tried a little campaign in his diocese by talking to meetings of church councillors. All but one of the meetings were polite.

While he was a bishop he never altered his mind about the separation of Church and State. When the commission on Church and State reported in February 1936 he thought nothing of its diverse recommendations and said so at Church Assembly in a devastating speech of thirty-five minutes. He made no converts. They clapped him to heaven but it was the expression and not the opinion that captivated. The Archdeacon of Stoke-on-Trent agreed with him, but everyone valued the archdeacon as an eccentric of harmless opinions and a big heart.

His national influence was further burdened, at least with one important group in the Church, by the load of a notorious phrase: *the Protestant underworld*. He withdrew all that was untrue about the phrase in a speech in the House of Lords. It did not satisfy his critics. He was pressed again to withdraw, more unreservedly. Even his wise old lawyer stepped out of the normal line of duty to beg him to withdraw because the phrase so lessened his influence in the affairs of the English Church. Henson refused to withdraw. If men understood him to apply it to all Protestants they were guilty of wilful polemic. The fact existed, *a volcano in English society, liable to explosions of No Popery fanaticism, which carries politicians off their feet by its violence, and stains the national record with the crudest exhibitions of fatuity and bigotry*. If this fanaticism existed, which no sensible observer doubted, why should he not call it by its proper name?

Because he would not withdraw, henceforth he carried a label around his neck. Evangelicals never trusted him again. That was a sad diminution of his national influence in the Church everywhere outside his own diocese of Durham. In part it was due to a childhood experience of the sects; in part due to the hardly controllable tongue of a brilliant conversationalist; in part due to his training that men should speak the truth, and if no one else said it, that was because they lacked his courage as well as his imprudence. The world of the Ian Paisleys really existed, too easily forgotten by those moderate reasonable godly men and women who were the norm of the Church of England.

In 1932 he became the aggressor by a pamphlet *Sibbes and Simeon* which assailed evangelicals for their administration of patronage trusts, asked for the abolition of such patronage trusts, and hoped that meanwhile no self-respecting clergyman would accept the offer of a benefice from such a trust. This was a declaration of war, for these patronage trusts were important to evangelicals as a way in which they maintained continuity in scriptural teaching in evangelical parishes. The evangelical newspaper the *Record* even printed a note that Henson's *mingled loathing and contempt for evangelicals is displayed on almost every page*.

In these conditions his mind, as in the 1880s, moved towards Catholicism. This too was hard. His memory of the fights in Ilford; his watching of the Dreyfus case; his arrival at the sober conviction that the doctrine of apostolic succession divided the Church; the countless condemnations from his pen or mouth against Roman Catholics or Anglo-Catholics – these stood on the record and he wished to retract not a syllable. But where was he? He could not be a Modernist for he had too devout a faith in the incarnate and crucified Christ. If he could not be an evangelical or an Anglo-Catholic, what was he? He asked himself whether he would ever be able to understand himself.

In July 1833 John Keble preached that assize sermon in Oxford which was commonly taken to be the start of the Oxford Movement with such mighty influence on Catholic

opinion within the Church of England. In July 1933 high
churchmen all over England organized commemorations of
that centenary to which they owed so religious a debt. Keble
and his heirs taught the Church of England not to be so insular,
to lift up its eyes to the faith and devotion of the centuries.
They revived sacramental life, were strong that the Church
had inherent rights apart from the State, and cared for the
beauty and dignity of ways of worship.

The managers were very bold. They invited Henson to
preach two centenary sermons, one in Durham Cathedral (11
July) and the other on the very day of the centenary (14 July) at
St. Mary Abbot's, Kensington. They were bold because they
wanted to give thanks for a Catholic tradition and Henson
sounded so anti-Catholic. No doubt they needed a historian,
and wished for a speaker who would say what was worth
hearing. But they could hardly have issued such invitations
unless they failed to take Henson's anti-Catholic prejudice too
seriously.

The invitations cast Henson into a quandary. At first he
thought the centenary silly. Then he wondered how he could
speak without seeming to be the partisan of a party to which he
did not belong. Then he accepted – both invitations.

He confessed that all movements are oddly mingled. But he
thanked God for the Oxford Movement, and its beneficent
consequences in the Church of England. His old love of Dean
Church poured back into his heart, and Dean Church was the
historian through whose book most of England liked the
leaders of the Oxford Movement. Henson praised them for
their protest against the materialism of their age, their ideal of
consecrated living, the severity of life, the simplicity and
sincerity of character. The new Henson burnt what he had
adored by demolishing a saying of Mandell Creighton which
once he would almost have approved: 'I am an Englishman
first and a churchman afterwards' – *a saying,* said Henson,
*which is either a mere platitude, for every man must be born before he
can be baptized, or the very essence of spiritual treason.* These men
of the Oxford Movement called the Church back to the sense
that it is a Church; and therefore not the creature nor the agent
of the State; but free, independent, holding a divine truth
given by its Master, and linked by its ministry to the apostles

through ordination. *Is a State-created State-controlled establishment even a tolerable version of that Society which, to the inspired thought of St. Paul, was 'the Body of Christ, the fulness of Him that filleth all in all'?* The Oxford Movement reasserted the Catholic nature of the Church, and so revived from long disregard a cardinal truth.

These two centenary addresses marked the new phase of Henson's life. This hammer of the Catholics recovered, and stated nobly, the sense of what the Church owed, for all their faults, to Catholics. The Church is a body of people with its own order, and way of life, and teaching, and manner of worship, which no State can touch; in its inner life free because it is the Body of Christ.

This side of Henson – we may call it his earlier side, or his young priest's side – was strengthened by the appearance of a new religious movement.

Frank Buchman was already an unsuccessful evangelist of thirty when he had an experience of conversion at a little Cumbrian church near Keswick. He was an American and a Lutheran; jovial and brisk, clean and outgoing, with a strange magic in the personality which some resented and some could not understand and some revered. His Lutheran tradition was pietist; that is, biblical, not very churchy, believing more in groups of holy and like-minded men and women than in congregations organized ecclesiastically, not frightened of mysticism, and not far from near-Quaker doctrines of inner light, or of the leading of God in the heart. The experience near Keswick came when he visited the Keswick Convention, an annual meeting of evangelical Christians for prayer and the encouragement of practical holiness. The Keswick Convention attracted numerous British leaders of religion including Anglicans. But it could not easily fit the restrained Anglican tradition, for its members used the language of 'perfectionism' – under God's grace and in His hand we may *now* live perfect lives.

The basis of a religious movement was present; an American evangelist who understood the techniques of mass evangelism, and wanted to bring all good people together in a movement of holiness which crossed the border of denominations. At first, like the early Methodists, it was simply a society to encourage holiness. Revealingly Buchman called it the First Century Christian Fellowship. The pietist meetings for common devotion and encouragement were called house-parties; a name which suggests the lay, unchurchy stress of the new movement. Soon the mark or message of those meetings was the old Keswick perfectionism cast into the form of four absolutes: absolute honesty; absolute purity; absolute un-selfishness; absolute love.

During the 1920s Buchman visited both Oxford and Cambridge. He found ready hearers among groups of under-graduates. They were not content with the cynicism of post-war Britain or with the university of Evelyn Waugh. They saw Churches quarrelling over trivialities, and longed for ideals, and heard a man who talked of absolutes here and now, and who cared nothing for the disagreements of Churches. And the odd magical touch in the prosaic personality played its part. He knew how to use the men who sat at his feet. He turned them into leaders of groups.

At first the devotional method was in embryo. When it took shape, it included 'the quiet time', a silent meditation early in the day when the soul listened for the direct leading of God and resolved to act accordingly; a 'sharing', group therapy before group therapy was invented; a sharing which included public confessions; and this was the principal innovation, for it seemed like a revival of the public confessions of the primitive Christians. Since these were confessions by men in their late teens or early twenties they frequently concerned sex. The words 'absolute purity' and 'absolute honesty' were not mere sound. The difficulty, the embarrassment, the revulsion of public confession under such conditions could and did disgust. But for others it made an overwhelming new experience of the coming of the grace of God to forgive.

Using a group of undergraduates on a tour to convert, Buchman acquired by accident a name. In South Africa a railway porter chalked on the luggage the words Oxford Group. Buchman accepted the chance nickname. By 1933 the name Oxford Group was widely received to describe a move-ment which at base was American but rapidly became inter-national. And it gained adherents in high places; the heads of two if not three Oxford colleges, an Oxford Professor of

Divinity, the Primate of Denmark, an Indian bishop bearing the historic name of Westcott, the sister of an English bishop, and one of the holiest missionaries in India. Men thought of it as a new kind of Methodism, and were anxious that this time the Church of England should not lose its enthusiasts but should bless and baptize whatever in the movement could be seen to be of the hand of God. Archbishop Lang of Canterbury received and blessed Dr Buchman and a hundred of his workers at a meeting in Lambeth Palace. Three days later (7 October 1933) Bishop Winnington-Ingram held a commissioning service in St. Paul's Cathedral, which was filled with 7,000 people. Young men under the dome challenged the journalists about their personal faith. Five hundred men and women marched down the aisles to receive communion and the blessing of the bishop. Winnington-Ingram compared himself to Pope Innocent III, giving his blessing to St. Francis of Assisi despite his fear of the new methods.

The movement came into Henson's life in three ways. It affected people in his diocese, and parish priests asked the bishop what ought to be their attitude. Henson loved Oxford, and some in Oxford resented the name Oxford Group, as though this controversial evangelism was a child of the university. And thirdly, far more emotionally for Henson, one of the young men for whom he cared much, the young man whom he thought to be the most promising of 'his' ordinands, became a disciple of Dr Buchman, went off to Canada as an evangelist, and seemed to Henson to lose his way and destroy a promising vocation. Henson began to collect evidence of the damage which this emotional movement could do to emotional young men. And when he discovered public confession he was afflicted with revulsion. About sex Henson was a Victorian. Sex was intimate and sacred, and he was sure that the right attitude was reverence. Flaunting of sexuality filled him with nausea.

In March 1933 he published *The Group Movement* as the first part of his charge at the third Quadrennial Visitation of his diocese (new edition with new preface, December 1933). He kept saying that not for a moment would he question the good which the movement did to individuals. But the charge was a sustained indictment of the Oxford Group. And as such it fits into a new mood of his life since he passed into the wilderness after the rejection of the Revised Prayer Book.

Here was the confessional, *exposed to its worst risks and stripped of its protective discipline*; here were adolescents acting as father–confessors, the blind leading the blind; here was the fascination of prurience as well as a moral ideal; here was an idea of guidance as immediate inspiration, taking the place of reasonable discussion and sensible judgement; here was a movement which seemed to have little place for the poor but went for Oxford undergraduates and political leaders and capitalists, its work done in *hotels* and *centres of fashion;* here was a movement claiming to be above denominations but like all such movements turning already into another denomination.

The charge on the Oxford Group showed in one booklet the weakness of Henson's pugnacity and the virility of Henson's faith. On the one hand this is the hunter of Birkenhead come back to life, the prejudiced fighter, as when he compared Buchman's 'dictatorship' in the movement to the dictatorship of Stalin. He was not well fitted for the impartial critique which would have helped because his inner revulsion from any such movement ran too deep. The *Times Literary Supplement* (16 March) called the booklet brilliant and convincing. Other reviewers were less kind. One amused him because the word 'sharing' appeared as 'shaving'.

At the other end the charge gave him the chance to wear sackcloth and ashes for his Church. History shows that all such movements of enthusiasm in religion stem from a failing Church. Men cry for otherworldiness because the Church is worldly. They suffer illusions about the Holy Spirit because the Church fails even to tell them of the Holy Spirit. They engage in public confession because the Church fails in its quiet and private care. Ought we not to be led by this exaggerated talk of guidance to listen in quiet far more than we do? Ought we not to remember that our Prayer Book provides for private confession and to make that easily available to all in such a need? Are we not as a Church being *formal, faithless and futile?* He refrained from using this moment for another attack on the establishment. But is it not right, he asked, that we are conventional, compromising, unreal? Is not Christian witness respectability? *Perhaps no Church in Christendom has . . . been so completely despiritualized as the Church of England.* We need new resolution to self-surrender, new commitment to discipleship, a new sense of the brotherhood of servants of Christ which is the Church.

And so, in this charge, the Savonarola who was inside Henson could again be heard; the cry of the ascetic of Bethnal Green, the voice of the Barking priest; against fashionable Christianity, and rich Christianity, and respectable Christianity conformed to this world.

Naturally Anglo-Catholics were surprised and pleased at this strong recommendation of private confession from so notoriously anti-Catholic a bishop. Between 1928 and 1934 they came to recognize that Henson was not the foe that they thought, and that sometimes he could say what they wanted to say better than they could say it for themselves.

This attitude of the Catholics was confirmed by an accident. A famous Unitarian, L. P. Jacks, gave three sermons in Liverpool Cathedral at special services. Henson preferred to take no notice. But his friend and enemy, truculent Lord Hugh Cecil, embarked on a prosecution of Dean Dwelly of Liverpool and demanded that the untruculent Archbishop Temple of York should try Bishop David of Liverpool in his court. This threw all the Churches into confusion. Were Unitarians Christians? Even if they were (which all but extremist bigots refused to deny) would the Church compromise its soul by allowing someone who did not believe in the divinity of Christ to preach in its pulpits? The argument raged up and down the country.

Inside his vast bubbling frame Archbishop William Temple had not only a very kindly nature but a fund of common sense. He refused to hear any case in any court. But when pamphleteers said that the Church of England no longer minded about the divinity of Christ, he could hardly do nothing. He told Lord Hugh Cecil that he would bring the matter to the Upper House of the Convocation of York. He brought it thither on 7 June 1934.

Henson wanted none of this. He believed Lord Hugh Cecil misguided. But since the matter must come to the Convocation of York where he was the senior bishop, he was forced to declare his mind. And when he inspected his mind he found it unhesitating. Bishop David was wrong.

Some Catholics and some evangelicals wondered whether Henson was a Christian. The Hereford Scandal caused scruples. He refused to affirm two great miracles of the New Testament, and some doubted whether this refusal to affirm was possible for a Christian. In their eyes he stood for laxity in Christian teaching. They expected him to want Unitarians to be able to preach sermons in pulpits of the Church of England.

They did not know their Henson. Before his ordination in Cuddesdon church and again before his consecration to be a bishop in the abbey, he examined his soul and realized that the incarnation of the Son of God, and his death for the redemption of the world, were the heart of the faith by which he lived and without which Christianity was nothing. He preferred not to be asked whether a Unitarian could preach in a Trinitarian pulpit. If he was asked, he knew that to answer *yes* denied his conviction about religious truth.

The Upper House of the Convocation of York met in the hall of St. William's College in York. It was a fine panelled room, with portraits of bishops on the walls, and a refectory table where the archbishop sat at one end and the junior bishop at the other. The morning started chilly, and the windows were kept shut, and despite the month a fire burnt cheerfully in the grate. But the morning grew warmer, the room turned stifling, and this affected Henson, who was a fanatic about fresh air. He began to feel poorly.

In his pleasant soft voice, and with his charming manner, Bishop David argued that all the anxiety had a touch of hysteria. The faith is a mystery which words cannot sufficiently express. Must we now insist on the words of the creed? May a bishop take into account the reverent intentions of a man like Jacks, whose goodness everyone recognizes? In our churches we sing hymns by Unitarian authors ('Nearer my God to thee, 'Thy kingdom come', etc.). We recommend people to read books by Unitarians. Is not the anxiety due to the history of the word Unitarian and a certain prejudice arising from that history?

Suffering the discomforts of asphyxiation, Henson read a

long and prepared speech. He thought that he read it very badly. To himself he sounded brutal and unpersuasive.

He said that he had no desire to cast aspersions on the Bishop of Liverpool. He only desired to affirm that the bishops *would endure nothing that seemed to throw doubt on the cardinal verity of the Incarnation*. Not only the *credit* of the Church of England was at stake but its *very character;* for if this new departure became a precedent it *would compromise even fatally the claim of the Church of England to be a true part of the Holy Catholic Church*. We use Unitarian hymns rightly because we read into them the faith by which we live. *Belief in the divinity of Christ was not the peculium of the Church of England, but the constitutive belief of the Church Catholic itself*. Christianity is a religion of redemption and Unitarians accept neither the fact nor the need. *Jesus . . . has the same absolute* claim upon all men's worship and loyalty as belongs to God. A persuasion of this sort of uniqueness attaching to Jesus seems the *essential characteristic of what has in the field of history been Christianity*.

Bishop Burroughs of Ripon, sounding as though he had a bad cold in the head, supported Bishop David. Everyone else was strong behind Henson. So the matter ended; and Henson's former mortal enemy the *Church Times* raised him to lofty heights, his old friend *The Times* found his logic irresistible, and his old friend Dean Inge lamented that he deserted the cause of liberty of opinion.

The speech was persuasive. He devastated no one, pulled the leg of no one. The Bishop of Liverpool could not resent, the Unitarians could hardly deplore, Lord Hugh Cecil could bask. The speech had no sparkling phrases, no brilliance, no jests. The orator declined to use his oratory. To the reader of what he said the reason is obvious. He talked of what to him was the most sacred of subjects. He spoke of the cause of his way of life, the *raison d'être* of his existence as a Christian pastor. He wished only that he did not feel asphyxiated, and lamented the inadequacy of his words, and had no idea that he persuaded as seldom in his life.

Dean Inge thought that this was only another of Henson's turnabouts. Henson felt himself consistent with his past. We who see the inwardness of that past confess that Inge was wrong and Henson right. But this also must be said. The change in Henson's doctrine of Church and State, forced upon him by the rant of Rosslyn Mitchell and by the coming to power of the Labour Party, turned him to think again of the spiritual nature of the Church. Always he had known the Church as a body which in its essence no State could touch. Driven into the wilderness by the events of 1927–8, he realized how he stood in kinship with those high churchmen who asserted the rights of the Church as a divine society. Confronted with the establishment which he now rejected, he sought for the difference between the Church and the world, and so to affirm the Christian gospel whether the world cared to listen or to close its ears.

His national reputation rose again. The lone wolf of 1930 became the elder statesman of 1936. No longer a possible archbishop, no longer a leader in Church politics, no longer the adviser of a primate, still seen as exceptional and sometimes wrongheaded, this astringent unprelatical prelate was at last known to have compassion, and to be a pastor. This revival of reputation made a difference to two causes, vital for the nation, on which he now began to engage.

# 9. DIVORCE

A. P. HERBERT

England had a divorce law which many experts condemned. The 1857 Act introduced the possibility of divorce only for adultery, which was the one case allowed by the words of Christ reported in St. Matthew's gospel. But as economic prosperity pushed more and more citizens to join the middle class and gave them a measure of social freedom, and as women gained more social and political equality, partners were no longer so willing to put up with the miseries of a failed marriage which might fail for other reasons than adultery. Since they could only get a divorce after proving adultery, they either committed or pretended to commit adultery. In hotels on the south coast of England a brisk trade was conducted by managers whose servants were willing to testify in court that they found so-and-so in bed with so-and-so; and these arranged 'adulteries' were grossly repugnant to those who had no desire whatever to commit adultery but resorted to this corrupt sexuality or perjury to free a woman who no longer wished to share their bed and board. Lawyers who practised in divorce courts, and some social workers, and some clergymen, were sure that the law was intolerable and must be changed. A strong royal commission under Lord Gorell, before whom Henson gave evidence, reported as early as 1912 recommending wider grounds for divorce than the ground of adultery. But the bill founded upon this report, and introduced into Parliament after the war, failed to commend itself to a majority of the legislators.

Leading churchmen were among the enemies of change. Christianity stood for the sacredness of family life. If divorce were permitted for the sake of adultery, no other ground could be allowed, on the express authority of the New Testament. The Roman Catholic Church, represented in the House of Lords by a respectable body of peers, could not allow divorce on any ground and fought to the end a widening of the grounds for divorce. High Anglicans in the Church of England shared the point of view. But it was also shared by a large body of opinion which believed in the home and the family as the basis of the State, and regarded easy divorce with abhorrence, and was informed of the evidence that children of divorced parents might suffer disadvantage in their upbringing.

In 1935 Henson's old All Souls friend, Charles Oman, retired from one of the two seats representing Oxford University. The Conservative caucus at Oxford chose a dim candidate to succeed; and the electors refused, and astonished the world by returning not the Conservative but an independent, who though an Oxford man had not bothered to take his degree, and was famous for nothing more serious than light-hearted articles in *Punch*. A. P. Herbert, hastily taking not one degree but two, dedicated his parliamentary career to the reform of the law of divorce. Since government refused time he started with every disadvantage; and since the years 1936 and 1937 were the years of Edward VIII and Mrs Simpson, the ice on which he skated was at times as thin as a wafer. Men thought him too light a weight for the task. They accused him of making the most solemn subject trivial by turning it into fun. But, like all great clowns, he mocked the follies of the human race because he wanted to change their ways.

Underneath the cap and bells worked a serious reformer. His moral sense was not specially religious. Though the son of a lapsed Roman Catholic father and a mother who was a Selwyn and very Anglican, he called himself 'a non-playing member of the Church of England', with a respect for Cranmer's Book of Common Prayer and an affection for sentimental hymns of his childhood, but only a foul-weather worshipper, an 'inferior religious species'. His mind was more practical and more mocking. He just saw that a law which drives a man to get into bed with a woman whom he has never seen before is a silly law. And more than that; something deep inside him felt moral nausea at the collusions and prying chambermaids in the hotels of Brighton and the South Coast.

By persistence and good fortune he pushed his Marriage Bill as a private member's bill into the House of Commons. It widened the grounds of divorce to include cruelty, desertion for three years, and incurable insanity; and in the last months of 1936 the House of Commons (though not by a majority of its members, for more of them abstained than voted) passed the bill. The question therefore came before the House of Lords. And this debate was expected with the more trepidation because the House of Lords contained three groups less well represented in the House of Commons or not represented at all: a strong and respected body of Roman Catholic peers; a group of law lords who practised in the courts and knew the sufferings of marriage and divorce in their seamiest consequences; and the archbishops and senior bishops of the Church of England who were expected to give a lead on a decision which touched the Church and its moral law so intimately. Many clergy were known to be disquieted in conscience, especially at the thought that they might be compelled to allow the use of their churches for the remarriage in church of divorced persons. The bill tried to still their fears by a wise clause of relief. Under the 1857 Act they need not themselves marry a divorced parishioner but must lend their church to another clergyman if the marrying parties could find one to celebrate their wedding. Under Herbert's bill the clergyman need neither marry nor lend his church for the marriage. Thus it could be said that the conscience of no clergyman need be troubled unless he wished it to be troubled.

Henson's position was clear. The nature of the human race is such, that if divorce is prohibited, adultery and prostitution flourish exceedingly. The sexual drive is the strongest of human appetites. Facilities of divorce *may have their origin not in licentiousness, but in a high standard of marital obligation, in a jealous regard for the quality of the home, and in a keen sense of what equity requires in the treatment of the individual.* A large increase in the rate of divorces does not necessarily tell that the moral standard of the nation declines. It may simply tell that many more marriages were intolerable than we knew. Conversely, divorce must not be easy. We need to be sure that men and women do not wed frivolously and trivially; that young married folk do not suppose at the first breath of a quarrel that they must end their partnership and make no effort to be reconciled. For the sake of the State and the moral welfare of the people, husband and wife must be seen to be united by a strong and lasting obligation. This is the right belief which leads some Christian moralists to refuse divorce altogether. Therefore we need a middle way, which neither refuses divorce in such a way as to foster adultery or collusion, nor makes divorce so easy that it weakens the social fabric of the State which rests upon family life. This middle way, Henson told his diocesan conference, is attempted honestly by the Marriage Bill now before Parliament.[1]

After this diocesan conference Henson received a vast and moving mail from unhappy people whose predicament could not be healed under existing law, and many whose predicament could not be healed under Herbert's law.

The bill came for its second reading into the House of Lords on 24 June 1937. Henson went to the House intending to speak in the debate. He spoke more impishly than he intended. The reason was that he lost his notes for the speech. Though he spent the morning at the Athenaeum preparing, he preached a well-prepared sermon at Clerkenwell in the afternoon, and this circumstance caused him to forget his notes so that he arrived at the House of Lords needing to speak from what he could remember; and he always spoke best – if it is best to electrify an audience – without notes.

Two speakers spoke before him from the Bench of Bishops: Archbishop Lang of Canterbury and Bishop Michael Furse of St. Albans. Henson admired Lang as the finest orator after dinner whom he knew; but the man was for him just a little too pontifical – and he once refused to take part in the consecration of a Bishop of Hereford. Furse was everything which Henson distrusted in bishops – Anglo-Catholic, a man of emotion rather than reason, enthusiastic, and of a very large stature.

Lord Eltisley introduced the bill with moderation and good sense, the kind of speech which is the best type of speech for the House of Lords. A Roman Catholic peer said that the bill was un-Christian. And then came Lang.

Lang had persuaded himself into a peculiar position. The bill was good for the nation so he could not vote against. But it contradicted the mind of the Church, so he could not vote for. 'I must simply stand aside.'

Watching from the bar of the House, A. P. Herbert listened with pleasure to the beautiful timbre of Lang's voice and

---

[1] The address was reprinted in *Bishoprick Papers,* 12–21: conference of March 1937.

admired the ease of his command of words and the limpid clarity of his expression. But he described the speech as a 'stately feat upon a tight-rope'. Henson, who never in his life sat upon a fence, was offended by the balancing act.

Then, after a lawyer critical of the bill, came Michael Furse. To read his speech in Hansard is to know that the speaker understands not the first thing about collecting votes in a public assembly. He filled it with digressions and introduced his childhood as the seventh of ten children and his thirty-four years of happy married life. He asked the House to throw out the bill because it weakened marriage, but gave no rational motives for throwing out the bill. Furse was a missionary, an evangelist, a stout fighter of the old school, a foursquare Victorian. But he was ill adapted to a legislative assembly of the twentieth century.

So, after a good defence of the bill by another lawyer, Henson rose. He started naughtily by accusing the Bishop of St. Albans of not having read the bill, and more naughtily by demolishing him with the sarcasm of a single sentence: 'he also delighted us with much intimate and curious information'. So far from the bill bringing the law of England into conflict with the law of Christ it will bring it into a deeper and truer harmony. He assailed the Roman Catholic opponents – the corruptest communities known to the world have been those in which divorce was absolutely prohibited. Divorce may mean a desire not to degrade but to raise the standard of human life. He assailed Lang's use of evidence from the New Testament, which was curiously vulnerable. Not for many centuries, perhaps never, had an argument over the New Testament, put forward by an Archbishop of Canterbury, suffered such instant destruction from one of his bishops. *I believe if we pass this bill we shall rebuild a great many broken homes, and shall once more enable many children to have strength and comfort in an ordered domestic life, and shall, in that measure, strengthen the State by helping to rebuild it.*

Listening at the bar, A. P. Herbert was carried away by this torrent of argument. The bill was his baby, he loved and cherished its welfare. During the year he listened to countless speeches for and against the bill. He knew that this was his top moment, that never had he so enjoyed a speech. 'What art!

what ease! what dignified mischief! what scholarly sincerity!'
Herbert wished that Henson was a member of the House of
Commons.[1]

The secret of Henson's skill in debate was not merely the
manner, the humour, the boldness at times almost brazenness,
the tone rising up to passion, and the crystal clarity of his
structure. He mastered his subject beforehand. He read the
papers, old Blue Books, the pamphlets by contemporaries. He
always wrote several letters to friends whom he knew to be
experts asking for their opinion. To leave his notes behind was
no disaster, for he had the subject at his fingertips.

A. P. Herbert to the Bishop of Durham – Monday 28 June
1937

My Lord

May I very heartily congratulate and thank you for your magnificent speech on Thursday, every sentence of which was a work of art
to all, a joy to me, and a stout and inimitable blow for the cause.

                              Yours sincerely,

                              Alan Herbert.


Herbert was right to think it no small gain, when both archbishops ostentatiously refused to vote for the bill and sat on a
moral fence, that a bishop of the calibre of the Bishop of
Durham should argue with such conviction and persuasiveness,
that the bill was a Christian bill.


## KING EDWARD VIII

King George V several times had Henson to preach, despite a
hesitation when he began to propagate the idea of disestablishment, which the King regarded as attack on the interests of the
Crown. Henson gave heartfelt loyalty. The King died at
Sandringham on 20 January 1936. Henson happened to have
arranged to breakfast next day with the prime minister.

Baldwin spoke with feeling of the King's death. 'The great
question now', he said, 'is, how will the young man carry

---

[1] *The Ayes have it* (1937), 176.

himself?' He told Henson that yesterday King Edward VIII came to Downing Street. When Henson wrote his diary that evening his record of Baldwin's words ran as follows:

I had him here yesterday, and talked to him gravely. I told him that the king's life was really a dog's life, so incessant and monotonous were his official tasks. His intentions are admirable.

When seven years later Henson wanted to print an account of this interview he sent the text to Baldwin, then in retirement. Baldwin redrafted. When it was printed it read differently:

He the king came quite unexpectedly to see me yesterday, and we had a most serious talk for over an hour. His intentions are admirable.

Like everyone else Henson had unease but hope about the new King. He had met him twice and liked him, the boyish charm and tact and public service. Now when Edward was summoned to a high vocation Henson gave him all the benefit of the doubt.

Henson first heard the rumours on 28 October 1936. Accustomed to being undisturbed in his study, he was indignant when Ella broke in, *under the aspect and manner of a prophetess,* armed with a morning paper which reported the second divorce of Mrs Simpson.

*What seemed to me the silliest of gossip seems to her a matter of cardinal importance, something which would justify me in abandoning my work and devoting the morning to discussion! I drave her from my study with all the vehemence permissible to a Christian husband, and with something more than the decision of an Anglican bishop!*

A fortnight later Dean Inge sent him a report on the talk of London. Henson mentioned this to Archbishop Lang of Canterbury, who replied (6 November 1936), 'As to those other considerations to which you allude I can only say that they are in my mind night and day, and they darken all my hopes and wishes about the Coronation.' This letter of Lang's brought it home to Henson that the gossip was not idle. A fortnight later Lord Londonderry told him a lot more, and how the King was hardly on speaking terms with Archbishop

Lang. Henson still tried to believe that nine-tenths of the gossip was fiction.

In mid-November 1936 Henson went to London to attend the Church Assembly. On the late afternoon of 17 November Archbishop Lang asked all the bishops to meet him in his room; and told them that his plan for a religious preparation for the coronation was now out of place, that the King was much in the company of a twice divorced American lady whom the American press openly called the Queen-designate of Great Britain. The British newspapers were responsible but could not be silent for ever. The government hoped to get assurances from the King. Bishop Winnington-Ingram of London and Henson spoke in support of abandoning any appeal for a religious preparation for the coronation, and then Henson left because he found the atmosphere of the room asphyxiating.

Wherever he went, friends or acquaintances, lawyers and peers and anyone who might or might not know, told Henson other stories, about the King's behaviour, or the King's gardener, or what Walter Monckton, the King's lawyer, said at dinner.

On 1 December 1936 Bishop Blunt of Bradford made a speech to his diocesan conference. He talked of the coming coronation, and of the self-dedication of the new King, and of his need of God's grace; and then he said that it could be wished that he showed more awareness of this need. This was a severe public rebuke from a junior bishop to a new King. In the original draft he had no intention of referring to Mrs Simpson. Evidently he was well organized for he composed the address six weeks before, at a time when he had never heard of Mrs Simpson. At the Church Assembly in November Bishop Furse of St. Albans showed him American press cuttings about her. He wondered whether to alter his draft, and decided to leave it unchanged. If he thought that it would not be taken to refer to Mrs Simpson he was guilty of *naïveté*. The evidence shows that though he wrote the text without an inkling of Mrs Simpson, he could not but have her in mind as he delivered his speech.

The utterance at Bradford happened to coincide with that moment of time when the national press, which held its silence miraculously for more than five weeks, knew that they could hide no longer. They pitched upon Bishop Blunt's rebuke as the excuse to disclose everything; and so the affair of Mrs Simpson, the King's love, the question of divorce, the very future of the monarchy, burst upon an astonished nation.

Archbishop Lang was angry with Bishop Blunt. Henson, who had a less anxious responsibility than Lang, was more moderate but still cross. A bishop's homage to his sovereign meant that he undertook to guard his sovereign's reputation. If anyone should remonstrate with the King on his behaviour it should be the Archbishop of Canterbury and/or the Cabinet. *Nothing is more likely to harden the King in an unwise course, than that he should be publicly 'warned' by a bishop.*

Bishop Blunt, who was a good man, never recovered the esteem of the nation nor, quite, of all his diocese. The author of this memoir once had the honour of speaking from the same platform as Bishop Blunt; and was left with a puzzled resentment as he watched the audience while the bishop was on his feet, because the words were powerful and the audience would hardly hear.

The press assailed the bishops for moral comments. Some bishops were talkative and gave them what they sought. Henson kept his mouth shut, and persuaded his clergy to do the same. The *Sunday Sun,* which tried to persuade Henson to write an article on the monarchy, got a negative answer in two words. Half an hour after he listened to the King's broadcast announcing his abdication, two reporters came to find out Henson's views. He refused to see them. *Those ghouls can see nothing but 'copy' in the pathos of failure.* When the next morning Henson read the prime minister's speech to the House of Commons he could hardly restrain his tears.

So the King left for France and lifelong exile.

On the evening of Sunday 13 December Archbishop Lang gave an address on the radio and pointed the moral. He showed the draft of the speech to no other eye, not even to one of his chaplains, who afterwards thought that they might have saved him. The speech was a disaster. From it Lang's reputation in the nation never recovered.

The speech had moments of pathos and moments of grandeur, for Lang was a true orator. But this was not what came out of the loudspeakers as Britain listened to what he said. He blamed the King for giving up his trust, for choosing to put private happiness before a high calling. He has sought this happiness 'in a manner inconsistent with the Christian principles of marriage, and within a social circle whose standards and ways of life are alien to all the best instincts and traditions of his people. Let those who belong to this circle know that today they stand rebuked by the judgement of the nation which had loved King Edward.' These were not the only words in the speech. But they turned every friend of King Edward into a mortal enemy of Lang. And they made many more men in the nation think that the archbishop kicked a man already on the floor.

The best plea for Lang was, that he was very close to Queen Mary the Queen Mother; so close that he even drafted the very dignified and moving statement which she issued to the nation. Therefore he was touched by the severity of her attitudes to what had happened.

Some eminent persons wrote to thank Lang. But Lambeth was deluged with larger baskets of vituperative letters than the staff had ever known.

Of the larger number of critics Henson was not untypical. The press watched Henson. In their eyes he was always good for a ringing sentence. They could not accept that he said nothing. He soon found that he was widely rumoured to have sent a personal message to the Duke of Windsor. Two reporters came to find out if this was true. He had made a remark at his visitation address about the Church of England being governed by the two archbishops and the BBC. The hint was plain enough for the press. The *Daily Express* ran a headline '*Sensation behind Dr. Henson's Sarcasm*'. Letters started to arrive thanking Henson for making a protest against the archbishop's broadcast.

Other bishops were not so reticent as the Bishop of Durham; who did not like the way they followed the moralizing example of the primate. He was therefore more than a little astonished to receive the following letter from Archbishop Lang:

The Archbishop of Canterbury to the Bishop of Durham:

Old Palace, Canterbury
23 December, 1936

My dear Bishop,

I have reason to know that the continuance of personal criticism of the late King is giving some pain to those of all others whom we would naturally wish to spare. This must be my excuse for venturing to suggest to the Bishops that it would now be well to refrain from further public direct criticism of his conduct or allusion to the unhappy circumstances of his abdication. I think that enough has now been said on this painful matter and that the time has come for reticence. You may well think that this suggestion is unnecessary. But I trust that you will not misunderstand or resent it.

From this letter Henson inferred that the Palace had protested to Lang and that he had received a *wigging*. The inference was almost but not quite correct. On 22 December the press reported a strong rebuke from Archbishop Temple of York. This hurt the new King, because every such utterance gave new fuel to the newspapers. King George VI complained to his secretary Lord Wigram, who telephoned Lambeth, which telephoned Lang at Canterbury. This telephone call was the direct cause of the letter which the guiltless Henson received from Lang.

Still men commonly assumed from Henson's silence that he was the bishop on the side of the abdicated King. Someone wrote from Newfoundland to accuse him of 'defending the Simpson crowd', and warned him against the influence of Lord Beaverbrook. An American clergyman wrote him a grossly insulting letter because of his 'protest' against Lang's broadcast.

Henson was rueful. *If things go on in this way, I shall wind up by being hailed as one of the late King's 'social set' myself! Yet it is the case, that I have never knowingly made any public allusion to the Archbishop's speech.*

In April 1937 Henson was invited to stay at Windsor Castle. Both the invitation, and the conversations which took place while he was staying there, show that the new King and Queen were quietly grateful to Henson for his silence at the time of Archbishop Lang's speech. They talked very frankly to him about all that had happened. He found the new Queen perfectly charming.

But now the national argument struck him unexpectedly.

How should the ex-King be married to a lady already twice divorced? Early in the exile there was talk of a religious service in Vienna. The inner circle slowly grew aware that the ex-King, or Mrs Simpson, or both, badly wanted a religious marriage. One of their advisers got in touch with Canon Leonard Martin Andrews, who was a rector in the diocese of Truro, had an official connection with the duchy of Cornwall, and became chaplain to the King under Edward VIII. Confronted by the question whether he would marry the Duke of Windsor to Mrs Simpson with a religious service, Canon Andrews said that he was willing, on two conditions: that neither King George VI nor Archbishop Lang objected.

Walter Monckton therefore went (5 April 1937) to Lambeth to see Alan Don, chaplain to Archbishop Lang, and to find out what was likely to happen. Don said that all four houses of Convocation had lately passed resolutions deprecating the use of the marriage service in the case of all persons with a former partner still living. He was certain that Archbishop Lang would feel bound by these resolutions, and that Canon Andrews should be told.

Monckton said that the Duke of Windsor was very obstinate, and was determined to satisfy his bride with a dignified ceremony.

Whether Canon Andrews withdrew in the light of this information is not certain. But it was soon clear that his other condition was likewise impossible. King George VI decided not only that no member of the royal family should attend the wedding but that no chaplain to the King should take part. And Andrews was chaplain to the King.

Though by then several other clergy had offered their services, the Duke of Windsor and his circle seemed to reconcile themselves during May to the need for a wedding solely at a French registry office.

On 2 June 1937 Henson confirmed boys at Durham School; and after lunch a journalist came to tell him that the Vicar of St. Paul's Darlington, the Reverend R. Anderson Jardine, was reported to be at Tours to officiate at the marriage of the Duke of Windsor to Mrs Simpson. Had Henson given him permission? Enquiries started to come in from America along the same lines. Henson dictated a tough answer:

*The Rev. R. A. Jardine has no authority to officiate outside his parish and diocese. If the Duke's marriage were to take place within the diocese of Durham the Bishop would inhibit him, but the Bishop has no jurisdiction outside that diocese, and must presume that Mr. Jardine has obtained permission from the Anglican bishop who has authority over English clergymen on the continent of Europe.*

Jardine was educated at Liverpool College and apprenticed to an architect. At the age of nineteen he experienced a conversion and became a street-preacher, and then took charge of a chapel at the Yorkshire mining village of Denby Main. According to his own account his father disinherited him at his conversion, and in the village two attempts were made to kill him. By then he was a kind of Methodist, and was sent to a pastorate among the fishermen of the Shetland Islands, and later to Coniston in the Lake District. He met an Anglican vicar who in 1920 persuaded him to join the Church of England. In 1923 he was ordained and after a curacy was appointed (1927) by evangelical trustees to the living of St. Paul's Darlington.

The appointment was one of the cases which led to Henson's critique of patronage trusts. For even when he went to institute Jardine to the parish he found him an *unattractive and illiterate fellow*. This first unfavourable impression was confirmed. The man was *impudent, disorderly and tiresome*. He visited Anglo-Catholic parishes and made scenes. He had a parish of 13,000 but was usually out of it in some nonconformist chapel in someone else's parish; he invited a famous ex-medium to preach in his own pulpit on '*The Witch of Endor*' but Henson banned the pulpit and forced him to turn it into a talk in the schoolroom. He started to put himself forward as a faith-healer. He caused trouble at the diocesan conference of 1932. While Henson preached in the cathedral the sermon commemorating the centenary of the Oxford Movement (July 1933), Jardine arranged to hold a meeting in Darlington to denounce the Oxford Movement and did not fail to refer to the Bishop of Durham. In short, from the bishop's point of view, and from the point of view of several vicars, he was not a model clergyman. This was not compensated for by parish work, for the statistics show that the number of confirmation candidates halved.

When the newspapers announced that Jardine would marry the ex-King to Mrs Simpson, the local papers proclaimed him a notable clergyman, renowned for his preaching and beloved by the people.

Jardine read in a newspaper that the ex-King could have no religious blessing upon the marriage. He was shocked, and could eat no more breakfast. He cut out the article, and went down his garden to an old army tent where he always prepared for Sunday and said his prayers. He found the newspaper headline a 'voice', and knew that he must offer his services. He wrote a letter to the Duke's friend Herman Rogers and expected no answer. Rogers talked on the telephone to the Duke of Windsor in France. The Duke was overjoyed at the idea. He had a faith that this was the most wonderful of marriages and must be sanctified by more than a mayor in a French registry office. He leapt at the prospect of being married by an English clergyman according to the Book of Common Prayer. He told George Allen, his legal adviser in England, to interview Jardine and, if he found him suitable, to arrange that he be sent to Tours. During the children's service next Sunday Jardine received a telegram from Allen asking him to telephone.

So one of Henson's clergy found himself in his best suit at the Château de Cande, shaking hands with an ex-King who said 'Thank God you've come, thank God you've come.' 'Pardon my language, Jardine, but you are the only one who had the guts to do this for me.'[1]

The blessing on the marriage took place next morning, in a room like a flower garden, with an altar of an oak chest fronted with fat female figures. Jardine refused to have a crucifix on the oak chest and no one could at first find a plain cross, so there were minutes of embarrassment until they fetched a cross from the Protestant chapel. Jardine read Cranmer's immortal

---

[1] R. G. Martin, *The Woman He Loved* (1974), 329–30.

words in a strong voice, with Edward saying 'I will' in so high-pitched a tone that it startled the company, and Mrs Simpson almost inaudible. Jardine wondered whether the congregation would smile as he said 'Edward Albert Christian George Andrew Patrick David wilt thou have this woman to thy wedded wife . . .?' But no one in the room thought this roll of names other than solemn.

The lines from Tours hummed, and the press of the world invaded Darlington to find out everything about Jardine. Reporters offered Jardine large sums for the inside story of the wedding, and Jardine, who was no man of straw as the incident of the crucifix showed, found it a great temptation (for he could not at that moment pay his rates) but refused the offers. The reporters met him at Victoria Station with a riot, and woke him up at 4 a.m. next morning. He found 3,000 letters waiting for him at the vicarage.

The world seemed to think that Henson could have stopped Jardine, and Henson found himself at the centre of unwanted international publicity. One book of history even printed a telegram from Henson to Jardine which was alleged to arrive at Tours the day before the wedding: 'You are without episcopal licence or consent to unite the Duke of Windsor and Mrs Simpson. Since your licence has been revoked, under the circumstances you are unable to legally solemnize the marriage.'[1] Even the Duchess of Windsor in her memoirs wrote of Jardine defying his bishop.

Henson sent no such telegram. Apart from the split infinitive, which was hardly Hensonian, the fake telegram betrays ignorance of the law of the Church and the law of England. Henson perfectly understood that he was powerless. If it happened in the Durham diocese he could act. The legal marriage of the Duke was conducted by a French mayor. No one could stop an English clergyman at Tours saying afterwards what prayers he liked. Henson did nothing. The Bishop of Fulham, who was responsible for Anglicans in the northern continent of Europe, sent Jardine a message disclaiming all authority for what he did.

The International News Service asked Henson whether he

---

[1] Iles Brody, *Gone with the Windsors* (1953), 244.

would take disciplinary action against Jardine. Henson was faintly amused that at the same time he received a letter from Archbishop Lang which disclosed irritation. He was less amused by the letters of abuse which began to pour through the post. Some of the letters were obscene.

A few days later Lang wrote again about Jardine: 'No doubt you will deal with him as you think best when he returns.' Henson considered this and thought that Jardine was best left alone. Jardine had committed no illegality. He had used words in a context which gave them no legal force. Henson could do nothing but censure. He knew that to be censured would help Jardine. It *would only bring grist to his mill*.

Nevertheless he disliked the vehemence and obscenity of his mail, and expected Jardine's return to his parish with foreboding. He wondered if the people would make Jardine's life uncomfortable and decided that the contrary was more probable. The Mayor of Darlington said that he was disgusted and that the town would not approve. But Henson realized that a royal wedding touched waves of sentiment. From all over the country young couples wrote to Jardine asking if they might be married at his hands. When he conducted a wedding in his church on 5 June, 2,000 people besieged the church, and Jardine gave the bride and bridegroom a slice of the Duke of Windsor's wedding cake, which the bride said she would carefully preserve all her life. An admirer of Jardine started raising a fund to help him but Jardine stopped the fund.

Interviewed by the press, Jardine said 'I simply went to give the Duke and Duchess the desire of their hearts. They wished for a religious service, and I was proud and glad to give it to them. Now that it is done I feel extremely happy.' He described some of the Duke's conversation, how he talked of his visit to the distressed areas, and how he expressed great admiration for the Bishop of Durham. 'My action needs no defence, because I have not married a divorced person. They were already married' (*Northern Echo,* 5 June 1937). He proudly showed the gold cuff links which the Duke gave him, with the monogram of the initials of himself and his wife. They asked him whether it was true that he would become the Duke's chaplain.

On 6 June the congregation at St. Paul's, Darlington,

usually about sixty, was 600; mostly women, and from all over the country. He announced beforehand that he would preach on what he had done. In the pulpit he held up the newspaper headline which said that no religious ceremony could be held. He asked whether we are to require innocent parties in a divorce to do penance, and whether we are going back to the Middle Ages when popes kept kings shivering in the snows.

Did not one greater than any in authority in the Church say, 'Let him who is without sin cast the first stone'? I believe that I have stopped the government of this country and the Church of this country from the inevitable regret that would have followed in some years to come that they had not authorised a religious ceremony for His Royal Highness. . . . Through this action faith has been restored to many people in God and his Church.

Next Sunday, to Henson's intense relief, Jardine announced from the pulpit that he resigned the parish. That put him again into headlines. Why? Were the people offensive? Had Henson persecuted him? Was he to be promoted? Would he visit the Duke and Duchess of Windsor in Austria? Jardine told the reporters nothing. He said it had nothing to do with the marriage at the Château de Cande. His wife's health was weak. He could not wish her to face another winter in Darlington. He was fifty-nine and should make way for a younger man and had received many letters from America and he and his wife would take an American holiday. Many years later he confessed that the motive for resignation was ostracism in the parish.

Rumours about pay for silence were not slow to begin. People wondered whether the duke's advisers were perturbed by the publicity of last week. That comparison in the Darlington pulpit to the woman taken in adultery, suggested a lack of taste or tact. But what evidence there is suggests that his fares were paid by East Coast Radio, the managers of which wished him to broadcast.

Jardine and his wife arrived in New York on the liner *Queen Mary* on 5 July. There he entered a world which was far beyond him, the pressure of the international media. He enjoyed publicity a little too much for his own future comfort.

The unsophisticated ex-evangelist fell into the hands of men who wanted to use him for gain. He started to speak a little too freely, and his managers started to use sensational methods, down to or up to streamers from aeroplanes and banners floating above cars.

The Duke and Duchess of Windsor could not complain of his utterances. Of the married pair he had the highest opinion, he was sure that they were deeply religious people. But the Church of England he lashed; and especially its archbishop. He suffered from an illusion that the abdication of Edward VIII was caused by a plot between Stanley Baldwin the prime minister and Archbishop Lang. But the sentiment of the American people was wounded by hard-faced men making capital out of a personal tragedy or affair of the heart. To everyone's astonishment charities started refusing to receive the proceeds of Jardine's meetings, audiences were small, halls empty, the American public stayed away with ostentation. They felt it not only to be distasteful but unethical. And after Jardine was foolish enough to try to attract the failing crowds by saying, on the station at Lake Placid, that he was going to 'blow off the lid' about the abdication, and that Archbishop Lang behaved 'scandalously' and that his speech after the abdication was 'caddish', Jardine was finished as news. He made a lecture tour; returned to England to settle his affairs – the Darlington magistrates had issued a warrant for payment of his rates of over £9 – and returned to settle in America during February 1938. His American agent absconded. In Atlantic City gangs went round tearing his posters from shop windows. Two years later he was given charge of a little independent church or chapel at Los Angeles, which seated 150 but which he renamed appropriately Windsor Cathedral; and the loyal Duke of Windsor promised him a cross of gold for its altar. Being near Hollywood he ventured into the film industry and tried to make a film which would 'wake up America to indecency' and assail pornography but his financial backer died and everything collapsed. His neighbours supposed that he must keep half a million dollars salted in the bank but for most of the time he was broke. In May 1943 he and his wife were arrested on a charge of outstaying their immigration permit. The Duke of Windsor, who was at Palm Beach, was asked by the press whether he would help Jardine, but he could not remember who Jardine was, and when they told him, he said that he had no power to help. That year Jardine told his own story of the wedding in a book, called *At Long Last*. He called Henson an ecclesiastical weathercock, but it sold few copies, and Henson never read it or even heard of its existence. To the end Jardine regarded Edward as a possible saviour of Britain and its Empire and as a man among the front rank of the world's leaders.

On 23 July 1979 the auctioneers at Sotheby's in London sold for £2,290 the order of service used at the wedding of the Duke of Windsor. It is inscribed 'To the Rev. R. Anderson Jardine in remembrance of 3rd June 1937 Edward Duke of Windor'; for so, in the excitement of that moment, the Duke misspelt his new name.

Thus a man in love, who wanted to consecrate his marriage before God, used the representative of a Church which repudiated that representative. As Jardine once said in an American speech, an ex-King should be married by a bishop. Yet who will blame any man who wants to consecrate his affection before eternity and finds a minister willing? Because he found a minister who did not quite fit the task, the Duke planted an earthquake under the road along which that minister was travelling, and destroyed his sense of direction, and left only the memory that he did right at the Château in France and nothing could take away that memory.

On 5 November 1937 Henson went to St. Paul's, Darlington, to institute Jardine's successor. He could feel the large congregation expecting him to say something about Jardine. He disappointed their hopes. But at the end he was relieved, and sensed how the congregation was relieved, that the service was marred by no untoward interruption.

# 10. THE DICTATORS

LIKE MANY intelligent Englishmen Henson was not pleased with the peace which followed victory in the Great War. The Treaty of Versailles failed to win a moral assent. It claimed money in reparations of such astronomical sums that even modest men suspected payment to be impossible without bringing down the economy not only of Germany but of Europe. It ostentatiously accepted the principle of self-determination on which the German armies agreed to the Armistice, and then flagrantly departed from those principles in several regions vital to the new Europe. Like many men of his generation Henson was uneasy – worse than uneasy, he read the witty and destructive indictment of the treaty by Maynard Keynes and was persuaded that the Allied victors committed *a great crime*. Grateful though he might be to Lloyd George for recommending him for a bishopric, he had no trust in his moral principles. *One can understand how great a calamity it was that the British Empire should have been represented by a shifty brilliant Welshman, advised by a cynical though charming opportunist.* They had started out with ideals. They had believed the war to be a moral cause. He had felt able to preach it as a crusade. And now the crusade ended in this *unworthy conclusion*; a treaty forced upon a beaten enemy, *engineered by hatreds* and *base ambitions*. Henson decided that he *loathed* the treaty. It was despotic, and he hated to think that his country took part in despotism.

In all this Henson was typical of his class and generation, if a little more articulate and vehement in his expressions. The morality of the posture is unshakable. But it was a mood which helped the coming dictators. A settlement failed to commend itself to large numbers of persons who must be the main supporters of governments which had to administer the settlement. If dictators claimed revision of Versailles, even at the muzzle of a gun, no one could say that revision was immoral. Good men will not risk a gunfight for a cause which they suspect to be tinged with immorality. The age of appeasement was born.

One widely accepted part of this feeling Henson failed to share. In origin Armistice Day was simply a commemoration of the dead. The silence of two minutes, the sudden cessation of work and noise on a weekday each 11 November from 1919, was so moving that the day became an annual commemoration, with parades, services, silence in the streets and in the mills, a unique expression of popular mourning by a nation where nearly every family had a young man who died. As the years passed the celebration of Armistice Day took on a new meaning; not only a lamentation for the past but a dedication to the future. The war ended war. Never again must we allow militarists to drive us into fighting. And as the young, who never knew war, grew up during the twenties, one wing of the celebration became associated with a mood of pacifism. It takes two to make a fight. We can end war by refusing to make war.

Henson thought pacifism a fad. This opinion he shared with most of the British people. But unlike most of the British people, he suspected the celebration of Armistice Day. With each revolution of the year it would grow more like Guy Fawkes Day, a national memory of something which ceased to have meaning. He thought that it exaggerated the idealism of 'our side' during the war of 1914–18 in the light of modern knowledge, and was cruel to the bereaved by reopening their wounds annually. By the end of the twenties he started to say so in public, a shocking doctrine to those who left a piece of their heart in the hills of Gallipoli or the mud of Passchendaele. He preached the Armistice Day sermon of 1928 at the university church in Oxford and said that the celebration should now cease; and as he walked back to All Souls a cadaverous-looking young man assured him that his message was the message of the fiend. This sermon got little publicity and so won little abuse. But two years later, when he made a speech at the Primitive Methodist chapel in Willington, comparing Armistice Day with Gunpowder Plot day, and the *Yorkshire Post* printed what he said, and the national newspapers took up the question, he received a stream of abusive and anonymous letters; and suffered the humiliation that when he attended the Armistice Day service at the cathedral the dean, Bishop Welldon, preached against his bishop. The British Legion passed a resolution affirming the value of the remembrance and sent a copy to the Bishop of Durham, and when the Lord Mayor of London entertained the bishops to the annual banquet his speech pointed, too severely for courtesy, towards an unnamed bishop among the guests.

Henson did not feel strongly. He did not argue, Armistice Day is linked to pacifism in the minds of the young and pacifism is dangerous in this jungle of a world. If men wanted the day he was tolerant.

But a provision of Versailles which won his whole-hearted assent was the League of Nations. In his eyes this was the only way of preventing war. Instead of settling disputes by the force of a powerful army, they must be settled by a supreme court of the nations, willing if necessary to enforce its verdict by sanctions against an aggressor. Many bishops of the Church of England thought it a moral duty to support the League of Nations and to appear on platforms to make known its ideals and encourage its supporters. In this Henson was in no minority of bishops. But as early as 1923 he won a name as the most convinced and articulate bishop to believe in the League of Nations. During that year, when the Germans failed on a payment of reparations, the French army occupied the Ruhr, and the French talked of securing the future by dividing Germany, and making a separate German state of the Rhineland under French protection. Like most of the British Henson thought the French action immoral. It was this resistance to the French which first brought Henson into public notice as the special champion of the League of Nations.

The newspapers were right to see him as a champion. And as he was one of the first of bishops to see the League as the moral hope of the future, so he was the last bishop to defend the League when everyone else deserted.

This was not *naïveté*. His papers show inner uncertainty even while he preached a mighty sermon at the Presbyterian church in Jarrow on behalf of the League (30 September 1923). When his old colleague Johnson of All Souls, who was present, doubted the League afterwards, Henson was irritated. Then he realized that the irritation was due to echoing doubts within his mind. *The difficulties of an international order would carry me to a complete pessimism as to the prospects of the League if I were not persuaded that the general conscience is moving in the direction of abolition of war, and that such abolition is in the line of God's manifested will.*

For a man who became a hammer of dictators, Henson was slow to start. Like most of the British, he had no special dislike of Mussolini before the summer of 1935. He accepted the doctrine that the man was a vigorous ruffian whose methods were sometimes lamentable but who did some good and prevented worse. When Hitler attained power in the spring of 1933, and the Nazis burnt books and beat or exiled Jews, Henson knew what he thought but was not quick to speak. He went to a meeting in Sunderland to protest against the persecution of the Jews (7 May 1933) but found himself curiously uncomfortable, almost as though a bishop was felt by the audience to be out of place on the platform. They listened politely to what he said, but their loud applause was given to the Socialist and former MP, Ritson. Henson had the odd sensation that the Jewish organizers of the meeting found his presence less of a help than an embarrassment.

The antipathy of Henson to Mussolini, and the antipathy to Hitler, and the two campaigns against the two dictators, were simultaneous in chronology and interacted, each upon the other. But each had its own logic; for clarity it will be convenient to treat them in succession, starting with that campaign which in time was just the later in its beginnings, the battle against Fascist Italy.

During the summer of 1935 the Italians built a huge army in their East African colony of Eritrea and made no concealment of the plan to conquer Ethiopia, which in those days was commonly called Abyssinia. To public opinion in Britain, the threat was immoral. It would be the first aggression since the Great War by one of the powers responsible for maintaining the League of Nations and its covenant; it would be the first serious test of the League as a keeper of the peace in Europe; it would be war by a well-armed modern State against primitive tribes, the type of colonial war which recent events made obsolete and which was now seen to be immoral; and if the Italians were allowed to do what they too evidently planned,

Europe would throw aside its ideal of world order and return to the killing-grounds.

The governments of Britain and of France saw that these moral judgements of public opinion might be right but overlooked the realities. The tiger in the jungle was Hitler. The giant of Europe – not at the moment but soon – was Germany with its larger population, industry, unsatisfied military demands, and hatred of the settlement at Versailles. Since they had no confidence in Stalin's Russia, and since America retired from Europe, they thought that the only way to contain Germany lay in the alliance of Britain, France and Italy. If Italy invaded Abyssinia and then France and Britain declared Italy the aggressor and went to a war of punishment, or imposed economic sanctions, they drove Italy out of their camp into the camp of Hitler and brought a Second World War ominously closer.

Here was a direct conflict between high policy and the moral sense of many educated men.

No one will wonder on which side Henson stood. Do what is right *now*, even if it risks present or later impolicy – that was the philosophy on which his career was built and which brought him many uncomfortable moments.

This moral argument was not however a conflict between common sense and irrational faith. Men of sense could argue that the diplomats erred in their prophecies. Here was an invasion without moral justification. It had excuse neither in frontier incidents (unless manufactured) nor in economic need, unless it be economic need to put too many men into an army to prevent them from swelling the numbers of unemployed. The Italian record as a colonial government in Libya was not creditable. Nothing was to be said for this invasion except Mussolini's political need of a triumph and personal need of an ego. Those who argue that we must not do what is right because we shall then throw Mussolini into the embrace of Hitler and worse will befall, assume that Mussolini is a reliable ally of France and Britain and that his nearly obsolete army matters against Hitler. Both these assumptions are improbable. We shall do better to stop a dictator now, at the first throw; and then, when we prove that the League has teeth to enforce the moral law among nations, we shall have a better chance of rallying the world against a more savage dictator when or if that time comes.

One argument was omitted from this debate, except among the diplomats. Could we succeed? If we assailed Italy and won, Mussolini would fall. If we assailed Italy and lost, the failure would rally all the Italian people behind their dictator and encourage every other aggressor in the world and destroy the League of Nations. So the practical question mattered to the moral answer. Had we the battleships, and could they foil Mussolini's front by closing the Suez Canal? Or had we the leverage to stop the Americans selling oil to Mussolini?

Henson well knew that practical possibility affects moral judgements. What he saw was clear: an immoral invasion which the powers had a duty to stop if they could. All else was cloudy, guesswork, betting on the future. Whether or not we could persuade the Americans we had a duty to try. Whether or not closing the Suez Canal brought war between Britain and Italy, we had a moral duty to close the Suez Canal. The duty was certain, the war was prophecy.

That August of 1935, as Italian intentions were shouted from fascist rooftops, Henson was melancholy and remembered the July of 1914 when Europe was on the brink of its suicide. He wrote to his friend and late chaplain Charles Pattinson:

*It does seem intolerable that we should sit by, and look on helplessly while an abominable oppression is planned, advertized and carried through in breach of treaties and in insolent contempt of the League of Nations.*

And again (20 August 1935):

*Mussolini is evidently bent on going through with his abominable project: and, as in 1914, the holiday season introduces civilisation to another of those up-rushes of aboriginal bestiality which we call war. It is impossible to avoid the darkest fears as to the developments which this Abyssinian war may have.*

He decided that the Italians modelled themselves on the Nazis, and was left with a *loathing* for Mussolini's Italians as *mean and cunning bullies.*

In *The Times* of 27 August 1935 appeared a letter from Lord Hardinge of Penshurst, a weighty authority, to argue that

Britain had no special moral responsibility in a fight between
Italy and Abyssinia, and to underline the risks of any effort to
restrain Italy. Next day this was followed by more letters of
which the first came from the pen of Lang, Archbishop of
Canterbury.

Henson did not now like Lang. Once friends at All Souls,
near each other when the Vicar of Barking sought to persuade
Lang to be his curate, Lang became a part of Henson's single
ineradicable resentment in life, the conduct of so many of the
bishops over his election to the see of Hereford. Their tem-
peraments were opposed. Lang was a witty speaker after
dinner, few better; in ceremonies magnificent; an orator, but
rather in the secular sense than the religious; a noble presence,
a courtly manner. Henson blamed Archbishop Davidson,
whom he greatly admired, for postponing problems by worry
and delay. He blamed Lang for postponing problems by
finding smooth-sounding formulas, and found this worse, for
Davidson's method was transparently honest whereas Lang's
seemed to Henson to gloss over. The best-known of Hensonian
anecdotes tells how Lang showed a group his portrait at Lambeth Palace, and said that he did not quite like it because he
looked proud and pompous and prelatical; and from the back
of the group Henson asked, *And to which of those epithets does
your Grace take exception?* The story may have grown but
carries truth about attitudes. The man seemed to him so
politic. And in one judgement of Lang he was wildly wrong.
He thought that they differed because Lang was never racked
with self-doubt, whereas he himself never knew any other
state of mind.

In view of these outward courtesies and veiled antipathies, it
was curious that Henson's passion for truth allowed him to
sign letters to Lang *affectionately yours*.

Lang's letter about Abyssinia appeared to Henson characteristic. It seemed to him canny, cautious, and non-committal
about the main question.

On Friday, 30 August, Henson's letter appeared on the front
page of *The Times* under the heading 'Justice before Peace'.
This letter assailed the still powerful pacifist movement. We
have perforce put up with many oppressions of weaker peoples
since the Great War, for we had no remedy. But here looms an

oppression which we can stop if we want. In the Mediterranean we are a great power, and have the force to interfere effectively. Justice is a higher concern than peace, for while justice can never be rightly abandoned, peace can never be unreservedly pursued.

This letter caused lively debate with the pacifist leaders.

On 11 September the British Foreign Secretary Sir Samuel Hoare made in Geneva a speech which reverberated round the world. It was mighty against the aggressor, and was received ecstatically. It gave an illusion that the world had teeth and was united in the determination to bite an aggressor. From the viewpoint of the diplomats with their eyes on the future threat from Hitler, this was a fatal speech; for its thunderous success and its capture of democratic opinion made it impossible to retract or to look for the compromise with Italy which prudence dictated. The diplomats knew as the people did not that the French government, whose co-operation was necessary, saw Germany as the one enemy that mattered and were determined not to lose their Italian ally for the sake of morality in East Africa.

This speech Henson, in common with most of England and France, admired.

Already in disagreement with an All Souls archbishop, Henson now discovered for the first time that he disagreed with the All Souls bishop, Arthur Headlam, Bishop of Gloucester. Headlam visited his family home at Whorlton Hall in the county of Durham. Henson went to see him and discovered that Headlam was *quite callous* about the morality of the Abyssinian question and was *sniffy* about the wisdom of Sir Samuel Hoare's speech to the League. For Headlam also had his eyes set towards Germany, and honourable friendship with Germany if it could be achieved. Henson thought him naïve.

The friendship between Headlam and Henson illuminates Henson's personality. The two men disagreed on all the vital subjects. They came into resounding public conflict, until their names were bandied about in German newspapers and cited by Dr Goebbels. In his journal Henson was repeatedly frank, at times even contemptuous, about the faults of Headlam. Temperamentally they were made for opposition; bludgeon and rapier, elephant and hawk, theologian and historian, heavy and light, flat feet and nimble toes, bumbler and master of language. Henson once said of Headlam that he was *a man better for a friend than an enemy, though infinitely trying in both characters.* Yet despite every obstacle of temperament; despite caustic exchanges in public as well as private; despite Headlam being a bishop and Henson could be the intimate of everyone but a bishop; despite passionate difference on the most agonizing moral question of the day – they remained in their hearts a pair of friends to the end.

It perturbed him, though it could not surprise him, that this uncomfortable ally cared nothing about the morality of Abyssinia and thought only about Hitler's Germany. To him the doctrine that we must jettison Abyssinia to save ourselves from Hitler was simply the old doctrine of Caiaphas the high priest, that to save the people an innocent man must die.

**Three weeks later the Italian army invaded Abyssinia. The** Emperor Haile Selassie appealed to the League of Nations. Between 7 and 11 October the members of the League resolved to apply sanctions against Italy, and started to ban imports from and certain exports to Italy. But Russian supplies to Italy remained much the same, American supplies rose sharply. British battleships were moved into the Mediterranean but the admirals were vehement that they should not shoot, and the French government did what it could behind the scenes to prevent sanctions being effective. Sir Samuel Hoare and Pierre Laval tried to agree a compromise with Italy, which revolted the common people as a betrayal of Abyssinia and lost them both their places (*Sir Samuel Hoare is reported to have broken his nose; had he broken his neck it had been more politically convenient*, 14 December 1935). After a display of military incompetence and the aerial bombing of tribesmen and the ineffective use of poison gas, the Italian army entered Addis Ababa (6 May 1936) and turned Abyssinia into an Italian colony. Hitler seized the chance of turmoil among his opponents and sent battalions to reoccupy the Rhineland from which the German army was banned by the treaty of Versailles.

During all this débâcle Henson was not silent. Uppermost in his mind, the subject kept pushing into sermons and speeches and letters, whether the moment was appropriate or not. He could think of little else. His mind was filled with melancholy whenever he thought of Abyssinia and that was often. He lay in bed with a bone in the ankle painfully broken – so painfully that even the journal ceased for more than a month. But in bed he was full of sadness at the cynicism of his country's politics, and stirred with martial spirit at the need to fight wickedness.

Abyssinia had lost the war. France and Britain had lost the campaign against Italy. The diplomats urged their governments to restore the anti-Nazi front by ending sanctions as quickly as possible. And as the argument over the end of sanctions sounded louder in Parliament and nation, it entered even Henson's household. He discovered that his wife agreed with the peace-makers. Vexed that she could not see his point of view over Church and State, he was distressed that she could not see his point over Abyssinia; for to him the morality of this cause was as clear as daylight. He regarded the policy of the British government as cynical and opportunist and was hurt to find that Ella, who was neither cynic nor opportunist, should think the British government to be right.

He started to write. The little book which he published was the angriest that he ever wrote. He called it simply *Abyssinia: Reflections of an Onlooker*. Just after Baldwin's government ended sanctions against Italy, Henson sent off his manuscript to the printer and on 8 July posted copies to everyone he could think of. On his orders the publisher sent a copy to every Member of Parliament. It had twenty-four pages. Its price was 6*d*.

He had no expectation that his policy would be adopted. He knew now that he had no practicable policy. But he had to say what he had to say.

Abyssinia, he said, was the last home of African freedom. It was still a country with barbarities, where might be found the slave-trade and the use of torture. But its king, Haile Selassie, was a man of intelligence and culture who only needed time to bring his country into the modern world. Already he had promoted schools and hospitals.

But he was not allowed this time. Mussolini established his power in Italy by methods of craft and violence which recall the age of the Borgias. He looked upon Abyssinia with the eyes of King Ahab looking upon Naboth's vineyard. He invaded the country like a modern barbarian Alaric, bombing Red Cross hospitals, scattering poison gas, and waging war with brutality. He was destroying the League of Nations, which could retain neither reputation nor force if he were allowed to annex Abyssinia.

And what had the Pope to say? What protest has come from the Pope's lips? . . .

Intelligent prosecutors may be as angry as they wish but are not shrill. This unusual defect in Henson's indictment was due to an unexpected cause. The little book seems as though its enemy was Mussolini, or the weak-kneed British and French politicians who let him get away with villainy. But the real enemy was elsewhere. It was the Pope.

Henson was shocked at the stentorian silence which came out of the Vatican. In his conscience no issue could be clearer. An Italian dictator committed an international crime against a helpless and innocent sovereign. This dictator was the ruler of a Catholic country, his absurdly numerous army was full of Catholics, the taxpayers who financed his war were Catholics. The Pope was a Christian leader and had a claim to be a judge in international morality. Then why the silence? When the Archbishop of Milan and other ecclesiastics made martial speeches, why no repudiation? When churchmen brought gold from the churches to the war effort, why no rebuke? When poison gas, which the world agreed to be barbarous, was used on tribesmen, why no condemnation?

*Abyssinia* was the anti-papal pamphlet of Henson's life. The affair for him began with the crime of Mussolini and ended with a Pope who preferred the interests of the Church to the clarity of moral conscience. And this was the reason for the shrillness. This was the Henson not only of the thirties. He was the child of a father vehement against popes, the warrior of Ilford against papists, the impassioned observer of the Dreyfus case.

The pamphlet flopped. Very few members of Parliament bothered to acknowledge the gift. The generous William Temple called it *most impressive*, Lord Wolmer said it was a masterpiece. Hardly anyone reviewed it, the *Guardian* treated it seriously, Roger Lumley said that he could not even read as

far as the end, the Roman Catholic *Tablet* rebuked him gently
for superficiality, the *Catholic Times* printed an 'Open Letter to
the Bishop of Durham'; and the lowest moment for Henson
came when he made the humiliating discovery that his only
ardent supporters were the *Protestant underworld,* if that phrase
is stretched to include Henson's least favourite bishop,
Burroughs of Ripon, who immensely admired it and asked all
his clergy and laity to get it and read.

Henson confessed to himself that *Abyssinia* was not the
happiest of his publications. But he had to say it because only
so could he relieve his mind or satisfy his soul. He came to
regard it as *a wreath placed on the coffin of African liberty*.

In March 1938 Hitler overran Austria and Czechoslovakia
was obviously the next victim. In this crisis the British and
French must at all costs woo Mussolini from Hitler. On
16 April 1938 they agreed with Mussolini to recognize the
conquest of Abyssinia in return for an end to Italian pressure
on the British in the Middle East and for an undertaking to
withdraw Italian troops from the Spanish civil war.

George Trevelyan, Regius Professor of History at Cambridge,
the historian of Italian unity and politically a famous Liberal,
long a friend of Henson, appeared on the front page of *The
Times* next morning. His letter welcomed the Anglo–Italian
agreement, and said that we should say no more about
Abyssinia; as Henson described it, *throwing over Abyssinia with
alacrity*. On 12 May Lord Halifax announced in Geneva the
decision of Great Britain to abandon the cause of Abyssinia.

Here were the two moralities. Was it an absolute moral
obligation to go on supporting the oppressed when no help
could thereby reach the oppressed and when such support
might make further oppression easier? The deeply moral
Halifax had no doubt on that side; a moral judgement is always
conditioned by what can be achieved practicably. The deeply
moral Henson had no doubt on the other side. These were the
oppressed. To throw them overboard opened us to the charge
of playing political games in our own interest. And in any case,
in any circumstances, how could a Christian man end his
backing for justice against injustice, or tolerate one villainy
because thereby he might hamper a second villainy? He spoke
his mind in a letter which *The Times* printed on its front page

(21 April) but he got nothing except letters of thanks and a *Times* leader which sustained the government. *Diplomacy,* he commented to himself, *is a dirty business, and the sons of this world are for their own generation wiser than the sons of light.* He provided on request a stout letter which was read from the platform at a public meeting of protest in Caxton Hall (5 May). He could not persuade Ella or Fearne. They seemed to care nothing, he mourned, over the *betrayal* of Abyssinia.

And now the question came to him in a troubling form. The government's decision must be debated in Parliament. Should he speak? Bishops are only acceptable as speakers in the House of Lords if they speak on the issues of moral life, or matters touching the Churches, or a social evil like unemployment which touched the people of their diocese. Lay peers resented them if they talked on large matters of public policy where they had no expertise. Henson knew that if he spoke in the debate, *I shall make myself very odious.* He saw that the speech could achieve nothing, because the government was certain to get its way. But he found it a duty. *It can do nothing but good to raise a protest . . . After all one owes something to one's own self-respect.*

The subject was debated in the House of Lords on 18 May.

Lord Snell rose to move a censure on the foreign policy of the government, in conniving at the subjection of Abyssinia to a new form of slavery. Lord Brocket argued that the government needed support and that its agreement with Italy was a long step on the road to European peace.

And then spoke Archbishop Lang of Canterbury. His speech was sensible. But it reads now in the pages of Hansard, and it sounded to Henson as he listened, too smooth a speech. Lang said that no one had seen the invasion of Abyssinia with more repugnance. No one felt more bitterly the humiliation when the League failed to protect the Emperor Haile Selassie. But facts are facts. Italy has most of Abyssinia. Agreement with Italy is not pleasing but is a step towards lessening fear in Europe. We must build bridges before Europe is divided into two camps. Nothing can stop the armaments race 'except an increase of appeasement in Europe'. Lang said that he felt a 'reluctance almost amounting to pain' to have reached this position. 'I do not think I ever made a speech in the House with more distaste, but I cannot believe it is a sacrifice of principle for expediency. . . . I am not conscious of having made any bargain in my conscience with Mephistopheles, because it seems to me that the cause of general peace is something greater than mere expediency.'

The formulas of the speech betrayed uneasiness. Henson, who thought the policy immoral, felt internal disgust at hearing it defended on pseudo-moral grounds by the leader of his Church. So he rose in the best and worst circumstances for one of his great orations; prepared but unable to read a text; angered by a previous speaker; and with the anger given point because that previous speaker was Lang.

Henson started by saying that Lord Halifax had spoken in Geneva the funeral oration of the League of Nations, and that his speech there was marked by *the cold sophistry of a cynical opportunism*. The League was the one good thing which came out of the treaty of Versailles. Masses of thoughtful people set their hopes for the world upon the League. He was one of that multitude who were cut to the heart by seeing the collapse of this great combined effort to escape from the recurrent tragedy of war by the only conceivable means. . . . It is not so clear as the prime minister (Chamberlain) seems to think, that this appeasement will be lasting, if it is founded on a gross and acknowledged wrong. This volte-face by Britain, from resisting Mussolini to accepting his conquest, is shameful.

*What you can do, by conceding now this point and now that point, is to put off the immediate conflict, but you are only making sure that when the inevitable strife does at last occur you have conceded the strategic points to your adversaries and made it as certain as you can that you and your civilization will be destroyed. . . . My Lords, really, as practical people looking coldly at the world and weighing facts calmly in the scales of reason, is it reasonable to trust the word of these dictators?*

These quotations give little idea of the passion with which the words were delivered. One reporter said that it was scorching, another that the speaker was hot with anger. At one point in the onslaught he swung round on his heels and confronted Lang face to face, in what an observer called one of the most remarkable dramas that the House of Lords had witnessed in years.

He had the comfort of a little praise afterwards from two of the succeeding speakers. But most speakers dismissed him – no realist, unfair to the government, unfair to the foreign secretary. And yet the way they dismissed him showed that he needed to be dismissed – that is, this was a formidable piece of persuasion which spoke for a body of opinion in the country and which was represented in Parliament. Two peers professed 'horror' at Henson's attitude – a bishop saying that war in Europe was inevitable. The Earl of Mansfield said that the Bishop of Durham seemed to have such a hatred of the totalitarian forms of government that we must have war with these governments not only sooner or later but the sooner the better (Henson said nothing of the kind) and mocked Henson by quoting the old tag about prelates who:

Prove their doctrine orthodox
By apostolic blows and knocks.

He said that Henson's doctrine was a creed of despair. Lord Allen of Churtwood said that 'it is the pleadings for righteousness which have sometimes been the preludes to the most terrible catastrophes'. The Earl of Glasgow said that he regarded Germany and Italy as bulwarks against Bolshevism in Europe. And finally Lord Halifax, summing up for the government, dismissed Henson's speech as literary in flavour, chided him for his rudeness, and said that he did believe the word of Mussolini. 'I do not think' said Halifax, 'that the kind of statement that the Right Reverend Prelate made with great conviction this afternoon, that neither the word of Signor Mussolini nor that of Herr Hitler was ever to be believed, is the kind of statement, coming from one in his position, that does assist the cause of peace.'

In the country the critics of Henson thought that he represented the mass of people who placed an exaggerated hope in the League of Nations as the only way to end war, and now paid in disillusionment for that defective sense of justice which imagined that a new international order could be founded on a basis of privilege for France and Britain.

Henson knew that his speech that evening destroyed whatever popularity he possessed in the Painted Chamber. Never again could he feel that he commanded the ear of the House of

Lords. Never again did he make a speech in the House of Lords. In a few months he had a big chance to make such a speech and refrained from taking that chance.

Nevertheless, this was the third of the three speeches which the long memory of the old man looked back upon with a special gratitude.

This time, he could not have the satisfaction that he was in a minority of one. Scattered through the country he had many warm-hearted supporters. Not least, Winston Churchill. And Churchill did not forget.

Henson and Abyssinia are last glimpsed together at a dinner party in Magdalene College, Cambridge (20 May 1939) where Henson went to preach a sermon to the undergraduates. To meet Henson the Master invited George Trevelyan the historian and his wife, a Member of Parliament, George Kitson Clark the historian from Trinity College who was a member of the Conservative Party, an unknown spinster, and a young clergyman whose name Henson never gathered, but who was Michael Ramsey the future Archbishop of Canterbury. With Trevelyan and Kitson Clark in the party, Abyssinia became the debate across the table, and waxed warm. We have two accounts of what followed:

Henson: . . . *I found myself something of a storm-centre. George Trevelyan is not, I suspect, quite at ease in conscience over his acquiescence in the destruction of Abyssinia, and he disclosed the fact by his declamatory vehemence.*

Michael Ramsey: Henson talked vehemently at the Master, and said that we ought to have stood out to the end against Mussolini. I thought that the monologue went on too long, and interrupted. I said 'What does Dr. Trevelyan think?' Trevelyan, thus appealed to, asked laconically 'Wasn't Abyssinia a slave-owning country?' And this checked Henson's flow.

In the same months when he became known as a champion against Mussolini he was as well-known as a champion against Hitler; but for different reasons.

His German stepmother Carissima had lived with him in Ilford after Thomas Henson's death. When he married Ella she

moved out with his sister Marion, first to Horley and then to
Birchington, until she aged and took to her bed. Then to
Henson's lasting grief Marion, on whom she now depended,
died first; and for the last few months of her life Carissima
lived in her bedroom at Auckland Castle. She died on 26 July
1924. Her stepson never quite had the intimate affection for
her which he felt for his sisters of the flesh or for the mother of
his babyhood. But to her he owed what boyhood and youth he
experienced, and his school, and Oxford. Always he looked
upon her as the greatest of his benefactors.

Germans therefore were not all bad Germans. Henson could
never identify the German people with the Nazi Party.

Among English bishops the expert on German affairs was
George Bell, formerly chaplain to Archbishop Davidson, now
the Bishop of Chichester. Bell knew most of the German
church leaders, and understood better than anyone else in
England their predicament under Nazi rule.

Was it the duty of a Christian man in Hitler's Germany to
resist the regime, so far as he could in tyrannical circumstances? or might it be his duty to work with, even if necessary
within, the Nazi Party and bring the State back from the
brutalities of revolution to the rule of law and a moral government? Honest men in Germany might give different answers
with sincerity. But since the first answer had more frightening
consequences than the second, it naturally demanded a more
total sincerity.

The British people were not at first much offended by the
ending of democratic rule in Germany. They allowed that
Hitler's more democratic predecessors might have failed the
country and that in the German crisis a stronger government
was inevitable. They were horrified by what they heard about
concentration camps, but many believed, what they were told
from Germany, that these restrictions on liberty were the
temporary needs of an insecure regime after revolution and
would slowly give way before the normal rights of the citizen.

But two acts of the German government shocked them as
they shocked the rest of the world: the near-persecution of the
Christian Churches and the maltreatment of the Jews.

To fathom the complexities of the religious crisis in
Germany needed expertise which Henson did not possess. By

request, partly from Archbishop Lang, he sent a letter to *The Times* on the subject, printed 4 June 1935. But here he acted as a mouthpiece for others. He was disturbed to find his friend Headlam befriending the Nazi leaders. Headlam thought that the right course for Christians was to co-operate with the Nazi State so that we could help it to more civilized courses. He showed Henson a long and friendly letter which he received from Rosenberg, the minister of state for racialism in the German cabinet.

In the Church Assembly on 20 November 1935 George Bell proposed a motion to express sympathy with the Jewish people in Germany and to ask Christians in Britain and other countries to make plain to the rulers of Germany that the continuance of their present policy would arouse wide-spread indignation and prove an obstacle to good will between German and other nations. The wording of the motion sounded, and was, mealy-mouthed, because Bell knew that ferocity with Nazis could produce the contrary effect to what was intended, and might hurt Jews.

An English layman who was the German consul at Plymouth rose to move that the motion be not put. He said that the Church Assembly was not for politics; that the English should be the last people to dictate to another country how they should handle the question of race, when Australia excluded Japanese and the difficulties in South Africa were well-known; and that during the fight inside Germany between moderates and extremists it was important not to strengthen the hand of the extremists. The passing of the motion might increase the difficulties of Jews in Germany.

Henson had not come there intending to speak. This speech of the layman from the west country stank in his nose and brought him to his feet.

To read the minutes of the debate of the Church Assembly when Henson spoke is to experience sudden refreshment of the mind. The tone of discussion feels different, the printed word looks fairer, the mind leaps to attention. George Bell was the most Christian bishop of his age, but had little idea how to commend the points which he wanted to press; and this lack was important historically, for his causes were always the best, and yet he could not make men listen unless they wanted to listen. The backbenchers of the Church Assembly were not more leaden in speech than the backbenchers of the House of Commons, but they seldom sparkled. In the moment that Henson rose to speak, the reader has the illusion that the volume of minutes changes colour.

He was offended; and he had not prepared – the two circumstances in which he always spoke most powerfully. Civilization is not the property of this nation or that, but is a common possession, and carries with it obligations. The Germans are hypnotized by a fiction about race which is without foundation. When he read the news from Germany he *felt a kind of blind rage* within him that they could not draw the sword and go to the help of the low against the mighty. He talked movingly about the vastness of the obligation which Christianity owed to the Jews. He told them how when he was a boy in the Isle of Thanet he lived within 2 miles of Sir Moses Montefiore, the Jew who was the famous benefactor of East Kent. When he sat down, the assembly gave him an ovation, with loud and continuous applause.

Whether George Bell would think it wise, for the sake of German Jewry, to be so outspoken, he did not care. That Nazi newspapers accused him of *warmongering* by his talk of drawing the sword and going to the help of the low was hardly a matter of interest, certainly no matter of regret. When he spoke unprepared, on matters where he felt strongly, he could slip into some terrible phrase which afterwards gave him cause to repent. This speech had not a word in it which he saw reason to withdraw. He discovered that so far from his normal plight of being the *lone wolf,* he spoke for the large majority of the Church Assembly – indeed, as the newspapers next day showed, for the vast majority of the nation. The *Manchester Guardian* praised the speech to the skies, the *Daily Herald* had a flaming headline, the *Daily Telegraph* and the *Yorkshire Post* carried pictures of Henson; and when that evening he attended service at Westminster Abbey many people came up and thanked him for what he said.

Four days later he arrived back at Auckland to find a heap of hostile letters from *German Anti-Semites and Italian Fascists.* He was startled to find that Britain contained so much racial hatred.

This was the second of the speeches of his special memory when he was old.

Putumayo – German Jews – Abyssinia: the three speeches which in his antiquity he remembered with gratitude had a common thread. It was not quite that in each of them he spoke for the nation, for though in the first two he spoke for most of the nation, in the third, on Abyssinia in the Lords, he spoke only for a party. But in all three debates his sympathy was hot. In each he felt an overwhelming compassion for a suffering people; South American Indians helpless before exploiting traders, German Jews helpless amid nationalist fanaticism and racial delusion, African tribesmen helpless beneath the bombs and poison gas of colonial conquest. Critics who suspected the Bishop of Durham to be born without heart mistook their man.

The speech had two personal consequences in Henson's life.

First, it brought him back to the centre. Since the débâcle over the revised Prayer Book and his extreme reaction, and since the change in the headship of the Church from Archbishop Davidson to Archbishop Lang, Henson found himself a back number; at least in the sense that he was Bishop of Durham, concerned with his county and his people and his clergy, but not important in the general policy of the Church; and so far as he came into public view, only a waspish critic of movements like the Oxford Groups or organizations like the evangelical patronage trusts; and not everyone thought that patronage trusts or the Oxford Groups were worth this expenditure of print and fury. But now he was again the leader of a cause. This could not mean that he was again adviser to an archbishop. He distrusted Lang as a compromiser, Lang distrusted him as an extremist. In the age when the nation engaged on a policy of appeasing dictators, because the foreign office and the army chiefs told government that it must at all costs gain time, responsible men could not take into their counsels the only bishop in England who from start to finish thought the policy of appeasement to be cowardly and immoral nonsense. In a measure, he was still a lone wolf; or rather a voice crying in a wilderness; yet with words which could not be dismissed, in the way that a few years before they were dismissed, as the utterance of a crank; for the words awoke uncomfortable echoes and suspicion that he might be right.

Secondly, he was a hero to the British community of Jews. Their officers sent him letters of heartfelt gratitude, they designed to print his speech as a pamphlet to circulate in Germany, especially as German propaganda claimed that he clamoured for immediate war with Germany. In the United States American Jews included the name of Henson in their prayers. German Jews began to write him pathetic letters, asking him how they could get their children out of Germany. From Vienna he received a letter of reverent praise addressed to *Your Eminency*. Sir Wyndham Deedes returned from a visit to Germany and reported that the pamphlet was read there widely and did good for the Jews – 'all Jews and non-Aryans now look to you, my Lord, to espouse their cause'. The English publisher Victor Gollancz, whose firm was the most anti-Nazi among English publishing houses, collected documents on the killing and beating and bullying of Jews in Germany and when he published it as *The Yellow Spot* (1936) it carried a weighty introduction from Henson. The binding was bright red. Most of the book was a nauseating series of extracts, with pictures, from the vilest newspaper ever to disgrace a modern nation, Julius Streicher's *Der Stürmer*. Henson was not pained to appear in such a book, he found it salutary to expose an obscene fanaticism. It pained him aesthetically, however, to appear in a book of so vulgar a colour.

This business began to proliferate. On the day of the funeral of King George V (28 January 1936) Henson's attention was drawn to the celebrations at Heidelberg. The university was about to rejoice in the 550th anniversary of its foundation. It conformed to the usual courtesies by inviting other universities and learned societies to send delegates. Other universities would normally send delegates. But – the question was raised with Henson – ought they to send delegates to this festivity? Heidelberg was forced to drive out its Jewish professors. The present heads of the university must be either Nazis or co-operators with Nazis. Jews could not now be undergraduates. And it was likely enough that the Nazi government would use a non-political ceremony, with many foreigners present, as an occasion for political propaganda. Eighteen months before, they had not scrupled to use the historic passion-play in the village of Oberammergau to party ends, and to foster an anti-semitic slant.

Henson knew himself to be no expert in German affairs and consulted a number of friends, including George Bell and George Trevelyan. Trevelyan, though he detested the German government, was not in favour of breaking academic links with Germany which afforded the possibility of reasonable criticism. George Bell's letter was decisive: 'Is it not a case for a rocket in *The Times* from the Bishop of Durham?' Next day, which was Sunday, Henson wrote what became to historians his best-known letter. It appeared in the columns of *The Times* on Tuesday, 4 February 1936.

The links of international scholarship are precious. Across the frontiers men pursue the same truths and value the liberties which make that pursuit possible. But

*it cannot be right that the universities of Great Britain, which we treasure as the very citadels of sound learning, because they are the vigilant guardians of intellectual freedom, should openly fraternize with the avowed and shameless enemies of both. The appearance of British representatives at the Heidelberg celebration, and the presenting by them of congratulatory addresses, could not but be understood everywhere as a public and deliberate condonation of the intolerance which has emptied the German universities of many of their most eminent teachers . . .*

Not everyone approved of the Heidelberg letter. In *The Times* of 7 February Sir Arnold Wilson was rude to Henson, the German papers picked up Wilson's letter, Henson again became a figure of demonic quality in Berlin. Professor Armstrong accused him of not turning the other cheek and of recommending un-Christian action. A Briton in Heidelberg wrote pleading that the university was justified in removing from their chairs professors who were out of touch with the national reawakening.

But the men whose opinions Henson really valued sent messages of approval – Trevelyan, Edwyn Bevan, many others.

The aftermath vindicated Henson. The speech of the Nazi

minister of education at the Heidelberg celebration hurt those who cared for the historic ideal of universities. Not long afterwards the title of the head of the university was changed from Rector to Führer. The Institute for Jurisprudence, which had a Jewish endowment and a Jewish name, lost the name but not the endowment. New courses included much military history, much racial philosophy, and a course of lectures entitled Germany's Right to Colonies. The Nazi student organization was all-powerful in the lecture rooms.

This championing of the down-trodden, Henson found exhausting work. It had no end. Every sort of group wanted to use his name. A Dutch society wrote to Mr Herbert Dunelm that they sent 1,000 copies of his letter to all professors in Holland. A 'British non-sectarian Anti-Nazi Council to champion human rights' asked him to join in convening a conference but he refused (*I didn't care to associate myself with a cohort of cranks*). The Friends of Europe asked him to write a foreword to a grotesque book by a Nazi professor Bergmann, but he refused (*I did not care to waste my time on such tasks*). The publisher Constable was successful in getting him to blow a puff for the biography of Hitler by Konrad Heiden. Henson thought the book good. It could hardly fail to lower Hitler's reputation.

He had a little local difficulty. His friend, the chief magnate of Durham county and Chancellor of Durham University, Lord Londonderry, wanted to be friendly with the German leaders in the hope of being able to influence their behaviour. Mostly Henson and Londonderry kept out of each other's way when controversy was imminent.

For the year of the coronation Londonderry was elected Mayor of Durham and for the weekend of his inauguration service in the cathedral had the German ambassador, Herr von Ribbentrop, to stay. On the Saturday evening he gave a dinner-party at Wynyard. But Henson, not through his fault, misunderstood the invitation and did not go; and afterwards was relieved, because he did not see how he could have failed to be rude to Ribbentrop. Londonderry took Ribbentrop to the mayoral service in the cathedral next day and they sat side by side. The preacher was Henson's suffragan, Geoffrey Gordon, the Bishop of Jarrow; who did just what his master would have done, by preaching at Ribbentrop on freedom and human rights.

Ribbentrop knew all about Henson. He asked a member of Henson's London dining-club Grillion's, what kind of a man was the Bishop of Durham; and got the answer that 'he was known to be a very eloquent man, who spoke his mind freely.' Ribbentrop said, 'He doesn't have a high opinion of us. I read a speech of his in which he used very strong language.' The Englishman said that in what he said Henson expressed the mind of the majority of English people.[1]

Londonderry's next move was still more embarrassing. He helped to persuade Durham University to send a representative to the bicentenary celebrations of the University of Göttingen. Henson was the visitor of the university. After what happened over Heidelberg he must persuade the university to rescind its decision. Moreover he regarded Göttingen as *a Jew-baiting university.*

Nazi students had raided the university library (one of the historic libraries of Germany) and burnt a lot of books by authors whom they hated but had not read; and the Rector failed to protest against the young men's vandalism. By the time of the invitation to Durham 22 per cent of the staff of Göttingen University had been dismissed, to the benefit of universities in America and Britain, which gained scientists and scholars of an international fame. No university suffered more than Göttingen from Nazi depredations.

The letter which Henson wrote to the Vice-Chancellor of Durham was strong:

*. . . If Durham university were to take a course so inconsistent (as I must needs think) with its duty as a seat of sound learning, and so unfavourable to its public credit, I should certainly find myself in the unhappy situation of having publicly to make known my personal disapprobation.*

*Surely in this year, when our university will celebrate its centenary, we must be specially vigilant to avoid any procedure which could give countenance to the suspicion that Durham is unregardful of its primary duty as the guardian of truth and intellectual liberty.*

[1] Lord Castlereagh, Londonderry's son, told the Durham MP Ritson, that one night at Wynyard Henson at dinner took on the combined hosts of Ribbentrop, Alba, Ronald Graham, etc. and 'floored them in debate'. This is not an incredible event but it did not happen. Despite two or even three near misses, Henson never met Ribbentrop.

He sent Lord Londonderry a copy of this letter with a covering note that he regarded the proposal as *a condonation of the academic policy of the Nazi government,* and that if the decision were not rescinded he must refuse to take any part in the celebrations of the Durham centenary.

Thirteen days later the university rescinded its decision to send delegates.


An extraordinary thing about Henson was the rapidity, even the instantaneousness, with which he reached moral decisions that took other men years of anxious meditation.

Inside Japan the civil government was locked in a secret struggle for power with its generals who were divided into more than one faction. In February 1936 this broke out into a *coup d'état* in which officers of the army murdered the prime minister and another cabinet minister. When Henson read of the assassination he was afraid that it would strengthen the war party in Japan; and he was afraid with reason, though no one in Britain knew that the officers had opened secret negotiations with Ribbentrop. But the murders caused him to think about the ethics of murdering.

We know now the agonies of conscience through which Christian Germans passed when they met the conviction that the only way to end tyranny was to kill the head of state. The pros and cons of tyrannicide were long debated in Christian ethics; the special difficulty that if the act is regarded as moral any eccentric or fanatic can justify himself on a plea of morality; the attempt to limit the moral decision to approved authorities in the State, like a Parliament versus King Charles I of England; the growing conviction that in a modern repressive society these traditional restrictions are unworkable; the debate on the nature of loyalty to one's people, which is an extension of the moral duty of loyalty to one's family – the debate went on and on, weakening the arms of conspirators and continuing long after Hitler was dead and Mussolini murdered. All this torment of the conscience was foreign to Henson. Within an hour he reached the conviction that tyrannicide was right; that tyrants were obviously tyrants; and that no restriction against the fanatic or terrorist need be built within the moral theory. *Who could deny the morality of a patriotic Italian who, for public reasons, killed Mussolini? or who would not applaud the German who, in the interest of elementary morals, killed Hitler? I should give them Christian burial without hesitation.* This was February 1936. Henson must have been the only bishop in England, and perhaps one of the very few moralists in all the world, who reached such a conclusion at so early a date. It took Christian moralists three or four years more to contemplate this possibility; and some are undecided to this day.

This stance was not without hesitation when war came. Men wanted to justify reprisals morally. Henson never doubted that under no conditions could reprisals be justified. When he was consulted by one of his 'sons', he said that by casuistry you could justify almost any extreme of wickedness morally, and then gave a list of crimes which must be condemned and which could only be justified by false argument. This list of crimes includes torture of witnesses, breaking treaties, and tyrannicide.

The letter appears to condemn plots to murder Hitler or Mussolini on the ground that good ends cannot justify bad means and the Christian must wait on God's time for the vindication of justice against tyranny. When consulted as a moralist, Henson could not reach a violent conclusion with abandon. Less than nine months later (September 1941) he wrote to a correspondent, *Unfortunately assassination appears to be a lost art on the Continent of Europe.* He surprised himself by this judgement. He gave himself a note of exclamation, though only one such note. *Imagine that a respectable Christian bishop should have been brought to the pass of giving bed and board in his ethical scheme to ASSASSINATION!* When a Vichy politician Henriot was murdered in June 1944, Henson treated it as a *well-deserved punishment*. He did not criticize Stauffenberg when he put the bomb under Hitler's table.

But his moral antennae stayed sensitive. On the question what was to be done when we captured Hitler after the war, he preferred that he be sent to a lunatic asylum. He did not condemn Mussolini's murderers, but thought that the orgy of hatred afterwards, with the corpses of the dictator and his mistress hung upside down before a jeering crowd at Milan, *a revolting exhibition of bad taste and worse morality*.

During the summer of 1937 the conflict between Hitler and the more resisting part of the German Protestant Churches, known to history as the Confessing Church, came to a head with the arrest of all the leaders of the Confessing Church, of whom the best known in England was the former submarine commander Martin Niemöller, pastor of the important church of Dahlem in the suburbs of Berlin.

Niemöller's trial after arrest was long delayed. When he came for sentence before a Berlin court in March 1938 the moment was tense because England was filled with fury at the Nazi pressure on Austria before its occupation a few days later. The court substantially acquitted the defendant, inflicting a small fine and a term of imprisonment so derisory as to mean immediate release. As Niemöller left the court a free man, he was picked up by the Gestapo under the powers of emergency arrest and confined in the concentration camp at Sachsenhausen. At this moment Adolf Hitler himself used the occasion to thrust at Henson. The two English bishops vocal in their protests were Henson and George Bell of Chichester. Hitler told the British ambassador in Berlin that he would brook no further interference from English churchmen, and that it was their meddling which caused him to order the sending of Niemöller to concentration camp.[1]

To Christian Britain Niemöller symbolized the soul, standing for the ethical and religious foundations on which Europe was built, beaten down into the ground by a tyrant, but still dauntless. He seemed to be a free soul in a state where all freedoms were destroyed, a conscience unshakable among men without conscience; a light of the long heritage of civilized Europe threatened by pagans; with that unique combination of moral and physical courage needed by anyone who stands up against a reign of terror. Henson was so deeply moved that for a time Niemöller was the subject which pushed willy nilly into all his addresses at moments suitable or unsuitable, at confirmations, institutions of clergy, speeches. From the pulpit of St. Cuthbert's Darlington he called Niemöller *the freest man in Germany in spite of his confinement in a concentration camp* (20 March 1938). Franz Hildebrandt, Niemöller's former

---

[1] Nevile Henderson, *Failure of a Mission*, 73–4.

assistant now an exile, heard of these speeches and gave Henson a copy of a message of courage which Niemöller sent to his son out of concentration camp, and Henson used the message with moving effect at an institution in Stockton.

That summer of 1938 war loomed over Czechoslovakia. On 1 July Ella and he gave a garden party half-ruined by a thunder storm, and remembered that this was the anniversary of Niemöller's imprisonment and that he was still in gaol. He had been reading a piece of German propaganda called *Germany Speaks,* with a frontispiece of Hitler and a preface by Ribbentrop, and a chapter on future friendly relations between Britain and Germany, a chapter which offended Henson by failing to mention either the German Churches or the German Jews. He decided to commemorate the anniversary with a letter to *The Times*, to the effect that agreement between England and Germany was possible only on a foundation of mutual respect, which must mean agreement in the foundations of civilization. These foundations *are rejected when justice, toleration, freedom, and good faith are set at nought. The treatment of Pastor Niemöller involves precisely that rejection of the fundamentals.*

On the same day George Bell conducted a service of prayers for Niemöller in St. Martin-in-the-Fields. He spoke of the preaching of silence; the pastors who in their cells could not preach were not dumb, their very silence spoke. On the same day in Niemöller's own church in Dahlem the congregation held another service of prayers for their pastor, and were joined by seventy pastors and 2,000 people.

Arthur Headlam, the Bishop of Gloucester, spent June 1938 in Latvia and Estonia, on ecumenical discussion with churchmen there, and visited the house of his ancestor, Tsar Peter the Great. On the way back he stayed a week in Berlin. He met German pastors and laymen, up to the editors of newspapers and Ribbentrop, who was now the German foreign minister. While in Berlin he picked up a copy of *The Times* and read Henson's letter on the anniversary of Niemöller's imprisonment. He talked to a lot of pastors in Berlin and thought that they seemed to be free. He also thought that a letter like Henson's put the German government against the Churches. For Henson to say that Germany rejected justice, freedom, toleration, or good faith seemed to him not only unwise but untrue. He mentioned Henson's name to Ribbentrop, who replied that he knew about Henson and did not take him seriously (Headlam to Henson, 16 August 1938). The moment that he arrived back at his palace at Gloucester he took up his pen and wrote a counter-blast to *The Times*.

He started by accusing Henson of inaccuracy. That the Christian Churches are treated with insult and injustice is untrue. Government fusses them with undue interference and petty regulations but that is all. Pastor Niemöller is in prison because he stubbornly defied the law which bans the use of the pulpit for political ends. 'He might, I am told, be released at once if he would undertake to avoid using his pulpit for political purposes. Even in this country we do not like political sermons.' He called Niemöller a 'troublesome clergyman'. The German government is not approved by many in this country but our government is not approved by many in Germany. The German people want our friendship, and

I doubt whether letters like those of the Bishop of Durham do any good to those on behalf of whom they claim to be written. They certainly do not help the cause of peace or of friendliness between nations. They do not, I believe, help the influence of Christianity in Germany. Would it not be better to abstain from the pleasing task of continuously scolding other nations and attempt to understand them? (*The Times*, 14 July 1938)

This was a direct attack on Henson; and by its contents an old friend delivered himself into his hands. Henson immediately wrote back to *The Times* with a challenge.

*Does the Bishop of Gloucester think that the Church of Christ ought to keep silence in face of the doctrines and procedures of the German State? Does he think that the Church of Christ in England ought to regard the situation in Germany as a merely domestic affair, with which none but Germans are concerned, when the victims of Nazi tyranny, Jews and 'non-Aryan' Christians, are streaming out of Germany and Austria in crowds so great that the statesmanship of Europe is at a loss how to provide for them?*

He said that he had good evidence that the expression of our moral indignation affected politicians in Berlin and is welcomed by their victims (*The Times*, 16 July 1938).

From the pulpit of Dahlem Niemöller's brother said that no

one there had heard of this condition, alleged by Headlam, that if Niemöller promised not to use the pulpit for politics he would be at once released. On the following day (17 July) Henson addressed a crowded meeting of Jews in the town hall of Leeds and was given a standing ovation by an audience of more than 3,000 people.

Headlam returned to *The Times* with a letter which in the unjust perspective of hindsight, and even in the just perspective of many contemporaries, has a claim to be the most lamentable letter ever written by an Anglican bishop to a newspaper. He said that the pastors who co-operated with Hitler were good orthodox evangelical pastors, even 'the Thuringians' (the Thuringians were a revivalist group of Nazified clergymen but to call them 'orthodox' was stretching the word far beyond its broad limits). Headlam said that the one thing needed was a united German Church and that it is 'the one thing Hitler desires'. (Although Hitler once desired it, he had long ceased to do so, and we can guess at a number of other things which at that moment of Czechoslovakian time he desired more.) Headlam wrote 'I have just been at a Scouts service, at which we were bidden to be courteous. I venture to think that it would be wise to be courteous even to dictators . . .' (*The Times*, 20 July 1938).

The argument was a bigger argument than the clash resounding over the country between two elderly bishops of the established Church, and taken up and discussed by other men who wrote leaders or gossip columns or letters to the newspapers. Should Churches refrain from interfering in politics because their eyes are fixed upon another world? Or is it their duty to take a moral stance in politics whenever politics touches moral issues? And behind this perennial argument was a subtler tension of mind which plagued Christian leaders, from Pope Pius XII downwards, for the next seven years. Is it the duty of a Christian leader to maintain Christian ideals of justice against villainy even when these public proclamations will do no good and are likely to hurt those at the mercy of villains? Is it better to make friendly Headlamish noises at the villains because this is the only way that practical good can be done to help innocent men under the sword of tyrants? The argument was not yet quite so clear. Headlam did not yet think

Hitler a villain. Henson knew that he had a duty to maintain the moral law, and had assurances from Germany that this might help Niemöller and not make him suffer worse. But those who know their Henson know that more information would have made no difference to his conduct. Even if he were persuaded that his cry for justice could help Niemöller no whit, he would still have cried for justice. Come storm or hail, you must speak.

To Headlam's letter about courtesy to dictators Henson thought it unwise to reply, though he saw how easily he could devastate his opponent. He received a few abusive letters but on the whole was pleased to find that most people were on his side, and he could not resist a twinge of delight at being sent an article from *Truth* entitled 'Heil Headlam!'.

Meanwhile George Bell was busy from Chichester. While Henson thundered out the general principles from the north, he did what he could, on his habit of doing good by stealth whenever possible, to weaken Headlam's influence. Headlam might say foolish things; he might not be highly regarded at that moment by the great British public; but he was one of the best known of all British churchmen abroad, partly because he was a genius at ecumenical meetings, with a long list of gains to his credit in different parts of Europe, and partly because he held an official position, which made him a foreign secretary for the Church of England. He was the chairman of the Council of Foreign Relations. Men in Basle or Paris or Constantinople or Berlin would think that when he talked about Niemöller he talked for the whole Church of England. Bell could not bear this idea. His first scheme was to persuade Lang to force Headlam to resign. Lang told Bell that Headlam was too stubborn a man to resign. So Bell and Lang agreed on a public exchange of letters which would show that Headlam spoke neither for Lang, nor for Bell, nor for the English bishops as a body, nor for the Church of England as a whole, but solely as any other individual entitled to his personal opinion. The exchange of letters appeared in the press on 26 July, 1938. Henson thought them well enough, but they left Headlam in office and did not cancel the damage which he did by sitting in that chair. In public (*The Times*, 12 August 1938) he raised the argument to higher ground; not the fate of a par-

ticular individual but the principles of justice on which rested
European civilization.

> . . . *It is no mere question of persuading the totalitarian State to mitigate its
> treatment of individuals, but rather the cardinal issue of affirming the
> essential principles of the Christian religion against a policy which grossly
> violates them.*
>
> *Pastor Niemöller is the embodiment of a protest which no Christian
> Church could refrain from making without forfeiting its claim to be Christian
> at all . . .*

Henson asked Headlam what a Christian minister was supposed to do when confronted with the anti-semitism of Julius
Streicher or the paganism of Rosenberg? *Ought he to secure his
own safety, and connive in the corruption of his people, by keeping
silence . . .?* Was he not to resist the Nazi Youth Movement as it
tried to de-Christianize his boys? What message would he send
to Pastor Niemöller in his concentration camp? *A cold intima-
tion that English Christians hold him (Niemöller) to be mistaken in
his opposition, and advise him without scruple or delay to obtain his
release by signing the pledge never again to criticise the proceedings of
the totalitarian State?*

On the contrary, Niemöller will be heartened by the knowledge that he has the prayers of English Christians. To bring
England and Germany closer together – a cause which everyone must make their own – is best served by making clear to
the rulers of Germany the moral nausea which we feel.

> *No policy of political co-operation can be sound or permanent if it be not
> based on a community of sentiment with respect to those principles of social
> intercourse, historically drawn from the Christian religion, which are the
> ultimate bases of genuine civilization.*

To this noble letter, challenging him to say what advice he as a
Christian bishop would send to Pastor Niemöller, Headlam
avoided a public reply. No reply was possible. For this demolition Henson received several letters of thanks, one from a
grateful anonymous in Leipzig.

The Bishop of Chichester to the Bishop of Durham,
27 September, 1938: 'The evidence of the damage which he
[Headlam] has done to Niemöller and to Christianity is overwhelming.'

The wild build-up of Nazi propaganda convinced the world that a declaration of war against Czechoslovakia was likely to coincide with the Nazi rally of 12 September 1938. Dean Inge, Henson's former intimate, now more a past friend than a friend but valued because of memories from the time before they were sundered, was staying with Henson in Auckland. Breakfast on the morning of 12 September was almost an explosion. For Inge said that he wished Labour would organize a general strike against the government; that we had no interest in Germany's aggression against Czechoslovakia; that France was the cause of all the evil in Europe. Henson could not bear such language. *I believe that the timidity of our academics and the pacifism of our enthusiasts are the most potent forces now making for war.* It pained him that Fearne Booker was found to agree with Inge – but *she has at least the excuse of her sex.*

Should Chamberlain meet Hitler? Henson thought it wise, and yet he dreaded. His mind was so perturbed that he could not prepare the address for his candidates before their ordination, normally his most solemn utterance of the year.

*My anxiety is twofold, for while I shrink with horror from the prospect of war, I dread even more, and with deeper loathing, another effort to avert war by dishonour. Is Chamberlain designing to placate Hitler by the betrayal of Czecho-Slovakia, as he designed (but failed) to placate Mussolini by betraying Abyssinia? I try to assure myself that so gross a treason is incredible, and yet, when I take account of the grovelling 'realism' which now prevails, I fear.*

After that it is not necessary to record what Henson thought of the Munich settlement and the abandonment of Czechoslovakia to its fate. Many voices called for Sunday 2 October to be a day of national thanksgiving in the Churches. Thanksgiving for peace and thanksgiving for Munich did not seem easy to distinguish. What should he do? *Peace is welcome but may be disgraceful. War is disastrous but may be just and honourable. How does the matter stand in respect of this agreement which was signed at Munich? What precisely are we to thank God for? . . .*

At service that morning he refused to include a special thanksgiving but still prayed for peace.

But Munich left him unusually hesitant. When a cabinet

minister resigned because he could not bear Munich, the Bishop of Durham, who could not bear Munich, failed to speak.

At the debate or post-mortem in Parliament Archbishop Lang lauded the prime minister and the foreign secretary in courtly language, and then asked himself and the world whether it could ever be right to base peace upon an act of injustice. He said that Britain had no obligation to help Czechoslovakia. We 'undertook friendly mediation' and 'it is not our fault' that it failed. If war came the Czechs would have been crushed before Britain and France could help. Therefore, 'I find it difficult to believe that any such injustice has been inflicted as would morally tarnish the peace which we have received.' He hoped that this act of appeasement would bring other acts of appeasement in its train.

In the House of Lords, Lord Lloyd, hater of the Munich settlement, assailed Lang as a Gallio, who cared nothing for a moral issue because it was a long way away, and who dismissed the Czechs by saying that war would destroy them, and by not remembering that nations also have souls. But the weight of opinion among the peers supported Lang; and in the country also.

Henson was not in the House of Lords that day. When he read the words of Lang he thought them *almost cynical casuistry*. Afterwards many regretted that the Bishop of Durham was not able to be present to speak in that debate.

But the private papers show that he could have attended. He spent a quiet morning at Auckland working on a book (not a good book). In the afternoon he walked round the Park with his chaplain, and interviewed an ordinand who travelled from Bristol to be inspected. The ordinand remembered only the care and courtesy of the bishop and the pheasant sandwiches which Ella cut for his journey and was unaware that the bishop's mind might that day travel far. Nothing on that day or the next day stopped Henson from being in his place in Parliament. That betrays uncertainty. And he was right. Too sore an anguish troubled the nation. The moral issue, though not so simple as Archbishop Lang portrayed, was an agony: war with honour and horror, peace with dishonour but still peace. Bishops ought not to look like warmongers. This was no time for fireworks in Parliament, nor for taking Lang's 'casuistry' to pieces. So he worked on a book during hours when his disciples thought that he should have caught the train to London.

In November 1938 a young Jew murdered a member of the German embassy in Paris. In revenge the Nazis organized that pogrom through Germany known as the Night of Glass. They smashed Jewish shops, beat Jews, killed Jews, burnt synagogues, and for the first time awakened many ordinary Germans to the disgrace of their own government. Henson was not at all silent. The Jews were deeply grateful to him for everything that he did and said. A deputation of fifteen Jews came to the state room at Auckland Castle and Mr Toparoff of Sunderland presented a framed copy of the page of the Golden Book in Jerusalem which records the names of the friends and benefactors of the Jewish people (21 December 1938). Almost his last speech as Bishop of Durham was made at a meeting in Darlington where he appealed for families to receive into their homes Jewish children who were refugees. He started writing to experts, and to the Home Office, about the reception of Jewish refugees – including one relative of his stepmother, whose sister married a Jew.

That November he invited George Bell of Chichester to address the Diocesan Conference at Durham about the persecution of the Church in Germany, and the two anti-Nazi allies stood shoulder to shoulder on a platform. This was a happy occasion and very unfair to Bell; first because Henson was known to be resigning and therefore was bound to win more attention than the main speaker; secondly, because Henson introduced Bell with a personal indictment of Hitler's persecution of the Jews. This speech from the chair cast into the shade everything that Bell had to say. Bell's speech made no impact upon the audience; nor even upon most of the reporters, for although *The Times* distributed its favours equally between the two prelates, most newspapers printed Henson and did not bother to print Bell.

Bell resented this treatment not a whit. His collins to Henson for having him and his wife to stay was a tribute from one anti-Nazi stalwart to another. Bell had come to feel, what he had not always felt, that this was a leader and a champion whom the Church of England was blessed to possess (Bell to Henson, 18 November 1938).

The friendship between Henson and Bell is of special interest. Henson found it hard to revere a bishop. He applied higher standards of criticism to them than to any other of God's creatures. All the bishops whom he admired were intelligent, gentle, kindly, not slow, nor foolish, nor sentimental, nor over-emotional. George Bell passed this highest of tests. His mind was not fast. Henson could not see him as a considerable thinker, and thought little of him as a public speaker. When Bell spoke he always saw what mattered, but took roundabout routes to say what mattered. Henson made rude comments on Bell in his private papers, and ruder comments to his face. *I suspect* (he wrote congratulating Bell on becoming a bishop) *that your head is a very menagerie of all the crankdoms which during the last decade have turned the (Anglican) world upside down.* Later he accused him of having lived too long in *the heated atmosphere of committees, conferences, congresses, and the like debased outcrops of modern democracy.*[1] Although this was said in fun, Henson really wondered whether Bell was *narrowed* too young by serving so long as chaplain to the Archbishop of Canterbury. Yet he approved Bell's Life of Davidson; and it was the bishop rather than the biographer whom he came in the end to admire – the stalwart against Nazis, the defender of Germans against men who said that they were all vile, the assailant of reprisals by British and American aircraft – the man had courage and determination and the kind of high moral conviction at the cost of popularity which could not but win Henson's allegiance. Bell, summarized Henson to himself, *is a greater man than his aspect and manner suggest.*

[1] Jasper, *Bell*, 248; *Letters* 2.56.

# 11 THE DIOCESE OF DURHAM

THE EPISCOPATE at Durham lasted eighteen years and two months. At two points men talked of him as a possible Archbishop of Canterbury, at another point as a probable Archbishop of York. To the eye of posterity Durham was where he ought to be.

The Bishop of Durham lived in a magnificent castle, the palace of Bishop Auckland, with a glorious chapel the size of a small parish church, the best collection of pictures in any episcopal house and in most houses of any kind in the north of England, fifteen bedrooms, a state room 40 feet long, every sort of incident from northern history recalled by its stones, and breathing the names of English history, English thought, and English scholarship, Tunstall and Cosin, Butler and van Mildert, Lightfoot and Westcott. The Park was 800 acres, with delightful country walking, a ruined deer-house but no longer deer, and in normal hours open to the public. When Henson saw it as a place to live in, he was gloomy: *hardly tenable by the Bishop by reason of his poverty.*

The great dining-room was used only for meetings. But its windows rattled when one person walked across the floor, and Henson could see the floor sagging whenever a meeting happened. The historic pictures were dry and in need of varnishing. The east wing of the house was derelict. The Welsh slates on all the roofs were in poor condition. The clerestory windows of the chapel were held only by plaster and could be blown out by a storm. Some of the pinnacles above the chapel were broken. The house was lit by gas and oil lamps, and had no electricity. Throughout Henson's tenure drainage ran to a cess-pool through questionable pipes.

The chapel of Auckland was a noble church not an intimate domestic oratory, but it had tombs and memories, coats of arms and carved mitres and poppyheads, and a unique screen. Could a modern bishop with a sense of history dare to desert what Pudsey built as a banqueting hall and Cosin turned into a chapel and Lightfoot adorned? *It would be indecent and profane.* Yet, must he camp in squalor amid yards of corridor and freeze in dining-rooms which he could not heat, despised by his neighbours and always uncomfortable? He did not enter the occupation of his see until nearly five months after he was nominated; and a reason was the long and unsettling argument behind the scenes (and not altogether behind the scenes because it pushed its way into the newspapers) whether he should, or could, live at Bishop Auckland. He decided to try to live there, and if he found that he could not, to look for a smaller house.[1]

*I shall live in Auckland, if I manage to live at all, as a ruined hidalgo of ancient lineage and historic name in the vast and crumbling palace of his ancestors. The dignity and exceeding beauty of the chapel impressed me greatly, but over everything, within and without, is written Ichabod.*

Guests who dined with them in winter were likely to grow icicles during meals. Ella wore a woolly garment above her dresses. She kept a stock of shawls which she gave out to guests who went to chapel in the evening. That the former lord of most of the coal in the north of England should shiver for want of enough buckets of coal was an incongruity.

From time to time he made arrangements with the Ecclesiastical Commissioners to make the house habitable. Electricity from the mains first came in 1924. He persuaded the Leeds City Art Gallery to clean the great Zurbaran portraits, one by one in return for the right of temporary exhibition. Nearness to a very poor and unemployed population meant depredations; open-face coal stolen from the Park, the fences of the Park torn down for fuel, once lead stolen from the roof, lead drain pipes carried off and perforce replaced with iron.

Henson revelled in the size of it and thought that only a man from such narrow origins would enjoy living in a palace. He liked to show every sort of visitor round the house, especially miners whom he picked up in the Park, but he always wondered whether they criticized a bishop for living in apparent splendour and was sure that they had no idea that he (*poor embarrassed phantom*) could hardly survive in so many

---

[1] Year 1931: Income £7,000; outgoings – rates and taxes £2,000; upkeep of garden £500; car £500; chaplain, secretary, office, £500; diocesan contributions £500; income at disposal *including repairs of house* £3,000.

rooms. He realized for the first time the merit of not having children.

From his predecessor he inherited a butler Ernest Alexander, who lived there so long that he owned the place and looked on succeeding bishops with a proprietary air, as passing protégés to be cherished. He was far more than a butler, for he also attended to the external reverence of the great chapel, and though Henson had nothing in him of Wooster, Alexander had a touch of Jeeves. He preferred things in the castle to remain as in past times and since Henson preferred the contrary, he looked upon his new bishop much as Jeeves looked upon Bertie Wooster when he selected a suit of too loud a pattern. The successive bishops attributed to Alexander the virtue of omniscience. He was already famous in the history of Bishop Auckland. Driving through the Park on a Sunday, Bishop Handley Moule was horrified to see boys of the town playing football, and ordered Alexander to stop the game. Alexander leapt out, seized the ball, and carried it off to the castle in the bishop's carriage. Then there was the cook Mrs Berry and six or seven maids, and a boy or two called footmen who came thin and left fat. Henson could not always apply the right name to its proper face, but he was considerate and they were devoted. He tried to keep in touch with them after they went. When he celebrated the sacrament in the chapel on Sundays, he afterwards wrote down the names of the communicants, maids and all.

To live at Bishop Auckland had disadvantages by reason of its 11 miles from Durham. At times he felt remote from the centre of his work, or suspected that the real bishop of the diocese was his suffragan bishop who lived in Durham. He compared the bishop out at Auckland to St. Simeon Stylites sitting aloft and solitary on his pillar among the sands, contemplating from on high the spectacle of the Church of England; or he said that the palace resembled *a lonely boulder, deposited on some plain, to which it was carried in a previous geological epoch, and which has no affinity with its present surroundings.* This sense of solitude came into the fairly regular moods of melancholy. Auckland *is as deserted and derelict as the pillars of Palmyra in the Syrian desert.* This mood was deepened by two private discoveries. One was the pedestal on which bishops were set, and how difficult to distinguish a friend from a suppliant, and how hard to be completely free with companions. The second was the affliction of Ella's deafness, which began to make communication difficult even with his wife. She carried now a large spiral ear-trumpet known as the Cobra. It was not long before he might even need Fearne Booker's soprano to convey to Ella what he said. This last he found very isolating, as though he was alone in his own home. On top of all it must not be forgotten that some people with whom he had to work looked on him with suspicion or active dislike, and still more that by his lack of assurance he temperamentally imagined that people suspected him more than they did truly.

But part of the isolation he loved. He kept his morning hours undisturbed for reading books, writing sermons or speeches. If he had guests in the house he went to curious lengths to make sure that he would not have to entertain them in the mornings. Most reluctantly would he consent to serve on a committee which met in the morning.

He cut himself off from one link to Durham, or to his clergy, or to other bishops, by refusing to let a telephone into the house. Because a telephone was necessary his chaplains and Fearne Booker spent many hours and bags of coins in the call-box at the market square of Bishop Auckland. If he sent a telegram, he drafted it in the orotundity of Hensonian prose for he had no notion that there exists a language called telegraphese.

But one invention changed the lives of all bishops and the entire pattern of administration as dramatically as any change since Samuel Wilberforce used the new Victorian railways to alter the ideal of a bishop's work. Henson was the first Bishop of Durham to use a car systematically. In later years Moule used a car but is recorded to have *run* 2 miles to a village church, in pouring rain and at the age of seventy, because his car broke. Henson was therefore the first to be able to visit outlying parishes easily. He had no inkling how a car worked, and no notion how to drive, and could not understand why his chauffeur would not overtake round corners. Though his car was comfortable and episcopal-looking, he was just as happy if his chaplain drove him in his little Morris Minor. Twice he

suffered small collisions, once he ran into a mound of road-
works unlit at night and was painfully late for an engagement,
the car would sometimes refuse to move and in 1931, for this
reason, he travelled for the first time in what he called an
English *motor omnibus* and found that its motion made him feel
sick. With the car he would be out to two or three engagements of an afternoon and evening, and showed little signs of
weariness or inability to sleep when he returned.

The chauffeur became one of his 'sons'. William Badham
worked at a garage in Hereford and was hired as an occasional
driver. Henson liked him and offered him the regular post of
chauffeur at Durham. Much together, they grew to be more
father and son than employer and employee. Henson prepared
him for baptism and confirmation and himself administered
the sacraments. When in summer 1924 Badham decided to
emigrate to South Africa to seek his fortune, Henson paid his
fare and later sent money at a bad time.[1] Badham's successor
Leng never attained the same intimacy.

Still more necessary as personal friends were the chaplains.[2]
He chose them carefully, gave them unstinting loyalty, and
made them companions as well as chaplains. He expected his
chaplain to type with at least two fingers and to learn shorthand, but when he dictated spoke so slowly that they hardly
needed the shorthand. Since he said whatever he thought he
required reticence and was not disappointed. They organized
his programme, times of departure, trains to catch, reserved
seats.

For reasons which the reader knows, the relations between
bishop and dean were respectful but cool. Welldon at last grew
infirm, collapsed one day in the cathedral and could hardly be
raised, appeared henceforth at services in a bath chair and once,
sitting still in the shadows after a service, was mistaken by
tourists for one of the monuments. He retired to the south and
the Crown chose Cyril Alington the Headmaster of Eton

---

[1] In 1947 he published as a pamphlet (he did not quite live to see it printed) a long
letter of advice which he wrote to Badham on his 21st birthday; entitled *Coming of
Age*. By then Badham was dead.

[2] Charles Norcock, inherited at Hereford, who was Fearne Booker's cousin; Jack
Clayton 1921–5; Lionel Trotman 1925–9; Charles Pattinson 1929–36; Martin
Ellingsen 1936–9.

(1933). Alington cared about beauty in worship and therefore wanted to make more changes than Henson could quite approve. But he liked Dean Alington very much and respected him; and Alington was a humane man who rejoiced to have on the face of his bishop a mouth which could be trusted not to utter a platitude. The link between Bishop Auckland and the cathedral was much closer after the coming of Alington.

The solitude at Auckland was not solitary, for visitors thronged the house. Ella was very hospitable, too hospitable with her feminine Scottish relations. Local magnates, high ecclesiastics, parish clergy to consult or advise, candidates for ordination, Fellows of All Souls, a constant stream of people came and were only a nuisance if they interrupted his mornings or talked like donkeys during a meal. Favourites were Dean Inge in earlier years, Arthur Headlam who had a family house near by, William Temple despite Henson's disapproval of his 'Socialism'. They found him alive. He reminded one visitor of the tang of a twitching bow-string, all the more in contrast with the dark tapestried room and carved ceiling and heavy furniture. More absurdly another visitor compared him to Voltaire, a rococo sage with aquiline features and a self-assured precision of manner.

He woke early and might be reading by 5 a.m. He had a hot bath during which he whistled or even shouted (he was not tuneful enough for his airs to be deemed singing) his favourite psalms. He regarded the bath as a fertile seed-plot of ideas. Occasionally he tried to memorize a sonnet, or a psalm, while he dressed. He was careful, his clothes were always spick, his hair always in place, and sometimes he would go all the way to Sunderland to get his hair cut with artistry. At 7.45 the post arrived and he and the chaplain set to work answering letters until the time for morning prayer, and he liked to finish, but often answered more letters after breakfast. Important letters he liked to write in his own beautiful hand, and himself copied them into ledgers, if possible with a goose quill, otherwise with a steel pen which he resented and with which he made as many blots as a schoolboy, never with a fountain-pen which he loathed. He almost always answered letters by return of post. The copying took an amount of time which would astonish posterity with its xerox machine. Then he settled

down to prepare his next, or next but one, public utterance, or
to draft one of his too frequent letters to the newspapers, or
simply to general reading of books which caught his interest.
He typed his sermons on a typewriter with large letters and
carefully used capitals for words like GOD and neatly under-
lined the weightier phrases. Sometimes he tried out lectures or
sermons on his wife (before deafness made this impossible)
and she listened with a peaceful encouraging affection which
failed to make him proud of his draft. This scintillating
extempore orator regretted the occasions when an accident
forced him to speak without a written text. He was willing to
preach old sermons of his own, but this practice became
uncommon as he grew older.

The study had a huge desk which he bought from Armitage
Robinson the Dean of Westminster and was otherwise a scene
of jumble which he allowed no one to tidy. The shelves
reached to the ceiling, and were double-banked, books on
chairs, books on the floor. He read whatever took his fancy
and had no systematic plan for study, a neglect which he
continuously lamented and as continuously did nothing to
alter; except by acting on the principle, to read books old and
big is better than to read books new and small. He read little
theology; a lot of church history; a lot of current affairs; a
mingling of celebrated books from the past (Butler's *Analogy*
being a favourite) with controversial ephemera of the present.
When struck by a passage in a book, he drew a pointing hand
in the margin, and after he was bishop the wrist was often clad
in a lawn-sleeve. By his bed he kept a long shelf of books on his
current interest. In free evenings he read a surprising number
of novels, Walter Scott still the king but otherwise not the
classical novelists. On train journeys to London (which in
private he usually called Babylon) he took two suitcases, one
with episcopal robes and personal luggage, the other full of
books. On the train he read steadily and often seriously but
sometimes relieved the journey with a novel. He resented his
addiction to novels, because most of them were worthless, and
he was so constituted that if he began a book he had to finish.
He still liked poetry, at least Browning and Matthew Arnold,
and every Christmas Day he read aloud to Ella and Fearne
Milton's *Ode on the morning of Christ's Nativity*.

The day's activity was punctuated with cups of tea. At dinner he usually drank a glass of wine, even when an eminent teetotal campaigner came to stay.

If a guest with a problem came to lunch, Henson would after lunch walk him round the bowling green and discuss. If the afternoon was free he always went for a long walk in the Park; with company if possible, if not, without. He carried a pointed stick with which he prodded at litter. He argued with the visitor, or his chaplains, or one of his 'sons', treated them as equals and wanted to know their opinions; picked up miners or lads whom he met, and found out about them and their philosophy, treated them also as equals, sometimes brought them back to see the house or the chapel and then wondered whether they would think bishops too grand. The young clergy with whom he walked round the Park sometimes found the experience formidable, but never found it other than memorable.

Lovingly he watched over the common birds in the garden, their habits, mating, nesting, quarrelling, fledglings. He listened for the first cuckoo and watched the swallows building nests in the porch of the chapel. *A blackbird with a white head . . . disports itself before my dressingroom window. It suggests an aged clergyman by its appearance, but its activity belies the suggestion.* In his private prayers he often thanked God for nature. The chief reason for his lament at the coal-stealing from the Park was his love of the trees and grass and stream. He revelled in tints of autumn. He had a religious sense about wallflowers and lavender. He must be the only bishop in history who listened with ecstasy to the cawing of rooks and heard the raucous cries as though they all shouted a hymn of everlastingness to their maker.

If he had free time in the evening, he often demanded that the cards be brought, and played coon-can, which was the only card-game he knew, and usually pretended that he thought Ella cheated. When one of his chaplains, Pattinson, married a true violinist, he would persuade them both to play duets. Every evening he liked to write his diary for the day. In childhood someone must have told him not to waste paper. Whether much had happened in the day or little, the entry must go on to the end of the (usually quarto) page.

At meals with the visitors he would talk; and this talk varied according to the mood but always fascinated the company even when they disapproved. Once he dined at Trinity College Cambridge and held the company spell-bound by his talk; and caused the vice-master a fit of ruefulness, for he disliked what he heard of Henson, had not known that this talker was Henson, and afterwards had to admit that he vastly enjoyed his evening. Occasionally, when carried away, Henson could be guilty of a monologue. Occasionally, when trying to entertain a shy or solemn young man, he could shock by his droll humour and absurdities. More than occasionally he would be penitent, after an evening's talk, that he spoke so recklessly before the immature. These were the necessary accompaniments of such talk. He was informed in history and literature; held the strongest opinions on most subjects and no diplomatic desire to hide what he thought; and was kind, and friendly, and underneath compassionate. Unless his hearers were disturbed by the recklessness, or held opposite opinions of equal strength, they enjoyed the conversation so keenly that if they sat at Ella's end they preferred her not to talk, and might even be vexed if she did talk, so that they need miss no word that came from the other end. Occasionally he could be formidable to a companion at table. Out to dinner he was put next to an Australian girl whose finger-nails were painted bright vermilion. He said to her, *There are few fairer things than a lady's hand. If you have pretty hands, why spoil them? and if your hands are unpleasing, why draw attention to them?*

Whether from heredity or experience he was uncomfortable with bishops; especially Welldon, Lang, Furse of St. Albans, Burroughs of Ripon. He admired Archbishop Randall Davidson, but could hardly enjoy a talk with him because he felt that his senior was always on his guard and wondering what it was prudent to say – the opposite in conversation to Henson. *I made desperate efforts to provoke him to indiscretions but am almost always baffled by his wariness.* Nevertheless Davidson was one of the small number of bishops whom he deeply respected. They were not many – Burge, Ernest Pearce, Temple, George Bell, and of the younger generation Mervyn Haigh. With leading laymen he had no such discomforts, his critical standards were lower. He put Lord Salisbury at the top, and Arthur Balfour and Stanley Baldwin not far away (Conservative leaders all) and then Asquith close behind. Winston Churchill he liked but did not trust him until the Second World War showed a different Churchill.

On high social occasions he often felt uncomfortable. At a feast like the Lord Mayor's banquet he never failed to feel a prick whether such junketing became one of Christ's apostles. *I have just enough religion to make me unable to enjoy 'the world', just enough to make me awkward and uncomfortable in 'Society', not enough to make me avoid it. Thus I am at perpetual cross-purposes with my own conscience.* Select dining-clubs in London he enjoyed, for there he conversed with the leaders of the country in law or politics and found opponents worthy of his steel. But the inherited puritan feeling never let him be quite comfortable with the world. When he breakfasted in bed on holiday he asked himself whether an apostle would have breakfasted in bed. His conscience was ill at ease when Ella and Fearne Booker went off to a dance and he asked himself whether the scruple was rational. Sherry parties he condemned as *a squalid form of entertainment.* Visitors who came to the house were expected to smoke in a hole called smoking-room.

He soon defined what he liked, and what he disliked, about being a bishop. He loved the spiritual, and abhorred the business. If he could get out of a committee he would. He had to preside at the diocesan Board of Finance, but the solicitor recorded that the members of the committee were not encouraged by the chairman to talk. He hated the necessity to raise money. He thought most diocesan conferences a waste of time, and the meetings of central Church bodies in London worse than a waste of time. He had no faith that truth or wisdom is to be found among majorities. As he set off for a meeting of bishops, or for Church Assembly, his prayer at starting was very modest – *that we may do no harm.*

But the man was a preacher, and preaching he loved. Formerly he addressed people whose hearts he knew, now he talked to strange faces in strange village churches; and knew too exactly when his utterance was unintelligible, or bored, or offended in a way which he never intended. He found that he loved confirmations, the directness of communication between himself and the children or their parents, the too heavy sense of responsibility that he was privileged to be part of a solemn moment in so many lives.

*I think that of all the oblations which poor humanity offers to its Creator, the hopes and fears of Confirmation candidates are perhaps the most accept-able.*

Then he discovered that, though he had a low opinion of the value of his advice, he took a pleasure in giving his opinion, when he was asked, on a moral or religious problem; though, if the problem was too gravely personal, his heart was miser-able. To this rule he made one large exception, crusaders for a cause; for temperance, or purity, or foreign missions, or boy scouts; campaigners whom he mourned as *the flies and mosqui-toes of the spiritual life.* Zealots in the Girls Friendly Society caused the lament about such crusaders, that they were *moral scarecrows in a field of virtue.*

He was proud to be Bishop of Durham. He often talked of the *Palatine see,* for the old Bishops of Durham were Counts Palatine, charged with defence of the realm against Scots. The pride was partly a sense of history, that he sat in so ancient a chair with so eminent a place in English history; partly a sense of surprise that the ill-educated boy from Broadstairs rose to such a height; partly a pleasure that he followed a long line of men like Butler or Lightfoot. He took a comic satisfaction in one or two of the outer trappings – that he should be able to write to his stepmother with the signatures *H. H. Hereford* and then the signature *Herbert Dunelm;* and when he made out the list for a dinner-party, even in the privacy of his own diary, he would write out the list of guests and then add his own name in full, *the Bishop of Durham*; almost as though he savoured the title because he could hardly believe it to belong to himself. The night before one ordination he set an ordinand next to him and through dinner told him about the men in the portraits on the walls, and ended *prince-bishops all;* and the ordinand took marks off the bishop that in such a moment he should think of the secular glories of his see. But mostly this pleasure in the past, which was also a pleasure in the present, could not offend. Henson had a strong sense of fitting dignity but noth-ing of pretentiousness. One of the reasons for his distrust of

Archbishop Lang was a fear that Lang could not distinguish dignity from pomposity. If Henson sat on high in the magnificent bishop's throne in Durham Cathedral, observers might suppose that the occupant would be tempted to suffer from a sense of his importance. But this occupant was liable to think, as he sat there splendid, that he resembled some archaeological ruin of the Near East with an equal influence upon Bedouin tribes in the surrounding desert.

On his visits to parishes he was not generally thought by the people to be a great preacher; for his rigid refusal to depart from a written text might be a barrier, and he thought sermons of twenty minutes very short; and if his mind was full of a subject – say, the morality of contraception, or of divorce, or of Mussolini in Abyssinia – he could not help but talk about it even though the occasion was not relevant to contraception or Abyssinia. Usually he was crystal clear but he expected his hearers to know as many words as he, and one of them once came away from a sermon treasuring the phrase *an invariable concomitant phenomenon.* Moreover he had an agony about coughing in church. If a choirboy could not check his coughing while he preached, he stopped the sermon, waited for silence, or asked the culprit to leave; and once when he asked an adult cougher to leave, the victim passed the bishop's chauffeur outside with the words 'I hope that Bee dies of whooping-cough.' This habit is universally agreed by those who remember it to have been a mistake, because everyone remembered the bishop and the cough and forgot what the bishop said.

At Christmas 1934 Henson's mind was full of the British purchase from the Russian government of that treasure of Christian history and Biblical study, the Codex Sinaiticus. In Jarrow he dismayed a congregation, which expected the message of Christmas, by a disquisition on the Codex Sinaiticus; and when on top of this he asked a cougher to leave, another indignant worshipper clattered out noisily, and later abused the sermon as 'the dry chaff of remote scholarship with ill-concealed patronage'. The clatterer could not know what we know, that the rector asked the bishop to tell them about the Codex Sinaiticus. Still, other bishops would have obeyed the request by knowing so little about the Codex Sinaiticus that they could easily insert the comforts of Christmas. And probably the comforts of Christmas – even though Henson was uneasy if religion made for comfort – rose above the horizon after the clatterer left. At Pelton parish church he found obscene pictures drawn inside the hymn-book at his stall. Any other bishop in England would have said a quiet word to the vicar afterwards. Henson took the book to the pulpit and spoke with severity on the moral state of the parish where this could occur.

But though they might not understand what he said, or like it when they understood it, or think that he went on long, the country parishes saw more of their bishop than they had seen before. And sometimes, on big occasions, they heard an utterance more powerful than they could have heard anywhere else in England. He had a friendly touch with the choir, and on high days went round after service shaking their hands and giving each of the boys a shilling. For educated young men the words could be compelling. One believed that he learnt the beauty of the English language from listening to Henson. Another changed his course of study from classics to history because he heard Henson speak on the importance of history. Another found it remarkable that when he heard this preacher he should feel a desire to clap in church. More than one learnt of the importance of Christianity as a way of life. After he preached to a numerous congregation at Loughborough College, a crowd of students pulled him in a lorry to the station and then carried him on their shoulders from the lorry to the train and 1,000 students on the platform cheered his parting – though he lost a rug in the mêlée. A girl in one congregation is recorded as afterwards making this judgement, which rings true in all its three sides – too educated speech, strong impression, high calling of clergy – 'I could not understand it, except he seemed to tell the parsons to blow the Lord's trumpet and not their own.'

He had the advantage of a striking appearance; the little **stature with the bushy upturned eyebrows which could make** him look sometimes forbidding, sometimes quizzical, sometimes like Mephistopheles. The hazel eyes were brilliant, and though the sensitive mouth could take a grim line, when he smiled the face was enchanting and the humour infectious.

One of his young men said of him 'He seemed to grow as he spoke, until one had the impression of being in the presence of someone one can only describe as majestic, and yet benign. I suppose that in these days one would describe his presence as charismatic.'

In his earlier years he led processions through the streets on Good Friday, an older custom of the county; 2,000 or 3,000 marchers, mostly men, to a town hall or hired auditorium, with a mayor, and the ministers of all denominations, and a band, even a Salvation Army band; and ending with an address by the bishop. At Sunderland in 1921 it was like the good old days at Barking, though the rain fell and he eyed his bedraggled lawn-sleeves. At Gateshead in 1922 it was almost rained off by a drenching downpour; at Hartlepool in 1923 it was truly an event of all the people; at Sunderland in 1925 he was escorted through the streets by the two MPs; and then it failed. In the year of the General Strike he was ill, alone and comfortless in his private chapel. He walked again through Sunderland with the mayor on Good Friday in 1928. But the event was fading, more went away for Easter, people lost interest, he never walked again and spent his Good Fridays quietly.

He had much interest in Christian unity, no interest in Christian unity as churchmen of his generation understood the task ahead. All schemes for unity have a concealed axiom, the other side is not so good a Christian society as ours. The only thing needed is for everyone to abandon their pretensions and recognize the others as equal to themselves. Christian unity does not need manufacturing, it exists. Ecumenical men try to manufacture. He voted for the South Indian unity scheme at a Lambeth Conference, but gave his vote with scepticism. And when the negotiations touched traditional Churches which hardly counted the Church of England as a Church, he was not indifferent but hostile. At the celebrations of the anniversary of the Council of Nicaea in 1925 an exchange was reported between Henson and Bishop Headlam of Gloucester (who at such work was a master) because eastern patriarchs would kiss the Anglicans in their customary sign of fellowship:

Henson:  Well, Headlam, have you kissed these prelates?
Headlam:  Not in my line.
Henson:  I deplore your aloofness, Headlam, because I am credibly
informed that our relations with the Orthodox depend
upon the fervency of our osculations.

Could Christian unity depend upon outward forms? Hence he
led the protests when Archbishop Davidson (1923–4) allowed
discussions about unity with representatives of the Church of
Rome of Malines.

The Anglicans celebrated the 1,250th anniversary of
Benedict Biscop's foundation at Monkwearmouth. Cardinal
Bourne came to Sunderland and was rude to the Anglicans,
calling their claim to 'continuity' an impertinence. Several
clergy appealed to Henson for an answer. Henson promised to
speak on the subject in a sermon at Bishopwearmouth, Sunday
14 September 1924. (*This wrangling of Churches, this insistence on
claims and names, this careful delimiting of ecclesiastical frontiers, is
all beside the mark.*) He drove to Bishopwearmouth and found
the church crowded and many outside unable to push in. He
preached for forty minutes and no one slumbered. Many
newspapers gave prominence to the sermon. The churchwardens and at least three clergymen asked that it be published. When it was printed (as *Continuity*) it was bought over
the country. One of his young friends told him that in the
general view the cardinal had been put in his place. On the
whole Henson was pleased. And the people were well pleased.
I met a very old man from Durham, who told me that Henson
was a 'wonderful' bishop. I asked him what he remembered
about Henson. The only thing that he knew was that Henson
rocked back Cardinal Bourne and gloriously vindicated the
Church of England.

In 1922 about one and a half million people lived in the
Durham diocese which was the county of Durham. Henson
judged that about 40 per cent were nonconformists or Roman
Catholics, for the area contained a large number of Irish immi-
grants. To serve these people Henson had 272 parishes – that
is, an average population of about 6,000 to every parish but in
such conditions averages are meaningless – 388 clergymen of

whom more than 100 were curates. If the people were divided by clergy, each clergyman ministered to 3,866 people. But this again was a meaningless statistic.

The number of these clergy, and especially the number of curates, fell drastically since before the First World War and still fell slowly (sixteen fewer by 1927). Henson's first general view of the clergy as a class, both in Hereford and in Durham, was unfavourable. He entrusted to his journal sweeping generalizations which superficial historians will use without discrimination. They were usually married (and Henson's ancient and private doubt about the marriage of clergy made him painfully sensitive to what he thought unsuitable in a vicar's wife), they were poor or very poor, many were of humble origin, and had an inferior education. The scholar among them (outside the Canons of Durham) was Espin, the Vicar of Tow Law, an astronomer famous among astronomers. That they came of humble origin was in his eyes a sign that they were likely to have been forced into inferior education, and that they would not easily rise above the normal culture or absence of culture among their parishioners. Knowing that the dream was wild, he hankered after an exclusively graduate clergy; and knowing that the dream was wilder, and having in his own experience but one university, hankered after an exclusively Oxbridge clergy, with exceptions indeed for the University of Durham. And when he met for the first time the clergy of the diocese of Hereford, and then the clergy of the diocese of Durham, he was pained beyond reason. A man whose academic interests lay in the history of the English Church ought neither to have been surprised nor pained. He soon discovered that some of the best of his Durham clergy were sons of miners and that several had been miners. But it took him time to adjust his standards; and to realize that the parson whose hands smelt because he milked his own goats was not necessarily an impossible priest, and not to be astonished that *an undersized hirsute plain man* named Marr, who had ministered in the *unlovely slum* of St. Cuthbert's, Hebburn, for twenty-three years, was of the stuff of which calendared saints were made. He started recording the professions or trades of the fathers of the men whom he ordained.

For a long time he was not popular among the clergy

because, as one of them said, he showed them the rough side of his tongue. His brother was the rudest man in Calcutta and he himself had been taught to speak the truth especially when it would displease. Since he had high standards he conceived it his duty to thrust these standards upon the clergy. When he saw a parson idle and a parish neglected, he said what he thought when he got the chance. This tongue aroused resentments. He wanted to abolish the parson's freehold which gave vicars and rectors security of tenure in their parishes because he saw it as an invitation to the idle to stay idle. He hated impunctuality. The daughter of his friend the Swedish archbishop came to stay in 1922 and said that she heard he was always quarrelling with his clergy and asked him whether it was true. Henson could not remember a quarrel.

The astringency made him a few enemies: Milner, the Vicar of Elton, who publicly refused to shake hands because he disapproved the bishop's rule that confirmands have not less than fourteen years; Watts, the Vicar of Shildon who was a Socialist and denounced the bishop as a Tory; Hodgson, the Vicar of Escomb, sympathized with the Bolsheviks and made plain his antipathy to Henson; Merryweather, the Vicar of Pelton, who excommunicated three of his parishioners – and apart from such few cases, a number of other men, too courteous to reprove their bishop in public but who nursed criticism in private.

He gave them handles. A group of ordinands in the chapel at Auckland were embarrassed when the bishop saw a man of humble origins and limited wardrobe wearing a light grey suit with a pullover, and said sternly, *Young man you are not properly dressed for an ordination,* and caused another candidate to press chin into breast in the effort to hide a spotted tie. Arriving at St. Oswin's church in South Shields he found all the clergy in the vestry wearing copes and ordered them to take them off and had an altercation with the vicar and thereafter the spirit of the service was not devotional.[1] The parsons thought him odd

---

[1] He wore a cope himself in York Minster by request of William Temple (25 July 1934). *The thing is not illegal, and there may be as much pettiness in refusing as accepting.* He wore a cope when he escorted the new King, in the ancient privilege of Bishops of Durham, at the coronation of King George VI. He wore vestments, uncomfortably, at an episcopalian chapel in Scotland. He never wore them in England.

to denounce parsons' motor cars in the national press (on the ground that cars took them too easily away from their people) when he went everywhere in a chauffeur-driven car. Countless stories went round about his stage whispers. He was not always aware when he was audible. In a solemn procession with mayor and corporation through a churchyard, the consecrating bishop could be heard saying *Those tombstones look like lavatory pans*. When a worthy councillor bored the company infinitely with his speech, the bishop on the platform was heard to say, in what he fancied to be a whisper, *If only I were nearer I would make that man feel my episcopal foot*.

The curates thought him a Victorian, outmoded in his ideas; because he condemned cars for clergy, or votes for women, or trade unions for miners. His anti-union stance complicated their pastoral lives and made some of them think him a disaster. But they could not deny that he had presence. Gervase Markham, looking back after many years at his curacy under Henson, wrote: 'My impression is that nowadays (1979) curates think of their diocesan bishop as a fellow human being. Forty years ago our bishop was a man from another world, who shed an aura round him, a Shekinah of formidable glory into which one hardly dared to intrude.' Henson was not in his element at walkabouts or bunfights after service.

Curates summoned to see their bishop trembled as the butler Alexander showed them with all the courtliness of the centuries into Henson's study. But this did not mean that Henson was prelatical. On the contrary. Lady Frances Balfour had an extensive acquaintance among bishops. The Bodleian library has a letter from her to the Earl of Selborne (Selborne MSS 90/135) in which she lists the bishops whom she found specially unpompous. This list was caused because she met Headlam and thought him buttoned in his gaiters. At the head of her 'human' bishops she put Charles Gore and Fish Cecil, and in the past the holy Edward King of Lincoln. 'Henson, of course, I love, but he is in a class apart.'

He thought much about the wives of the clergy, and disliked it when young clergymen got married. He inspected fiancées when he could, and the interview for the engaged couple was likely to be formidable in prospect and delightful in experience. When his chaplain Charles Pattinson was about to become engaged, Henson summoned her for inspection, and at first quite frightened her, and soon won her total and lasting affection. Towards the end of his episcopate he grew far more friendly to clerical marriage, and allowed that in certain circumstances clergy might be better priests if they were married – though he still preferred his curates not to rush into matrimony.

He helped clergy with a fund which was described as 'a fund at the bishop's disposal'. This money came from various generous donors, a lot of it came from himself. He was specially glad to cover debts and would give an interest-free loan with no date set for repayment. Perhaps he remembered how in the bad days for his family, Fellows of All Souls used to keep him from the clutches of his bank manager.

A bishop who disliked committees depended more than many bishops upon his suffragan bishop, who lived in Durham and had the titular see of Jarrow. After his predecessor's suffragan died he appointed two efficient suffragans in succession, both of whom were good at committees and good chairmen and tireless workers.[1]

From time to time, in one of his melancholies, Henson decided that his suffragan and not himself was the real Bishop of Durham. In such moods he would never decide to remedy by attending more committees in Durham even though he might again lament the isolation of Bishop Auckland. But in 1925, partly because his difficulty was not imaginary, he began a venture which was the best way for a man of his equipment to unite the diocese. He took over the expense and management of a diocesan magazine, *The Bishoprick* (first number, 5

---

[1] He inherited Quirk. His first choice was Samuel Kirshbaum, a Jew by race who changed his name to Knight during the war with Germany. He was curate at Barking where Henson then at Ilford helped him. Thereafter they were inseparable; and Knight became curate of St. Margaret's Westminster, incumbent in Herefordshire, incumbent in Durham county and so suffragan. The choice was so Hensonian that at first it was not liked. Knight wrote the Saturday religious article for *The Times*. Then Henson chose Geoffrey Gordon, who was equally Protestant and still more Modernist; and since Henson's Modernism was mild, they began to diverge. But he filled Henson's needs for a good chairman and pastor among the parishes. He died suddenly in 1938. Henson had every right to choose his successor, but postponed the choice for many months so that his own successor might choose.

November 1925). The arrangement of the business was left to his suffragan and his chaplain and the diocesan secretary. But Henson wrote everything that mattered. He printed his weightier sermons or charges to ordinands or obituaries or speeches to diocesan conferences or attacks on those enthusiasms which currently aroused his indignation like the Oxford Group Movement or Faith Healers. This was the kind of writing at which Henson shone; topics of the day treated with a vigour and a frankness and a range of reading which made them examples of the highest form of journalism and the most intelligent mode of propaganda. Many clergy found them compulsive reading. Curates looked forward to the coming of the next number. The magazine became known, subscribers outside Durham joined, London newspapers printed extracts, it began to pay its way, and finally cost its author nothing. After ordinations, confirmations, and institutions of new clergy to parishes, it was his agent for reaching out to the diocese. Half a century later bits are still readable even by persons who know nothing about Durham.

In judging Henson's episcopate, no one must forget that he was the first bishop in all history to make a diocesan magazine bought in other parts of England.

Because he read widely, and could not fail to finish even a worthless book which he started, and wrote so many letters with his own hand, and copied so many with his own hand, and took hours of trouble with sermons or speeches or lectures, and worked slowly because he had high standards, and put the best of his mind into the *Bishoprick* – he could not have time for fundamental study. In this he resembled all the other bishops. Yet even here he was like none of the others.

Cambridge University invited him to give the Rede Lecture. This is a prestigious lecture and Henson was the last-but-one ecclesiastic to deliver it during the twentieth century. The vice-chancellor probably expected a theme appropriate to a churchman. Henson chose to lecture on Byron.

The lecture, delivered on Saturday 3 May 1924 in a full Senate House, is one of Henson's best pieces of writing and one of the rare moments which make the student wonder whether after all this hard reader could have sat happy in an Oxford chair.

Why should a Bishop of Durham choose Byron? Because men should talk about what interests them. Why was he interested? The liberator, the martyr for freedom – once the boyish Henson inspired audiences with his eloquence on Gordon of Khartoum, Gordon dying to free blacks from slave-dealers, Byron dying for Greek freedom against the Turks. Then the editor of Byron's letters was his old friend Prothero and therefore the theme had an aura of All Souls. And Byron was nurtured in a narrow Calvinist faith and grew to be notorious throughout Europe for immorality. This last juxtaposition puzzled and fascinated Henson for reasons of which the reader is aware but the vice-chancellor was not.

His conscience was not quite clear. *For a Christian bishop to be devoting Lent to the study of Byron's poems and letters is a proceeding entirely congruous with All Fools Day* (1 April 1924). He resolved to accept no future proposal which would turn him aside from diocesan duty. (He soon broke the resolution.) He imagined gossipers saying that the Bishop of Durham was an idle fellow who neglected his diocese to indulge his hobby. We have no evidence that anyone gossiped anything. Probably the diocese if it cared at all was glad to have its bishop deliver the Rede lecture.

The lecture attracts. That is not so frequent an occurrence in Henson's writing (sermons excepted) that it can pass without comment. His vocation was that of gadfly among the Churches, to blast at folly, low standards, idleness, woolliness, sentimentality, pomposity, excess of emotion, injustice and bigotry. Therefore nearly all his writing was combative. He intended to rile for the sake of reform. *Byron* is rare because it had no wish to reform anyone or anything.

St. Andrews University invited him to deliver the Gifford Lectures on the philosophy of religion. He decided to refuse. He was a historian not a philosopher and anyway had no time. Then William Temple, himself a philosopher who gave famous Gifford Lectures, persuaded him to accept. So he delivered lectures on *Christian Morality* (published Oxford 1936) to a diminishing audience. The result is his only solid academic book.

Civilization, and all that is highest in society, rests upon Christian moral standards which are a natural morality framed and developed and transformed by Jewish ethical thought and the person and teaching of Jesus. These principles are applied in changing circumstances of society, so that St. Paul's attitude to slaves or women becomes obsolete in new conditions. The foundation of Christian civilization is the home and the family, which is natural but has been powerfully conditioned by the Christian exaltation of the woman and the child. Henson was the first systematically to apply these principles to the problems of a coming world – racial equality and racial mixture, the pressure of too many mouths, the duty still to fight a just war though any war must have horrendous results, the rightful use of divorce and contraception.

Friends reviewed the book wisely and generously, but few people bought copies. It was not quite fundamental enough for the ethical philosophers, its common sense not quite theoretical enough for the theorists, its exposition too academic for the general reader, and those who expected Henson to be always brilliant were disappointed at his self-restraint. Henson afterwards felt the venture to be unhappy and wondered whether he was right to spend the time. What stands out of the book is his conviction of the unequalled nobility of the Christian ethic and its absolute necessity if the world is to survive.

That the two senior bishops of the York province, Temple and Henson, could both enter the realm of the professional and give Gifford Lectures must help the Church of England and might even help Christianity. But the help so given to the diocese of Durham was indirect and would not be seen as help by some hard-pressed clergy.

During the last spring and summer that he was a bishop he worked at a book, *The Church of England,* written by request for a series of *English Institutions*. It appeared at the end of 1939. It was a melancholy book. The mood of sadness in a world of looming war, and of an old man of seventy-five near the end of his active work, can be felt in its pages. He took all the ecclesiastical structure apart, and when he held the pieces up to the eye of the beholder they looked more like a contraption of one-armed engineers than like the shadow of a celestial city. It could hardly be denied that in certain lights and from certain angles this was how the Church of England looked. Friends threw appreciative noises into their reviews, George Bell said that it was a first-class book, Charles Smyth said that it was exceptionally shrewd, Raymond Mortimer thought it extraordinary to find a bishop able to take so detached a view of the Church he served, Evelyn Underhill said that the Establishment as here portrayed was about as exhilarating as a workhouse, and the gloom of the *Church Times* was blacker. Just occasionally the old fire reappeared, for example in an eloquent prose-poem in honour of one of his heroes, Archbishop Cranmer. But this experience of authorship perturbed him sufficiently to abandon an agreement to write a book on *The English Bible* for the Home University Library.


The people multiplied, the number of clergy fell. Henson needed fresh men, ordinands. He cut himself off from part of the supply by a sudden rise in the standards for ordination. He thought his predecessor Handley Moule to be a very good man and a bad bishop; and in the latter capacity worst, in being too kind to suppliant and ill-educated ordinands, so that Henson was left with responsibility for a number of men whom he thought impossible. He said so publicly, and caused himself a sudden period of sharp unpopularity in the diocese, where Moule was justly beloved. He broke some men's expectations; and his most disliked decision was a refusal to ordain the blind – disliked with reason, for Christian history contains examples of blind priests delicate for all their disability in the direction of men's souls. Therefore, by requiring quality where quality was seldom to be had, he lessened the supply of men for whom his parishes clamoured. He would never lower his standard. He personally examined the deacons in the classics of the English religious tradition, John Jewel, or Joseph Butler, or Richard Hooker.

The reputation of a bishop may draw or repel young men or their advisers. Henson started by knowing that his name repelled. The country might care nothing about the Hereford Scandal, but those who cared for ordinands cared much. He was a Modernist bishop. Nearly all the best ordinands were either Catholic or evangelical, and not likely to admire a Modernist bishop or to wish for ordination under his hands. Of every variety of Catholicism he was a biting critic. And though he stood for the union of Protestant churches on the basis of charity, something about this language made evangelicals uneasy. The heads of the theological colleges, who advised future clergymen, would direct them elsewhere. Young men hesitated, or were advised by their families to hesitate, before applying to such a bishop.

In his first few years at Durham Henson lost this doubtful reputation. Yet he did not change his mind.

He was elected and consecrated after a national storm against his Modernism. Dean Inge, the ablest journalist of all the Modernist leaders, preached the sermon at his nerve-racking consecration. The Cambridge Professors of Divinity, who were committed to restating orthodox Christianity into intellectual respectability, looked to Henson expectantly. The Modernists needed a bishop to head their cause.

An American bishop resigned his see and became a Roman Catholic, and justified this behaviour by quotations from Henson. Another American resigned office in the Church and justified his behaviour by large quotations from Henson. G. K. Chesterton turned Roman Catholic from being Anglican, and justified his behaviour by quoting Henson and Inge. This was Modernist fame.

That expectation was shattered within a year of Henson coming to Durham.

In his autobiography Henson failed to mention the Modern Churchmen's Conference at Girton, Cambridge, in August 1921. Here the Modernist leaders gathered and talked in provoking language, which the press printed.

Under the same historical solvents which led Henson to his turnabout in 1899–1900, some Modernists began to want to free faith altogether from its origins in history and make Jesus a symbol or myth, and refuse to allow that faith depended in any way on enquiry into a person of the past. This was not however the principal rock of offence. Everything depended on whether the enquiry was conducted in a reverent and religious manner. Modernists were immature, in the sense that they felt to be rebels against a tradition; and therefore some of them talked brashly, or gleefully, or even scornfully. Their lesser men suffered from the illusion of second-rate minds that to shock conservatives is the way to persuade.

At Girton Henson's friend Rashdall threw overboard the Christian creeds. Rashdall was not second-rate, nor brash, nor scornful. But reading this speech in the newspapers, Henson examined his own mind and knew that he could not agree.

Agnostic about the birth from a Virgin or the resurrection of the body, he knew that his Christianity depended upon Christ as the incarnate God, and could see no way to state this except by the old Nicene creed. The crucifix which he bought in the slums of Poplar so long ago still faced him from his shelves and still spoke to his heart. As he celebrated the sacrament on 11 September, the thought swept over him that Rashdall's theory of the Christ was not compatible with the sacrament of holy communion. Though he liked Rashdall with his *shambling bonhomie* and allowed him to be a learned man, he condemned the *lesser fry* as *shallow, dogmatic, provocative, and almost incredibly foolish.* They belittled the scale and perplexity of the reconstruction to which they addressed themselves, forgot that a Church cannot proceed like a university, and that *it is an obligation of charity to make sure that the faith of the simple is not gratuitously disturbed.*

Henson was afraid that if 'the Modernist bishop' preached against Modernism in a Church Congress, he would be accused of *tergiversation.* He was right in this fear. Nevertheless he preached at the Church Congress.

These events began to distance Henson from the Modernist party.

In a national perspective this was not a gain. A bishop was needed to head the Modernists. Henson refused. The leadership therefore fell within a few years to Bishop Barnes of Birmingham, a Cambridge mathematician. This was a disaster for Modernism, for Bishop Barnes was too much of an individualist to guide or restrain his junior extremists. By the middle of the thirties the Modernist movement achieved the unenviable reputation of being the most arid version of religion ever to pretend to be a faith. In this decline Henson's refusal to lead had a little part. But he may have been right as well as wise. No one knew better than Henson that he was not

a theologian. The ultimate problems with which the Modernists struggled were profound.

The event had personal consequences. It separated him from
earlier friends. *I am like a circus-rider with a foot on both the horses!*
*The position is precarious, and very uncomfortable.* The painful
separation was a progressive alienation from Dean Inge, who
came to blame Henson as a turncoat, and whose attitude to
religion Henson came to doubt as journalistic and superficial,
whereas formerly he regarded him as the leading divine
among the Churches. This gulf was patched for a time.
During the thirties they ceased the old intimacy. Hensonian
sagas began to circulate among the clubs – how when Bishop
Barnes came late to a meeting of bishops and found no chair
left, Henson cried, *Anticipate the judgment of the universal Church*
*and sit on the fire.*

In the Church of England were three schools of thought,
now called Evangelical, Catholic and Modernist. He was
realizing that he could not accept the Modernist label, because
he found their interpretation of Christianity to be maimed.
The evangelical movement was impossible to him because it
was the religion of father and because his mind grew to be
remote from an evangelical pattern. Catholicism he was
brought up to see as dangerous; and then he fought in Ilford
and watched the villainies of the Dreyfus case in France, and
threw Catholicism to the winds and identified himself as its
critic. Then, where did he stand? What did he stand for? Was
he only destructive, and had no direction in which he could
lead? Was he all his life to see the weakness of other men, but be
unwilling to lead them forward? Was he only an individualist, a
*lone wolf?* These hesitations bothered him for the rest of his life.

But from the point of view of the diocese of Durham, this
distancing from the Modernist leaders had nothing but gain.
The ordinands continued to decline because ordinands continued to decline in the nation and most of them were
southerners and County Durham was a long way away. But
they did not decline because they wished to have nothing to do
with Henson. In his moments of melancholy he still thought
his repute to be a minus. He was usually wrong.

The new attitudes were symbolized by the principals of the
two theological colleges with most Oxbridge ordinands who

were not evangelical. B. K. Cunningham was the head of Westcott House at Cambridge, old-fashioned, charming, and with influence on many excellent ordinands. Henson took to him, he took to Henson, and set up a link between Westcott House and the diocese of Durham, so that Henson was very pleased that two of his own 'sons' went there to train for ordination. Odder was the link with Cuddesdon near Oxford, for by foundation and tradition Cuddesdon was Anglo-Catholic. Henson could hardly think that men received at Cuddesdon a proper grounding in the principles or practices of the Church of England. But it had men whom he needed; he had Anglo-Catholic parishes; and a delightful principal, Jimmie Seaton who was known as Friar Tuck, set up the link between Cuddesdon and the diocese of Durham out of which Henson said he received his best ordinands.

Henson was very fair. He did not like it if his Catholic ordinands refused breakfast on the day of their ordination but he would not interfere. He did not like it when the Catholic-minded archdeacon, the scholar A. E. J. Rawlinson, whom he selected as a counterweight to other diocesan officers like his suffragan, organized a retreat for the candidates before their ordination; but he blessed it. If the candidates came and asked him to hear their confessions, he always heard them; and usually he talked to the candidates about the place of confession in a pastoral ministry, and astonished some of them by his expertise. He always advised the men that if they were themselves required by their duty to hear confessions, they should themselves go to confession. They felt that this anti-Catholic bishop was somehow Catholic.

Two of his ordinands afterwards became famous throughout the world and in their careers we see the bishop at work.

Leonard Wilson later won the acclaim of the Churches as a confessor for the faith when he was tortured by Japanese in Singapore. Henson received him as an ordinand, encouraged him, found him a diocesan grant, advised him on work overseas, and kept in touch through his career.

Philip Strong was later the leader of the Churches, and more than the Churches, in wartime New Guinea and still later the Primate of Australia; a man of a stature seldom found. He always intended to be a missionary. He found an Anglo-

Catholic parish to which he wanted to go as curate, St. Mary's, Tyne Dock. This was 1922; and 'the only fly in the ointment' wrote Strong, was that it was 'in the diocese of Durham . . . If there was one Bishop I was not keen to be ordained by and to serve under it was Bishop Hensley Henson.'

With trepidation Strong went to Bishop Auckland and resented the majesty of Alexander the ancient retainer as he was shown into the study. *Sit down Mr Strong, I understand that you want to come to my diocese.* This was not true, so Strong replied that he felt called to go to the parish of St. Mary's, Tyne Dock, if the bishop would allow. Henson suggested that he look at other (less Anglo–Catholic) parishes. Strong persisted; if not to Tyne Dock, he had a possible parish in the York diocese. Henson then said that he must pass an examination on Hooker book V, gave him a discourse on Hooker, and asked questions. 'I soon found that I need not give very full answers as he seemed to like to answer them himself and I therefore tried to be a good attentive listener.' Henson then took him into lunch where he was made to feel a member of the family.

When he was ordained in the chapel of Auckland Castle, he sensed how the giving of holy orders moved Henson to the depths of his being. Strong was not mistaken. Henson felt this as a glory and an agony – the agony of sitting in judgement on fellow-men, the emotional exhaustion of the sacrament which sometimes prevented him from sleeping that night, the difficulty of interviews with ordinands when he was so reticent about religious experience and hardly liked to probe, the inadequacy which he felt as a guide of troubled souls, the worry that he sent them like soldiers into a long weary campaign of which neither he nor they could ever see the end. Strong could not perceive all this, which we can see from Henson's papers. But he was moved because the bishop was so moved.

A year later Strong was to be ordained priest in Auckland chapel. In his charge to the ordinands Henson warned them not to hear confessions during their inexperienced years as pastors. This troubled Strong grievously. He decided to withdraw from ordination next day unless his difficulty was cleared, and sought an interview with Henson. Strong said that he accepted thus far, a young priest should not sit in church at normal times for confessions, for this was the proper place of the vicar, but that in going about in the parish, ministering to the sick or dying, or healthy, there must come times. . . . Henson put both his hands on Strong's shoulders and said *My son, you can never refuse the ministry of reconciliation when it is asked of you*; and Strong thought that he remembered an added word of confidence in his pastorate.

With these ideals and emotions the charges which Henson gave to the ordinands cost him most in preparation and now make the best book which he ever put into print.

*Ad Clerum* was published in 1937 to mark fifty years since his own ordination. It contains twelve charges to ordinands on the eve of their ordination, and therefore his ideal for the Church of England.

Henson's parson is a quiet unostentatious man whose work is to lead his people towards the good life. This work is partly service to them; but not only by service, for he must hold before their eyes the Lordship of Christ, and affirm the reality and the everlastingness of things unseen amidst a secularizing world where the affirmation is not easy. He is not to court unpopularity, but neither is he to court popularity. He ought to be in a manner marked out from the people because they should feel he has a special commission from God; and so he ought, at least in his parish, to wear the clerical collar. He ought not to use irreverent words, or descend to slang in the pulpit, or smoke tobacco in the streets, or use words which offend unnecessarily (like *mass*). He is to be careful in the duties of life like paying bills to tradesmen. He is a reading man who does not waste much time on newspapers but keeps his study of Scripture, and needs another intellectual interest or hobby to keep his mind alive. He stays in his parish, and is seldom seen rushing away in a motor car, and visits his people from house to house, and is contented with his lot. He is a member of a profession as the world regards professions, yet he knows that it is more a vocation than a profession, and remembers as he looks back that he hardly chose his course of life, he seems to himself to have been able to do no other. If he marries he chooses a wife who can share his vocation, and if that happens she becomes a great influence for purity and kindness and devotion. From his pulpit he speaks rather of another world

than this, so he should not use the pulpit for political programmes or a discourse on current affairs. He is a man of
discretion who is interested in human beings, and tries to keep
a sense of proportion, and is modest, and knows his own
limits, but wants to live strictly by his own better standards.
He feels the weight of the responsibility, the difficulty of the
fight; yet he is not overburdened by it because he knows that
he was sent to these people by a commission that stems from
the apostles, and that he takes rank as one of Christ's
ambassadors.

The portrait is austere, without a deep feeling of glory or
grace. The speaker cared too much about realities to idealize
into utopia. No one saw more penetratingly how the ideal was
not lived out. But for all its severity, the portrait is kindly, and
practicable, and honest. It stands in an authentic tradition of
the English pastoral ideal, from Richard Hooker to George
Herbert, from John Keble to Richard Church.

He cared nothing for fashion. Contemporary rages or
phases of thought left him unmoved or hostile. That is what
makes parts of him readable still. The classical divinity of the
Church of England was the ground on which he stood, and by
which he judged the intellectual excitements of an hour. The
faculty was a superb though destructive gift of seeing through
every sham. The ideal was that of pastoral care in its dedicated
single-mindedness.

The more men he ordained, the more clergy knew the man
and sentiment in the diocese altered in his favour. By the time
he resigned the see he had ordained some quarter of the clergy.

Because he could not use the telephone he kept in touch by
print, by interview or by letter. The channel of print consisted
of more than the *Bishoprick*. By the door of his study he kept a
bench piled with copies of his writings – they were not widely
bought by the public – and would often speed the parting cleric
with a gift duly inscribed. If the interview was troublous or
tragic he was tormented about the circumstances or the person
or what he could do to help. He felt penitent that because he
had such a fear of emotionalism in religion, he could not come
close enough to the hearts of people to whom he ought to be
close. Religion was so secret in the personality that it
demanded reticence, and he was embarrassed to talk with a

man about his religion and then sorry that he felt embarrassed. Therefore letters mattered. With his pen he could say what he could hardly bring himself to say with the mouth.

His letters never fail to look fair on the page, and hardly ever fail to interest.

On whatever subject he wrote he was worth reading. Whether he charmingly refused a bride's hope that he would wear a cope at her wedding; persuaded a sacked schoolmaster not to sue his school; regretted the departure from the country of its landowners, feeling that society was thus deprived of its natural leaders, and the bishop was left solitary, *like a lodge in a garden of cucumbers*; used a humorous ferocity of language to his equals; tried to get preferment for good men in his diocese, like a bishopric for his learned archdeacon, Rawlinson; wrote the most withering of rebukes to an idle and impertinent curate; reproached the growing practice of selling pamphlets on a bookstall at the back of the church, a practice which he thought to stink of commerce in a sacred place; coped with a rare case of homosexuality and, for a man with such revulsion, coped with wisdom; congratulated a vicar on his morning service; tried to raise money for good causes (these letters he hated writing, but he did more than anyone to preserve Durham Castle); sent the fare to a priest asked to preach before the King (an invitation which he had quietly caused) and with the fare sent excellent advice on how; covered the debts of a former confirmation candidate; stirred a clergyman not to give up visiting his people house to house; protested to a member of the Sunderland Corporation against the squalor of houses for which they were responsible; helped ordinands over difficulties of faith; kept in touch with former curates or incumbents now missionaries or bishops overseas; tried to stop a priest from nagging at his people – *don't scold;* fiercely protested to another bishop because he ordained a man whom Henson rejected as far below standard; struggled to hearten a man with thoughts of suicide; sent his compassion to the bereaved; sought vainly to make an idle Oxford undergraduate sit to his books; refused a request to dedicate the shield of a victorious football team, or a regiment's silver bugle (*a line has to be drawn somewhere*); encouraged a young church historian to make church history the work of his life; demanded from the vicar of a sizeable parish why he presented only two for confirmation and both girls; or protested at the sudden new use of a gong in the midst of a parish liturgy – whatever he was at, every word counted.

A special though large group of letters are those to his friends; which include his 'sons', his protégés, his former chaplains, some of his former ordinands. These letters show the best side of Henson; care, trouble taken, affection, charm, an hour of time on a busy day sacrificed to a 'son' sailing across East Indian seas. In these letters – unlike the letters to equals, to William Temple, or George Bell, or Archbishop Lang – the caustic streak never intrudes. They are like the letters of a father concerned for his children's welfare and friendship.

He had a theory of writing letters, and a model. The letter is a true means of personal communication. It must never be dry information. It must bring the writer closer to the reader. The writer must not only say what happened, he must say what he thought about what happened – that is, he must disclose something of his private attitude and so allow the receiver a little piece of his personality. His model was the eighteenth-century *Letters* of Lord Chesterfield to his son. The model was not the ethics of those letters, which Dr Samuel Johnson condemned as teaching the morals of a whore and the manners of a dancing-master. Chesterfield's letters were written out of a full affection; they were designed to aid the growth of the receiver; they aimed to illuminate and interest; and they were meant to bring the writer and receiver closer together in spirit.

Whether a bishop can afford to spend an hour of his day writing to a former choirboy of Durham now in Borneo or a former chauffeur now in South Africa was a question which Henson could not fail to ask, and to answer with doubt. But he kept up several of these correspondences. Partly he felt the duty of a man to keep in touch with his 'family'; partly he found a pleasure in writing letters to friends; and partly he cared for those friends' welfare and wanted to help or encourage or remind them of their roots and ideals.

Three of the 'sons' collected the letters, one even had them bound and indexed. If no one can like Henson after reading his autobiography, no one can do other than like him after reading these collections of letters.

Every year he summoned the men whom he had ordained to a reunion at Auckland: holy communion, tennis, croquet, bowls, clock golf, walks in the Park, lunch with ample food and very strong ciders and all ending with an address from himself at evensong. By the end they were about a hundred strong. He button-holed them for conversation (not always welcome to the young, who could tremble even at a party) or seized them to see the roses or the pigs, and finally replied to a speech of thanks with memorable witticisms.

Such charming replies to a speech of thanks were unique to these annual reunions. For at no other time could Henson bear to be thanked publicly. He knew the world to be full of insincerity. He despised flattery. He was at his worst when he needed to stand on a platform and hear compliments about himself. If men made pleasant remarks to his face, he assumed them to flatter and looked sour, or aloof, or ill at ease, anything but the gracious recipient of a well-meant kindness.

## 12.  RETIREMENT

On 8 November 1938 Henson reached his seventy-fifth birthday. Fits of giddiness troubled him, his teeth constantly needed the dentist, his stomach was uncertain. His brother Arthur, rich and curmudgeonly and in favour of dictators, died the previous August and left him £5,000 in his will. On the summer holiday of 1937 Ella and Fearne and he found Hyntle Place, an Elizabethan house at Hintlesham, which belonged to a dentist of Ipswich. It cost £1,850, and he built on a big study for his books (cost with smaller alterations £1,547) and even installed for Fearne's sake the telephone which Ella could not hear and he could not understand how to use. The process of saying farewell to the diocese of Durham was painful and twice brought him very close to public tears; but the tears were not only of sadness but of amazement at the wave of affection and reverence and gratitude which swept his clergy and laity in the county of Durham, for he still worked under the illusion that he was the most unpopular of bishops and suffered from an overwhelming sense of failure. He refused to accept any parting gift. The one jar was the conspicuously meagre attendance by the corporation of Durham, most of whom were strong Labour men, at his farewell service in the cathedral.

A lot of books he gave away, some very valuable, and sold a lot more at a ridiculously low price. He destroyed vast piles of letters that would have been valuable to the historian, and quite a number of old sermons. The move was difficult because Ella was too old to take the decisions which she alone must take. The vast study table which he bought from Armitage Robinson he sold for only 5s. and was never afterwards content with smaller desks. But some precious things went with him, the armchair and the barometer which the curates of Barking gave. Even when they had rid themselves of a lot of monumental furniture suitable only for persons who live in castles, Hyntle Place gave an air of congestion. Not all the move was well organized. He found himself with five left-leg gaiters which sighed for partners.

Friends wrote generously. Henson was specially pleased at

the kindness of William Temple, and the words of his friend Lord Charnwood, who thanked him because he had made the Church of England a *more habitable place for honest men*. News-papers marked the occasion and ranged from what Henson thought to be absurd flattery to the *Evening Standard* (2 September 1938) which portrayed him as a man of small stature and saturnine countenance, with a passionate adherence to High Tory principles, but which also mentioned how some still thought his Prayer Book speech of 1927 to be the greatest parliamentary speech of modern times. Lang could not imagine why he decided to retreat to so remote a spot, and showed himself nervous at the prospect that he might have leisure to write an autobiography. Various commentators suggested that he be made a peer to keep him in the House of Lords. He acquired the fifth in his long line of signatures: H. H. Henson; H. Hensley Henson; H. H. Hereford; Herbert Dunelm; H. Hensley Henson, Bishop.

What should he do? He had books to write, sermons to preach, lectures to prepare. He still accepted invitations to preach, for on 21 May 1939 he preached to the undergraduates of Magdalene College Cambridge on *A War of Ideologies;* and the organist, who was Henry Chadwick and hardly likely to sympathize with Henson's divinity, could not afterwards remember what was said but knew that he listened to a rare utterance. Henson disliked the new discomforts of not being an official person. For the first time since 1912 he travelled third class on the railway and found it *horrible: The carriage was filled, and I had to sit with my back to the engine: and some fat coughing females insisted on having the window closed*. (It was February.)

He smiled to find a resentment in himself when he received a letter from his successor signed 'Dunelm': Dean Alington's news from Durham half amused and half pained. The *Bishoprick* was instantly duller, and the Bishop of Durham's sermons, but everyone thought the new man good and humane. It distressed Henson that he so quickly changed Henson's rules and was willing to confirm children below the age of fourteen and to wear a cope and to allow collections at confirmations. Still, Henson approved of his successor, and that was a comfort.

Seventy-five is old to move house. To abandon work, and friends, and a position where he was respected, and a home which he enjoyed, and a historic chapel where he loved to say his prayers, and a garden about which he had religious feelings – all that made it hard to adjust. He had hoped to find work in the new leisure to write, and to lecture, and to preach. These hopes were destroyed by Hitler. War cancelled his engagements to lecture, hampered his travelling to preach, and made the publication of books doubtful. He felt himself to have lost the chance of doing the work which he hoped to do in his retirement. He was an old man on a shelf and he longed to be able to help; and all he could do was to give occasional addresses, or write letters to his 'sons', or help the gardener dig an air-raid shelter, or send weekly religious articles to the *Sunday Times*. Occasionally he went to London, festooned with a gas-mark, and would again enjoy ecclesiastical gossip at the Athenaeum. But if he found it hard to accept the change from Durham to Suffolk, he found it harder to accept the isolation in Suffolk caused by war.

He had no doubt that Hitlerism was foul and that Christians should fight and the war was a crusade; and he said so to troops and undergraduates and congregations. When Dean Inge came out strong against the war, Henson was angry. He wrote a letter to *The Times* about the crusade, and expanded it by request into a little tract called *The Good Fight,* price 1*s*., which put Niemöller into the calendar of saints and declared Christianity, with its conscience and its family and its home and its Church and its respect for the individual, to be the formidable opponent of dictators.

This public crusading activity had a most unexpected consequence. When the British scrambled out of Dunkirk, and France fell, and invasion was feared or expected, and morale was at its lowest, Winston Churchill offered Henson, now aged nearly seventy-seven, a canonry of Westminster Abbey.

Henson knew Winston Churchill for many years because they conversed from time to time at the dining-club Grillion's. He liked him and enjoyed his extravagant talk and his wit, but his view of Churchill the politician veered with the views of the rest of the country. Five years before the war broke out he thought it would be in the interests of everyone if Churchill retired from politics and devoted himself to literature. Two years before the war they found themselves in warm agreement on the government's policy over Abyssinia. Confronted with the crisis of 1940, Henson wanted Churchill for prime minister. He contrasted Churchill with Halifax as possible candidates: *The one has genius without character, the other has character without genius. I incline to think that we are in one of those unpleasant situations in which genius is the unum necessarium.* (7 May 1940; altered for *Retrospect*, 3.96)

Churchill could not quite like the Archbishop of Canterbury. Lang was as identified with the policy of appeasement as Chamberlain. Lang was nominated by Baldwin, now in unjust national disgrace, and in a manner was Chamberlain's archbishop. Other appeasers Churchill could send to be ambassador to Washington or into the wilderness. Lang he could not remove. The awkwardness was not made easier by Churchill's almost total ignorance of ecclesiastical affairs. By godly custom the prime minister always consulted the Archbishop of Canterbury before making nominations to bishoprics.

Looking round for clergymen in Britain who were untinged by the doctrines of appeasement, Churchill saw Henson, diminutive but head and shoulders above the rest. Henson behaved with discretion over the abdication, his attitudes to Mussolini rejoiced Churchill's heart, he thought Hitlerism villainy, the war a crusade, and pacifism woolly-mindedness, and all these things he said in the English language – a language which Churchill well understood. Churchill toyed with the idea that Henson back in London might help him with that choice of persons which was a weighty responsibility of the Crown.

On 31 July 1940 Brendan Bracken, who acted as Churchill's private aide, came to see Henson by arrangement at the Athenaeum. They sat in the portico at tea-time. Bracken said that Churchill wanted Henson to be canon 'as a piece of war work.' He wanted Henson in the Abbey pulpit and wished for his advice on church appointments. He thought that after the war disestablishment might be one of the necessary readjustments. Henson liked Brendan Bracken.

Henson found that Lang was not quite pleased. But they

agreed that he could not refuse the appeal to war work, and that he could resolve not to hold the canonry after he was eighty years old; and that Henson, who had his pension as bishop, would take only his expenses out of the stipend of the canonry. At no point in this argument did it cross Henson's mind that a man who disapproved establishment might hesitate over accepting a canonry from a prime minister.

No clergyman was ever treated worse by prime ministers in their disregard of the kindnesses of protocol. He was offered six appointments by the Crown and only in the first two was courtesy observed. Asquith offered him the deanery of Durham through the Dean of Westminster, though being Asquith he followed it with a personal letter; Lloyd George offered him the bishopric of Hereford in a personal letter indeed, but scandalous in its wording; Lloyd George offered him the bishopric of Durham through a secretary who had the impertinence to ask that the reply be sent to himself; and now he had the offer of a Westminster canonry in a letter not from Churchill but from Brendan Bracken, whose official position was obscure. However, Henson consoled himself, Churchill was busy winning a war. And then Churchill consoled him by sending a personal letter.

The *Church Times* lamented. His old enemy Hannen Swaffer in the *Daily Herald* asked what war work Henson was supposed to do which younger men could not do? Henson was even more consoled when Churchill suggested that Henson's installation as a canon in the Abbey should be 3 September as it was the anniversary of the outbreak of the war, and that the whole Cabinet should attend; and later when the King and Queen announced that they intended to come; and later still when Churchill insisted that Henson's address be broadcast.

The Cabinet attended the service, but not the King nor Queen, nor hardly anyone else; for as the congregation assembled the siren went for an air raid and the Abbey was cleared and Churchill advised the King not to come and the BBC could not broadcast the service or sermon.

Henson was for the second time a Canon of Westminster between 2 September 1940 and the end of April 1941. This does not show the full extent of the fiasco. His installation coincided with the beginning of the blitz on London and the

Battle of Britain. Suddenly it was a world of guns, and sleep-
less nights, and broken windows, and cellars, and of no one
with time to listen. He lived in Hintlesham till the time came
for his residence in April 1941. As soon as he arrived at the
beginning of April, he was horrified to find that he could
hardly read the lessons properly, even with a magnifying glass
as well as spectacles; that his sermons were to tiny congregations and in the blackened church he could hardly see his notes;
that he fumbled his way up the steps. After his first six days as
an active canon the oculist ordered him to resign.

Brendan Bracken came again to see him. He tried to persuade
him to continue. He was foolish enough to suggest that if
Henson stayed the prime minister had it in mind to confer an
'honour' upon him, and so clinched Henson's resolution to go.
Once this was agreed, everything was made easy, and Henson
miserably lasted till the end of his duty in April.

He never afterwards disclosed the feeling in public, but
those who knew him best agreed that this felt a far greater
wretchedness than he tried to show. The turmoil of mind was
not so much that he let down Churchill and perhaps the
Church and perhaps the nation. He discovered that he was an
old man. He resigned his see at a time when he still possessed
physical vigour and a powerful utterance and a lively step, still
a man who looked young for his age. And now he could not
even see the Bible to read it, could not see his sermon to
preach, and he a man who must preach from notes and could
never now learn the trick of talking extempore. In February
1939 he left Durham for Suffolk with plenty of plans, much to
do in his years of leisure. In April 1941 he left Westminster for
Suffolk, realizing that it was time to go back to his quiet corner
and wait for the release of death. When he went to Westminster
he was old in years and young in spirit, when he came away he
was old in both.

Early in the morning of 29 April 1941 Alan Don walked
across Dean's Yard on his way to celebrate the sacrament in the
Abbey. He met Henson deep in thought, wearing an old
shovel hat. Henson was taking a last look at his place of work,
during his last day of active career. He was sad, and knew that
he had nothing to look forward to but solitude in Suffolk. Alan
Don found him at that moment pathetic. But he was sorry to

lose his company, for he had found his tongue sparkling and his personality lovable. Henson came into the Abbey and made his last communion there. 'I counted it a privilege', said Don, 'to have thus ministered to him on the last day of the residence among us.'

Canon Donaldson of the Abbey, who was famous as a Christian Socialist and a leader of working men's demonstrations, and of whom therefore Henson could not approve, asked if he would publish the sermons which he preached in the Abbey during April. In his first melancholy he thought them unworthy and refused. But when he was further away and considered maturely, he published the sermons as *Last Words in Westminster Abbey*. They are a surprise. For these four sermons, spoken to tiny congregations by stumbling lips, are the most moving sermons which he ever printed. Though they do not lack Hensonian phrases (*the woeful pageant of moral turpitude*) they have not the force, the energy, the cutting power of the old Westminster sermons. But they have mellowness, and ripeness, and with the gentler tone a new persuasiveness.

He began to draw his world inward. He started to refuse invitations which needed distant travel. He began to live more and more in the past. He dedicated his time to autobiography.

The autobiography had a history behind its genesis. As a young Fellow of All Souls he began to keep a journal. This was partly a religious exercise, partly a record of work or in Barking of parish activities. It was not literary. As it developed he used it for religious reflections, for composing prayers or doggerel verse, as common-place book for useful quotations from books, for copies of awkward letters, for thinking on theology. He did not regularly maintain the record. Once (to March 1894) there was a gap of ten months and it is certain that no record of the interval was lost or destroyed. In 1892 he said that he only put pen to paper if he was otherwise bored.

As the keeping of it became a habit – during his first period as a Canon of Westminster – he came to feel something missing about the day unless in the evening, or at least soon afterwards, he made the record. He found it devotionally helpful, especially as a source of penitence. He advised young men to keep such journals. Whenever he read his own he found it a saddening experience. He also began to find that as the years passed it fascinated.

This casual or religious attitude to his journal first changed with the Hereford quarrel. When the Bishop of Zanzibar ex-communicated him before all the world, and he thought it best to reply by silence, he wondered whether some time he ought not to write an apologia for himself, for such odd if not scandalous judgements about him were spread. This was only a vague notion, never defined.

But as he thought about the past, it dawned on him that his record might be interesting, at times, to some historian. To the see of Hereford was consecrated a bishop who was agnostic about the two great gospel miracles. This was a stage in history and the controversy shed light upon the ideas of the time. Nevertheless he steadily destroyed letters. Occasionally he asked himself whether he was right to throw away letters which a future historian might value; and always answered his own question, that if his son had lived it would be different because someone would care for such letters. He wondered whether the notebooks of the journal ought not to follow the letters. But he found it too interesting, at times too useful, and still a source of penitence. *If . . . a diary be frank enough, and kept for many years faithfully, it provides such a record of tergiversation inconsistency and folly as gives it real disciplinary value.*

He began to question himself over the morality. Could a diary be honest? Was a man always posing, even to himself? Was he writing down rather how he liked to appear than how he appeared? Was there always *an imaginary audience*? And was it morally legitimate to record conversations in a diary? At dinner in Grillion's one night he raised the moral scruple among the company. Lord Hugh Cecil said that it was 'fair enough' to keep a private diary 'so long as you did not publish it during the lifetime of anybody whose reputation could be affected, or whose feelings might be wounded'.

But whatever the morality, he could not now stop. It was a habit, almost a drug. He accused his journal of being *grotesquely egotistic. Diary-keeping is like dram-drinking, a habit ill to form and hard to break.* He wondered if his addiction to the diary was a symptom of loneliness, an offspring of the egoism liable to afflict the man without a family. He kept wondering whether to destroy the notebooks. He showed an 1890 piece of it to his archdeacon, Rawlinson, and said that he was minded to be rid of it all, and Rawlinson begged him to commit no such destruction. It survived his death, with a few exceptions. The entire diary for January to May, 1935 is missing and was missing when he moved from Durham to Suffolk. Doubtless he destroyed it because it contained the record of the tragic case of immorality with which he had to deal; and certain single pages here and there have been torn out but few.[1] In his last years Henson even used his journal as a way of telling his wife, whose deafness he could no longer penetrate, what he thought or did during the day. After his death Fearne Booker wondered whether she would be right to destroy the journal. She wrote to ask Henson's successor as Bishop of Durham, who thus bore the final responsibility for the decision that it ought to survive.

The events of 1928 revived in Henson the sense that he must explain himself. Accused of instability, thought to be a crank, the bishop who one minute was the ultra defender of establishment and the next minute its ultra enemy, he could see that the plea of consistency could only be made convincing if he resorted to personal history. Archbishop Davidson wrote a charming Christmas letter (1928) which was the first suggestion from outside that he should write an apologia for his life. He began to think less of writing an autobiography than of leaving his journal behind for posterity. But then the journal was so voluminous, and often so trivial, that on reflection he expected posterity to burn.

In the autumn of 1935 George Bell published a biography which became the standard history of the Church of England in the twentieth century, the Life of Archbishop Davidson. Naturally this biography contained a narrative of the Hereford Scandal, for which Henson allowed Bell to consult his papers. The publication brought Henson into unwanted prominence, reminding the old of what they had forgotten and telling the young what they never knew. Henson thought that the narrative was not quite fair to him and that some of the reviews were still less fair. But the trouble was not only prominence. After

---

[1] In the earliest volumes quite a number of pages have been removed. From one of the Letter-books, April to December 1927, 183 pages are torn out.

childhood this was the sorest place in his memory. *There are some things which had best be forgotten, and that gratuitous and unscrupulous controversy is one.* That comment is not from the mind of an intending autobiographer.


On 17 June, 1938, when his forthcoming resignation of the see of Durham was news, he received a letter from Norman Sykes, who was not yet Professor of Ecclesiastical History at Cambridge. The object of the letter was to persuade him not after all to retire because the bench of bishops needed a historian. But, if he resigned, Sykes begged for autobiography. As he read the lives of other bishops, Gore and Talbot and the monumental Davidson, he reflected how 'some autobiographical reminiscences from your hand would have enlightened many a dull page, and lightened up many a disputatious scene'. This was a new idea to Henson; that quarrels better forgotten might be meat and drink to a historian.

A month later the Dean of Westminster, engaged in founding a *Westminster Abbey Quarterly,* asked Henson for reminiscences of his time as a canon. Henson went to his journal and enjoyed the extraction of material, from which he made an interesting article. This exercise caused Ella to read aloud parts of the journal. From that moment his wife was convinced that he ought to record his memories.

The exercise also brought him against a new obstruction. He was a little alarmed to discover how frank were his comments on the Dean and Canons of Westminster. Brought up to speak the truth especially when it will displease, he had not been able to carry this out into the social conventions; and he therefore used his journal as a release for the 'truth', or for the irritations, which he felt but had not liked to express. Kindness to other people or the 'rule' that you speak only good of the dead, forbade him to utter what he thought at the time. But if he wrote at all, he ought to try to write the 'truth'. The claim of charity versus history started to bother him – *I was not born for so mealy-mouthed a generation as this.*

Three months after his retirement from the see of Durham he happened to meet at the Athenaeum Humphrey Milford, the publisher of the Oxford University Press. Milford courteously regretted that the Cambridge Press were to publish Henson's book on the Church of England. Henson then asked Milford whether he would like to publish *some kind of autobiography* if he wrote one, which he thought was an *unlikely event*. Milford jumped at the suggestion.

Eight days later, on 11 May 1939, Henson spent the morning at Hintlesham seeing whether he could start an auto- biography. He was at once confronted by the bar. How could he begin? He would have to speak frankly about his father – and how could he *without falling into impiety*? As he rummaged in his journal the idea of parading himself was at first painful. The best possibility seemed to be a narrative of his ministry with an introductory chapter about upbringing and character. He made little progress. That September he consulted several friends, and found that they were in favour. The Archbishop of Canterbury, for understandable reasons, was not. 'Will you forgive me if I express the hope' wrote Lang (19 November 1941) 'that you will keep under due restraint your great gifts of trenchant and caustic criticism, and not indulge too freely in the very natural pleasure it must give you to exercise those gifts?'

The experience and pain of the second Westminster canonry in the blitz aged him and drove his mind inward upon itself, so that he more easily began to live in the past because he had nowhere else to live. The sore places of childhood he could not bear to write. But other scruples vanished. He would speak the truth; if it hurt, that was how he saw it at the time; the Hereford Scandal should be laid out in its fullness before the public, if he could not avoid it he would print his whole journal of that agony and men should see at last how it looked in the eyes of the victim. Occasionally the doubts returned. Sometimes his journal as he read it felt to be only *an exhibition of stuffed birds*. Sometimes he realized that he was engaged on a public confession, a public act of penitence. At moments he decided that the whole journal was better burnt. But Ella and Fearne Booker were steadily in favour of the autobiography, and they were now the weighty influences in his narrowing life. Like other wives and daughters of ageing men who have lived lives of intense activity, they saw that the old man had not enough to do, and needed work to occupy his intelligence.

But they were not alone. Ten separate publishers enquired with hope.

The first volume, taking his life to the Hereford diocese, was finished during the summer of 1941, and copies arrived on 4 July 1942. Fearne's accuracy, typing, and indexing were necessary to the production of all three volumes of auto-biography. The second volume, containing the Durham episcopate, appeared in 1943. The plan was to stop. But he lived on, his mind still commented and reminisced, Milford was willing if not eager, the women wanted him to have work to do, and so the third volume, of his years of retirement, was almost finished just before his death and published post-humously (1950).

After the end of the first volume he dictated to Fearne and this caused errors when she misheard what he said.

With his publisher he had disputes.

The first was the title. Henson's original idea for a title was the simple *An Autobiography*. Confronted by the pain of memory, he decided that he was not writing an autobiography. He was concealing certain things, and they were important. Then it started to have a curious title: *Memories, personal and professional, confirmed and corrected by a Private Journal. By an Outsider.* The pseudonym expressed his sensation that all his life he was a *lone wolf*. But then he realized a pseudonym to be ridiculous, since everyone would know who was the Out-sider. Then he suggested to Milford that it be *Retrospect of Thought and Life;* and finally the familiar title – *Retrospect of an Unimportant Life*.

Against this title Milford protested. 'This title won't do at all; it is much too modest.' But Henson got his way. After-wards everyone commented on the hypocrisy, or if they were kinder the folly, or if they were still kinder the error, of this title. Was the man fishing for compliments? A man who was the ablest orator of his day in one of the Houses of Parliament had not the option of declaring that his life was unimportant unless he professed a cynicism about existence which is not open to a Christian bishop.

This was a signal of the looming calamity of Henson's career. The apparent Uriah Heepism had complex sources in his character. He had a truly humble side, and also an 'umble

side, a self-depreciation which no one took quite seriously.
Passages about his existence as lived among the *froth and foam of
current ecclesiastical life* appear from time to time in his journal.
Usually they are part of one of the waves of melancholy which
were his burden. Yet the cool-headed reader does not always
believe that Henson believes in his own writing. And, mixed
up in it all, is something from the Calvinism of childhood, the
nothingness of the soul before its Maker, the only true form of
Christian humility.

The next reason is, that by a fault of authorship he made
parts of his first volume boring. With the exception of his early
life, and the Hereford Scandal where every word grips the
reader, the first volume was ill organized. Lord Roche told
him that no one should be allowed to write a book after the age
of sixty. That was a hard saying. Henson was seventy-nine
when the first volume appeared, eighty when the second
volume, eighty-four when still working at the third volume.
He had just written a poor book about the Church of England,
he was now in danger of writing a poor book about himself,
because his antiquity diminished the power of self-criticism.

So he made the main part of the first volume a record of
forgotten controversies. It felt to him, and not without reason,
unimportant.

He wrote while France fell and a few hundred airmen won
the Battle of Britain and the American fleet was sunk at Pearl
Harbor and Malaysia was lost to the Japanese and bombs never
ceased to thud down on London. Those who accused the title
of hypocrisy forgot the feelings of a man who read of world-
shaking events in his newspaper at breakfast and then sat down
at his desk to describe how thirty years before he rid himself of
a too musical organist. Nevertheless even Henson confessed to
using the word *unimportant* in a Pickwickian sense when for
once in his life he perpetrated nonsense, and called himself *an
obscure but prominent English ecclesiastic.*

The existence of the journal was a heavy burden. Its weight
of information blinded the author, as he sometimes complained, to the essence of the matter. If he could have thrown
all the journals away and written from memory and then
checked with the journals, he would perhaps have written a
better book. But he would not have been able to finish. His

constructive power declined, and left a selective faculty. Before the end of the first volume the journal took charge of the author. In the second volume the journal dominated. The third volume was almost nothing but extracts from the journal. The *Retrospect* started as the author's reflections on his life and ended as extracts from his contemporary journal.

The reader enjoyed this change. The first volume is the dullest. Just at the end it fascinated because it contained the journal of the Hereford Scandal. The reader found himself in a source of contemporary history, graphic and hardly bowdlerized. He found brilliant phrases, satirical and comic; penetrating comment and beneath the veil of discontent much wisdom, expressed too frankly, even belligerently. These controversies might be dead but the man who recorded them was alive. Something of the pleasure of all three volumes was derived from their *indiscretions*: the lasting resentment of a bishop when men opposed his election; the half-derogatory portraits of Armitage Robinson, or Burroughs, or Winnington-Ingram, or Furse, or even Gore. In the argument between history and charity, history won; and history won partly because of Henson and his upbringing that truth is truth though it does not please; but also because the autobiography turned into extracts from a document of the past, written only for the private eye. But let us not exaggerate. In the affair of Hereford, or the failure of the Revised Prayer Book in Parliament, or the proceedings of two Lambeth Conferences (secret, but Henson obtained a dubious kind of leave to publish from Archbishop Lang) the autobiography/journal instantly became a source for history. Henson eschewed no technical terms. He revelled in the ecclesiastical arguments which laymen could hardly fathom. One lady who enjoyed volume one, found that the physical effort tired her because she needed to keep on her knees a prayer book and volumes of the encyclopedia in order to understand all his language.

Milford the publisher protested at the typescript of volume 2. As the author's constructive power faded, the selection of extracts became the work of authorship; and the further the book went from memory and the nearer to old extracts, the easier to add length. Milford said that the book was 50,000 words too long; and 'what should, I fear, go first, are many of the comments on eminent colleagues who are happily still with us, e.g. . . . Lang, Temple, Talbot, Barnes (passim), Headlam. My impression is, that a lot of space can be saved, with the loss, I admit, of many pungent criticisms in this way' (Milford to Henson, 18 February 1943). It is odd to see a lay publisher pushing towards charity a Christian bishop too old to see what damage he was about to do to himself. Henson disapproved but perforce obeyed.

*The value of the personal comments and criticism of contemporaries which you think violate charity is to my thinking historical. The modern tendency to a kind of hagiological 'mutual admiration' is so disgusting to me, and so obscuring of the truth, that I am prepared to risk some personal odium in order to correct it.*

A breath of recklessness touched his spirit. Only four years before he knew that to publish the journal was wrong, it was too intimate and egotistical. Now he even told a friend that he would pay to print the entire journal if he had enough money. In obedience to Milford he omitted sentences, and other sentences he changed, so that the process made the diary not quite reliable as history, since it was still printed as the contemporary record from the past but was altered in 1943. Very few of these changes were historically important. One instance will be enough. Henson described the behaviour of his friend Fish Cecil of Exeter at a bishops' meeting (*Retrospect, 2*, 170).

Print: *Exeter excelled himself.*
Original: *Exeter excelled himself in muddleheaded irrelevance.*

Each volume was well received and well reviewed despite the usual handful of savage damnations. That was to be expected: an able man, writing always good English, commenting on the events of his lifetime with a shrewd and critical judgement. That was the merit of the book, and most people saw it to be high.

But Henson achieved this at the cost of his reputation.

Rab Butler told the author of this memoir:

When I was a young man, I read a fine book by Henson about Christianity. It helped me much. Afterwards I always regarded Henson as my leader in religion. I said to myself, what is good enough for Henson is good enough for me. When his autobiography came out I bought it with pleasure. It was a terrible blow. It seemed to be all name-dropping and controversy and he seemed conceited. The autobiography shattered my admiration for the man.

This feeling was understood by Henson's friends. Here was a bishop whom they loved as an affectionate and generous friend, who cared for his people and his diocese; and now he represented himself as a wasp.

E. F. Braley wrote to him: 'When I see what purports to be the record of someone's life which omits the most important part of it, I see that for the sake of veracity and completeness some of the contents of your letter-book ought to be divulged.' The *Times Lit. Supp.* (25 July 1942) awarded volume 1 'the prize for causticity among Anglican episcopal autobiographies. Yet the complete absence of rancour. . . .' *Punch* said 'His estimate of other clerics is altogether unwarped by forced cordiality. . . . This plain dealing with others is made palatable by his unpretentiousness about himself' (8 December 1943). Kindly reviewers commented on his dislike of wearing his heart on his sleeve and his fear of emotional display and therefore his refusal to recount the affection which he inspired.

Was the caricature deliberate? One at least of his 'sons' thought that he intended caricature beause he could not bear that men should think well of him. This is hard doctrine. Probably the judgement errs. The truth must be spoken, that is much more likely to be the reason, combined with an old man's inability to see that a historical record, which looks so fresh, is already selected from the very moment when it is committed to paper.

The distasteful bits of the autobiography are not the attacks on other bishops but the praises of Henson cited from other men's letters or leading articles. No historian can hurry, eyes averted, past this wart. The reviewer in the principal Methodist organ was nauseated, quite beyond reason, by a very trivial instance; when Henson, just made Bishop of Durham, called at the bank to explain that he must sign cheques with a different signature, and the cashier is quoted as saying, 'That's a proud signature, my Lord.' This Methodist critic whipped what he called Henson's 'purring self-complacency'.

Since the preface to this book shows that a similar instance – the letter from Lloyd George quoted at the end of the third volume of the *Retrospect* – offended the author of this memoir and almost made him refuse the invitation to write it, let us see what can be said to extenuate.

First, Henson was proud with a sense of wonder, which is the best way to be proud. That the little boy from an odd home and no school to speak of should rise to be Bishop of Durham filled him with astonishment.

Secondly, he was convinced that the world regarded him as a bad bishop. Why he was so convinced we leave to the guesses of the psycho-historians. But the trouble was not only that he fancied the world to think ill of him – and this was partly true, for some of the world did think ill. The trouble was his deep-seated suspicion that the world might be right; that he was indeed a bad bishop, and was liable to change his mind inexplicably. More than anyone else he needed to prove to himself, as well as to others, that he was not so bad as 'everyone' fancied. So he noted when someone said that he wrote beautiful English, and someone else said how Hereford regretted his loss, and someone else said that Durham felt an outburst of joy at his return.

Thirdly, this self-praise is recorded only for three subjects:

(1) the brilliance of his oratory – and he could not need this praise to bolster his ego because no one who holds crowded audiences can be unaware. The little child in Broadstairs who memorized sermons from his father's bookshelf and preached in his nightgown had come to fruition and could not but know;

(2) the excellence of his prose style – possibly this is like the Latin titles of several of his books, connected with the continuous distress at the lack of a formal education;

(3) the approval of a majority in both his dioceses – this an apologia against those who held the contrary opinion and said so in press or Parliament.

But pastors receive letters of thanks on other subjects; more private and intimate; from souls troubled, and anxieties helped, from men lifted out of debt or encouraged to faith. That Henson received many such letters we have evidence. He destroyed almost all. He cited none by way of self-praise.

Thus the only puffs which he allowed to vainglory were the superficial – good speech-making, good writing, and popular approval which in his heart he despised as showing that the approved person could not be a true apostle.

The letter from Lloyd George might have another excuse. It comes almost at the end of volume 3. A letter of Fearne Booker shows that only about three-quarters of the third volume was ready for the press when he died. Henson is not to be blamed for all the contents of the third volume.

Still, it was a failure of judgement, thus to print. In 1939 at the age of seventy-six he knew that it was wrong to print – autobiography yes, journal no. Three years later at the age of seventy-nine he was printing the journal; partly because it had become the only way he could write an autobiography now, partly because he was more careless of his own repute as he grew nearer to death, but partly also because of the illness of the very old, where their mind seems to be as good as ever but their judgement is impaired. The defender of Henson may claim for him that charity which younger men feel it right to pay to the very old.

Several reviewers commented on the vein of sadness in the book.

He was a man with all the constituents of happiness – bodily health, a successful marriage, work that filled his time and satisfied his inclinations, and a strong faith in God's provi-dence for the world. Those who wrote him down after reading the *Retrospect* fancied that he must be a disappointed man because he never became an archbishop. Nothing could be further from the truth, either that he cared about being an archbishop, or that the circumstance could account for the sadness, which lay at a deeper level of the soul.

Something came from a scepticism, or a ruefulness, about his own situation. He never doubted God, unless extreme pessimism about the future is equal to a weakened faith. His commitment to the discipleship of Christ never wavered. The ruefulness rested upon the Churches. He found himself not only an apostle of the Lord but a mainstay of a public organization in society. He neither denied the necessity of Churches, nor was ever disloyal to his own Church, unless it be disloyal to criticize a Church savagely and its leaders trenchantly. But the fabric of institutional Christianity felt to him, at times, more like a house of cards than God's castle upon its rock; as much a means of corrupting as of transmitting a gospel. He did not feel this all the time nor even most of the time. But it lay underneath his fear of popes, and suspicion of archbishops, and cold appraisal of bishops, and sweeping judgement on clergy as a class, and horror of campaigns, and absence of interest in ecumenical schemes of reunion, and nausea at little chapels propagating the truth of Noah's flood. God made him an apostle, and so put him into an organization. The gulf between the organization and what it was supposed to do kept troubling his heart.

He valued the past heritage and did not like what he saw happening to Britain and the world. He saw the social unrest of the twenties and the growing challenge of the young to conventional Christianity. He saw Russians destroying Churches, and Stalin murderous, and Hitler sickening in his anti-semitism and Mussolini repressing liberty and another war looming to end the society in which he grew. Against a new Dark Age Christendom was the solitary bulwark, and where went Christendom? He seemed to himself to live in a tide of self-destruction by Europe, and everything that he stood for was the breakwater, and that breakwater was cracking in the flood. This pessimism about contemporary society was a constituent of the vein of sadness.

There for better or worse were the three volumes. To them he added a collection of essays reprinted from the *Bishoprick,* under the title *Bishoprick Papers* (1946); important because his essays on issues of the day were among his cogent pieces. He was one of those writers whose ephemeral comments bear reading by posterity out of the context in which they were delivered. The review of the book in *Theology* (November 1946, 346 ff., Frank Bennett) included the best epitaph on Henson:

'He stood with head erect among the ostriches.'

The little family in Hintlesham, of childless father, childless mother to whom he could not talk, and acting daughter, suffered another loss. The 'son' who came closest of all the 'sons' to them, the one who alone turned from a 'son' into a son, was Derek Balfour Elliott, known at first as Derek, later as Dick. His father died after being maltreated by the Russians, and mother could not afford to keep him at Sedbergh School. Henson undertook his education, moved him to Durham School, had him to stay and read and walk round the Park in the holidays, paid for his fees at Oxford, was excited when he decided to seek holy orders, paid for his fees to train for the priesthood at Westcott House, and finally ordained him. Dick became an army chaplain in the Green Howards, and won the MC at Dunkirk for ministering serenely and without hurry to wounded men while they lay under heavy fire. He went out to the Middle East, was captured at the fall of Tobruk, and died a prisoner in an Italian camp. Henson was proud of this son's character and achievement, valued his judgement, treated him as an equal. It was the last of the 'family' deaths before his own.

Dick Elliott's death hurried the last cairn on the mountain of autobiography.

Dick wanted Henson to write a credo. Reviewers of the first two volumes of the *Retrospect* demanded the same more unkindly. They said that Henson showed himself a destructive critic, who pilloried weaknesses in Papists, Anglo-Catholics, Modernists, Evangelicals, Protestant sects – what then did he believe? Henson found the demand just. Because Dick asked it, he conceived the idea of a last Open Letter after many Open Letters, this time *An Open Letter to a Young Padre*. When Dick died he did not abandon the idea. He selected Gervase Markham, also a service chaplain, and also one whom he ordained, and asked whether he might send him the letter which he intended for Dick, as though Markham as well as Dick asked for his credo. Incidentally it enabled him to begin with a tribute to Dick's character.

But wrapped within the attempt at a credo lay an aim still more personal. He had not quite made a clean breast. He had written a vast autobiography, and yet had found it too painful to tell all the truth about childhood, and undergraduate years, and even the years at All Souls. The Open Letter took on the air of a self-purgation. Now at last he could bring himself to tell of his repugnance to his father's religion, and the Congregational minister at Broadstairs, and the absence of baptism as an infant, and his miserable preparation for confirmation, and his flight or expulsion from school, and his escape from home; and he needed also to purge himself by telling the world that he, the hammer of popes and Anglo-Catholics, sat wrapt under the pulpit of a Jesuit preacher, and under the disreputable Father Ignatius, and how he suffered the doubts of his age on the truths of religion, and contemplated abandoning his boyish desire to be ordained; and how he was led by men whom later he fought, like Charles Gore or Father Puller, and how he engaged with Jimmie Adderley in plans for a group of monks to serve the slums; and how he seriously considered whether to be a Cowley Father, and how he came to use confession regularly and regularly to hear confessions.

When he came to think of his own faith, it was surrender to the historic Christ who still lives among men; more a surrender to a person than to a creed, but always a crucified person, through whom men found pardon and peace; a person of whom the convincing evidence was the life and faith of his best disciples, both then and through the centuries and now; in whose light Henson saw purpose and providence in history. Of Churches he cared little in comparison with this crucified Lord. But he could exchange his own Church for none other, and thought the Church of England a Protestant Church, aligned with the Reformed tradition, shedding extreme Anglo-Catholics who could not be Protestants and Modernists who clouded the faith of Christ into mist. Asked directly whether he, vehement critic of clergymen, regretted becoming a clergyman, he answered with a resounding *No*.

So the last utterance – the Open Letter – was a kind of purgation. Here was an evangelical boy who came to loathe his father's religion; and all his young adult years he was an ultra-Catholic assailing his father's Protestantism; and all his older years he bit extreme evangelicalism, Protestant underworld, with its party trusts and its Jardines; and, when forced to say in ancient years what he believed, found that he was after all a kind of evangelical, a man of the Reformation. He could tell the truth about himself finally, and be at peace with the faith of his home.

He helped with the services in the parish church at Hintlesham. This was uncomfortable. The rector, an old Durham man, was Anglo-Catholic in a way which suited neither rustics nor bishop. Not to worship happily on Sundays was a trial. Then he had disabilities, with eyes or gait, he stumbled over sermons, grew absent-minded so that he shocked himself by forgetting to lead them in the creed. On his walks in the country lanes he would stop to talk to the ploughmen as once he talked to the miners in Auckland Park, and would turn aside into the village church to say his prayers.

The rector died, and a long interregnum troubled the parish as men refused the post and the bishop could not fill. For the second time in his life Henson became a country parson. This lasted for eleven months (October 1944 to September 1945). He found it very salutary for his soul; preaching week by week to a tiny congregation, forgetting his place, fumbling over his notes, doing his best for a dozen people. At various times in his life Henson recorded compliments to himself. He never recorded anyone praising him for what was one of his most generous acts, the consent to care for a tiny parish for nearly a year at his age eighty-one and state of health. He wondered whether as bishop he was kind enough to some of his country priests now that he understood their predicament from inside. The old man took a little pride that he stood in the tradition of a historic ideal of pastoral care – and the heroes which sprang to his mind out of the past were not quite expected – George Herbert, John Keble, Richard Church.

None of the three in the house was used to cooking, cleaning, washing, gardening, improvising repairs; and therefore the quest for help, for servants, ways of lightening the unaccustomed burden and trying to maintain the old way of life during the war, had part-comedy and part-melancholy. A faithful girl from Durham, Sarah, came for a time and returned after the war. The old couple could not have survived without Fearne Booker as a Poo-Bah. She became Ella's ears and Henson's eyes. Life was complicated for a few months by a too talkative *evacuate* – the rest of the country called them *evacuees* but Henson thought this grievous grammatical error, and that an *evacuee* is someone who took too strong a laxative. The sacred hours of morning study grew less sacred when they had fuel for a single fire which must be in the study, and his endeavours were interrupted by the presence of others, who did not realize the beauty of silence.

After years of war he found that his clothes were shabby and he would not go out to a fête because the *idea and aspect* of a shabby bishop was repulsive. He would mourn about these things and then realize that he fell into the besetting sin of the old and tried to remember his blessings and count them before the Lord. At night dreams drifted up the past – he once found himself in the House of Lords laying about him with a hammer and *just as their Lordships were rising in their places, unspeakably scandalised,* he awoke. He would dream of his sister Marion and wish that she would come back. He dreamed that he was a chaplain in an officers' mess and an officer described how a German held up his hand in surrender and the officer shot him – and Henson was just denouncing the British officer, (*Sir, you disgrace your country and your cause, by what was nothing else than a base and brutal murder*) when he awoke.

In the pulpit or to local lecture societies, or to local wounded or troops, or in conversation, he would do what he could – denounce any hint of anti-Semitism in a conversation, counter every suggestion that all Germans were bad Germans, do all he could against the doctrine of reprisals. He thought the use of the atomic bomb wicked and it shocked him, in more ways than one, when he found that in this matter he agreed with the Pope and not with Archbishop Fisher of Canterbury.

He watched the Church move on, but mellowly. He thought William Temple the right choice when Lang retired, though his faith was shaken when the newspapers showed the new primate wearing a mitre. He thought Geoffrey Fisher the right choice when Temple died, though his faith was shaken when the newspapers showed the new primate smoking a pipe (*Is it seemly? is it spiritually serviceable?*). He had long opposed the ordination of women and read that the Bishop of Hong Kong ordained a woman to be a priest; but he could see nothing against it on principle, he just preferred it not to happen, and so hoped that his Church would not recognize what the Bishop of Hong Kong did. He was more disturbed to hear from Durham that his successor licensed deaconesses to preach, for if you concede the ministry of the Word, how shall you refuse the ministry of the Sacrament?

He kept in touch with Durham friends. Dean Alington wrote him charming letters, and told him how Arthur Headlam, preaching in Durham Cathedral pulpit, coughed out his false teeth, caught them at some distance from his mouth, and thrust them back. Henson wrote charming letters to Alington in reply, and when he heard that the Socialist leaders were to dine at the Durham deanery, advised the dean of many respectable ecclesiastical precedents for poisoning the enemies of our Cause. He was sad as his contemporaries, Headlam among them, died and he wryly made his private obituaries. He read Roger Lloyd's *History of the Church of England in the Twentieth Century* and specially hated its praise of himself. His brother Arthur's widow died and relieved him of all anxiety over money by her bequest.

He watched the sparrows in the garden, and the partridges. The page numbering of his journal kept going wrong, but it was kept up nearly every day, even in winter. In the winter of 1946–7 he needed to wear mittens *which have always seemed to me the sure preliminary of approaching departure.* When he went out he had to lean on a stick and found himself panting after a hundred yards. 7 April 1947 was the day of spring that year when Sarah first saw partridges. He wondered if they were members of the same covey that nested there successfully last year. *Anyway they are heartily welcome. I essayed a walk in the garden, but had at once to abandon my attempt because of the violence of the wind, which made me pant. What a spring, and what a winter!* These are the last words of the journal. Depending on the nature of the calculation, it was volume 107 or 108.

That evening he suffered a heart attack. For nearly six months he was in bed, or down in a chair, on warm days outside. Almost to the last day he could still be fierce about books read to him, could still dictate to Fearne trenchant letters.

He had two more heart attacks. He was well cared for, by two nurses and a good doctor. Gervase Markham and his wife went to see the invalid, and found him in bed, hair snow-white, face lined but very gentle –

The pugnacious warrior had been sublimated into a gentle saint. He seemed touched by our visit, and we talked of spiritual things, and before we left we knelt beside his bed, and he gave us a quiet blessing. We crept out as from a holy place, and left the house knowing that we should never see him again.

On 28 September 1947 he had a heart attack in his invalid chair in the garden. The doctor came but he died in his sleep just before midnight.

In a manner he died childless. His son of the flesh died at birth, his son of affection died in what he saw as a crusade against vileness. His wife looked on Fearne Booker as her daughter. Whether or not he ever came to see Fearne as a daughter, she came to look upon him as a father. She afterwards said that the man with whom she fell in love was not the eloquent dean nor the militant bishop, but the little old parson stumbling in a village church. It was Fearne Booker who was at his bed when he died.

# INDEX